Acclaim for *John Joseph Mathews*

"[Michael] Snyder's meticulous biography explodes long-standing myths about Mathews, documents his personal secrets and traces his extended family from Osage, French, Welsh and Southern slaveholding ancestors to descendants from his two marriages who carry forward Osage-influenced forms of creativity. It also provides glimpses of early twentieth-century Indigenous networks in Mathews's encounters with writers, artists and intellectuals of many tribes and nations across Oklahoma, Europe and Mexico. In filling gaps both personal and cultural, the book does fine service."

Times Literary Supplement

"This is a critical biography, delving into both the literary and the personal sides of Mathews. In the end the story is edifying. . . . I was transfixed by the interactions of literary legends traipsing through the narrative—Savoie Lottinville, . . . J. Frank Dobie, . . . Carter Revard."

Plains Folk

"*John Joseph Mathews: Life of an Osage Writer* is a major contribution to the growing field of biographies of American Indian literary figures. Students of Native American literature will find this a significant addition to the canon of Mathews scholarship. Others will find it an engaging read."

Daniel F. Littlefield Jr.

author of *Alex Posey: Creek Poet, Journalist, and Humorist*

JOHN JOSEPH MATHEWS

American Indian Literature and Critical Studies Series

JOHN JOSEPH MATHEWS

LIFE OF AN OSAGE WRITER

By Michael Snyder

Foreword by Russ Tall Chief

University of Oklahoma Press : Norman

This book is published with the generous assistance of the
Wallace C. Thompson Endowment Fund, Univerity of Oklahoma Foundation.

Portions of chapter 5 of this book ("Osage Literary Man") were adapted from "Friends of the Osages: John Joseph Mathews's *Wah'Kon-Tah* and Osage-Quaker Cross-Cultural Collaboration," *Chronicles of Oklahoma* 88, no. 4 (Winter 2010–11): 438–61.

Library of Congress Cataloging-in-Publication Data
Name: Snyder, Michael, 1973– author.
Title: John Joseph Mathews : life of an Osage writer / by Michael Snyder
Description: Norman : University of Oklahoma Press, 2017. | Series: American Indian literature and critical studies series ; volume 69 | Includes bibliographical references and index.
Identifiers: LCCN 2016044311 | ISBN 978-0-8061-5609-5 (cloth) | ISBN 978-0-8061-6052-8 (paper)
Subjects: LCSH: Mathews, John Joseph, 1895–1979. | Authors, American—20th century—Biography. | Osage Indians—Biography.
Classification: LCC PS3525.A8477 Z75 2017 | DDC 813/.52 [B] —dc23
LC record available at https://lccn.loc.gov/2016044311

John Joseph Mathews: Life of an Osage Writer is Volume 69 in the
American Indian Literature and Critical Studies Series.

The paper in this book meets the guidelines for permanence and durability of the Committee on Production Guidelines for Book Longevity of the Council on Library Resources, Inc. ∞

Dedicated with much love
To my daughters

Ivy K. Snyder
Cora A. Snyder

They are invaders and I am indigenous.

—John Joseph Mathews, *Talking to the Moon*

CONTENTS

ILLUSTRATIONS

ACKNOWLEDGMENTS

I offer my deep and hearty thanks to the following people: Pamela S. Stout, Christine Hadley Snyder, Marci Shore, Timothy Snyder, Lori Anderson Snyder, Dr. E. Eugene Snyder, Philip Snyder, Mary Moore Snyder, Mary Lou Anderson, the late John Hopper Mathews, Mary Abigail Mathews, Laura Mathews Edwards, Chris Mathews, Sara Mathews Dydak, Sam Edwards, John Clinton Hunt, Peter H. Brown, Sam P. Brown, Henry C. Brown, Harvey Payne, Philip Blair, Raymond Red Corn III, Milton Labadie, Judy Taylor, Rhonda Kohnle, Romain Shackelford, Mongrain Lookout, Pauline Allred, Kathryn Red Corn, Lou Brock, Russ Tall Chief, Carter Revard, Charles H. Red Corn, Veronica Pipestem, Thomas Kraus, Alessandra Jacobi-Tamulevich, Emily Jerman Schuster, John Lovett, James H. Cox, Strat Tolson, Bobbie Tolson, Melvin Tolson, Frederick F. Drummond, the late C. D. Northcutt, John W. Raley Jr., the late William H. Mattingly, Stanlee Ann Mattingly, Phillip Fortune, the late Shockley Shoemake, Bob Burke, Bob Gregory, Bob L. Blackburn, Craig S. Womack, Phillip Carroll Morgan, Ryan Slesinger, Timothy S. Murphy, Robert A. Warrior, Geary Hobson, Alan Velie, Garrick Bailey, Chief Geoffrey M. Standing Bear, Sean Standing Bear, Judge Marvin Stepson, Paul Jordan Buck, Father Chris Daigle, Steven Poe, Tiffany Poe, Elizabeth Thompson, Hallie Winter, and C. Cali Martin.

Thanks are also due to the librarians, employees, and volunteers who helped me at the Western History Collections, University of Oklahoma Press, Bizzell Library, and Carl Albert Center at the University of Oklahoma, Norman; the Osage Tribal Museum, and Osage Language Center on the Osage Nation; the Osage County Historical Museum, Pawhuska Public Library, Osage County Treasurer's Office, Tolson Agency, Grandview Inn, and Immaculate Conception Church in Pawhuska, Oklahoma; the Keith Leftwich Memorial Library, Oklahoma City Community College,

Oklahoma Historical Society Research Center, and Oklahoma History Center, in Oklahoma City; Oswego Historical Society and Oswego Public Library in Oswego, Kansas; the W. W. Graves Memorial Public Library and Osage Mission–Neosho County Museum in St. Paul, Kansas; the Ponca City Public Library; Harry Ransom Center at the University of Texas, Austin; KTUL TV, Tulsa; Sterling Memorial Library, Yale University; and the Nature Conservancy's Tallgrass Prairie Preserve.

FOREWORD

Russ Tall Chief

The kinship I feel with John Joseph Mathews and the subjects and characters of his books is complex and multilayered. I was so impressed by the depth of his exploration of Osage history and cosmology in *The Osages: Children of the Middle Waters* that, after reading just the first few chapters of the book, I recognized he was one of the premier culture-keepers of our tribe. The details Mathews marshaled in this account required me, as a young reader, to revisit the book, and even then I still did not understand the complexity of the early history of our tribe. My great-aunt Maria Tallchief, my father Tim Tall Chief, and I confided in one another with humor that none of us really "got" the book, especially the cosmology and origins of our tribal history. I plan to continue rereading *The Osages* until I comprehend the abstract qualities of our tribal structure, which Mathews explains with the same poetic language found in his creative writing.

Mathews's prose is poetic, whether he is explaining the history of our tribe, narrating the biography of E. W. Marland, or creating nuanced characters in his novel *Sundown*. His poetic style informed my approach to writing once I started publishing nonfiction on a regular basis in *Native Peoples* magazine and elsewhere. An analysis of Mathews's writing reveals the immense palette of rhetorical devices with which he paints his stories. Mathews's writerly style makes his works particularly appealing to those of us bold enough to risk publishing, but sufficiently dense that some readers, including writers such as myself, might not "get it" upon first reading. His work, however, is worth revisiting since it continues to inspire me to elevate my prose, infusing poetic devices sometimes to the point of conspicuity. I am grateful to Mathews for providing me with the courage to alliterate without apology, for example, or to interpret aesthetics in and on my own terms, as opposed to limiting my vocabulary to a distilled perspective designated by and for art critics. Mathews showed me that interpretation derived from my own perspective and revealed through respect and gratitude for the chaos and order of the natural world is most important—not the diction quizzed by college professors who view the application of terms from Western critical theory as informed and therefore most trustworthy. "Piss on 'em," I heard him say to me in my mind. "Create your own vocabulary."

In addition to Mathews's influence on my own writing style, I found personal qualities in his characterizations that I shared both proudly and with regret. Challenge Windzer, protagonist of *Sundown*, and I share strengths and flaws, which I own now as an adult but denied during my youth. As a young military aviator, "Chal" tried to conceal his mixed-blood Osage heritage by passing as Spanish American. I also went through youth embarrassed at times of my heritage, and especially my last name, because I felt it was too "Indian." I grew up during the heyday and aftermath of the American Indian Movement (AIM), which in my opinion equally inspired pride in Native heritage and incited hatred of it by many non-Native people—the same people resentful of the civil rights movement that preceded and helped spark the flames of AIM. I was too young to internalize the "Native Pride" that resulted from the occupations of Alcatraz and Wounded Knee. Native Pride, especially when exercised with force, rhetorical or physical, still required a bulletproof vest, or more symbolically, bulletproof skin. In some areas of the country, Native people still needed to pack a weapon to protect themselves from the rage still resonating on both sides of the domestic warfare between Natives and certain racist non-Native groups.

My older sister Amy fought her way through school during the 1970s as a minority among minorities even more than I did, fighting the "dirty" and "greasy Indian" attacks with both words and fists. Somehow Amy even managed to deflect the "greasy Indian" insult issuing from the non-Native side of our family. While this continual assault on our Native half seemed to make Amy stronger, it also made her meaner than a hornet, as my granddad, George Tall Chief, would have said. (George was the eldest son of Eves Tall Chief, who knew and respected John Joseph's father, William S. Mathews.) I recall even Amy's boyfriends were afraid of her, as was I. Anyone who knew Amy knew that if justice needed to be served, regardless of whether she was right or wrong in a conflict, she would not hesitate for a second before flattening someone's nose with her fist before they even finished uttering the word "greasy," with no regard for breaking her own fingers or any other noses in the process. Perhaps Amy most closely resembled Mathews's older sister Josephine when it came to getting her way. I, on the other hand, was intensely sensitive of snickers over my name, mockeries of Indian dances and expressions, and popping lips travestying the beautiful "lulu" that Native women vocalize to honor someone.

"While working as an actress in New York City during the 1990s and early 2000s, I almost changed my last name," my sister Amy says. "I couldn't get work as an actress because my five very reputable agencies would only send me up for Indian roles. I called them *'ooga booga'* roles because they would ask me to talk more like an Indian! I spoke to them and asked them not to put me in that file because I was not the stereotype these casting directors were looking for. In hindsight, I should have insisted harder. But by the time I realized what was happening, I was making good money producing events and hosting shows."

Many of my youthful experiences caused painful identity struggles, and the results were similar to Chal's self-hatred depicted in *Sundown*, including his passing for something other than Indian. I was embarrassed each first day of class, or when I was introduced to a group, since giggles would follow my name. I was very often the only Indian in the room, as I imagine Mathews was at the University of Oklahoma and Oxford University. I could feel my face flush blood red when a teacher, coach, camp counselor, or other adult announced my name in roll call. Although Tall Chief (and the name is two words, although my family and I often intentionally combine the words to avoid becoming, in my case, "Mr. Chief") was pronounced correctly for the most part, many times my name would be announced as if it were a question: "Tall Chief?" Since much of my youth resembled Chal's, when faced with an embarrassing situation because someone laughed at my name, or asked if it was my "real name," I would more often than not try to diffuse the situation with humor. Often still, I have to explain my name to people as "'Tall,' as in big and tall, and 'Chief,' as in the leader of a tribe."

Whereas Chal enlists in the Army Aviation Section, Signal Corps during World War I and has a series of adventures, I, on the other hand, ran away to Boston at the age of eighteen to "find myself," which I did in the theater scene. I had not genuinely committed myself to theater in Oklahoma due to false self-expectations about what a former football player, wrestler, and pole-vaulter, who also embarked on brief boxing and bareback bronc riding careers, should be. In retrospect, the theater was the perfect place for someone in an identity crisis to try on numerous personas, from heroes to romantics, foils to villains. Like Chal, upon my return home, my own inner conflict exploded into recklessness on an epic scale that led to countless broken bones, broken promises, and broken hearts, before I finally reached self-acceptance.

As readers of Mathews learn, many of his characters and plots are based on his own experiences, as well as his own understanding of Osage history and culture. Thus, my sense of kinship with the writer flourished after I learned we shared a similar ethnic and cultural heritage, including Osage, French, Scots-Irish, Welsh, and English ancestry. My grandfather told me we were also Cherokee on his mother Rose's side ("a smidgen"), and it is believed we are Choctaw on my mother's side, in addition to being English and Welsh, an eclectic mix that the older I get, the more I appreciate. Like Chal, my struggles for self-acceptance drove me to hell and back, where I danced with the devil on more occasions than I would like to admit, sometimes with unsuspecting passengers who soon understandably turned around and ran for their lives. But fighting my way back to the surface from the darkness below is what is most important, as I believe it is for Chal. Just as we may sell or lease the surface land of Osage County, the minerals underneath the surface remain Osage in perpetuity. Concomitantly, as human beings, we can put on any mask we want in life or on stage and pretend to be someone or something that we are not on the surface, but inside—underneath—we will always be Osage by blood and by culture.

I don't want to speculate too much on how closely Chal personifies Mathews the man, mostly due to the fact that much of what I learned about Mathews the man has proven incorrect. For example, for my entire life I was under the impression (and even bragged) that Mathews had an aerial dogfight over France against the famous "Red Baron," which I later learned never happened. However, as Michael Snyder shares in this revealing biography, after years of legends such as this being perpetuated by family and friends, even Mathews himself gave up trying to set the record straight. I have faith, nevertheless, that Dr. Snyder has set the record straight in these stories, or has gotten as close to the truth as possible. Thank you, Michael, for your zest and quest for the truth about a man who, despite his complex identity, is perhaps best understood as a faithful servant to his country and to his Osage people in his struggles for the preservation of our American and Wah-zha-zhe ways of life.

JOHN JOSEPH MATHEWS

Chapter One

SILVER SPUR

> Could it be that Indian blood mixing with other bloods will create a new type of Indian. If this be true, then the Osages will not be engulfed by present day society but a new type of Osage Indian will emerge from the propagation.
>
> —Kenneth Jacob Jump, *Osage Indian Poems and Short Stories*

John Joseph Mathews was a respected Osage author who lived his life the way he saw fit. He held a clear vision of what he wanted out of existence and pursued his ideal diligently. Mathews was proud to be Osage Indian, one-eighth by the crude standard of blood quantum, and was thus invested in a collectivist tribal community. Yet he was a staunch individualist who cherished his autonomy and personal agency. This seeming paradox extended across his life: the embrace of Osage communalism by an author who, like Thoreau, embodied classic American individualism. Complicating this characterization even further is the fact that Mathews, as an Oxford University graduate, avid hunter, traveler, and pipe smoker, in several ways subscribed to the ideals of a leisured English aristocrat and was something of an Anglophile, despite his Native roots. In the 1930s, a reporter visiting The Blackjacks, his small sandstone home on an Osage prairie ridge, thought Mathews resembled "an English gentleman vacationing at his hunting lodge." In the 1950s, another visiting journalist stated that with "flawless diction and command of language" that "belied his western garb and mud-spattered boots," Mathews seemed "an English country squire dressed in the garb of an Osage County rancher." As Mathews grew older, however, he increasingly identified as Osage and was increasingly perceived and recognized as such by other Osages.[1]

Mathews was a keen observer of the natural world. He received academic, empirical, or military training in ornithology, taxidermy, geology, biology, archaeology, botany, zoology, aviation, history, literature, tribal governance, and even chicken raising. In five books he published in his lifetime, Mathews distinguished himself as a literary nonfiction writer, novelist, biographer, and tribal historian. He holds a secure place in literary history as an early American Indian author who helped clear a path to the Native American Renaissance underway by the end of the 1960s. His semiautobiographical novel *Sundown* (1934) is one of the first novels written by a Native author to feature a Native protagonist. According to Choctaw-Cherokee critic Louis Owens and Potawatomi critic Terry P. Wilson, *Sundown* established the paradigm of the modern American Indian novel. The trope of the alienated Native veteran returned to his home community is similarly deployed by N. Scott Momaday in *House Made of Dawn* (1968), a late-modernist novel credited with inaugurating the Native literary renaissance, and Leslie Marmon Silko's masterful *Ceremony* (1977). Anishinaabe (Ojibwe) critic Gerald Vizenor writes, "*Sundown* was the start of a new vision in native literature, a modernist presentation of a dialogic presence over a romantic absence." Mathews's biography of oilman and governor E. W. Marland is one of a tiny number of books published in the 1950s by an American Indian author.[2]

Mathews was born in Indian Territory in Pawhuska, the capital of the Osage Nation, located in the northeast of what in 1907 became the state of Oklahoma, not far from the Kansas border. According to Osage Tribal Agency records, he was born on November 16, 1894. Citing the family Bible, however, Mathews claimed several times that he was born in 1895, including on draft cards and his Guggenheim application. Jo Mathews, as he was known to friends (first spelled "Joe," then by the 1930s, "Jo"), was born in the house his father built next to the Osage Agency, overlooking the Pawhuska Indian Village. His parents were the wealthy, influential William Shirley Mathews ("Will") and his pretty, young wife from a French Catholic family, Pauline Eugenia Girard ("Jennie"), who married in 1887. The couple had eight children, three of whom died very young. Those who survived were Jo, one older sister, Sarah Josephine (b. 1888, known as Josie), and three younger sisters, Marie Imogene (b. 1897), Lillian Bernard (b. 1899), and Florence Julia (b. 1902). All three children born between Josie and John Joseph died in early childhood: Susan Frances (1889–91), George Martin (1891), and William N. (1892–95). The fact that little John Joseph thrived after Will and Jennie's three painful losses, and was the sole male heir, afforded him special treatment. In retrospect he called himself a "princeling."[3]

Mathews felt mixed emotions about his sisters. He described Josie, the eldest, as "didactic and histrionic." After she repeated a fabrication a few times, to her it became fact. Almost seven years older than Jo, Josie had a hard time accepting that her younger brother stole her spotlight. As a little girl, Josie was pretty, imaginative, but willful, frequently getting her way with her parents. One time when he was about five years old, and Marie was about three, Josie persuaded them to become "REAL angels," since they had not yet reached the "age of reason" according to Catholic dogma. Jo and Marie agreed to be closed up in a bran box so that Josie could send them to heaven, but they begged to be released when they ran short of oxygen. Josie, perched atop the box, only gradually and reluctantly acceded. Later, Jo, whom Josie disparaged as a "clod," teased her about her near murder of her little siblings.[4]

In contrast, Jo described his favorite sister, Marie, as tranquil, and guided by wisdom, logic, and a strong sense of justice. Because of illness, Marie became almost totally deaf at age twelve. Quiet, intelligent, and kind, Marie studied local history, wrote poetry, and like her sisters Josephine and Lillian, played piano. As an adult, like Jo, she shared her love of nature and birds with children. She was aided in school by younger sister Lillian, who was later known to relatives as difficult and disapproving, and according to Jo, was concerned with being "the first with the latest." Marie and Lillian frowned upon many of their brother's life choices, including his abandonment of Catholicism, but like their brother, they became historians of their tribe and Pawhuska, specializing in the Osage relationship with the Catholic Church and early white settlers. All three shared their knowledge with the community and historians. All the Mathews sisters were attractive young women, but neither Marie nor Lillian married, and eventually Lillian was labeled a spinster. Prominent Osage County rancher Frederick Ford Drummond reported that his father, Fred G. Drummond, dated Lilly. Deeply in love, Lilly believed she was destined to marry Fred, and when he married another woman, she was so devastated that she renounced marriage entirely. From 1937 to 1943, Lillian was the first curator of the Osage Tribal Museum, which Jo largely established. She then pursued a career with the Osage Agency, retiring in 1969.[5]

Florence was Jo's adoring baby sister, a flattering tagalong he nicknamed "Dooley." Florence's daughter, Florence Feighan Jones ("Fleur"), said the nickname derived from the popular Irish American character Mr. Dooley, created by humorist Finley Peter Dunne. Like Mr. Dooley, intelligent Florence "always had an answer for everything." Since her sisters played piano, Florence took up the harp. As for Jo himself, he said that he was born happy, if slightly confused, but had a "terrible temper."[6]

William S. Mathews, one-quarter Osage, was by turns a successful rancher, trader, merchant, banker, tribal councilman, and judge, and he and his family became one of the most prosperous in Pawhuska. For his son, growing up in a booming Osage oil town adjacent to the traditional life of his ancestral Osage culture was exciting, enriching, but perhaps also disorienting. In both volume 1 of his unfinished autobiography and the opening of *The Osages*, Mathews evoked the sounds of tribal songs and death chants that entered his upstairs bedroom window and his little ears. The poignant, climactic "sob of frustration" on which the chant suddenly terminated filled his impressionable mind with perplexity and wonder, and haunted him throughout his life. He pondered humankind's frustrating struggle to comprehend the infinite mysteries of God (Wah'Kon-Tah) and existence.[7]

The name "Osage" is a corruption of Wah-Zha-Zhe, an English rendering of the French phonetic transliteration of the name that the French thought pertained to the whole tribe, but which actually referred to a specific subgroup, the Hun-Kah, or Earth People. Long ago, the Osages referred to themselves as Ni-u-kon-ska. Humbling themselves before Wah'Kon-Tah, they modestly called themselves "Children of the Middle Waters," which Mathews used as the subtitle of *The Osages*. According to Mathews, the tribe was divided into two groups, the Tzi-Zho, or Peace People, whose names came from the Sky, and the Hun-Kah, a warlike people whose affinity was to Earth. Mathews's ancestral line, the Buffalo clan, was of the Hun-Kah. Given that Mathews was an erudite gentleman-author, his belonging to the warlike Earth People may seem ironic. But he was also something of a warrior: he served his country in World War I, tried to join the war effort during World War II, and became a "hawk" in his geopolitical views.[8]

Centuries ago, the Osages were Woodland Indians, part of a large group of Dhegihan-Siouan speakers who lived in the Ohio River valley. By the mid-seventeenth century, this group gradually began moving west, having tired of war with Haudenosaunee (Iroquois) invaders or searching for better game to hunt. Over time, this large group separated into the Osage, Ponca, Omaha, Kaw (Kansa), and Quapaw tribes. The Osages transformed into a buffalo-hunting Lower Plains tribe, and for centuries their homelands stretched over vast tracts of what are now the states of Missouri, Kansas, Arkansas, and Oklahoma. Rennard Strickland wrote that his people were often praised for their "steadfast resistance to white influence." Early Euro-American visitors described them as strikingly tall, dignified, handsome, fierce, and sometimes imperious or aloof. Successful in "taking advantage of their strategic position athwart the navigable Missouri River system," the Osages played "one European power against another before finally succumbing to the overwhelming tide of immigrants streaming from the new American nation," Terry Wilson writes. Throughout the second half of the nineteenth century, Osage homelands gradually shrank through a series of treaties with and land purchases by the federal government, until Osages were relegated to a diminished reservation in what is now Kansas. The tribe sold that land in 1870 under the Drum Creek Treaty, and over the next few years moved south to their present reservation in Indian Territory.[9]

An Osage, Jo's father, Will, was a storehouse of tribal knowledge, and served as a trader and merchant to the tribe. In most ways, however, he raised his children as upper-class Catholic Euro-Americans, and hired servants and a driver. Jo's mother, whose parents were born in France, was devoutly Catholic, so the family went to Mass regularly. Jo did not attend the local boarding school for Osage boys; instead, he and his three younger sisters were enrolled at Mrs. Tucker's Preparatory School, an institution established to educate the children of white traders, clerks, and Indian agents. Mrs. Tucker's school was very close to the Mathews home, located on a hill on Grandview Avenue across from where the white-frame Osage Agency building once stood. Laura Tucker was one of Jo's most formative influences. "From the first grade to perhaps the sixth," Mathews wrote, "Mrs. Tucker, with her brightness and her rugged certainties, laid a wonderful foundation upon which later I was to build my formal education and culture." Though strict, she encouraged Jo's fascination with words. Perhaps surprisingly, he was not an outstanding pupil; he believed he was "ranked rather low in effort and interest." When Tucker was interviewed after her student had achieved recognition, she simply recalled Jo as shy. This failure to assert his talents was typical throughout Jo's educational career, and his grades were uneven. This pattern derived from the privilege he enjoyed: being the sole male heir in a relatively wealthy family encouraged complacency. After Tucker's school, Jo enrolled for two years of junior high at St. Joseph Mission School, a parochial school in Pawhuska, and then attended Pawhuska High School, a public school.[10]

Although Mathews and his younger sisters attended Tucker's school, Josephine attended the Osage Boarding School, funded by the tribe, and the St. Louis Boarding School for Osage girls, run by the Catholic Bureau, which two of her sisters also attended. St. Louis School, which boarded up to two hundred girls, was a four-story, native stone structure lying south of Pawhuska. Also underscoring the Mathews family's Native heritage, Jo's cousin Owen Mathews, son of Uncle Ed, attended Carlisle Indian Industrial School in Pennsylvania, but ran away and lived with Jo's family for a time. Josie later attended Mount St. Mary's Academy in Oklahoma City and graduated from Loretta Academy in Kansas City, Missouri. One June, after returning from boarding school, she annoyed Jo with lessons on how to eat soup genteelly and other such niceties, causing him to spill his soup while resisting her grabby hands.[11]

Growing up, Mathews was not closely connected to full-blood or traditional Osages, partly because of discontinuity in his family's Osage backstory. For the most part, the relatively traditional "village Indians" (as opposed to "town Indians" and mixed-bloods) did not regard Jo as Osage, and outside of his family, few Osages in the community recognized Jo as a relative. Yet as Osage author Charles H. Red Corn eloquently writes, "the Buffalo Clan blood flowing in the veins of John Joseph was not apparent in the tone of his complexion or in the color of his hair. However, Osage was abundantly present in his heart and mind and in his soul." He derived his Osage ancestry from his paternal great-grandmother, A-Ci'n'Ga (or d'Achinga), also called Wind Blossom. She was full-blood Osage, part of the Great Osages division, a member of the Big Hill band and the Buffalo clan. Tradition states that long ago, all Osages dwelt together in one village. At some point, a great flood separated the people, and the group that found safety atop a hill became known as the Pa-ciu'-ghthin (Big Hill band). A-Ci'n'Ga resembles the traditional Osage name for a third-born or subsequent daughter.[12]

As a young woman, circa 1813, A-Ci'n'Ga married William Sherley Williams, a Welsh American. Williams, John Joseph's great-grandfather, was a missionary to the Osages who helped compose an Osage dictionary and translated parts of the Bible and several hymns into the Osage language. Later he "went Native," more or less converting to Osage beliefs and culture. Williams spoke Osage fluently, hunted and trapped with Osages, and danced with them in ceremonies. According to biographer Enid Johnson, the Osages gave Williams the name "Red-Headed Shooter" and even wrote songs about him. A prodigious trapper and trader, and an interpreter for missionaries and the government, he much later became renowned as "Old Bill" Williams, legendary Mountain Man of Old West lore. Bill Williams courted A-Ci'n'Ga in Osage fashion, giving horses to her parents and gaining their consent to his proposal. For part of the year, the couple lived in an Indian village called Big Osage Town in what is now west-central Missouri.[13]

Their first daughter, Mary Ann Williams, was born in 1814, and Sarah followed two years later. Mary Ann attended the mission school at Harmony. Both Mary Ann and Sarah became brides of Jo's grandfather, John Allen Mathews. A-Ci'n'Ga died sometime between 1819 and 1825, at which time Bill Williams left the Osages, heading for the mountains, having previously served as translator during negotiations of the tribe's unfortunate treaty with the U.S. government. That year, 1825, was a bad one for the tribe because, arguably, they were swindled out of their rich, fertile lands in Missouri and Arkansas, and relocated to southern Kansas, having been persuaded to sign a dubious treaty. According to Johnson, before leaving the Osages, Williams took his daughters to live with his sister Mary in St. Louis, where they encountered a new world and were compelled to pray to the white man's God. Alternatively, according to John Joseph Mathews, Williams sent them away to a boarding school in Kentucky, where they met

John A. Mathews.[14] In the mid-1830s, Mary Ann married Mathews, a Kentuckian with Virginian roots, in Jackson County, Missouri. She had been previously married, and Mathews gained a young stepson, Bill Nix, also called Red Corn. Red Corn's father, Lorenzo Dow Nixon, had disappeared shortly after the birth of his son in 1832.[15]

Jo Mathews was fascinated by his great-grandfather Bill Williams and his mythos, and some ironic parallels can be drawn between them. Mathews grew up reading adventures of famous Old West traders and Mountain Men: Kit Carson, Jim Bridger, and Bill Williams himself. These fearless, rugged men became models of masculinity. In 1912, Jo went on a hunting excursion into a remote area of the Colorado Rockies with friends and fellow high school football players Floyd Soderstrom and Leo Bellieu, the latter also mixed-blood Osage. They chose the spot because nearby mountains were named after Williams, and Jo's father was delighted at the news. In 1929, Mathews wrote his mentor and friend Walter Stanley Campbell, "I am much interested in that old sinner, Williams." He felt empathy for Williams's character and viewpoint: "I feel that I should have done the same things he did under the same circumstances. His love of solitude I can understand thoroughly." Visiting Taos, New Mexico, in 1952, Mathews wondered where Bill had his store when he was a trader there, opining that Williams instead of Kit Carson could have become "the symbol of the hero and scout of the Old West." If only Old Bill had used his education and literacy, he could have "pumped himself into a hero" that endured. Williams and Mathews both possessed rich knowledge of the land, Indigenous peoples, and animals of the West, and during long periods of their lives, they opted to live alone. According to Enid Johnson, peers called him "Old Solitaire" and Natives dubbed him "Lone Elk." Both prized independence and autonomy. Campbell, using his pen name Stanley Vestal, wrote, "Bill Williams, dean of the free trappers, had always come and gone at his own will, without consulting anyone," an ideal Mathews shared. Both tended to avoid cities and often "civilization" in general.[16]

Mathews's identification with his great-grandfather is ironic, since some regarded Williams as vicious, cruel, and treacherous. Old Bill degenerated as he aged, becoming increasingly dirty, drunk, and dishonorable, a known horse thief and worse, a bloodthirsty "Indian killer." At the very least, he was considered eccentric, just as his great-grandson would be viewed by many townspeople. Both men were fervent, even insatiable hunters. According to biographer Alpheus Favour, Williams's "sole ambition in life seemed to be to kill more game and catch more beaver than any other trapper," and this fact, "along with his other eccentricities, made many believe that he was crazy." Although Williams "went Native" among the Osages and the

Utes, he was later hired by expeditions whose men wantonly slayed Indigenous people. During an 1833 expedition in California, Old Bill and company showed "utter disregard for the rights or the lives of the Indians," Favour states. In one incident, the men killed twenty-five harmless, curious "Digger Indians" (Maidus). During this period, stealing horses from Spanish missions and killing Natives was par for the course for Old Bill.[17]

After many years of separation, Old Bill paid his daughter Mary Ann and John A. Mathews a visit. The couple was living in what is now southeastern Kansas at an Osage settlement named Little Town, after members of the Little Osage band living there. The settlement was later resettled and dubbed Oswego. John A. Mathews had previously served as blacksmith to the Senecas, in 1839. Circa 1840, John A. Mathews was appointed blacksmith to the Osages of Little Town, who called him Mo'n-ce-Gaxe (Metal Maker). Much later, he was celebrated as the first prominent white settler on the future site of Oswego. Jo Mathews in fact visited Oswego twice to speak at events celebrating the history of the town. How diligently John Mathews pursued his duty among the Osages is a matter of some controversy. Osage historian Louis Burns writes that Mathews and a second man were appointed blacksmiths by the Osage subagent, and while "they drew the pay," they "rendered no service" to the tribe. Adding "insult to injury, Mathews's seven-year-old son and a small Negro slave were appointed to the striker positions." Burns claimed this exemplified perversion of Osage treaty benefits. Little Town abutted Mathews's 140 acres of cultivated land, which boasted a large double-chimney house, trading post, water well, blacksmith shop, stables, and sizable horse racetrack, all supported by the labor of African slaves. Horse racing was this Kentuckian's passion and calling card, and he even raced in other states. Little Town was but one of three trading posts that prosperous John A. Mathews operated.[18]

At the time of Old Bill's visit, John and Mary Ann had one daughter, Susan ("Sue," b. 1841), who was terrified of her grandpa's weird, unshorn appearance. Fast-forwarding to 1870, Sue married Kentuckian farmer and stockman James Simpson, and they built a home on the current Osage reservation, the home of two of her half-brothers, Ed and Will Mathews. Jo fondly recalled pleasant boyhood visits and picnics at Aunt Sue and Uncle Jim's rural property. Jim died in an accident in 1903 and Sue, though known for her sophistication, remained in Pawhuska.[19]

Sue's parents, John and Mary Ann also had a boy, Aloysius Allen Mathews, Jo's Uncle Allen. Allen was educated at Osage Mission in St. Paul, Kansas, and at St. Louis University, and never married. Promptly after Mary Ann died, circa 1843, John A. Mathews married her sister, Sarah Williams. A son, John, was born in

1843, and Anna Elisa ("Annie") arrived two years later. Another child, Jane, was born in March 1848. The correct date is probably earlier, though, because the next child, William Shirley Mathews, Jo's father, was born on September 15, 1848, in Fort Gibson, Creek Nation, where his father owned a trading post. Edward Martin Mathews arrived in 1850. In 1856, Sarah became ill, was hastily baptized, and died. On Sarah's baptismal record, Father John Schoenmakers labeled her as Mathews's "quasi wife," indicating they were not formally married.[20]

John A. Mathews was successful as a trader and businessman, and Little Town peaked in the 1850s. He gradually gained a reputation for fair dealings with Osages, then rare, and earned the respect of whites and Osages alike for his equity. He was a Southern slaveholder, however, and during the horrific period of Plains history known as Bleeding Kansas, he was so adamant about Kansas becoming a slave state, "he wanted to fight about it," historian W. W. Graves writes. Mathews antagonized his former friend, Father Schoenmakers, who was an abolitionist loyal to the Union. By 1860, Mathews was working to sway the Osages to support the Confederacy, persuading the chiefs of the Big Hill band and the Buffalo-Face clan to do so. The community's loyalty became split between their trader Mathews and the "Black Robes" (priests). Making matters worse, this strain occurred amid a terrible drought that brought suffering to the Osages. Mathews spent a great deal of money to help the tribe through the winter. Tragically, he had already lost his daughter Annie to a prairie fire in 1857. Once the Civil War reached Kansas in 1861, the region descended into chaos, becoming another bloody battleground. Some Osages joined the Union while others marched with Chief Stand Watie's Cherokees, Muscogees, and Seminoles fighting for the Confederacy. Incessant mayhem, raiding, and exploitation during the Civil War period nearly ruined the Osages.[21]

Jo's father, William Shirley Mathews, enters the story at age twelve. Educated by Jesuits at the Osage Mission School in St. Paul, Kansas, young Will was sympathetic to the priests. Even though his father had broken his friendship with Father Schoenmakers, in June 1861 William rode furiously to warn the mission of a gang of guerrillas—led in part by his own father—who aimed to terrorize them for favoring the Union. Having done his utmost to influence his old friend Schoenmakers to support the South without success, John Mathews "became angry, raised a band of adventurers, called them soldiers, and started for the Mission to kill the priest," Graves writes. According to O'Connell, upon learning of the plan, his son "mounted the fastest horse his father owned and raced to the mission. The Neosho was flooded far out of its banks; nevertheless, the boy plunged the horse into the stream," and bravely crossed at Trester's Ford. "The marauders followed a short time later but were afraid to attempt the crossing for several hours," allowing Schoenmakers time to escape to St. Mary's, Kansas, where he took refuge for eight months.[22]

Infamously, Mathews led raids upon Free State towns and settlements. As early as 1856, he formed a posse of pro-slavery partisans to avenge the burning of his barn by Free-Staters. Jo Mathews wrote that in August 1861, his grandfather "recruited Cherokees and Creeks from his trading post at Fort Gibson," and persuaded Osage Big Hill men to aid him in pushing Free-Staters out of the Cherokee Neutral Lands. Sixty pro-Union families fled to Humboldt and other Union communities in Kansas Territory. Mathews was accused of leading a September 1861 raid on Humboldt, burning, looting, and kidnapping freed slaves. A Free State newspaper denounced him and his followers as "devils in human shape," John Joseph Mathews noted. According to Louis Burns, such raids fomented by Mathews and his ilk drew retaliation and distressed the Osages. "Due to their location, their villages were to be vulnerable in the years ahead to invasion and looting. Thus, a high proportion of warriors had to remain in the village to protect the women, children, and aged. This reduced the hunting force and, consequently, the meat supply."[23]

While Mathews had personal and political motivations for leading the Humboldt raid, he asserted to his friend Dr. George Lisle, a Free-Stater, he had not been involved. Lisle later claimed Mathews counseled others against participating in raids and was unfairly accused of being an agitator. Yet contemporary newspaper accounts and historians such as Graves unequivocally state that Mathews led the Humboldt raid. The Sixth Kansas Cavalry, led by Lieutenant Colonel James G. Blunt, mounted a retaliatory expedition that located Mathews on September 18, 1861. Mathews was killed by a single shotgun blast fired by the ironically named cavalryman Pleasant Smith. Mathews's possessions were seized, his property burned, and the white residents of nearby Chetopa were arrested and court-martialed but later freed. To avenge Mathews's death, poor Humboldt was sacked and burned yet again.[24]

Left orphaned at ages thirteen and eleven, respectively, William and Edward Mathews swiftly fled following their father's sticky end. Assisted by two slaves—"Old Aunt Millie," the nurse, and "Uncle Ned," the stableman—with only the shirts on their backs, Will and Ed journeyed south to Texas where for a time, the Confederate-sympathizing Audrain family protected them. But soon they were left to their own devices. Jo Mathews said his father suffered deprivations that left a "scar not of the spirit, but deep in the animal." As teenagers in Texas, the brothers became ranch hands and cowboys, and later went on long trail drives north along the military road that led to Fort Gibson, Indian Territory, near Muskogee, Will's birthplace. For a time, they lived with "Mr. Adair," a Cherokee friend of their late father's (possibly this was tribal leader and Confederate colonel William Penn Adair), and worked as ranchers on the Cherokee nation.[25]

After the Osages moved from southern Kansas to their last reservation in what is now Oklahoma, Will and Ed rejoined them there in 1874. They wanted to establish a ranch on the communal acreage, which they were entitled to do as members of the tribe. They explored the Osage reservation on horseback, searching for an ideal location, which they found on a floodplain on Beaver Creek. There the brothers started their ranch, building headquarters in a dugout on the creek bank. William spent his first two years in Pawhuska as an employee of Isaac T. Gibson, a Quaker and the first resident Indian agent for the Osages there. Unfortunately, William suffered an accident: his horse fell on him, and one of his legs was amputated and replaced by a prosthetic leg. Thereafter, he gradually withdrew from ranching. Edward became a deputy U.S. marshal, while Will became interested in mercantile, milling, and banking opportunities.[26]

Will Mathews was a fair and ethical man, and he and his relatives fascinated his son. They radiated a glow of honesty and equity, and Jo saw their sense of honor as a hereditary trait. "My father's and his brother Edward's unostentatious and unconscious fairness was so much a part of them that no vicissitude of their barbaric teenage environment could influence it," Mathews wrote. Family friend Violet Willis said that Will "exemplified the unselfish citizen," possessed "compassion and understanding of the needs of his people," even of strangers, and was "a Christian gentleman, who took the command of loving one's neighbor as a prime law in every endeavor." Will held much responsibility and power in his dealings with Osages as merchant, banker, city official, and tribal councilman. He resisted the temptation of exploitation, unlike many white Pawhuskan professionals and guardians who were supposed to protect the interests of full-bloods. Jo had a lot to live up to.[27]

Four years after Ed and Will established the ranch, Will formed a partnership with John Soderstrom to operate a gristmill built by the U.S. government to grind corn into meal and wheat into flour for the Osages. A few years later, Will Mathews and Soderstrom bought this property at auction and built a larger mill, which they ran together until Soderstrom drowned in 1903, after which Mathews sold it. John was the father of Floyd Soderstrom, Jo's close friend who later owned a grocery store in Pawhuska. By 1907, Will was founder and director of the old Osage Mercantile Company, the premier grocery and general store in the Osage Nation. With its high, shady porch, the mercantile served as a meeting place for many traditional Native customers and early white traders. Raymond Red Corn III said that during this period, William wrote poetry on Osage Mercantile stationery. This engagement of the poetic amidst the commercial is revealing of Will, who read Shakespeare, Byron, and Yeats. His literary interest surely influenced his son.[28]

Focusing on banking and finance, Will gradually sold his other interests. He played a key role as banker during a period of great growth and economic development following the discovery of oil underneath the Osage Nation in 1897. He was one of the organizers and a president of the First National Bank of Pawhuska. In 1905, he helped organize the First State Bank (later First National Bank) in Hominy, plus the bank at Greyhorse Indian Village, which became the Osage bank at Fairfax. He later sold his interest in these banks to establish and serve as president of the Citizen's National Bank of Pawhuska, and remained a bank director until his death. In 1906, Philip Dickerson wrote in *The History of the Osage Nation*: "Mr. W. S. Mathews is of Osage ancestry, born and reared among them, and for many years honored and prominent in their tribal affairs. He is now a member of the Osage council. His family is one of the oldest and most prominent citizen families. His children are enjoying the best literary schools of the states." Part of a group that founded the first local telephone office in Pawhuska, Will was synonymous with progress.[29]

Will was proud of his Osage heritage, and used his tribal knowledge and language proficiency to serve his people's interests in his various roles. He was the Osage Nation's treasurer from 1882 to 1886, the chief justice from 1890 to 1892, and the prosecuting attorney from 1894 to 1896, even though he possessed no degrees. Prior to Osage allotment in 1906, he served on the Osage National Council multiple times. He lived next to the tribal agency, with twenty Indian agents as neighbors, whom he advised and introduced to tribespeople. These included Major Laban J. Miles, a Friend and friend of the family. The major's notes and remarks became the source for John Joseph's first book, *Wah'Kon-Tah: The Osage and the White Man's Road* (1932).

The U.S. government violated Osage tribal sovereignty when it declared it would cease acknowledging the Osage National Council's authority beginning in 1900. In 1904, when Jo was nine, Will joined Agent Oscar Mitscher's Allotment Delegation to Washington, D.C., to discuss what became the Osage Allotment Act. This group included many prominent Osages, including Bacon Rind, Fred Lookout, W. T. Leahy, Eves Tall Chief, James Bigheart, Heh-scah-moie, Black Dog, and Shun-kah-mo-lah. According to journalist Violet Willis, William's "composure, wise counsel, and understanding were needed especially during the turbulent days" preceding and during allotment and the preparation of the final roll of the tribe. From 1910 to 1912, Will served on the third Osage Tribal Council. Respected by tribesmen and government officials alike for his integrity, he made at least four trips to Washington, D.C. as a delegate of the tribe; his son later followed in his footsteps.[30]

In many other ways, William set a pattern that Jo followed. Will was an avid hunter who developed a love of horses as a boy from his horse-racing father. He passed down these passions to his only son, with whom he hunted. Like his father, Will owned stables, and he catered to hunters who wanted to visit the desirable hunting grounds of the Osage Nation. Along with the family house in Pawhuska, William owned property in the country. In *Talking to the Moon*, Mathews wrote, "my father built the first house in the blackjacks by the spring at the head of the canyon." E. E. White, a special agent to the Osages during the 1880s, wrote, "The Osage reservation is a picturesque country. The uplands are high and rolling, and the valleys broad and fertile. Building stone is abundant, and there are innumerable streams fringed with timber." On this unspoiled land, young Jo Mathews whiled away his hours with his dog, Spot, and beloved horse, Bally. Growing up, he "rode all over the northern part of this reservation" on his horse, camped, and "just had a wonderful time." Aspiring to become an ornithologist, he studied birds as much as he could.[31]

Judge Mathews, as Will came to be known, was a perennial fan of games and sports, and heartily supported his son's athletic abilities. He helped finance a semi-professional baseball team in Pawhuska, and he and Mrs. Mathews cheered them on. Jo, who had played shinny (similar to field hockey) and other Indian-derived games, baseball, and a soccer-like game at Mrs. Tucker's school, went on to play basketball (center) and football (fullback) for Pawhuska High, being elected captain of both teams. Tall and lean, he was a natural at hoops. In Osage style, Jo identified with an animal, the outsized sandhill crane. As Jo played football, a glow of pride spread over his father's face as Will vicariously played along. His father attended every basketball game with that same glow.[32]

Jennie Girard Mathews was a compelling person in her own right, and her family's history is also fascinating. She married William in 1887 in the Osage Council House, which became Pawhuska City Hall. Father Ponziglione, one of Will's teachers, traveled south from the former Osage mission at St. Paul, Kansas, to conduct the ceremony. Born in April 1866 near Linn, Missouri, Jennie was nearly eighteen years Will's junior and "looked like Mademoiselle Liberté on the French five-franc piece," her son wrote. Her parents were born in France and settled in Missouri. Jennie's mother, Jeanne Frances Regnier Girard, was "trained in the best schools of Normandy, France, before moving to America at age sixteen," eventually becoming a registered nurse at the Osage Boarding School. Back in the 1850s, during the yellow fever epidemic, Jo's grandmother Jeanne Girard traveled to New Orleans to be of service. In 1886, sometime after the deaths of Jeanne's first husband, Joseph Eugene Girard, and her second husband, disreputable Joe Lade, Jeanne Girard moved from

Missouri to the Osage Nation with her children and a half-sister. She remained in Pawhuska until her death. Mathews recalled his grandmother talking with his parents on the front porch on a hot summer's evening, fanning themselves with palm leaves. Jennie and Jeanne switched from English to French when unwrapping gossip, motivating young Jo to learn to understand French.[33]

Jennie Mathews was a compassionate, cheerful person who was active in the early social life of Pawhuska. She was beloved by Pawhuskans, some of whom revered her piety. She was an unwavering Catholic, and the Mathews family attended Mass at Immaculate Conception Church in Pawhuska. Among its many gorgeous stained-glass windows, the church boasts two sponsored by the Mathews family in 1919, in memory of William. He was less religious and, as an Osage, more attuned to what Anishinaabe critic Gerald Vizenor calls "natural reason" than was his French Catholic wife. Once, when Jo was a boy, Will wanted his son to learn a lesson about nature, so he arranged for Jo to view a mare foaling. Jennie frowned upon this, her disapproval mirrored by Lillian. In a 1960 conversation with two compadres, author J. Frank Dobie and oilman Ralph A. Johnston, Mathews said:

> My mother was very devout and my father was more as a pagan I think; he wasn't sure about it. He didn't like anyone to leave a rocking-chair rocking; he was superstitious. That's the closest approach he made to religion. I remember my mother's brother, who was also a non-believer, came from Seattle, Washington, to visit us one time, and I came in from the university and my Uncle met me and came up to the house. I asked, "Where is mother?" He said, "Well, this is Sunday, so . . . she's at the temple of ignorance."

Such remarks, along with his father's brand of paganism, seemingly tied to his Osage identity, influenced Mathews. He would later define himself as non-Christian.[34] When Jo strayed from the church, Jennie prayed for her son. "I suspect she believed me to be a failure in life, since I had renounced both formal religion and money as a standard of happy living," Mathews wrote in his diary. A passionate gardener, she encouraged neighbors to beautify their yards, giving them flowers from her beds. Jo described his mother as a "remarkable woman of dynamic energy" who was deeply interested in flora and fauna, a passion they shared. Jennie never completely mastered English, since her schooling was limited to the "backwoods log schoolhouses of the Missouri French settlements."[35]

While Jo stressed his mother's positive traits, in his diary, he criticized his maternal bloodline, the Regniers and the Girards of France. Typically, scholars discuss only

Mathews's paternal ancestry at any length because of interest in his tribal lineage, but Jo found his mother's ancestry intriguing. In 1952, Jo and Jennie visited her cousins and other kin near Linn, Missouri. Jo reflected, "I find the subject of the Regnier-Girard family intensely interesting and worthy of novelizing under the title of *Gasconade*" (referring to a "Gascon characteristic of empty boasting"). Through conversations with his mother's people in Missouri, Jo felt that ancestral traits were powerfully revealed. In his diary, he recorded the story his mother's maternal relatives told of his great-grandparents, Joseph Regnier and Anna Cortot of Normandy. The Cortots were people of property and culture who boasted "outstanding members." Anna ran away to marry Joseph Regnier, causing her family, who had forbidden him to enter the house, to disown her. The young couple sought refuge in the United States, settling in a French colony between St. Louis and Jefferson City. Joseph Regnier was shunned because his people were "maybe even less than 'humble people.' Perhaps peasants of manure piles, pitchforks and sabots." Mathews enumerated the "Regnier-Girard" family line's shortcomings at length. Whatever misgivings he held about his maternal line, he expressed only high praise for his mother.[36]

Thanks to his mother and father, Jo enjoyed security, privilege, and leisure in an exciting time and place to be a boy. Growing rapidly, Pawhuska blended diverse social, cultural, and spiritual influences. Sitting inside his home one boyhood Sunday in June, Jo heard lively hymns emanating from a little Christian church, blended with the stirring sounds of the Osage I'n-Lon-Schka dances—high-timbred singing, rhythms of drumming, and tintinnabulation of small bells affixed to men's legs—sometimes syncing up with stridulations of cicadas in the family's front yard. The raucous laughter of callous freighters punctuated the ambience. Jo penned a wonderful, autobiographical story reflecting such boyhood experiences. Written in Pawhuska and published in June 1931, "Ee Sa Rah N'eah's Story" is set on the outskirts of the arbor where the I'n-Lon-Schka dances take place. "When the women were decorating their men for the June dances, he [Ee Sa Rah N'eah] could always be found on the edge of the camp, sitting cross-legged, in utter detachment, and there I always searched for him. Though I loved the kettle-drum and its circle of singers, and of course was fascinated by the gyrations of the gorgeous dancers, I grew weary of this spectacle through long familiarity," explains the narrator. Even more than Ee Sa Rah N'eah, Mathews was on the periphery of traditional Osage life, in the metaphorical "grass at the edge of the camp." Jo observed, studied, and mimicked the movements of the dancers with his fingers, but never participated. Arguably, the June dances are more inclusive today than they were then.[37]

Jo's boyhood home was not the striking, tiled-roof house standing today at 611 Grandview Avenue. Built by his father, the first home was moved from the property in 1927 to allow construction of its splendid successor. Blessed by large Osage headright payments, the Mathews family employed an Italian architect, whose style is manifest in the home's arched doorways, niches, and balcony overlooking a fountain on the back patio. Elegant furniture was imported from China and Europe. This second home, next to the old Osage Agency, is where Jo's mother and his unmarried sisters, Lillian and Marie, lived all their lives, following the years his sisters spent at Saint Mary-of-the-Woods College, a women's school in Indiana that Florence also attended. For decades, the Mathews home was vibrant with family and friends, and Mrs. Mathews was a gracious host.

Marie and Florence's travels abroad influenced their choice of architect and furnishings. Circa 1925, Jo bade Marie and Florence bon voyage as they embarked on a trip around the world. According to Jo's son, John Hopper Mathews, Jo, Marie, and Lillian originally planned to travel together, but big brother got married (April 1924) and "spoiled it." Lillian backed out and Florence took her place. They reportedly stopped in Rome, had an audience with the pope in Vatican City, and visited China. Florence's daughter, Fleur Jones, told a family story originating in Marie and Florence's globetrotting. On an ocean liner, James Cash Penney, founder of J. C. Penney stores, became smitten with the much younger Marie Mathews. Marie learned Penney had already been married twice and had children, and apparently, she rebuffed his romantic overtures. Penney's first wife had died in 1910, his second in 1923, and he had three sons from these marriages. The age difference may have also kept Marie from reciprocating his affections, and possibly her deafness made her feel self-conscious. Returning to the States, Penney, still enamored, promptly opened a store in Pawhuska, creating a pretext to see lovely Marie. He visited Pawhuska for the store's grand opening and attempted to visit her. But Marie refused to see him or even leave the house, breaking his heart. Lending credibility to this story, J. C. Penney really did open a small store in Pawhuska in October 1925.[38]

The Mathews's neighbors to the north from 1900 to 1904 were the Mitschers. Oscar Mitscher was agent to the Osages, and his son Tom became a good friend of Jo's, but liked to fight, goading Jo by calling him "Curly," in reference to his hair. Marc, Tom's older brother, later earned fame as a naval aviation pioneer in World War I and a World War II hero; in 1961 Mathews read a biography called *The Magnificent Mitscher* (perhaps a country cousin of *The Great Gatsby*) about Marc. Tom and Jo interacted with traditional Osages. They loved horseback riding over to the village of the Thorny Valley Osages to race horses and play with Osage boys,

The Mathews family home on Grandview Avenue, Pawhuska, Oklahoma, 2014.
Photo by the author.

among whom there was no fist-fighting, arguing, or accusations of unfairness. The Natives played silently, unlike the grackle-like white and mixed-blood boys. These Osage boys, Jo recalls, were "inherently dignified and courteous and extremely cruel," ridiculing misfits and the inept. He visited lodges of traditional Osages, and learned something of their lifeways.[39]

On Jo's thirteenth birthday, November 16, 1907, the Osage Nation became Osage County in the new state of Oklahoma. The tribe was feeling the unfortunate effects of the Dawes Allotment Act, which was finally passed for the Osages during 1906. "Now town lots would be sold in the agency village, at the trading post of the Upland Forest People and at the village of the Big Hills, and town lots would be sold on the high prairie and at the settlement of a chieftain of the Heart Stays People," Mathews wrote. Non-Osages could now enter the reservation as they pleased without permission from the agent or the Osage Council. Fortunately, thanks to the efforts of James Bigheart and others, the tribe held on to their subsurface mineral rights during the negotiations surrounding the Dawes Act. Regardless of surface land sales to non-Osages, tribespeople with headrights would receive a share of the profits from the oil that was increasingly being found under the nation. Mathews wrote that on the day of Oklahoma statehood, the bell of the old Osage Council

House was rung so vigorously, it became stuck upside down, most symbolically. "This was the first time it had been rung by the excitable French-Osage mixedbloods and the euphoric Amer-Europeans, and this proved too much for the old bell that for years had called with dignity to the dignified chieftains to convene in council." The mixed-bloods were ecstatic, filled with incipient glory, while the full-bloods continued their accustomed dancing and feasting. Will Mathews, as a Progressive mixed-blood, also shared in the glory, though he did not speak of this to his son, unlike the father of protagonist Chal Windzer in the novel *Sundown*.[40]

Although Jo was fairly popular as a pre-teen and high school student, he was a loner by choice, a pattern he would follow during later periods. Throughout his boyhood he preferred to observe animals and birds—the red-tailed hawk being his favorite—and to ride Bally over the Osage prairie. On one jaunt, he met an outlaw train robber. On another, he sheltered in a cave to avoid a tornado, an occasional nuisance in Indian Territory. Fascinated with ornithology, Jo also took a correspondence course in taxidermy, and he stuffed a sacred golden eagle for Mr. Puryear, the druggist. Amateur ornithologist Judge Musseller of Pawhuska was so impressed with Jo's ability to identify birds, that he encouraged the youngster to become a natural scientist. Jo studied violin reluctantly but read enthusiastically: Ernest Thompson Seton's animal stories and Jack London's adventures stirred his soul.

Jo Mathews was greatly shaped by the literary, oratorical, political, and scientific gifts of his father and his mentors Laura Tucker, Judge Musseller, and John Palmer. The Sioux-Osage lawyer and politician John Palmer was a great orator who spoke with gravitas, quoted classical authors unpretentiously, and deftly wielded satirical wit. The Pawhuska newspaper identified him as a "Sioux Indian orphan boy who was adopted by the Osages more than half a century ago and grew into a leader and benefactor of the tribe." Palmer is credited with conceiving and advocating the communal plan by which Osage tribal members with headrights equally share the reservation's oil and mineral wealth. Will Mathews was also an orator who admired William Jennings Bryan; in many respects he resembled the mixed-blood Progressive councilman John Windzer, Chal's father in *Sundown*. Jo soaked up this influence, joining the Debate Club and becoming editor-in-chief of the Pawhuska High School yearbook.[41]

In many ways, Mathews experienced a normal adolescence, but he differed from typical teenage boys in one way: he did not have girlfriends, nor did he even date. Tellingly, in "Boy, Horse, and Dog," the first volume of his autobiography (published posthumously under its overall title, *Twenty Thousand Mornings*), he is consumed with the question of why he was uninterested in girls as a teenager and passive about

P. H. S. Trumpeter

Vol. 1. 1912 ANNUAL No. 4

PHOTO BY LOVE

STAFF

Staff of *The Trumpeter*, the Pawhuska High School yearbook, 1912. Mathews is in the front row, second from left. *Courtesy of Pawhuska, Okla., Public Library.*

them as a young adult. He repeatedly wonders why he never had a girlfriend or even a date for school dances, and why he never had sexual experiences with women until women aggressively pursued *him*, after he became a dashing aviator during the Great War. As his diaries and memoir reveal (and as is reflected in *Sundown*), throughout his life Mathews was concerned that others might have seen him as "queer" and "out of step." While sometimes this was a point of pride, it was more often the source of deep concern. "During this period of suddenly descended wisdom and sex arrogance, girls ought to have had special attraction for me," he writes—but they did not. In both his memoirs and the novel *Sundown*, he lingers on childhood experiences with girls and women that shaped him. He pored over his high school diaries looking for answers, insisting, "I was quite normal." He guessed living with four assertive sisters and an energetic mother may have cooled his emerging interest in the fair sex. Moreover, he concluded that because these girls and women doted on him, he thought he never had to work to garner female attention. Thus, he developed a passive attitude about girls and dating and did not participate in the usual rites of adolescence.[42]

Nevertheless, girls found him appealing. One summer, after Jo found a job as a soda jerk at Englishman P. J. Monk's pharmacy through his father, Will repeatedly stopped by, feigning medicinal needs. His deeper motive was to check up on a young regular, one Miss Newcomer. Later in the summer, he told Jo to give Monk notice so that they could freely hunt plover on horseback. He later revealed his underlying motivation: "That Newcomer girl'll get a fella into trouble." Jo was becoming an attractive, athletic young man. The biology-trained Mathews later reflected: "with full reproductive potential, the mysterious, ethereal chemistry working within me had by now created a definite aura, under which I walked and from which flowed the impulse which more and more influenced people to promote my leadership, my passivity notwithstanding." Jo's good looks and quiet charisma served him well.[43]

Mathews graduated from Pawhuska High School in May 1914, and he enrolled at the University of Oklahoma. Although he took little interest in current events, he realized the world was changing as a result of happenings across the Atlantic Ocean, particularly the assassination of Archduke Franz Ferdinand in June. With the declaration of war in July, Jo and Josephine had to cancel their planned trip to England with P. J. Monk and his party. After a full summer of horseback riding, hunting, and boyish adventure, it was time to become a college man.

Chapter Two

FLIGHT / SCHOOL

> Oklahoma is a sort of laboratory which invites experiment; a place not bound by tradition.
>
> —John Joseph Mathews

Mathews began his college career at the University of Oklahoma (OU) in fall 1914. Located in Norman, in the middle of the state, the university was then a relatively humble affair and the student body numbered fewer than a thousand. When he arrived, only a few red-brick buildings had been constructed in the style known as Cherokee Gothic, a term said to have been coined by Frank Lloyd Wright, but which Mathews called "bastard Gothic." Monnet Hall, then the law building, shone proudly in white limestone with its trademark owl perched high; today it houses the Western History Collections, which holds Mathews's papers. The Science Hall and the Library faced each other, tinted red by "winds that blew across the Redbeds" (the Red Beds Plains subregion of Oklahoma). Most of Mathews's classmates, progeny of settlers who fought droughts and grasshoppers in the land runs, were serious students who were not about to blow their chance at college. They were also collegial, though, enjoying solidarity in their common roots.[1]

In a 1917 article for the *University of Oklahoma Magazine*, Mathews explained the Indigenous history of the land on which OU stood. "Thirty years ago there weren't a dozen families within a radius of twenty-five miles of this particular spot," Mathews wrote. "The site of Norman and the University was merely a part of the great prairies grazed over by thousands of head of cattle and hunted over by Indians of a dozen tribes. Two miles distant was the 'Ten Mile Flat,' famous as the camping ground of the Kickapoos and other Indians as they wandered over the plains in search of game." The area was traversed by tribes of the northeastern part of Indian Territory that were visiting tribes in the southwestern part. The area that would become Norman was considered a safe place to camp along the way, "Holy Ground" where a tornado would never hit.[2]

Although the university was modest, a variety of athletics and clubs had started up by the time Mathews arrived. At first, he intended to maintain the athletic prowess he enjoyed at Pawhuska High. He tried out for and made the freshman football team, but never played varsity. In fact, when the freshmen scrimmaged with the varsity team, the tall "sandhill crane," assigned the unlikely position of tackle, was violently slammed by one of the touted Hott brothers, who was built like a tank. Mathews had an epiphany: he was not cut out to be a college football player.

During Jo's first semester, someone suggested the Land Run of 1889 be reproduced on the field during a big game. Thus began a tradition continuing to this day when a touchdown is scored. Ironically, the Native Mathews was part of the genesis of an event celebrating the opening for white settlement of "Unassigned Lands" that the Creeks and Seminoles had been forced to cede after the Civil War because of their support of the Confederacy. During land runs, settlers recklessly rushed land originally set aside for tribes that had been removed from their homelands, usually against their will. The land was promised to the aboriginals forever, but pressure from Boomers and Sooners coalescing at the Kansas border led to it being taken away and offered to whoever had the fastest horse to claim it.

During the inaugural replication of the land run, two horses were used (called today Boomer and Sooner). Mathews and another freshman team member "rode in a dead run, he down one side of the cinder path and I the other, and at the end of the run we reined in our horses, causing them to hook brake with their hind legs, then jumped off and planted our symbolical claim flags." William Mathews was in the stands, proudly watching this display. He may have harbored hopes of seeing his son play football, but this was not to be, since Jo was only a freshman and Will knew naught of Hotts or "coaches trying a sandhill crane out at tackle." He did not see a problem with honoring the land run, which was then only twenty-five years in the past. "Even though the princeling was only a freshman yet, and not suited up on this thrilling day," his father's attitude, when he visited Jo's fraternity house after the game, "seemed to say that anyway there was a hoss in the affair, and son had ridden him well." Will's face glowed during his visit, and the young men "naturally deferred to him," Jo recalled.[3]

Mathews generally found OU amiable. Along with his Pawhuska friends Charles Rider, Jack Ruble, and Jack Bird, Mathews joined the Kappa Alpha fraternity, Beta Eta chapter. Jack Bird was the son of John Lyman Bird, who worked for Jo's father at the Osage Mercantile and later, at his bank. Fraternity brother Howard McCasland, a football and basketball star after whom McCasland Field House was named, was a Big Man on Campus when Mathews joined. Initiated in February 1915, charismatic

Jo was immediately appointed an officer of the fraternity. Mathews enjoyed the chapter's annual dance at Oklahoma City's famous Skirvin Hotel, where author Ralph Ellison later worked as a teenager and gathered material later used in *Invisible Man*. At the frat house, Jo encountered "conscious maleness" manifested in hearty greetings and bear-paw handshakes, and endured hazing. In 1917, Mathews published a humorous piece on fraternity life, in which he described the entrance requirements: "To be qualified for membership in one of these exclusive organizations, you must have the recommendation of somebody who comes from the same part of 'the sticks' you hail from, and who knows you to be 'frat material.'" Jo's experiences in Kappa Alpha later inspired vivid scenes in *Sundown*.[4]

As a student, Mathews did not downplay being Osage. Because of his love of being outdoors, his skin tanned to a shade nearly bronze, lending him a more "authentic" Native look, as seen in youthful photographs. In 1914, the Oklushe Degataga Indian Club was formed, and Jo immediately joined. *Oklushe* means "tribes" in Choctaw, while *Degataga* means "standing together," or "stand firm"; this was the Cherokee name of famous Confederate General Stand Watie, whom Jo's grandfather John A. Mathews supported. By 1916, seven tribes were represented in Oklushe Degataga, including copious Cherokees, Choctaws, and Chickasaws, but only two Osages: Mathews and Sue Lessart of Ponca City, club treasurer and his sometime girlfriend. In spring 1916, Mathews dated Sue, with whom he felt comfortable. One of the few times he ever felt jealousy, he claimed, was when he could not find Sue at her sorority house and later discovered her promenading with a rival. The description of the club in *The Sooner* yearbook adopts the vanishing American trope: "Oklushe Degataga was organized for the purpose of preserving the relics and traditions of the rapidly disappearing Redman." The club edited two issues of the *University of Oklahoma Magazine* and sponsored several Native guests.[5]

While Jo was settling in at OU during his first semester, his big sister Josie was traveling in high style with two other Osage women from Pawhuska, touring eastern American cities, Cuba, and Mexico. Newspapers across the nation reprinted a story from the *Washington Herald*, "Indian Heiresses Invade Capital," which trumpeted the oil wealth (allegedly $3 million apiece) and Parisian haute couture of these "Indian maids" from Oklahoma. The article stated Josie, "distinctly a blonde" (dyed) had been named Little Deer by Chief Saucy Calf, prior to his mysterious murder. She was described as a skilled writer, an "authority on interior decoration," and the daughter of "Judge William S. Mathews, counsel for the Osage tribe," who was a frequent visitor to the capital. But Will's travels had stopped by 1914, due to his declining health.[6]

Josie's lifestyle and Jo's spring semester were interrupted by William's death. That term, Jo tried out for the freshman basketball team, but his plan was thwarted one night in March 1915 when Josie called and said their father was dying. Automobiles were then rare and travel between Norman and Pawhuska was challenging. Jo took a horse carriage to the train station and headed home by rail, reaching the family home around 4 A.M. the next day. There Josie greeted him and said their father, fearing he might sink into a coma, wanted to say goodbye. In that moment, Mathews saw her in a new light: "We stood and looked at each other for some time, then for the first time the beauty of soul that neither one of us had ever been aware of in the jealousy-dominated spoiled child, for the moment was ascendant in the young woman." As they waited for their father to pass, Jo recollected boyhood experiences with his dad, and was shocked to realize how old he was. Will was forty-six when Jo was born, not "almost fifty" as Mathews later wrote, but still older than the average father, when they went deer and turkey hunting together, camping, and sleeping under the "Indian wagon." William S. Mathews died on March 15, 1915, in his home. Mathews felt great familial pride in the abundant tributes that came from his town and tribe, of which he later felt ashamed. Since pride outweighed sadness, Mathews could not shake the feeling he had been somehow disrespectful of his father's memory.[7]

Jo disliked business and never wanted to take over his father's banking affairs. He was therefore gloomy when Elmer Grinstead, the family lawyer, said Jo ought to stay home to help his mother manage Will's affairs. Jennie, an "insouciant Frenchwoman," had neither taken interest in her husband's business nor learned the value of a dollar, having been accustomed to buying items from the Osage Mercantile at cost. In part because she "believed in the superiority of the male," Mathews thought his mere presence as a capable young man would aid and reassure her in her time of grief. Since Jo was not financially savvy either, the family was fortunate to have worthy advisors in Clyde Lake, cashier at the Citizens National Bank, and Grinstead, their honest lawyer. Ultimately, Mathews returned to OU a month later to finish out the term, but traveled home most weekends.[8]

Shortly after William's death, five or six Osages of the Big Hill band rode up on horseback from Greyhorse Indian Village. They were led by a member of the prominent Tall Chief family of the Buffalo Face clan, probably Eves Tall Chief, who served on the Osage National Council with Judge Mathews from 1900 to 1904. Jo held the door open for the full-bloods, who walked in as they would have on the trail, each stepping into the invisible footprints of the man in front of him. In silence they gathered in front of a portrait of William and sang the death chant that had so haunted Mathews as a boy, breaking off in a "sob of frustration, like a violin string breaking during an emotional crescendo." They turned heel and left the same way they had come, never acknowledging Jo. The Big Hill men returned twice more to sing the death chant after Jo returned to university, upsetting Jennie Mathews. This anecdote underscores the integrity of William's Osage identity and his recognition among Big Hill men.[9]

While Mathews was absent from school, he was assigned special papers to write. One was for Geology 1, on "the stratigraphy of the Redbeds on which we stood." Mathews, who became a geology major, earned an A. For English 1, he was charged with a humorous essay—an odd choice for a student absent for a funeral. Mathews gave it the old college try with "Wild Animals I Have Et," a parody of a book he had loved growing up: Ernest Thompson Seton's illustrated story collection, *Wild Animals I Have Known*. Seton, an English-born author and wildlife artist, was a founder of the Boy Scouts of America and the Woodcraft League. Young Woodcraft campers "played Indian," learning to live like Seton's idealized image of pre-contact aborigines. Twenty years later, Mathews visited the author at Seton Village camp near Santa Fe, which included a "College of Indian Wisdom" where Woodcraft leaders learned Native skills and crafts. There Jo delivered an impressive speech and befriended Southwestern artist and author Laura Adams Armer, who penned the Newbery Medal–winning *Waterless Mountain* (1931), peopled by Navajo characters. Although Mathews thought Seton's romantic project was doomed to fail, he still respected the elderly author. In 1959, while researching *The Osages*, Mathews reread Seton's *The Gospel of the Red Man*.[10]

In summer 1915, Mathews enrolled at Sewanee, the University of the South, a gorgeous Episcopal school whose campus overlooks the Tennessee Valley. Mathews cherished fond memories of that special summer, and hoped in vain to transfer to Sewanee for his sophomore year. He viewed Sewanee, with its classical and Heidelberg-like atmosphere, as a magical place where he could make good grades— and maybe even make the football team, since there was less competition. Mathews became more engaged in his studies than ever. Jo studied literature, but became bored by the "constant paeans to the literary effusions of the same old stable of American imitators of English writers and to the precious English novelists." He was, however, a top philosophy student along with Herbert Morris. Herbert and his brother Frederick had been Jo's classmates at Mrs. Tucker's school back home. Although they influenced Mathews to attend Sewanee, escape from home was also a factor, since he had already spent ample time in Pawhuska helping his mother after his father's death.[11]

Though Sewanee's students were men, Mathews found opportunities to meet charming southern women such as Charlotte Sessuns of Louisiana, with whom he "walked to the Point, filled with the glow of the potential creator, sublimated and euphoric." Another was Circe, the "lovely sophisticate" of "1915 vintage," more properly Miss Searcy of Atlanta, a "breathless and dramatic skirt swirler." She was impressed that Mathews refused to submit to a Homeric "swine" she transmogrified with her allure. The swine—that is, a booze-emboldened rival—demanded Jo stop dancing with Circe. They were on the verge of fisticuffs when a popular and gentlemanly football player intervened. Among southern college men at Sewanee, Jo discerned "conscious gentlemen" instead of mere "conscious maleness," a cut above their Oklahoman counterparts. By the end of the summer, both his mind and body had developed toward his late father's classical ideal of scholar-athlete. He wished to remain at Sewanee, but details of his father's estate still demanded his attention, necessitating a return to Oklahoma.[12]

Somewhat disappointed, then, Mathews returned to Norman for his sophomore year in fall 1915, leaving Pawhuska in time to avoid severe flooding that deluged downtown in September. At OU he tried out for the football team with no hope of making it, but with the goal of physical fitness. The best he could do was play with the Yanigans, "unlettered football pariahs," Mathews quipped, forerunners of the raucous Ruf/Neks. Before the football season was over, however, Mathews was out in the countryside instead of on the gridiron or yelling from the sidelines, hunting ducks along the Canadian River and quail on a local farm, and gazing upon gorgeous sunsets. Some weekends he was obliged to return to Pawhuska to assist his mother with finances and properties. These weekends at home, he said, yet again extinguished his hopes of playing hoops for the Sooners.[13]

During spring 1916, Mathews was a reporter for the student newspaper, then called the *University Oklahoman*, writing campus news stories, and in 1917 he published articles in the *University of Oklahoma Magazine*. The spring campus ambience was infused with groups of sorority women singing in unison under the elms, joined by bullfrogs croaking and peeper frogs chirping. As in high school, he was a "stag" at the dances. He attended these pleasant affairs, but arranged no dates himself. Jo's fraternity brothers, who seemed to note his relative disinterest in women, deemed him a safe date for their younger sisters visiting the university. Mathews thus found himself set up for several dates, much like Chal in *Sundown*. In the spring, high school seniors flocked to the university to visit fraternities or sororities in anticipation of the Greek rush the following semester. One sorority asked Jo, who owned a car, to escort their prospects during the next rush, leading Mathews to facetiously call himself the "Theta pimp" in front of some of his brothers. Such jocularity offended some, especially the upperclassmen: Mathews was chastised in a house meeting for his transgression against Southern Womanhood. Kappa Alpha had originated at the archetypally southern Washington and Lee University, and Mathews claimed their motto was "Dieu et les Dames." Thus his "flippancy was almost a matter of apostasy."[14]

In the summer of 1916, along with riding Bally on his old stomping grounds, Jo participated in an archaeological expedition at Honey Creek, near Grove, Oklahoma, though he actually spent most of his time hunting, fishing, and bird-watching. The organizer of the party was the historian and archaeologist Joseph B. Thoburn, who published *The History of Oklahoma* and was a founding editor of *The Chronicles of Oklahoma*. Among the members was Elmer Fraker, who sang bass in the Sooner Singers quartet with budding playwright Lynn Riggs and became director of the Oklahoma Historical Society. As the group journeyed to Big Mouth Cavern, they were soaked by rain and mistaken for gold diggers. Local residents, who had little concept of searching for sherds of pottery and arrowheads, began spreading rumors that the group was looking for gold, perhaps in the skulls of Indians. To thwart intrusion of curious locals, the party concocted a "Hecome-hicome story" about a monster in the cave, spreading word that their sleep was disrupted by bloodcurdling screams and howls emanating from within. Mathews told the story to hunters and fishermen he met, setting up an epic prank. Their curiosity sparked, a small crowd of rustics gathered around the cave's mouth. Thoburn lectured to them about the artifacts the expedition had found before suddenly switching, as planned, to an account of terrors they had suffered. Suddenly, groans and wails issued from the cavern, and all the archaeologists except Jo ran out of the cave, screaming, "The Hecome-hicome is coming out!" The locals fled in terror, and the pranksters circled back to the cave and congratulated their confederate, Jo, who was crawling out of the interior of the cave, "covered with clay, but clasping his Osage flute—the great Hecome-hicome." Other than Mathews nearly being shot by a brave farmer, the prank was a success.[15]

Later that summer, in August, Jo traveled by rail to visit his friend Floyd Soderstrom and the latter's teenaged bride, Rozie, for two weeks at their homestead in South Dakota, near the Wyoming border. He returned home only to turn around and head out again. This time, he traveled by car with Jack Bird and Jack Ruble to the Colorado Rockies, Wyoming, and Montana for hunting and skylarking. On their return, the Pawhuska newspaper announced their faces resembled "an old, peeled leather boot."[16]

Mathews returned to Norman for his junior year in fall 1916. Many know Mathews loved hunting, but few know he delighted in ballroom dancing! Jo joined the Tobasco

Club to trip the light fantastic with other campus dancers. These evenings are vividly evoked in scenes from *Sundown*. Jo's experiences at OU provided him with rich material, as they did for playwright Lynn Riggs, whose first play *Cuckoo*, a fraternity farce, debuted at OU in 1921. Jo fondly recalled pep rallies and festive bonfires in the streets of Norman on nights before big football games. He joined the Folk Lore Club, remained active in Oklushe Degataga, served on the staff of the *Sooner* yearbook, and wrote for student publications. Yet for some unfathomable reason, he flunked a journalism class for neglecting to write a required editorial. Later, Mathews wondered over his "incredible nonchalance and disinterest during this period." With a track record of "non-competed for and careless successes," Jo displayed the insouciant attitude of a young "princeling," as he put it, who, possessing looks, money, and charisma, rarely had to work for success and was accustomed to things being handed to him.[17]

Yet Mathews was a decent student in the natural sciences. Geology was his major and zoology his minor. OU had a strong geology department, and with oil strikes on people's minds in Oklahoma, a geology degree was practical and potentially lucrative. In 1915, Mathews joined the Pick and Hammer geology club, and he cut a cross-dressing caper during one coed geology fieldtrip. At night the professors transformed into Victorian chaperones, so Mathews and frat brother Charles McGaha played a prank. They dressed in borrowed women's clothes, then appeared by the fire before running into the darkness, causing a ruckus among the professors and prompting a count of the women. But even the chaperones could not contain a smile when the lark was revealed. Although he could be a trickster, Mathews was serious about his study of the natural world: in December he delivered a paper, "Hawks of Oklahoma," to the Oklahoma City Academy of Science. He returned to Pawhuska for Thanksgiving and for the winter holidays.[18]

In spring 1917, excitement over America's involvement in the Great War in Europe saturated every aspect of campus life, explicitly or implicitly. Mathews now read international news, not just the sports page. Trumpeted by newspapers and radio, the "romance of the war in the air" gripped him. The amateur ornithologist's heroes became European flying aces, celebrities such as Frenchman Georges Guynemer, French American Gervais Raoul Lufbery, and the dastardly Manfred von Richthofen, the Red Baron. That spring, buzzing energy filled the air with a strange euphoria. As war fever spread, the Greeks threw a military ball, with men in uniform and women in Red Cross nurses' garb. Jo borrowed an elaborate uniform from Oscar Jacobson, Swedish American artist and professor who in the mid-1920s famously mentored the Kiowa Five (or Kiowa Six) Oklahoma artists. He described the gifted artist as a role model, a man in whom "virility and ruggedness" comingled happily with attributes of the "classic gentleman." Mathews felt guilty about losing an epaulette from Jacobson's uniform. In January, Josephine traveled to Norman to visit her brother and friends, and attended a fraternity dance. Home ties were strong; Jo returned for Easter weekend and no doubt attended Mass with his mother and sisters at the stunning Immaculate Conception Church on Lynn Avenue, completed in 1915.[19]

Mathews learned that Plattsburgh camps were offering training for citizen-officers. When Oklahoma, Arkansas, and Louisiana received an officers' training camp, Mathews joined the First Cavalry of the Twelfth Provisional Troop, and waited to be transported to Little Rock, Arkansas. Before his departure, he took out an ad in the May 2 issue of the student newspaper, quipping, "patriotism is as high as the skirts in Hawaii," and he was leaving to do his duty. Therefore, he was offering for sale a dress suit in which he had "tripped many a dance (and girl) which still has the powder on the lapel where some lovely head has lain asleep through some dreamy waltz. Show your patriotism dear brother and buy it." He signed it "Brother Joe." After saying au revoir to college friends, Jo drove to Pawhuska to take leave of family and prepare for his trip. On May 9, Mathews and Jack Bird departed for the Citizens Training Camp of the Officers Reserve Corps, situated on Big Rock Mountain on the site of old Fort Logan H. Roots in North Little Rock.[20]

A hippophile, Mathews chose the cavalry, but ironically, he never rode a horse in the service. At Fort Roots, Mathews found an old-timey "Boots & Saddles" military atmosphere reminiscent of the stories of Bret Harte. Uniforms were antiquated and unstylish. Oddly, his troop "drilled in the manner of cavalry, but there was only one horse in the whole troop and he belonged to Captain Hays." There would be no horses. Being in a "horseless cavalry" appealed to Jo's sense of the absurd, but flying was never far from his dreams.[21]

In the meantime, his interest in young women became stronger. Although he had enjoyed some collegiate romances, he remained a virgin until he joined up. Jo's description of his initiation into sex is comical. At Citizens Training Camp, Mathews befriended men from New Orleans, whose "Southern male's chivalric haughtiness and dash" he admired. Jo was surprised to learn these men divided women into three categories: "lady and wench and Niggah." In contrast, his father had raised Mathews to honor the Cult of Southern Womanhood, to place all white women in the category of the lady, worthy of reverence and chivalry. This ideal, when combined with Jo's "inherent passivity," became Jo's "Achilles Heel when the female threw off her Victorian garments of hypocrisy and ignored the Moral Code (man-made), to which she had never given anything except lip service, and was forced to play the natural role of aggressor." On encountering handsome Jo, the passive princeling, young women "all seemed eager to escape the false pressures" of contemporary morality and reverted to "primitive female aggressiveness," he claimed. Interestingly, he represents himself as cool and passive, and women as desirous and aggressive. One Saturday afternoon in 1917, Mathews and his New Orleans friend, a smoothie named Chevalier Blanc, dressed, groomed, and went into town to meet two girls. From the way Chev primped in the mirror, Jo anticipated "sex adventure in company with this Don Juan." Mathews alluded to "khaki-wacky" women in his autobiography and in *Sundown*, and in Little Rock, he wrote, such women were as easy to meet as prostitutes, but the arrangements required "much more formality." Jo claimed to be unaware of any such arrangements, however, presenting himself as a compliant sidekick. Jo and Chev met the girls on a hotel mezzanine, then took them out for sundaes. With haste, since they had only a few hours to spare, they drove out to the country in a car Chev had arranged. Chev and his girl carried the backseat cushion into the brush, while Jo and his date remained in the roadster. Because Mathews thought the criterion of good sex was "ecstasy," that of "the prancing, whinnying, cajoling range stallion," anticipation of which filled him with "euphoric primordial excitement," he was rather disappointed in his "initiation into sexual activity." His date, however, experienced "light-headed glee, due partly perhaps to the thrill of her own naughtiness." After Jo climaxed, his date still clung to him with affection, making him wonder if he "had completed the ritual." Since Mathews believed no lady would yield so readily, he believed they had purchased sex that day. After Chev dropped the girls off on a corner in a nice neighborhood of "rolling lawns and elms," which Jo found disconcerting, he opened his wallet as if to pay Chev. Sizing up Jo as a naïve prairie boy, Chev simply remarked that the place where they had dropped the girls was down the road from a boarding school. Not only were these girls not sex workers, they were Catholic schoolgirls. For a few days Jo was shocked and felt he "had somehow sinned against Southern Womanhood." This did not keep him from seeing his date the next week, however, when the ritual was repeated. Such incidents challenged Mathews's assumptions about women. He admitted twenty-five years later, "I never knew much about women's souls."[22]

Mathews retained his dream of flight, and when his endomorphic friend Phil announced he had applied for ground school pre-training for the Aviation Section of the U.S. Signal Corps, Mathews was inspired. If Phil could learn to fly, and if his hero Georges Guynemer, with his "frail, feminine beauty" had done it with élan, then why on earth could not the "sandhill crane" himself take to the skies? After all, from boyhood Mathews had been fascinated by birds and had yearned to soar. When Jo was very young, he, like Chal in *Sundown*, had literally cried tears of frustration at his inability to fly. Captain Hayes granted his request for a transfer, and Mathews was accepted for ground school. His status changed from "citizen in officer training" to "cadet in training for a commission in the Signal Corps." After concluding his training at Fort Roots, he returned to Pawhuska and awaited orders.[23]

Mathews was sent to ground school at Austin, Texas, where he pursued an English-style aviation curriculum and drilled every afternoon except weekends. His routine was "classes, drill, lectures, wireless, meteorology, motors, alignment," from dawn until dusk. Mathews claimed four years of West Point regimentation were crammed into a few weeks of ground school, after which one was qualified to enter flying school. In August 1917, Jo made a brief trip home to see his mother, sisters, and friends, and he presumably also returned for Josephine's marriage to Henry Benjamin Caudill on Halloween. Born in Kentucky, Caudill had Oklahoma roots: his father, William J. Caudill, was one of the framers of the Oklahoma state constitution.[24]

Back at ground school, on Saturday afternoons Jo and his buddies took the trolley into Austin, mostly to chase women. University of Texas women, faced with a dude shortage, were charmed by suave aviators. Mathews soon found a steady "playmate," Mary Wilkins, who he said, "seemed to understand my idiosyncrasies so readily, especially my *joie de vivre* insouciance, which dominated my sense of humor." Whereas some people saw Mathews as arrogant or pretentious, Mary enjoyed his disposition, and they danced and laughed. Gore Vidal writes that early pilots, "temperamentally unlike other people," operated "above the earth in every sense." They were "uncommonly brave," if, in many cases "uncommonly disdainful of us earthbound ants." Jo was surprised by a bout of jealousy after he was assigned guard duty on New Year's Eve. By the time he was released at 2:00 A.M., Mary was dancing with some other charming, "arrogant" youth. "I had supposed that there would be no need for a display of jealousy where there is no competitive spirit and where passivity is the dominating characteristic and where there had ever been the assurance of being favored," Mathews mused.[25]

Mathews squeaked through ground school: motors were his nemesis, and even upon graduation he was hazy about the difference between a camshaft and a crankshaft. Nevertheless, he was accepted to flying school and assigned to Kelly Field, near San Antonio. Even though his first commissioned flight instructor was gruff and stingy with praise, this did not dampen Jo's thrill of flight: "I was at last brother to the golden eagle who circled so arrogantly above the Osage Prairies, taunting me for my earth-anchored stodginess." While flying, in his mind he became a bird.

Although the dream of flight is universal, his intense identification links deeply to his Osageness, his tribal interrelation with and connection to animals and birds. Mathews was a quick study: soloing in eight hours, he rapidly became a pilot. Once he moved into the cross-country flying stage, he was finally doing what he had always yearned to do. He made solo joy flights over the woods, gazing down on "the arterial system of earth." As he mastered flying, he came to think of his plane, a Curtiss JN-4 "Jenny," as a sentient being like Bally. Mathews felt thrill and ecstasy on solo and cross-country flights.[26]

Flying was extremely dangerous then, however. Mathews never flew in combat or served overseas, but he yearned to, and he was most courageous in his training and teaching of aviation. Accidents, many fatal, were common, and military planes were not then equipped with parachutes. Three of his bunkmates at Kelly Field perished in crashes. Once he had to make an emergency landing when a sparkplug misfired, and he and his plane attracted intense interest among ranchers and farmhands. While Mathews was stationed at Kelly, the base was hit by the 1918 influenza pandemic, and was quarantined. Jo did not become ill; nevertheless, his mother and youngest sister, Florence, apparently concerned over his health, managed to gain entry. Although the base was guarded, Jennie commanded their taxi driver to drive on, even if he had to run over the guard, who leapt out of the way! Jennie's insistence even persuaded Jo's commanding officer, who gave Jo a weekend pass to visit with family, and later seemed troubled by his own leniency. Mrs. Mathews had powers.[27]

In 1918, eagle-eyed Mathews was recommended for training in aerial bombing and was sent to a flyer's clearinghouse at Love Field in Dallas to await assignment. This extended layover was delightful, because he and two pilot friends were "adopted" by the Burtons, a prominent family who rented a suite at the famous Adolphus Hotel downtown after turning over their home to a patriotic wartime effort. One friend was classmate Ben Allan Ames, son of Judge Charles Bismark Ames. The Burtons's suite became a civilian home for the three flyers, who often dined with the family. The Burtons had three lovely daughters sweetening the whole deal, the Hotel had a ballroom, and Jo knew how to dance. Because of the Burtons and the vivacity of their social life, Mathews hated to leave Dallas.[28]

Eventually, Mathews was sent to Ellington Field, lying between Houston and Galveston, for advanced training in night bomb raiding. There, Mathews bunked with three other flyers in a tent. Quickly he became enchanted with night flying, which like cross-country flying, filled him with excitement and wonder, and his enthusiasm was mistaken for military dedication. Beyond night flying and rigorous bombing target practice, Mathews also indulged in skylarks such as buzzing the

Mathews in an Army Aviation Section, U.S. Signal Corps uniform, circa 1918. *Courtesy of the Mathews family.*

Rice Institute campus, waving and waggling his wings. His vision and ability were so keen, he soon became an instructor in night bomb raiding. He enjoyed this position, which he felt suited him perfectly. As other young soldiers died horribly in the trenches of Europe, Mathews lived the high life in Dallas, and at Ellington he "was free and playful" and "could take a plane off the line" at whim. Each flight was still risky though. Once because of a ruptured oil line, he was forced to descend from a moonlit sky, deploying landing flares. He spent the rest of the night attuned to the sounds of animals and birds. Another time, when he was an instructor flying with a student, horrifically, the student crashed into another plane. The smashed planes fell together, and Mathews hurt his ankle and suffered a severe burn on his right forearm from the exhaust pipe.[29]

Mathews was promoted to second lieutenant and moved to more comfortable barracks. He toned down his play, at least the aerial variety, when he became an officer. Instead of fighting the Red Baron, as his imaginative daughter Virginia would claim, Mathews flew over Texas towns in large formations of planes, dropping cards promoting war bonds, then landed and met mayors and beauty queens. Surrounded by "fluttering women," he enjoyed dances and balls, all part of the job. In his free time he reunited with Mary Wilkins, dancing at the Galvez in Galveston and on the roof of Houston's Rice Hotel. She and Mathews drove with others along Texas beaches in Jo's used car, and one moonlight night they drove too far out on the wet sand and became stuck. Though his memory was hazy, Mathews thought the car kept sinking and may have been lost. To the carefree young people joyriding that night, probably drunk, the whole episode was a lark. At the time, Mathews received a generous Osage headright payment plus his military pay, so perhaps the cost of a car did not worry him.[30]

Mathews indulged an Anglophile fantasy of flying for his hero, General Edmund Allenby, in Palestine. Allenby led British Empire forces against Turkish fighters of the Ottoman Empire, commanded T. E. Lawrence ("Lawrence of Arabia"), and conquered Jerusalem. Mathews mentioned Allenby several times. The fact that in the midst of war, Allenby was "imperturbably studying the botany of the region" held "special appeal" for him. In *Sundown*, Chal admires an Englishman, Professor Granville, whom he later encounters as Major Granville when the latter reappears to inspect Chal's piloting skills. After Chal lands a plane, Granville approaches him with a flower in his hand, much like a suitor. Identifying it as *Yucca elata*, Granville says he received a letter from Allenby, who was sure the flower could be found in the Middle East. "Yes, Allenby is writing a book on the flora of Palestine, and he had some very queer theories about the Yucca," Granville tells Chal. "I am gathering notes here and we are exchanging data." That night, Chal lies on his bunk, thinking of the way Granville brought him the flower and told him of Allenby's research. Chal figures the reason why he likes Granville so much, and the idea of Allenby writing down "queer theories" in a book on flora in "the middle of the greatest war in history" was simple: "he was queer himself." It is queer indeed that Mathews kept mentioning the possibility of flying for Allenby, for the simple reason that he was an American flyer in Texas, and the United States was not involved in that Middle Eastern front during World War I.[31]

Instead, Mathews was summoned to Langley Field near Hampton, Virginia, for duties unknown. He and another flyer were given four days to report there, so Jo briefly visited with family in Pawhuska before heading east. When he arrived just before the deadline, the commandant there was surprised, having received no orders. They lodged with a nice family, but soon it became "obvious the commandant might never receive orders" for them, so they concluded they were lost. Eventually, they became officers of the post, serving as "aerial chauffeurs" to militarized government scientists conducting aerodynamics research. Mathews joined the first experiments in cloud seeding to create manmade precipitation. He piloted photographers of bomb trajectories, and tested tinted goggles and other inventions. During one experiment with plane-to-ground telephony, Mathews nearly had to make a crash landing on water when his airplane caught fire. Fortunately, the fire extinguished itself and Mathew was able to pull up from the water in the nick of time. During this period, Mathews playfully circled the Statue of Liberty and the Washington Monument. While posted at Langley, he spent time in Richmond with a young lady, Ethel Ann Sutton. He and "auburn-haired, lovely voiced" Ethel danced at hotels and spent happy weekends driving around the Tidewater. He was still in touch with Sutton four years later.[32]

In August 1918 his sister Josephine gave birth to Henry Ben Caudill, Jr. A few months later, the Great War ended, and by summer 1919 Mathews returned home. His horse Bally now had a sorrel colt, suspicious of this bipedal stranger. His birddog Spot had died while he was at Ellington Field. While Jo may have been disappointed not to have seen aerial combat, the mounting lists of casualties and the stories he heard from friends who survived the front lines surely made him grateful for his domestic assignments.[33]

The War Department asked Mathews to join the Army's newly formed Air Service and retain his rank. Though flattered, Mathews opted to return to the University of Oklahoma in fall 1919 to complete his degree. On campus, war heroes were back in force and with a new sense of focus. The school was overwhelmed by a flood of returned veterans, and to alleviate this burden, Mathews believed the school rushed the men through the remainder of their education. Although Mathews left college for the military during the second semester of his junior year, the faculty of Arts and Sciences offered him generous credit for his ground school study of aerodynamics, wanting to graduate him after just one more term. Instead Jo decided to study for a full senior year.[34]

Now older and more experienced than the average senior, Jo was a Big Man on Campus and the top Kappa Alpha officer in fall 1919. When the 1920 *Sooner* yearbook devoted two illustrated pages to lists of "Sooner Vamps"—*vamp* being 1920s slang for a flirtatious, hip modern woman—"Joe Mathews," a sophisticated "Fifth Avenue Type," was one of five "He-Vamps." Due to his injured ankle, Mathews could not pursue athletics, regrettable since polo was now offered, probably thanks to Anglophile oilman E. W. Marland, a regent of the University. On the other hand, Mathews had time to pursue women and "seemed more interested in girls now." After his wartime experiences Mathews felt he saw women more "as they were, and this gave more confidence." He still felt the Cult of Southern Womanhood influence, but women's "wings had vanished and the nimbus was grown dim." He danced often and enjoyed several "playmates." Most of the campus women he had known prewar had married or had graduated. His last prewar girlfriend, Georgia Shutt, was replaced by Dorothy Prouty, Jo's "special playmate" and a member of Owl & Triangle, a women's honor society. Dorothy, who "walked across campus with long Junoesque strides," hiked with him to the Canadian River and danced the night away. During the "spring field meet" when Greeks rushed potential pledges, Jo brought the Mathews family car to campus in order to impress visiting high school seniors he chauffeured, hoping they would pledge to Dorothy's Kappa Alpha Theta sorority: "Again, the Theta pimp." Since Elizabeth Palmour, Jo's second wife, matriculated at OU the following semester and joined a sorority, it is possible they first met during this event.[35]

In 1919, Mathews again joined the staff of the student newspaper, and was on the staff of the *Sooner* yearbook. Shockingly, the 1920 *Sooner* staff (not including Mathews), allowed the Ku Klux Klan to have a full page, which simply said "KKK" and their motto, "Nemo Nos Impune Lacessit" (no one cuts me with impunity). The opposite page depicted the vengeful secret society DDMC (Deep Dark Mystery Club), looking sinister in leather hoods, gathered over a hooded, supine victim, apparently in the woods. The DDMC were a so-called law and order society who dealt harshly with supposedly wayward students. During Jo's college years and for decades afterwards, Norman was a "sundown town," meaning that African Americans were not permitted to remain there after darkness fell, nor were they allowed to drink from the water fountain in front of the Administration Building, as Mathews noted. In 1922, a black jazz band from Oklahoma City, hired by OU students, was run out of town by an angry mob clutching nooses and guns.[36]

During Jo's final semester, spring 1920, he got to know Walter Stanley Campbell, who became a crucial mentor. In 1915, Campbell was appointed a professor of English and started what became the Professional Writing Program. Beginning in 1927, using the pen name Stanley Vestal (his middle and given last name), he published many popular books on the Old West and Indians. He is notable for being one of the first Euro-American writers of the history of the West to consider the Indigenous point of view and use Native source materials. Partly for that reason, he was an honorary member of Oklushe Degataga. That spring, Campbell, who was a Rhodes scholar, World War I veteran, and faculty advisor of Jo's fraternity, was elected secretary of the Rhodes Scholar Committee for the state of Oklahoma. Soon after this appointment, he visited the Kappa Alpha house to talk to Jo about applying for a Rhodes.[37]

It is a widely repeated myth that Mathews either was a Rhodes scholar or was offered a Rhodes scholarship but rejected it because its terms were "too restrictive." According to his autobiography, however, Mathews did not apply for a scholarship, despite strong encouragement from Campbell. His grades were uneven, and he feared being rejected, thereby embarrassing his sponsor. Jo suggested to Campbell that he apply to Oxford and, if accepted, pay his own way rather than apply for a scholarship. Money was not an issue for Mathews at the time, since the Osages were affluent from tribal oil profits. In a 1972 interview, Mathews explained the misunderstanding, saying people naturally associate Oxford with the Rhodes scholar, and many stubbornly clung to the idea he was one. "Finally I just stopped saying I wasn't a Rhodes Scholar; I just let it go. I didn't correct," he admitted. Campbell helped Mathews gain admittance to his alma mater, selective Merton College. Mathews thought Campbell must have exaggerated his athletic ability, "dormant since high school," and his scholastics, "which like a hibernating insect came out only when sun-warmed by whimsical enthusiasm." He was accepted and expected for Michaelmas term in October 1920.[38]

Back in Pawhuska during the summer of 1920, Jo took a car trip to Yellowstone National Park with his mother and younger sisters. As he drove the Packard-12 through sage mesas and flats, he and his sisters sang together. "Lillian had a beautiful voice, but Marie, Florence and I were just expressing our sense of well-being, even as a coyote talks to the moon." Amidst mountains and in heavy rain, Mathews struggled with the vicissitudes of early automobiles, cooling the motor off after it overheated and putting on tire chains in soggy conditions while the ladies examined flowers or frolicked in a snowbank. At Yellowstone, he rode trails on horseback with Florence. In front of their hotel by himself, he witnessed a fistfight between two middle-aged men that dragged on until broken up by a police officer. Mathews was shocked and disillusioned to see roly-poly "businessmen with lodge symbols across their vests" brawling like beasts. His father had instilled in him a sense of respect for the "gentleman," a category that included nearly any professional. Mathews experienced a range of emotions, from vicarious shame and discomfort to mockery and disenchantment with "man's illusions about himself." Suddenly it seemed the concept of human dignity had little justification. He never mentioned this disturbing incident to his family.[39]

After such a major road trip, one might expect that Mathews would settle down to prepare for his voyage and studies at Oxford. Instead, he decided to embark on an elaborate, expensive big-game hunting trip in the Rockies, returning to the Wyoming Yellowstone area. He was joined on the first leg by Josephine's husband, Henry Benjamin Caudill, Sr. "We picked up our saddle horses and pack string at Holmes Lodge on the Shoshone River, on the trail to the east gate of the Park. Besides the five saddle horses, one for Bill the guide, one for Jim the cook, one for Wuff the wrangler and one each for Henry and me, we had a string of perhaps fourteen or fifteen pack horses," he wrote. They hunted nonstop and camped out in the snow. With beginner's luck, Henry bagged a wapiti (elk) bull the second day, but it took Mathews much longer to do the same. "Glad to be alive," Mathews thrilled to the sound of the "challenge of the bull wapiti," which filled him with ecstasy. "I was proud of my manhood," Mathews wrote in 1929, in Hemingway mode. "In his bugle there seemed to be virility, passion, power, courage, a primitive freedom, the will to survive, and a plaintive insatiable yearning." After he shot a bull wapiti, he was so anxious to ensure he would have a trophy that, fearful it would be ravaged by grizzlies, he insisted on decapitating it and dragging its gory head back to camp that night, against his guide Bill's good advice. In the dark he fell and rolled with a bloody, large antlered head down a snowy slope.[40]

After they returned to the lodge and Caudill departed, Mathews impulsively decided he wanted to hunt bighorn sheep in the Sunlight country of Wyoming. This would mean skipping his first term at Oxford, a rare privilege, but he cared not. In Cody, Wyoming, he took his unwieldy wapiti head to the taxidermist, and telegraphed his family and the Cunard Lines in New York to cancel his passage to England. Why was his desire to kill bighorn sheep more important than his first term at Oxford? It is a mystery. Surely he risked being denied a second chance. Yet Mathews followed his whim; even Oxford would not deter him from extending his already extravagant hunting trip in the Rockies.[41]

Before returning to Oklahoma, Mathews absorbed vibrant local color in Cody, a classic Western town. His guide, Bill Barron, introduced him to Caroline Lockhart, then a popular Western fiction writer and newspaper owner. On returning to Pawhuska in December 1920, Jo sent Campbell a copy of Lockhart's 1919 novel *The Fighting Shepherdess*, adapted into a film in March 1920, with a note explaining the fictitious town in the novel is Cody and the model for the novel's heroine was forced to sell her sheep at auction at low prices. Barron threw Mathews a rootin', tootin' party at the Irma Hotel, thick with Old West atmosphere. Jo hoe-downed with many girls and women to the music of indefatigable fiddlers and was invited into hotel rooms of sociable strangers. One wayward, drunken Harvard graduate, a would-be cowboy, whipped out a pearl-handled revolver and fired it through the ceiling. No one bothered to look in.[42]

Finally returning home in December, Mathews found a letter from Oxford awaiting him, hinting that Mathews did not properly appreciate the opportunity he had been offered and suggesting that more appreciative students were lined up to take his place. For freshmen, Michaelmas term was fairly unstructured and they were not obligated to prepare for exams; however, this period was seen as crucial, because, as Campbell's tutor had told him when he was at Merton College, this was when students became critical thinkers, learning the ropes of intellectual society. In spite of his transgression, Mathews was expected to appear for Trinity Term in the spring, and occupy the rooms at Merton left vacant since October. Mathews had previously told Campbell of his change in plans, and Campbell had alerted Merton that Jo had gone a-hunting, which possibly saved his spot. "He should have expressed disappointment, one might suppose," Mathews wrote, but instead, when he visited Campbell before leaving for England, the professor met him with a grin, and said with delight, "You're getting away with murder."[43]

Chapter Three

OXFORD AND EUROPE

> Oxford, in those days, was still a city of aquatint. Her autumnal mists, her grey springtime, and the rare glory of her summer days . . . when the chestnut was in flower and the bells rang out high and clear over her gables and cupolas, exhaled the soft airs of centuries of youth. It was this cloistral hush which gave our laughter its resonance, and carried it still, joyously, over the intervening clamour.
>
> —Evelyn Waugh, *Brideshead Revisited*

Missing Michaelmas Term and Hilary Term, John Joseph Mathews sailed to England via New York, reaching Oxford by mid-April 1921 for Trinity Term. From 1921 to 1924, Jo became a dashing Oxonian, cosmopolitan traveler, and husband of a talented young woman from a prosperous family. These years abroad affected his worldview, lifestyle, and even his speech. Jo matriculated at Merton College, Oxford, and traveled while a student and afterward in England, Scotland, continental Europe, and Algeria. During the summer of 1923, he took courses in international relations and French at the University of Geneva in Switzerland. In Geneva, Mathews in short order met, courted, and married his first wife, Virginia "Ginger" Winslow Hopper. Jo and Ginger's whirlwind relationship was interrupted by one post-undergrad term at Oxford, during which time she remained in Switzerland.

One of Oxford's oldest colleges, Merton offers gorgeous architecture, fields and gardens, and a strong academic reputation. With buildings originating in the thirteenth century and the oldest continuously operating academic library in the world, Merton evokes a timeless feeling. Campbell studied there in 1908–11. Modernist poet T. S. Eliot was at Merton during 1914–15, but preferred hanging with Ezra Pound in London. Following in Mathews's footsteps, mixed-blood Osage medievalist and poet Carter Revard, a Rhodes scholar, studied there in 1952–54, attending J.R.R. Tolkien's high-flying lectures and meeting visiting poet Dylan Thomas.[1]

At Oxford in the 1920s, "you could live in a way that was good for the spirit," Mathews said. Tall, handsome, and clever, Jo was a hit with the Brits. To many who learned he was an American Indian, he was the subject of keen interest.

He enjoyed drinking with friends and romancing young women, especially Beryl, or B.G., as he calls her in his diary, and planning holiday hunts and travel. At Oxford, where cultivation of the whole person was stressed, sport was obligatory, so he "fell in with the hunters." Oxford divided into cliques, including boatmen, rugby players, and aesthetes. Though he relished his expeditions with the hunt club, they were dismissed as philistines by higher-status clubs. A 1922 article in the *Oklahoma Teacher* said Mathews participated in boxing and rowing. His memory hazy, Mathews told interviewer Guy Logsdon he thought he wrote pieces for *The Isis*, Oxford's undergraduate magazine.[2]

Mathews's academic studies at Oxford were enriching, if his performance was erratic. Jo's first term introduced him to the system of weekly meetings with a tutor, and his writing developed through these critiques. "Whatever he had known about writing before, he now found under heavy siege, so that style, that personal state of grace, became identifiable as a goal worth hot pursuit. It would serve him well in the years to come," Rhodes scholar and OU Press director Savoie Lottinville wrote. During his first term, Jo's academic performance was lackluster. Late in the term, Jo admitted he habitually wasted time at local pubs instead of going to his morning lectures, which he usually found boring. When he finally walked to the Oxford University Museum of Natural History to attend a lecture, his professor and classmates were surprised to see him. In June 1921 he wrote, "even in the midst of Spring I have begun to deprecate my lotus-land existence. I haven't thought of a textbook or a lecture for weeks, nor have I written letters." Three days later, the term ended and he was called in to see his tutor for a "Don Rag," Oxford slang for when the faculty and a student's tutor, or don, gather to inquire of and apprise the student of how things were going. Jo's don told him he had been "very irregular" in his work and he "must do better next term, or [his] name would be scratched from the 'Books.'"[3]

Mathews may have fared better during Trinity Term 1922, since he did not require a Don Rag at the end of the term. Or maybe, as another student told him as he waited in the hall, the dons just "didn't want to see" him, because of his continued underwhelming performance. Although the term began in mid-April, Jo tended to sleep in and miss his 10 A.M. class at the museum, so he did not fully undertake his studies until well into May. He was out of touch: "I went out to the Museum this morning but found that everyone had gone out in the field—I returned and spent the morning buying books."[4]

At the end of the next Trinity Term, in late June 1923, Mathews took his final exams. After dancing and partying all night, Jo went for an early-morning jog. Back from the Meadows, he showered; threw on cap, gown, and white tie; and hurried to the museum for his first exam. He worked on his map, inspected by Dr. Thomas of Cambridge and Dr. Sollas of Oxford in flowing gowns. "My nights dancing and romancing seem to affect me little, my mind remained clear all day," Mathews reported with relief. That afternoon he traveled to Kidlington for a field exam, and from there hopped to the village of Wolvercote, on the outskirts of which Sollas and Thomas "sat like Sophocles on rocks and logs and gave us our 'vivers'—our oral examinations." Students and faculty returned to the museum and said their goodbyes. Mathews wrote, "Sollas looked up into my face, his mortarboard lifted, his shrewd eyes deep in the tortoise eye folds fixed up at me, said: 'Um-m-m-m, ye—yes—umh, Well, goodbye Mathews. Yes; you'll never set the world afire, but you've got so many other things. You'll get along; you'll get along.'" His professors would not have predicted his literary success, the "fire" he later kindled.[5]

By this time Mathews had outgrown his disinterest in women, and much preferred the ladies to laboratories. He dated multiple women, but Beryl, resident of the village of Woodstock, Oxfordshire, stood apart. For months, she intrepidly courted Jo in hopes of marriage. Beryl's mum did not approve of Mathews and discouraged her from seeing him ("What a brute I must be"). Only two months after Jo's arrival, Beryl devoutly pledged her undying love in a note. "She loved me beyond all reason," Mathews wrote, and "would fly to me if I sent the word, and I could tell her that I love her a little, at least." The note disturbed him. "I am quite upset tonight, but I am quite sure I shall never ask B.G. to marry me. All this will pass with the Spring, I dare say." He dismissed any notion of running away with Beryl and giving up Oxford.[6]

In some ways, though, Jo and Beryl's romance was idyllic. She rode in his motorcycle sidecar, and they took a romantic hike through the woods. Once they were sufficiently isolated, Beryl, "very kissable and charming as usual," reached "ecstasies." She fussed over Jo when he suffered a knee injury in a motorcycle accident, and sang and played the piano for him. "How lovely she looked there in the half-light. The emotion expressed in her song was deep, soft, and at times almost primitive." The next day was heaven and hell for Beryl. Their night began romantically as they walked down to Magdalen Bridge and "took a punt" (a flat-bottomed boat propelled by a pole pushed against the riverbank). Such an experience influenced his unpublished short story, "That Which Is Fairest." In his diary, Mathews wrote, "B.G. had just a touch of the moon on her pretty, strong face and she trailed her fingers in the water. Her face was partly averted and seemed thoughtful. I loved her dearly—I loved her golden hair and all the white fluffiness below it." But when she broke the silence, "the moment of love, of thrilling romantic love, in the spring, on a moonlight river, faded" and Jo was returned to "the earth and realities." When he "maneuvered the punt for anchorage," he saw again a "very pretty English girl," but a "rather aggressive," possessive English girl of whom he was "very fond as a 'playmate'" but whom he "loved not." At that moment Jo "decided to tell her the truth." He did not love her and would not marry her—or anyone, since he "didn't intend to marry, ever." He was "too much of a poet to remain with one flower till it wilted and died." Devastated, Beryl prophesied someday a woman would persuade him to marry her by appealing to his sense of chivalry, probably meaning she would become pregnant or claim pregnancy to leverage a proposal. The next day, Beryl was still terribly upset. Yet she continued to see Jo despite his frankness. "If I can't win in fair sportsmanship," then "I shall bear it," she sighed.[7]

Mathews was not the only bee buzzing about Beryl, however. Stung by his bluntness, she quickly accepted a rival's marriage proposal. In June 1921, a man identified only as C.F. visited Mathews in his rooms at Merton. Two days earlier, Beryl had consented to marry him, but subsequently refused to see him, explaining she loved Mathews and could "never love anyone else." Consequently, C.F. appeared, pleading for Jo to stop seeing Beryl. The light dawned on Mathews: Beryl "had been in a terrible dejection—she had a blinding desire to hurt me." But he was unsure, admitting, "I don't know the very elemental ways of the female of the species." Mathews thought C.F. pathetic, and his response betrayed anti-Semitism: "he is a Jew, I am sure—a gentleman, but a Jew, with all a Jew's characteristics of aggressiveness and tenacity—he was, after all, bargaining with me this morning. A real Anglo-Saxon would have died" before "whimpering and pleading," he opined. "Now I can never love B.G.—never; and of course marriage is more impossible than ever." Mathews refused to give in to her attempt to force his hand into a counterproposal. One must fight the biological urges of springtime, he reasoned.[8]

Despite C.F.'s plea, Jo continued to see Beryl. He found her as alluring as ever, but qualified, "I am glad the Term is soon over; she is growing worse each day." He knew continuing to see her was not right. "I feel that I ought never to see her again—I am terribly sorry that I can't return her love even though I have no desire to fall in love with anyone—marriage I fear is not one of my inclinations." Two days later he wrote, "B.G.'s love is now a form of lunacy. I can scarcely wait to get away—I fear such love." On June 23, he skipped town, setting out on his motorcycle with his friend "W.J.H." in the sidecar. W.J.H. was Rhodes scholar Wilbur J. Holleman, OU class of 1920 and a native of Stigler. Athletic Holleman was reading for a degree in international law at Merton.[9] Jo said goodbye to Beryl and motored away, feeling relief as he watched the distance growing between them. "When we were out of

Oxford and the wind rushed against my face, I felt wildly happy . . . how nice to be free!" He assured himself, "she will forget—anyway, one can't tell a girl of love just to please her—he must think of himself—of course I mustn't be a fool!—I'm away now, I can think how really close I came to doing something inevitable—I shall tell her the truth even if she suffers." Regardless of his resolution to flee and never see her again, he did see her in July and September.[10]

"Wine, women, and song" was often a theme for Mathews at Oxford and during his travels through Europe. Jo was fond of drinking in groups, usually alcohol but sometimes tea, at Buol's or Clary's Bar, while engaging in lively, enriching conversation. On a Sunday in June 1921, in his rooms he hosted four friends including Wilbur, "a wild lot" who drank "indiscriminately, at all times." In April 1922, Jo wrote, "I met Hazel during the afternoon and we began to drink about six and kept it up till we were quite 'under.'" After this passage, the bottom half of the page is snipped out, so it is unclear what ensued or whether Hazel is a first or last name, a woman or a man. A couple of days later, Mathews woke up late, drank tea at Buol's and there met "Mae" Lauthem, seemingly an Englishman, and Dick Dunlap,[11] a Kentuckian, and the three of them later took a pleasant stroll around Christchurch Meadows. Built on the site of the historic White Hart Inn on Cornmarket, Buol's was a favorite haunt. The hotel-restaurant offered a coffee and tea saloon, a dining room with a dance floor, and another dining room upstairs. His account of the trio's walk reveals casual racism: "Dick and I told 'Mae' nigger stories, which he enjoyed very much." Jo and Dick returned to Buol's and met another American acquaintance for dinner. Dick and Jo bought bottles of champagne. Later, two more jolly lads sat down and they ordered four more bottles, "and then two to take with us to Dick's 'digs' where we consumed them." During these carefree hours, drink spurred conversation, sometimes intellectual: "We all waxed happy, witty, and jovial, and talked much about 'futurist art' and other abstract things."[12]

During his Oxford years, Mathews enjoyed travel and hunting. With Osage headright payments skyrocketing, the early 1920s was a propitious time to satisfy his wanderlust. His first jaunt was a summer trip through England and Scotland on a motorcycle with Wilbur Holleman in the sidecar. They stayed at the village of Hornsea, Yorkshire, before proceeding north to Newcastle on Tyne, a city known for coal mining. Jo and Wilbur were wary when they encountered a gathering of miners listening to a speaker promoting an ongoing three-month strike, then on its last legs. Great Britain was in a postwar coal crisis; miners' wages had been cut because of an economic slump, and those who did not accept the pay cut were locked out of work. They felt betrayed on Black Friday, April 15, when they failed to receive a sympathy strike from transport and rail worker unions, who formed the Triple Alliance with the Miners' Federation. Mathews commented he was glad he didn't accidentally jostle anyone with his motorbike, since he and Holleman "might have been treated roughly." To an angry proletarian, a person who could afford a motorcycle was "a rich oppressor."[13]

The Oklahomans headed toward Edinburgh, Scotland, the next day. "The gloomy, wild desolation of a Moor is strangely pleasing to me," Mathews noted romantically, "and though the cold wind whipped through my clothes and the fog threatened, I wanted to stay and commune with nature in this wild, somber Moor. The plaintive call of the curlew fascinated and thrilled me—the sad melancholy of the place appealed strongly." But Wilbur was restless and "annoyed with the emptiness of the hills and Moors," so they sped down "a road twisting between bogs, stark granite boulders, and grey heather" until they "came down the last steep hill into Edinburgh." Jo and Wilbur played a game of golf at the Old Course at St. Andrews, northeast of Edinburgh, considered the original "home of golf."[14]

Jo's diary writing in the 1920s was often evocative and comical. One example is his account of what happened after he and Wilbur motored through Blair Atholl (notable for Blair Castle), Inverness, Wick, and Thurso, to a village named John O'Groats on the far northeastern tip of Scotland. In July, Mathews observed the behavior of *Homo sapiens* through a biological lens. "Crude country swains and rosy-cheeked, hearty country girls" danced to the music of an aged fiddler. Never having seen "such animal enjoyment," Jo watched transfixed as long as he could stand "the odor of their overheated bodies," pondering all the while "the fact that here was male and female—here was an excess of sex—sex dammed up and which one feared to let loose." Returning southward, they visited Dingwall, Fort William, historic Inveroran Hotel at Bridge of Orchy, Argyll, and Glasgow. Leaving the industrial city, Mathews found peace and softness in the home country of poet Robert Burns, who set "Tam o' Shanter" in the village of Alloway.[15]

Wilbur and Jo motored into the gorgeous English Lake District, home of the poets Wordsworth and Coleridge of the Romantic Movement, only to find hordes of Midwestern American schoolteachers. Two days later, in the port city of Liverpool, "a great, dirty, sprawling village," they were embarrassed to discover everyone stared at them and their motorbike as though they had "descended from the sky." Approaching Oxford, they dined and rested in Shakespeare's hometown, Stratford-upon-Avon. After meeting his Oklahoman friend Ann, Wilbur soon left for Vienna. Mathews recorded relief and love of solitude: "I am glad he has gone. I am extremely glad to be alone again. He is not a bad traveling companion, but I am of a solitary nature. Everyone does not like the things I like."[16]

Since staying at Merton was impossible, Jo left Oxford with two new friends from Philadelphia he met at Clary Bar, identified only as chubby C.E.L. and veteran S.G., who were entering Wadham College next term. The pair was so excited about being at Oxford they drank excessively and became "almost ridiculous." But since they were "very nice fellows," Jo agreed to travel to London and stay in Russell Square with them. He relished showing these Yankees around town, even if they found parts of London "rather queer," including Piccadilly Circus, where they visited "all of the Pubs in the vicinity." They decided to take a motorbike tour together through France, Germany, and Austria. Before the trio set out on their continental trip, they dined and danced the night away at the famous Savoy Hotel ballroom on the Strand.[17]

After seeing the castle and white cliffs of Dover, Jo headed to Paris to meet up with his Philly friends a couple of days later. Jo romanticized Paris. After having been there only one day, he proclaimed the City of Light "the gay, throbbing metropolis of the world." Life is not heavy; one finds "no Anglo-Saxon pratings about morals or uplift" since everyone lives "as he wishes, and indulges to the limit the liberties of the individual." He was fascinated by Parisian women (not ladies, he qualifies) he saw gamboling in the streets: "Women, no neater could one find in any country or clime, artistically dressed from head to toe, and versed in all the tricks of coquetry; every movement is a challenge to the male. Their *raison d'etre* is to please man." With a bit of misogyny, Jo figured women, whether ladies or otherwise, were more or less alike, paraphrasing the conclusion of Kipling's imperialist poem "The Ladies": "They're like as a row of pins / For the Colonel's Lady and Judy O'Grady /Are sisters under their skins!" The three young men saw a lot of skin over the next two days, taking in a show at the famous cabaret Folies-Beregère, where they ogled "a most unusual display of the exterior anatomy of woman." Shows featured risqué costumes and nearly nude performances; Jo found parts of the show to be appealing and clever, but was disappointed by a less artistic show at the Crystal Palace in Montmartre.[18]

Their travel agenda then took a serious turn. The next day, Jo and S.G. rode down dusty roads out to the ruined village of Château-Thierry, where a fierce battle took place in July 1918, one of the first fought by American forces under General Pershing. S.G. wanted to view the spot in the woods where he had nearly been killed. After eating a hearty lunch at "a Peasant's hovel," he and Jo wandered all afternoon. An elderly Frenchman and his daughter, who had married an American soldier, welcomed them emotionally. While they ate, their hosts saluted the bravery and kindness of Americans—especially the Marines who had saved their lives during the German advance. S.G. found the exact spot in Belleau Wood where he had been buried by a German shell, described the Marines' advance through the wood, and pointed out the position of enemy machine gun nests. They located the spot where S.G.'s friend had died, and visited his grave in the American cemetery. Though the Germans were driven back, the Battle of Belleau Wood was one of the bloodiest and fiercest of the war. Mathews philosophically wrote,

> The Wood lay in lazy, hot summer sunshine, in perfect peace. Here and there one saw a shattered tree, but from a view of the Wood as a whole, one could never guess that it had ever been disturbed in its profound peace . . . that at one time it had given cover to two armies, each shooting and slaughtering the other. Vegetation had begun to cover . . . ugly gashes of the trenches and the shell holes. . . . Belleau Wood has gone far in the process of healing her wounds and forgetting the summer of death and carnage. I saw the helmet and bits of the olive-grey tunic of a [German] soldier, and close by the skeleton of the owner. He was lying just as he fell, in a small depression. Already he was scarcely discernable in the growth. . . . I saw the flower first, and then was attracted by the half-hidden, gleaming pelvis.[19]

Perhaps for the first time, the full horror of the war sank in for Mathews. In comparison to his friend's experience, his wartime was a bowl of cherries, as he danced with War Bond Princesses and sweethearts, and took his plane out for joy flights. If S.G. was ever informed of the life Mathews had lived stateside while he lost friends and was almost killed in trench warfare, he must have thought Jo a lucky son of a gun.

Jo and S.G. then returned to Paris, where fun and games resumed. The trio went to a champagne party at the Café Jeunehomme in Montmartre, dined superbly, and danced with any willing woman. As they sat back and took in the show, their eyeballs nearly popped out of their heads as they gazed upon "the Apache passion dance, and the gyrations of an Algerienne half-caste." He would "never forget that Algerienne. She was at once an animal and human. She flashed green cat-like eyes at the audience, and twisted her body into impossible shapes; she whirled in ecstasy, and sang a barbaric song of the desert." Sated, they left Paris and visited Metz, Verdun, and Sedan, where they saw ruined French forts and war-torn cities. They also visited two Belgian cities before returning to Oxford by mid-September 1921.[20]

Although Michaelmas Term was approaching in October, Mathews had one thing on his mind: the sport of kings—hunting the red deer of Scotland. An opportunity to hunt highland stag had been felicitously arranged when he befriended a man who leased "forty thousand acres of deer forest in Argyllshire." Upon returning to Oxford, he began preparing for his next trip. Jo reconnected with Beryl, who accompanied him to the police station to register the rifle he would take to Scotland. She found Mathews's self-consciousness amusing as she perched pertly on a table at the station, "dangling her long silken legs and watching, as if she were waiting for [me to make] some facetious remark to the officer." At Merton College, Beryl donned his blazer while they happily packed his bag and "her laughter rang across Stebbins Quad, through the open window."[21]

Mathews traveled to Scotland with a new friend, Bertie Frazier, an older man who hailed from a diplomatic family. Bertie was courting Dolly, a winsome barmaid. Frazier's imperialist family for generations had possessed the "mahogany concession in the Crown Colony of British Honduras," Mathews wrote. "He lives 'like a king' with a lake, power boat, servants, and eats well." Jo had met Frazier at the Clary Bar in Oxford one day, where he also found C.E.L., Dick Dunlap, and "the inevitable C.W.": Cruce Warmack of Muskogee (OU class of 1920 and law student at Queen's College). The center of attention was Dolly, who sat calmly, faintly smiling as she listened to "man talk," voluptuous in a tight-fitting knitted dress. Jo was "immediately attracted to Dolly's lush body, so effectively female that she had to practice no female arts whatsoever." He viewed the dynamic in biologic terms. Dolly's mere presence, "her warm, soft, rounded, receptive femaleness," stirred the five men, among whom flowed "unconscious little competitive currents." Meanwhile, middle-aged Bertie evinced "vague uneasiness among four young men." En route to Scotland, Jo and Frazier visited Dolly at her pub. Frazier left only reluctantly, and for hours afterward sat quietly. Mathews was grateful for the silence that allowed him to focus on the gorgeous countryside. They headed north to Shrewsbury in the West Midlands, where Mathews noted the "Old Red Sandstone of the Shropshire Hills."[22]

Reaching a "red deer forest in Argyllshire," Mathews hunted "magnificent highland stag, black cock, and red grouse." Thereby he realized a lifelong dream, since to him the stag epitomized "the romance of hunting." The legendary red deer of the Highland moors had, in his words, "afforded royal pleasure" for the "kings of England and the chieftains of Scotland," and they afforded him material for three literary pieces. Capacious Auch Lodge, which his host was leasing, boasted a huge fireplace into which Jo "could have walked without bending, and very civilized conversation about horses and stags and grouse." In 1929, Mathews wrote of this experience for the *Sooner Magazine*, and later, the lodge and moors provided the setting for an unpublished short story, "Lady of the Inn," in which a young protagonist who is hunting red deer on the moors is haunted by the intense gaze of the lady innkeeper, beaming "primordial hunger" and "a pent-up primitive force that was relentless like death." In this spooky story, as the hunter becomes the hunted, Mathews again represents feminine desire as aggressive, this time in a work of fiction. Ultimately, the hunter flees in fear. Finally, in the early 1960s, Mathews drew from this setting for his animal story, "The Royal of Glen Orchy."[23]

Jo's desire to hunt seemed insatiable. In 1922, he found an opportunity to hunt in northern Africa. While he wasn't able to shoot mouflon (wild Barbary sheep), he likely hunted gazelles and shot a Barbary leopard.[24] He rang in the New Year quaffing champagne in Algiers, and in early January he was in Sidi Okba, which sits on an oasis in the Biskra province of Algeria. Sidi Okba boasts the oldest Mohammedan building in Africa. Here, in the religious capital of the Ziban people, he traveled on horseback with two friends, led by a guide named Ahmed. They rode among the sand dunes of the vast Sahara Desert, and appreciated Ahmed's hospitality. Mathews evoked the ambience in one scene from "Gallery," a series of vignettes or tableaux published in 1934 in the debut issue of the obscure experimental literary magazine *Space*, based in Norman and edited by OU professor and folklorist B.A. Botkin.[25]

At one point, Mathews found himself charmed by Ahmed's twelve-year-old niece, who sang and played for them on a bowed string instrument made from half a calabash attached to a long handle. Ahmed sternly chastised his niece when she played a particular song that, as he explained, women "sing to the groom, before the bride goes into the tent with him." As a lewd smile played over Ahmed's face, he said: "These women stand outside the tent where he is sitting waiting for his bride and before they let her in, they sing . . . that he must be bold and a real man, and not a little boy. They warn him to take her in strong arms of a man. It is alright if she sings the other verses but not that one; she is but twelve years." Mathews had sized up the niece, gaining "the impression of fully developed breasts, and her body was as ripe as a bee-buzzed fig. She would be an old woman at thirty. She is as beautiful as a range filly." Ahmed offered him the chance to "visit" with his niece. The notion intrigued Jo in the abstract, but he became disgusted with himself for considering it. "I must admit there was something rather thrilling about his proposition. There had been the desert and intrigue and romance, but when I thought of the twelve years of his niece, I thought also of the harsh poverty of the little cluster of mud houses and tents, protectively colored on the edge of the dun-colored desert, and a primitive emotion welled that horrified my cultured senses. I accused myself of abnormality, even though I had had no thought of accepting his offer. I protectively transferred my disgust from myself to Ahmed." This experience informed an unpublished story, "Allah's Guest."[26]

Ahmed made arrangements for Mathews to hunt with two guides. Jo bonded with one of them, Mohamed. Jo wrote that compared to Mohamed, his American companions now seemed artificial, "potty and even crude." He therefore kept his plans to hunt on his own with Mohamed to himself. "Their comments wouldn't have annoyed me, I just didn't care to evoke them," Mathews explained. His secretiveness is intriguing. Perhaps the Americans would have teased him for having a crush on the Arab. By mid-January, they had returned to England via Paris.[27]

Mathews had two profound experiences during his trip to Algeria's Biskra province. He considered one as an epiphany that pushed him to return home to Pawhuska and the Osages, to study and write about them. Mathews, accompanied by Mohamed and a cook on a hunting trip among mountains and sand dunes, asked his guide and new friend to take him to the famous Roman ruins at Timgad. Along the way, at midday, prior to dinner, Mohamed and the cook knelt down to pray, facing Mecca. Right then, a group of Kabyle tribesmen galloped toward them, members of a "wild," non-Mohammedan tribe. As they rapidly approached, they fired antiquated Winchester rifles, not out of hostility but from *joie de vivre*. After terrifying the trio, the tribesmen dismounted and joined them for dinner in a friendly way. Years later Jo's stepson, John Hunt, said this joy of shooting "recalled for Mathews the vision of Osage warriors, with only their breechcloths and guns, riding across the prairie and firing shots out of sheer exuberance." In such a manner they had once encircled him when he was a boy riding across the Osage prairie. Jo knew, or knew of, the men, and some of them in turn knew he was Will Mathews's son. After reflecting on these similar experiences, Mathews became homesick. In a 1972 interview with Guy Logsdon, he described questioning himself: "What I am doing over here? Why don't I go back and take some interest in my people? Why not go back to the Osage? They've got a culture. So, I came back, then I started talking with the old men." This is a wonderful story, but misleading, because 7½ years would pass before Mathews returned to live in Pawhuska.[28]

The second transformative experience occurred after his party arrived at the Roman ruins of a small military colony at Timgad (Thamugadi) near the Aurès Mountains, originally built using a grid plan circa AD 100. There, Jo encountered a Latin motto he later painted in "Chinese red" capital letters— still legible today— on his mantel at The Blackjacks sandstone cabin: "VENARI LAVARI LUDERE RIDERE OCCAST VIVERE." Translating the phrase as "TO HUNT, TO BATHE, TO PLAY, TO LAUGH—THAT IS TO LIVE," Mathews adopted it as the "motto of my life at the Blackjacks." In *Talking to the Moon*, Mathews claimed he discovered the motto by piecing together fragments of marble "lying broken among the tracks of jackals and gazelles." Sources predating his visit, and many references since, however, show that this phrase was a well-known graffito in the forum of Timgad, engraved on a whole stone, a *tabula ludoria* (gaming table), located near the entrance to the baths. Its words were arranged not in a row, but more logically in two columns to highlight its symmetrical construction:

VENARI LAVARI
LUDERE RIDERE
OCCEST VIVERE[29]

In this context the phrase can be translated: "The hunt, the baths, gambling, laughing: that's living!" Since this phrase was cited as the epitome of the epicurean ethos of the place and period, always with the gaming stone identified as its origin, his story of piecing the inscription together was possibly embellished. Mathews claimed it was "the motto of some unit of the Third Augustan Legion and was placed over the entrance of the officers' club, which included Roman baths." *Ludere*, which Mathews translates as "to play," according to University of Tulsa law professor Dennis Bires, has another translation: "to make love." Bires thinks it possible that Mathews privately "translated the inscription for himself 'to hunt, to swim, to make love, to laugh—that is to live,' though he was perhaps too discreet to put it that way in writing."[30]

After Trinity Term 1922 ended, Mathews was keen to resume his travels. He and his friend John O. Moseley, a Rhodes scholar studying at Oxford's Kingfisher College and Mathews's former classmate at OU, journeyed together to the village of Oberammergau in Bavaria, Germany, to see its famous Passion play. On the way they stopped in London and took some friends out for dining and dancing at a famous nightclub. They traveled through Belgium and Cologne, visiting cathedrals. Mathews enjoyed the view of the Rhine from the train, and found Munich's parks and fountains beautiful. The small village of Oberammergau was picturesque and hospitable. The Passion play affected Mathews unexpectedly. He was raised Catholic but was no longer a believer, despite a professed admiration for the religion and a belief in its value as a consolation. He wrote his sister Marie that where Catholicism "follows Jesus of Nazareth, I follow it, but Christianity as it has developed is one thing and the simple teachings of Jesus is another. Poor miserable humanity with her gropings and fumblings may become Christian someday, but at present, she is still setting up Golden Calves. Christ certainly would never know his own, just as poor Buddha Gautama or Mohamed would never know their own." Regardless, he found the enactment of the crucifixion of Jesus Christ at the Passion play to be the "most realistic thing" he had ever seen.[31]

During July, Jo and John journeyed northeast to Prague via Munich. Mathews described Czechs as friendly, thrifty, and proud of their new nation, Czechoslovakia.

Prague was beautiful and everyone seemed to be playing. That spirit was present in a young Czech woman named Wanda Trunk, whom Moseley met on the train. On leaving Prague, Mosley stayed in Wanda's compartment and was not seen again until they reached Dresden, Germany, where the trio played in the streets. In Leipzig, Jo and John met a lively group of girls and drank until 3 A.M. In Berlin, Moseley met some American friends and the crew descended on the Magnet cabaret, to which Mathews later returned alone. In this era, during the Weimar Republic, censorship loosened in Berlin, and it became a hub of cultural innovation. The song, dance, and satire of the *Kabarett* scene became more licentious as the 1920s progressed. Mathews remained in Berlin for a week, taking in a show at the Wintergarten variety theater, destroyed in World War II. He then parted ways with Moseley, whom he later saw at Merton.[32]

Back in Pawhuska, Jo's niece, Sarah Josephine "Sarah Jo" Caudill, was born in July 1922, the third child of his sister Josephine and Henry Benjamin Caudill. Tragically, Sarah Jo's fourteen-month-old brother, Billy (William Mathews Caudill), died two days after Sarah Jo was born. Jo received a cablegram in Paris with news of his passing, dampening his spirits. Within a few more years, the Caudills' marriage dissolved.[33]

Jo returned alone to Paris, where he spent two fabulous weeks. He looked up an Osage friend, Grace Soldani, who introduced him to Parisian aristocrats, the Comte and Comtesse de Sonis, and quickly developed romantic feelings for him. Soldani, who hailed from a wealthy French-Osage family from Ponca City, was staying with the couple and studying music. Grace was one of ten children of Amelia and Andrew Godance Soldani, who in 1925 built the Soldani Mansion, a meeting place for the younger social set. In the 1920s, the Soldanis, enriched by ranching and oil in Osage County, were part of the elite in Ponca City (in Kay County) that included oilman E. W. Marland, a future subject of a biography by Mathews, and his family.[34]

One day Jo was enjoying the ambience of a sidewalk café when George LaMotte approached him. A mixed-blood Ojibwe born in Wisconsin, who graduated from Carlisle Indian School and Haskell Indian School, LaMotte became a wealthy Osage County rancher and was connected with the Osage Agency until 1910. Later, LaMotte served on the first Executive Council of the National Congress of American Indians (NCAI). George had played double bass in the Wheelock Indian Band at Carlisle and later in touring bands, and his teenaged daughter Georgette inherited his musical talent. In Paris she studied piano repertory with two teachers. Over the coming days, Jo socialized with Grace, George, Georgette, and the count, countess, and their daughter, conversing over aperitifs, scrumptious meals, coffee, and drinks. Jo and Grace went to Mass at the monumental L'église de la Madeleine, a striking neoclassical Catholic church. Jo went on a boat ride on a lake in the Bois de Boulogne with the countess and Grace. It was a special time.[35]

Mathews then spent a month alone in Vichy, a spa and resort town in central France set on a riverbank, playing tennis, rowing, swimming, and practicing French. He reflected, "I can't decide whether I like the French or not," a curious remark given his maternal French ancestry. In Vichy he had intended to prepare for his final exams to be taken in June, but in late August he rued not having done any work, although he read H. G. Wells's *The Outline of History* (1920). Mathews wrote, "I walk nearly every evening along the quay. I rather like being alone. I am my own boss in that case and I do as I please. I have always been rather solitary in my habits." He saw his first bullfight in Vichy. He wrote a long letter to his sister Florence and one about love to Grace Soldani. He took a bus tour through mountainous southern France, then traveled in Spain for a few days. After Michaelmas Term 1922, Jo went home for the holidays, arriving in New York City in December 1922. He spent Christmas with his family and rang in the New Year 1923 at the Elks Club Dance in Pawhuska.[36]

Mathews presumably studied at Oxford during Hilary Term, January through March, and was present during Trinity Term, April through June 1923. He studied history in addition to geology and other natural sciences. In April, Mathews received a letter from Marie, concerned about her brother's morality and admonishing him to return to the Catholic faith. Jo replied, writing that her note perturbed and perplexed him, and dissipated "the atmosphere of mature study into which" he had "pitched during the vacation" between terms. He urged Marie to cease her diffidence and self-imposed isolation, assuring her that despite her "slight affliction" of being deaf, she was not abnormal but rather "the most mentally alert of the whole family." Mathews's niece and nephew, Fleur Jones and Bill Mathews Feighan, each corroborated their uncle believed Marie was the smartest in the family. They said Marie's younger sister Lillian used to take notes for her when they enrolled in courses together at Saint Mary-of-the-Woods College, but Lillian became vexed when Marie received higher grades. In big-brother mode, Jo urged Marie to engage the world, by nature competitive: "The world will not draw you out; you must obtrude yourself upon the world."[37]

When we next hear from Mathews in late June 1923, he had celebrated the end of his studies at Merton's Commem Ball and had two young women on his mind, one whom he called "The Viking," presumably tall and blonde, and Cissy, or "Miss Industrial Revolution," fancied by Jo's friend Arthur Hobbs. At 6:00 A.M. the ball finally ended and the revelers walked to Fellows Quad and to be photographed, after which Jo took off his tails and white tie, put on shorts, and jogged around the Meadows. "My Viking and I were empathetic, I believed, as I trotted. Perhaps there will be a note later. As I trotted I thought of Cissy, and the way she had got a position just behind me, with her hand touching my neckband, when the group photograph was made." He returned from the Meadows, showered, dressed, and reported at the museum for his exams. Despite burning the candle at both ends, Mathews managed to pass them all and receive an A.B. Oxon degree in June 1923, equivalent to a second bachelor of arts.[38]

Now graduated from Oxford, Jo wished to use his geological training to do reconnaissance work for an oil company. He had made a connection with Tulsa banker Harry F. Sinclair, who in 1916 founded Sinclair Oil. Mathews and another Oxonian, an Englishman, planned to work for Sinclair Oil in Portuguese West Africa (Angola), on an exploratory mission. But in 1922–23 the Teapot Dome Scandal hit, the largest American political scandal until Watergate, entangling Sinclair. President Harding's Secretary of the Interior leased navy petroleum reserves to private oil companies, including a subsidiary of Sinclair Oil, at low rates without competitive bidding. This was then legal, but Sinclair and another oilman gave the secretary illegal gifts totaling more than five million dollars in today's money. In the midst of Sinclair's troubles, Mathews's position was cancelled.[39]

Curious about the League of Nations and the internationalism of Geneva, Switzerland, Mathews commenced a short course at the University of Geneva, a *cours de vacance* (summer vacation course) on modern French and international issues, within less than a month after graduation. Jo studied from July 16 through September 1, 1923, earning a certificate. He attended meetings of the League of Nations, where world leaders lectured. Mathews was a part-time substitute correspondent for a short time, writing articles on the League for the *Philadelphia Ledger*. Critic Emily Lutenski has called Mathews an internationalist, and his study of international relations and visits to the League of Nations have been featured repeatedly in brief biographies of Mathews. Yet these experiences represent less than six months of his life, and he generally remained in the United States after returning in 1925. The only known exceptions were nine months in Mexico on a Guggenheim fellowship during 1939–40 and occasional visits to Canada during vacations.[40]

At the pension in Geneva where Mathews stayed, he met Virginia "Ginger" Winslow Hopper, an attractive young woman from a prominent family almost seven years his junior. An upper-class society girl from Newark, New Jersey, she lived in Geneva with her older sister Phyllis and her mother, Gertrude Louise Winslow Hopper. Virginia's grandfather, Inslee A. Hopper, had been president of Singer Manufacturing Company, famous for sewing machines, from 1863 to 1875.

Her father, Raymond Gould Hopper, a banker, remained stateside. He had been involved in efforts to raise money for Britain during World War I. Hopper ran an advertising service for banks, and was vice president of *American Banker* magazine from 1910 to 1916. After being diagnosed with spinal sclerosis, he began using a wheelchair. By late 1918, he had moved from New Jersey to Connecticut and was conducting all his business by mail.[41]

In 1923, Ginger and Phyllis became day students at Brilliantmont International School, a French boarding school in nearby Lausanne, where Ginger studied music and dance. Seventeen languages were spoken at Brilliantmont, which offered a breathtaking view of a lake and the Swiss Alps. In and near Brilliantmont and Geneva, Ginger and Phyllis enjoyed hiking, ice-skating, skiing, and horseback riding. Ginger was an excellent tennis player and competed in American and Swiss tournaments. Her son, John Hopper Mathews, said that over the course of one year, his mother defeated the top four women's tennis players in non-tournament games, adding that women's tennis in the 1920s was a different, more graceful game than it is today. Ginger also enjoyed writing and published several poems over the course of her life, collected in *Captured Moments* (1987). In a poem titled "England, July 1914," Ginger writes of her father bringing her family to Europe. In "Thoughts of Switzerland," she longs to return to the Alps. Even thirty years later, Ginger declared Switzerland her "second home." Her education had prepared her to be a cultured, sophisticated lady, an impressive wife for an upper-class husband. Ginger's studies in music, art, and dance at Brilliantmont didn't seem to yield the equivalent of a U.S. high school diploma, however, which is odd since she was twenty-one when she met Mathews. According to her daughter-in-law, Mary Abigail "Gail" Painter Mathews, Ginger had to complete a high school degree equivalency many years later in order to obtain a secretarial job.[42]

Mathews quickly fell in love with vivacious Virginia Hopper, and proposed to her by New Year's Eve 1923. It was a rapid courtship: they met in July and were married eight months later. Moreover, they did not spend much time together between their engagement and wedding, since in February 1924 Jo returned to Oxford for post-baccalaureate study in history. Despite expressing recurrent doubt about his imminent marriage, Jo returned to Geneva in April to marry. Given his previous rejection of Beryl and declaration he would never marry, Jo's behavior is perhaps surprising. On the other hand, the athletic, talented, and pretty Ginger possessed many attractive qualities. Plus, given Ginger's family and lifestyle, Jo assumed she was wealthy, a bonus. He had never needed to work, and marrying an affluent woman would ensure this pleasant state would continue regardless of the vicissitudes of

Osage headright payments. Ginger knew Jo was Osage, and given media fascination with the Osage oil boom of the 1920s and his lifestyle, she in turn believed Jo was wealthy. Two granddaughters, Laura Mathews Edwards and Chris Mathews, believe their grandparents each thought the other was much wealthier than was the case. Also, considering the timeline and his reservations, perhaps Beryl was prophetic when she predicted a woman would impel Mathews to marry her by appealing to his sense of chivalry. Considering Jo's past refusal of marriage, the speed with which he proposed to Ginger, and his subsequent doubt and regret over his engagement, perhaps Ginger thought she was pregnant.[43]

Jo celebrated New Year's Eve with his fiancée and Phyllis at a "fancy dress ball" at the Caux-Palace Hotel, in a village overlooking Lake Geneva. A dancer, Ginger "went as a pirouette" and Jo sported a blond wig, his bohemian disguise. The trio toasted Jo and Ginger's future happiness in marriage. Jo recalled that while he was happy in the haze of a drunken hour, his "rosy mood took no cognizance of the obstacles in the path of future happiness." He disparaged the revelers at the Palace as a "tacky lot" of "very middle class English and vulgar Americans" and claimed to be "quite sick of fancy dress balls at resort Hotels." Maybe this was just the hangover talking, one that made him just want to "die in peace." But by early evening on New Year's Day 1924, when he met Ginger for tea at the Palace, he again enjoyed life, wondering at "snow-covered mountains and the falling flakes of snow as they swirled and dropped." At the Pension Maria in Caux the next evening, as snow fell, he fantasized about living alone in a cabin in the Rocky Mountains, complete with "dog, fire, books, animal heads on the walls." Aside from replacing the Rockies with Osage prairie, eight years later he lived out this dream, building a sandstone home among blackjack oaks. But in the present, Mathews dragged his feet about announcing his engagement to Ginger: "I am delaying the day when I must write home and tell mother and the girls—She wants to be married just after Easter . . . in this little matter she may have her say, as it is nearly entirely her affair, although I dislike the idea of giving up my history studies at Oxford after the winter term." Acting as though the wedding had little to do with him, Mathews distanced himself emotionally. As Jo and Ginger spent much of their time together in Geneva conversing and playing, she didn't detect his doubts.[44]

In January 1924, Mathews, Ginger, and Phyllis traveled by rail from Caux to Geneva, and a few days later he said goodbye and headed back to Oxford for one more term, passing through Paris and London. Mathews admitted to himself, "I am anxious to get back to Oxford. I have a strange feeling that I wish to 'find' myself again—this should not be the case with one who has engaged himself to be married—I have made the mistake of my life." Breaking the engagement as tactfully as possible might have been the better choice, but the marriage seemed inevitable. Perhaps another factor was that later that year, he would turn thirty, an age then considered fairly advanced to be a bachelor. Having left Ginger behind, on the train journey to Paris he felt "rather free once more, and rather enjoyed it," but chastised himself: "Shame John you are supposed to be in love and lovers are not supposed to be happy away from their sweethearts."[45]

Jo moved into luxurious Canterbury House, where his friend John O. Moseley had lived. While studying history at Oxford, he enjoyed tea, dinner, and games of bridge while visiting the Hobbs family, whose hospitality he cherished. In March he had the family over for dinner in his rooms at Merton, and they drank to his future happiness. Jo felt as though Arthur, Phyllis, Dorothy, and Mrs. Hobbs were his own family, and relished their company. Jo socialized that term with several previously unmentioned friends, such as Cedric Brudenell-Bruce, Lord Cardigan, an automobile enthusiast. Cardigan later published several books, became the seventh Marquess of Ailesbury, and remained a close friend to Mathews, who saw the aristocrat as a kindred spirit. "Card" flew small airplanes, and his family members were the hereditary wardens of the Royal Savernake Forest, which appealed greatly to Jo's Anglophile tendencies.[46]

In March, Jo's feelings of regret and worry overpowered him, and he entered a crisis over his impending wedding to Ginger the following month. Feeling distressed and ill, he quoted Anatole France's *The Revolt of the Angels*: "Knowledge whither dost thou lead me? Thought, whither dost thou lure me?" On a dark, dull day, as wind whipped around the house, Mathews reflected:

> I am discouraged and blue, and life has never seemed so futile as it does at this minute. I have just come from the St. George Cafe where I dined alone . . . and to raise my spirit out of depression I had a bottle of 'fizz.' Despite all this I am . . . too dejected to read or write—In a little over a month I am to marry, but I am afraid of myself—what right have I to ask a girl to cast her lot with mine? I am nothing but a selfish dreamer, with moods of depression and elation—I am indolent and unbelieving and with not enough spirit to be really ambitious in any line . . . diffident and afraid of responsibility.

He had trouble imagining himself in the role of *pater familias*.[47]

The next evening, Mathews was invited to dine in the rooms of a friend he called "Jew" Jonas. Present were several ladies, including Irene Burnsides, who gazed longingly at Mathews, and the group danced in Jo's rooms afterward. Mathews later reflected that had Irene not been close with his friend "Tex" Richard, he "might have accepted the challenge of her very pretty eyes." Again, he scolded himself: "John you mustn't flirt; you are engaged to a little girl who loves you with all her dear little heart, and besides, you are going to be very much married on the something of April." Less than a month prior to his marriage, he desires Cissy Norton, and laments, "You are dammed queer John, and you don't even understand yourself."[48]

In March, Jo visited with Joseph August Brandt, a lifelong friend and Rhodes scholar who entered Oxford in October 1921. Joe Brandt attended OU from 1917 to 1921 and shared a common interest in writing. Their lives and careers were thereafter intertwined, and in the 1930s, Brandt became a key figure in Jo's literary life. Brandt finished Oxford with three degrees, studying modern Spanish political history, the basis of his *Toward the New Spain* (1932). In classic Oxford style, he rowed with the Lincoln College crew. In 1924, Mathews judged his friend as "not brilliant but quite energetic and some of his ambition lingers." They had dinner together at Brandt's digs that year and Mathews reckoned, "Old Joe has changed more than any other man from Oklahoma—his views are much broader and his outlook very different."[49]

In early April, Jo arrived in Geneva and over the next two weeks busied himself with preparations for his nuptials. John Joseph Mathews and Virginia Winslow Hopper were married on April 20, 1924, at the Hotel Beau-Rivage Palace, a historical luxury hotel in Ouchy, a park and lakeside resort south of Lausanne. At his wedding Mathews seemed detached, as though he were observing someone else's ceremony:

> I felt out of things, this was Ginger's day . . . her one day of glory, her day as Queen of Hearts—all present were her subjects. I at last saw the radiant figure in white come slowly up the aisle, alone and with confident tread—the figure stood in front of the altar, and I found myself beside her. Then the voice of Rev. Smith as he read the ceremony in exaggerated, melodramatic tones, which were more amusing than serious, and I should have laughed out loud [if not for] the seriousness of my position . . . I can still hear that wedding march . . . hammered out of the groaning old church organ by an unmusical but enthusiastic "helper."

Reflecting on "this great change from bachelorhood to married man," he was not sure how he felt, unable to feel emotions he thought he ought to feel over this "great event." Expressing his true feelings in the diary now seemed nearly "sacrilege or at least disloyalty."[50]

Jo's detachment persisted during what should have been a time of bliss, his honeymoon with Ginger Mathews. But on the train to the Italian town of Stresa, he experienced a "most 'lost' feeling" in a compartment with his bride, setting forth on a romantic Italian honeymoon. Despite what tender feelings he might hope would be present, Mathews confessed to his diary he desired solitude: "I should like to be walking into Italy with rucksack and, alone." It seemed marriage was a mistake; he felt inauthentic. The newlyweds traveled in the Stresa area, spending "several days along the shores of Lago Maggiore," on the border of Switzerland and Italy. He later wrote about an experience there in "Beauty's Votary," published in the *Sooner Magazine* in 1931, except he wrote Ginger out of the story! They hired a boatman to take them to Isole Bella, off the shore of Italy. At first the boatman seemed coarse, but after they had been on the island a while, he surprised Mathews by revealing the reason he insisted on making a timely return to shore. He wished to get to his hometown, Stresa, to meet three men with whom he would harmonize and strum guitars beneath the hotel window of a beautiful woman who had arrived in the city, with moonlight, romance, and the scent of flowers in the air. Ironically, such an atmosphere was missing for Jo on his honeymoon.[51]

The newlyweds visited Milan and stayed in Venice for a few days. They enjoyed two weeks in Florence, full of art treasures and tourists, before spending June in Rome. There, Mathews and Ginger randomly met Hermann Göring, the German World War I flying ace who became a Nazi leader, in the lobby of the Hotel de Russie. Göring and his wife had fled the disastrous Munich Beer Hall Putsch of November 1923. In spite of the fascist's vocal, strident hatred, their conversation actually "became warm and friendly." Göring declared the Nazis were going to imitate Mussolini's tactics and take over Germany. His belligerent invective upset Ginger, who afterward wept in their hotel room, afraid of another world war. Their daughter Virginia H. Mathews said she was conceived that night after Mathews attempted to comfort his wife.[52]

In July 1924, they returned to Geneva, where they set up temporary residence at hotels (Jo played tennis with Phyllis at one) before securing a five-room apartment in September. They were "quite happy to be settled at last, free from Pensions and Hotels," and he arranged his books with pleasure. They intended to stay for a while, but at some point, they realized Ginger was pregnant. Agreeing they wanted their baby to be born in the United States, they departed Geneva in November 1924 and traveled through Paris and London to Southampton, where they boarded the *America*. The voyage was difficult, since Ginger became ill and worried she might lose the baby. Her fragility and volatility on the trip deepened Jo's doubts about his path. The attractive couple, a bit unsteady on their feet, arrived in New York City on November 18, 1924, to begin their life as an American married couple and expecting parents.[53]

Chapter Four

FIRST FAMILY / CALIFORNIA DREAMING

> This is the real nature of California and the secret of its fascination; this untamed, undomesticated, aloof, prehistoric landscape which relentlessly reminds the traveler of his human condition and the circumstances of his tenure upon the earth. "You are perfectly welcome," it tells him, "during your short visit. Everything is at your disposal. Only, I must warn you, if things go wrong, don't blame me. I accept no responsibility. . . . Don't cry to me for safety. There is no home here. There is no security in your mansions or your fortresses, your family vaults or your banks or your double beds."
>
> —Christopher Isherwood, "Los Angeles"

Jo and Ginger lived for about a year in Montclair, New Jersey, before moving to Pasadena, California, where they remained until 1929. Their firstborn, Virginia Winslow Hopper Mathews, who shared her mother's name, arrived in March 1925. Beginning in late 1925, Mathews lived in California, at first with only Ginger. Later, little Virginia was brought out, and in August 1926, their son John Hopper Mathews was born. Ginger's sister, Phyllis, and their parents, Raymond Hopper and Gertrude Winslow Hopper, moved into the Pasadena home that Jo and Ginger purchased. The California years are relatively mysterious, since no diaries from California are known to exist, letters are scant, and Mathews was reticent about his first wife, daughter, son, and endeavors in Los Angeles.[1]

Ginger and Jo arrived in New York City from Europe in mid-November 1924. The couple, married for seven months, at first stayed at the Hotel Edgemere in East Orange, New Jersey, at the time a nice middle-class community. In December they found an apartment in Montclair, a commuter suburb close to Ginger's mother's family and her old stomping grounds, Newark. They moved in the day after Christmas, with their first child expected in less than four months. Their marriage was already stumbling during its first year. A few days after Christmas, they feuded over breakfast. Ginger started calling for him at 6:00 A.M. and thereafter at fifteen-minute intervals, causing him to recall "all of her shortcomings as a Wife and woman and to concentrate on these inherent defects until I felt that I had a real grievance, and wondered why I had married," Mathews wrote. She expressed "morbid thoughts of death during childbirth" and an "attitude of injured innocence" during a melancholy afternoon.[2]

The Mathewses did not seem to have financial problems at this juncture. In late December, they hired a servant, "one black Bobbie Green," whom Mathews said would come to them permanently. To Mathews, she embodied part of American 1920s modernity. "As gay and bright as her name suggests," Bobbie Green, an articulate, urban African American woman, represented changed times. "It is not 'Mandy' and 'Liya' in these days but 'Bobbie' if you please, who has diplomas and certificates for typewriting and shorthand and household management." He summed up contemporary American life as "radio, jazz records, synthetic gin, movies, tabloid, deodorized, 100% efficient, and Bobbies for servants." Mathews, who was never a big cinema fan and who saw jazz records as something to be spun as a last resort if conversation lulled, showed ambivalence toward the jazz age. In the 1920s, an increasingly urbanized nation was "homogenized by national advertising, chain stores, standardized products, radio networks, newspaper chains, and mass circulation magazines," signaling the rise of mass culture and "decline of regional variety," as Nathan Miller writes. Mathews's remarks are important since his five books published between 1932 and 1961—along with the writings of his friends and contemporaries, Stanley Vestal and J. Frank Dobie—were associated with the Southwestern regionalist literary and cultural movement responding to urbanization and standardization. The Southwestern movement influenced later generations of writers, including Kiowa author N. Scott Momaday, Larry McMurtry, and Cormac McCarthy.[3]

On New Year's Eve, Mathews reflected upon major life changes. Despite the rapid, total nature of these changes, they now seemed banal. "I attempt to think of a fitting résumé of the year just past with which to close this rather insipid annal. In fact, I should like to write something rather unusual, something striking" about the "mutability of circumstances and the uncertainty in one's life within the brief period of a year. But what is there to write about . . . the vicissitudes of existence?" His domestic scenario, already mundane, on this night felt suddenly strange as the wind whipped eerily around the corners of the building and New York trains rumbled distantly. Mathews experienced defamiliarization: "Tonight I look to my left and there see a mass of brown hair on a pillow, a childlike face, and childlike hands stretched out in a childish fashion over the covers. I hear the deep breathing and the vague mutterings of a child-woman, who is my wife—imagine my wife lying there asleep and I sitting here all unconcerned, as if she had always been there!" Mathews described marriage as an unpleasant duty, but mused that human beings can become used to any extreme:

> A soldier after a short time at the front feels he has always been at the front, a prisoner becomes accustomed to his stripes, and thinks of his condition not with shame but as unjust. A year ago I dreamed I was married and I remember waking up in a cold sweat—a prospective soldier might be perturbed in his mind before enlisting for active service, and most certainly a man on trial is nearly crazed when he visualizes himself as a prisoner. I have undergone the greatest change of my life—from carefree bachelorhood to responsible domesticity, and I scarcely realize that I have done so—my whole attitude toward life is changed and I don't recognize it—all seems natural.[4]

At midnight, as a cacophony of bells and guns rang in 1925, he recalled New Year's celebrations from the past three years: Algiers, Pawhuska, and Caux. But this year, Ginger drifted off to sleep and he wrote in his diary instead of frolicking. Formerly a tippler, Mathews quaffed grape juice while pregnant Ginger sipped milk. Noisemakers and revelers roused Ginger and she sat up squinting to wish Jo a happy new year.

In February, nearing the due date of their firstborn, Ginger and Jo moved into the Town House Hotel in Manhattan, near the hospital on the Hudson River where Virginia H. Mathews was born on March 9, 1925. After settling into life with an infant in the Montclair apartment for a few months, the new family spent the summer at Cape Ann, Massachusetts, where the couple rolled their baby in a fancy English carriage on a piazza overlooking the Atlantic Ocean. After returning from this holiday, the Mathewses remained in New Jersey for a number of months.[5]

In late 1925, Jo and Ginger sailed to Los Angeles via the Panama Canal to investigate living there, since Jo had heard about real estate prospects lying between Los Angeles and Pasadena. They initially left little Virginia with Phyllis and Gertrude Hopper in New Jersey. Jo and Ginger bought a splendid colonial house in Pasadena with palm trees and a garden, and eventually hired five servants. They lived there on a permanent basis by 1926. In Pasadena Ginger became active with the Junior League, gave dance recitals, and acted at the Pasadena Community Playhouse. Before long, she learned she was again pregnant. Subsequently, Ginger's family—Raymond, who was by then an invalid, Gertrude, and Phyllis—moved into Jo and Ginger's home, which increased the strain upon the couple's relationship. John Hopper Mathews was born in Los Angeles on August 3, 1926.[6]

Ginger and John Joseph Mathews, circa 1927.
Courtesy of the Mathews family

Virginia told a story of sitting on her father's knee after dinnertime, when he would read to her from the *New York Times* to improve her mind. One evening Jo told his little girl the subject of an article was being "facetious," and defined the adjective. On a later evening, when Jo was reading aloud to his daughter, Virginia said the person he was reading about was "trying to be facetious but he's not doing it," and proud papa Jo burst out laughing. Since Virginia was about three years old at the time, this was surely a story she was told and not a memory. John possessed few if any childhood memories of his father because he was only 2½ when Mathews moved out of the family home, and three when Mathews left for Pawhuska.[7]

In November 1926 Walter Campbell, who had just learned Mathews was living in Los Angeles, wrote to thank him for his help with Campbell's application for a Guggenheim grant. In February Jo had sent a clipping about a scholarship, and said his acquaintance Henry Allen Moe could help. Moe was the principal administrator of the Simon Guggenheim Foundation and, like Campbell, a Rhodes scholar. Campbell faced heavy debts: he began 1926 owing $3,500, then a great deal of money. Rejected by the foundation in 1926, Campbell, then working on four book projects he thought salable, asked Mathews for a loan of three hundred dollars for six months. He probably figured Mathews, then receiving generous Osage headright payments, was good for it. Campbell's successful publishing career as Stanley Vestal began the next year with *Fandango* and *Mountain Men*, and continued in 1928 with *Kit Carson*, followed by biographies and novels of Indians, mountain men, and the Old West and Southwest. In 1930 Campbell succeeded in obtaining a Guggenheim grant.[8]

By March 1927 and through early 1929, the man who had wanted nothing to do with his father's business was a real estate broker, buying and selling land. Mathews replied to Campbell four months later. Apologizing for his delay, he explained, "I have been put to tremendous expense during the past year getting my business started, not to mention an addition to the family, but I want to aid you, by all means." His stationery bore the name John J. Mathews; he rented an office in the Pacific National Bank Building. Virginia said her father learned of "barren land between Pasadena and Los Angeles" suitable for development, and began buying it up. Mathews "wasn't good with money," however, nor was his unnamed business partner. Mathews was destined to be a writer, not a businessman; in 1960, he told a reporter that when he was in the real estate business, he found most of the people he dealt with turned into "characters" to be analyzed, rather than business prospects.[9]

Mathews was always taciturn about his first family and his California dream. In a 1972 interview, he did not mention real estate as a reason for going to California—nor did he mention his first wife and two children. Instead, Mathews claimed he originally went west to find a job with Standard Oil of California, but the "head man," assuming Jo was a "waster," ignored his geological training. Mathews said he wanted to be sent to South America to do oil reconnaissance, but instead of being given a job, he received only sarcasm: the company didn't need any polo players, he was told. Jo's niece Fleur related a family story that Uncle Jo went to California because he wanted to try his hand at screenwriting in Hollywood.[10]

Virginia said her parents both acted at the Pasadena Community Playhouse, along with some Hollywood types. The playhouse, part of the Little Theatre Movement, was built in 1925, funded by Pasadena citizens. In April 1928 Ginger was among a mammoth cast of 159 actors playing 420 roles in the well-received world premiere of Eugene O'Neill's *Lazarus Laughed*, a biblical, philosophical play structured like a Greek tragedy. The Pasadena Community Playhouse later debuted works by F. Scott

Ginger as Anna Pavia, circa 1927.
Courtesy of the Mathews family.

Fitzgerald, Tennessee Williams, and James Leo Herlihy, author of *Midnight Cowboy*. When Ginger played Minnehaha in a performance of the story of Hiawatha at the nearby Rose Bowl, Jo asked Virginia ironically: "Isn't your mother the most beautiful Indian girl you ever saw?" Virginia agreed wholeheartedly. Ginger's performances influenced her son, John, who was involved with theater throughout his life. Other than Virginia's statement, however, there is no evidence that Jo Mathews acted.[11]

Drawing on her Brilliantmont School training, Ginger gave dance concerts in California and New York using her stage name, Anna Pavia. She appeared in joint recitals with then-famous American composer Charles Wakefield Cadman. Influenced by American Indian music, Cadman lived with the Omaha and Winnebago tribes and studied their instruments, publishing articles and touring a lecture on the subject. The most successful composer of the so-called Indianist movement in American classical music, Cadman merged tribal timbres with nineteenth-century Romanticism. Ginger's joint recital with Cadman, her role as Minnehaha, and her marriage to an Osage man all suggest she was fascinated by Indian culture. To her family, Ginger was a free spirit, a dreamer who embodied the spirit of the 1920s.[12]

By spring 1927, Mathews was making sizable financial gambles in the real estate market. In April, Jo replied to a letter from Campbell, saying he had just returned from the San Joaquin Valley. Jo praised Campbell's debut, *Fandango: Ballads of the Old West*, and said he could send $100 soon. He apologized for making the $300 loan in installments, but they were both experiencing financial crises simultaneously. "This happened to be my 'in between time' as well as yours," he explained. "I have done a lot of investing in the last year and only recently have taken a real daring gamble" that limited his ready cash. In retrospect, knowing the Depression was coming, one shudders at this line.[13]

In July, Campbell wrote from Yaddo, an artists' retreat in Saratoga Springs, New York. Walter and his wife, Isabel Campbell, a novelist and poet, spent time there with Rollie Lynn Riggs, the mixed-blood Cherokee and closeted gay playwright. Author of *Green Grow the Lilacs*, the source of Rogers and Hammerstein's musical *Oklahoma!*, Lynn Riggs began his college career at OU in fall 1920, one semester after Mathews graduated. Riggs worked closely with Campbell as a student writer, editor, and member of the Blue Pencil literary fraternity. Riggs was at Yaddo with Lange, a companion Campbell described in his journal as a blond, "somewhat soft young man" with whom Riggs could be spied rolling down hills, giggling. The Campbells became close with author and sculptress Tennessee Mitchell Anderson of Chicago (author Sherwood Anderson's second wife) and mixed with poets, painters, and a philosopher amidst what Riggs described as Yaddo's ambience of "decayed grandeur." With gratitude, Campbell told Mathews his "timely aid had made this all possible," and requested the rest of the loan so he could satisfy his creditors at last.[14]

Like Yaddo's grandeur, Jo and Ginger's marriage decayed. According to divorce papers, "on or about September 1928," Jo abandoned his home, never to live with his wife or children again. "Irreconcilable differences" made it nigh-impossible for them to cohabit as husband and wife. It is unclear where Jo stayed until November, when he drove to Pawhuska via the route of the old Santa Fe trail.[15] In Taos, Mathews sensed the spirit of his famous great-grandfather, Old Bill Williams. He spent a day with his pal, the Western artist W. Herbert "Buck" Dunton, who was collecting material for a portrait of Williams; Mathews predicted Dunton would become as famous as Frederic Remington. Jo asked in New Mexican bookshops about Campbell's recent biography of Kit Carson, which he was rereading; it was selling well. He told Walter he would soon be visiting. Beginning with Thanksgiving in Pawhuska with his mother and sisters, through most of January 1929, Jo stayed away from his wife and children over the entire holiday season.[16]

Along with visiting the Campbells, Mathews met Joe Brandt in Norman. Meetings with Campbell and Brandt paved the way to Brandt asking Mathews to become a contributing editor, then associate editor of the *Sooner Magazine*, which Brandt conceived in 1928 as an unconventional alumni publication. Between April 1929 and April 1933, Mathews published a dozen pieces in this periodical. Also in 1928, Brandt started the University of Oklahoma Press, which either originally published or later reissued all of Mathews's books. In January 1929, after Jo's visit, Campbell wrote, "now that you are the Associate Editor of *The Sooner Magazine*, you have an excellent reason for frequent trips to Norman, and we shall be very happy to have you and any of your family members whenever you can come." Campbell and Brandt were lifelong supporters of Mathews, prompting and nourishing his literary development. Later, Savoie Lottinville, who assisted Brandt and eventually succeeded him as director of the University of Oklahoma Press, and Frank Dobie joined them in a special circle of literary friends and champions of Jo's work and philosophy, forming a Southwestern regionalist circle.[17]

After this extended visit to Oklahoma, Jo drove back to Pasadena in early February. He told Ginger he was leaving permanently, gathered his things, and moved into the University Club of Los Angeles. He had been away about five months, but Ginger still loved him and hoped for a reconciliation. The timing of his declaration was unfortunate, since her father died on February 3. Valentine's Day was thus bitter. Jo wrote Campbell mid-month, telling him he had left his home and would receive mail at the club. "I have come to a decision which will in due course bring me again to the status of unmarried," Jo announced, although he would actually remain legally married for more than twelve years. The separation, he wrote, was largely caused by Ginger's "rare combination of incredible and impossible characteristics." Incompatibility had made their situation impossible for several years. Considering they were not yet five years married, this comment is striking. Mathews felt much better upon reaching a decision. After Campbell replied sympathetically, Jo stressed he did not mean to present himself as an "injured innocent" since "the whole thing is my fault of course; I shouldn't have married whom and when I did." Concerned about their brother, Marie and Florence visited California in June amidst their travels aboard the *Franconia*.[18]

Mathews dissolved his business partnership and expressed to Campbell his feeling that he needed to "make some sort of business connection as soon as possible. Having expended enormous sums in attempting to buy peace during the last three and a half years, I am at present concerned about the future." This was a new feeling for him. "In any connection I may make, I cannot hope to be my own boss as heretofore." He concluded introspectively, "Often I wish I were either an acquisitive man, or a dreamer and wanderer, and not both. I would do much better if I could be one these definitely." His letter caused Campbell concern over money he owed, but Mathews assured him that he remained "quite solvent" and his financial status was only relatively bad. In the past, however, he had always been "comfortably independent." In two letters, Mathews expressed a desire to accompany Campbell on a summer trip to investigate Sitting Bull, whose biography Campbell was writing, but ultimately decided he couldn't make the trip. Over three consecutive summers, Campbell interviewed many Lakota Sioux elders, including One Bull, Sitting Bull's nephew, who had fought at the Battle of Greasy Grass, or the Battle of Little Big Horn, in 1876.[19]

While staying at the University Club in early 1929, Jo wrote his first piece for the *Sooner Magazine*, "Hunting the Red Deer of Scotland," published in April; "Hunting in the Rockies" followed in May. The voice of these stories is hearty, literary, and slightly pompous. Two stories conclude flatly with Mathews committing the coup de grâce. But in "Admirable Outlaw" (1930), about hunting a wily coyote, Mathews expressed remorse for killing the animal, consistent with an Indigenous perspective that views animals as relations. A coyote lover, Mathews noted seeing and hearing them over the decades, and tape-recorded their howls. His third book, *Talking to the Moon* honored the coyote's call. Yet he killed animals he loved, and to him killing animals required no justification other than sport. He traveled great distances and went to substantial expense to invade remote habitats to hunt beasts such as bear, bighorn sheep, and wapiti. But after finally killing a notorious coyote with his dogs, Mathews reflects:

> Even in death he seemed defiant and unbeaten. He had fought and died silently, though mangled by the pack [of dogs]. . . . Each time one looks upon such a scene, he feels admiration for the little wolf that fights against such odds so grimly and silently. As he is the embodiment of cunning, fleetness and courage, one feels that such a death is a disgrace, and unfair to such high courage. One attempts to forget . . . that this little wolf's long quavering howl is the very voice of the night prairie, and tries to remember only that his victim is a chicken thief and a bandit.

Here Mathews questions the anthrocentric position he repeatedly took as both hunter and supposed ecologist. In 1963 Mathews wrote another coyote tale called

"Singers to the Moon," published posthumously in *Oklahoma Today* in 1996, in which he lamented the persecution of coyotes. Mathews uses the perspective of a coyote called Lineback, highlighting the animal's cleverness to evoke sympathy for the species, which was being hunted down mercilessly and killed by cyanide traps embedded in the ground.[20]

Mathews penned several more articles for the *Sooner Magazine*, which Brandt edited until 1933, when he turned his full attention to directing OU Press. During the early 1930s, Brandt encouraged Jo to write a book about Major Laban J. Miles and the Osages he served, and Brandt edited, published, and marketed the resulting book. Campbell likewise inspired and catalyzed Mathews, who held the author-professor in great respect. In 1929, Jo told Campbell he appreciated his sincere, knowledgeable advice, and asked his mentor to keep urging him to write: "Your interest is of great value to me, and your advice and prompting make me glow for hours after reading one of your letters." Many people had urged him to write, he explained; his family thought he was a "heavenly endowed genius, blushing diffidently on the very edge of eternal fame." Yet until Campbell saw potential in Jo's writing, he "had not even been interested in such advice." A letter of critique Campbell sent Jo on his short pieces gave him a "little thrill in playing with the idea" of becoming a professional writer.[21]

By October 1929, Mathews was back in Pawhuska for good. Late in the month, Mathews wrote Walter and Isabel from the Mathews family home on the hill at 611 Grandview Avenue, where he was living in a "complete apartment" above the garage behind the house. "I am not sure how long I shall stay, but I am planning to see the [OU] 'Homecoming Game' in November," he said. Jo had all his possessions with him except for a few pictures left in New Jersey. On the way home, Mathews visited Arizona landmarks named for his great-grandfather. Like Old Bill Williams 104 years earlier, Mathews left two children behind and headed for the mountains. "I climbed Bill Williams Mountain (a pied of course), and stopped a day in the White Mountains where I attended a Forest Ranger dance."[22]

During the heyday of the 1920s, when oil headright payments made many Osages wealthy, Mathews was one of many of his tribespeople who traveled widely but found funds short by the close of the decade. With his marriage to a woman he viewed as impossible in ruins, he returned alone to the reservation. Jo had spent about three and a half years in Los Angeles, interspersed with hunting trips to New Mexico or the Rockies and visits to family in Pawhuska. According to Gail Mathews, in late 1929, Ginger, Phyllis, Gertrude, little John and Virginia left their Pasadena home and returned to the Newark area. In 1935 they lived in Maplewood, and by the end of the 1940s resided on Beech Spring Road in South Orange.[23]

After Mathews returned to Pawhuska, he very rarely referred to his first wife or children. He tried to conceal them from the biographical record, perhaps embarrassed by the failure of his marriage and his absence from his children's lives. Jo and Ginger's granddaughter Laura said when her grandfather returned to Pawhuska, he presented himself as a bachelor. Many of his friends and acquaintances were not aware he had been married prior to his second marriage in 1945. It was not until his daughter, Virginia, began visiting during young adulthood that many learned Mathews had children. During one visit, Virginia introduced herself as Jo's daughter to Osage artist and sculptor Romain Shackelford, whom she knew was a younger friend of her father's. Shackelford replied frankly, "I never heard him say he had children." In 1943, when Jo introduced Virginia to Oklahoma Senator Elmer Thomas, the politician seemed annoyed and "rather caustic" because Mathews had never told him he had a daughter. Mathews had hardly any relationship with his children until they were teenagers, and his relationship with his son was always strained and distant on both sides. "I never knew my father that well," John H. Mathews told me.[24]

By all indications, Mathews did not see his children for about a decade, and he did not offer much financial support, according to Mathews family members. His granddaughter Laura commented: "It's not hard to understand that he and my grandmother didn't work out. What is hard for me to understand is that he just abandoned them, did not support them, did not acknowledge their existence. He just left." Since Jo and Ginger did not divorce until October 1941, until then he was not legally bound to pay support. In 1939, Mathews claimed he had been sending monthly allowances, but he could not be called generous, considering the family's struggle to pay bills after he left. Most of the Hoppers' remaining money, already diminished, was lost in the Great Depression. At some point following Jo's move to Pawhuska, when reliable support was not forthcoming, Ginger and Phyllis traveled there to call attention to their plight and to persuade Mathews to provide consistent support. Laura said they were righteous in their cause. At that time, she explained, to get alimony, the aggrieved had to sue the husband in the town where he lived, and this was difficult for Ginger as a strange woman from the East in a small town where everyone knew Jo Mathews. "He knew all the lawyers and the judges," so Ginger could not "get the time of day from anybody." In contrast, Mathews's niece Fleur Feighan Jones said Ginger and Phyllis tried to bring scandal and disgrace to Mathews to shame him into giving them money, but lacked a valid claim.[25]

Mathews seemed consistently indifferent toward his first wife and two children. Perhaps he assumed the Hoppers remained affluent. In 1939, after Jo traveled to Mexico on a Guggenheim fellowship, his payments to Ginger ceased, and she could not reach him. Having learned of the grant, possibly from a newspaper notice, Ginger phoned Henry Moe at the Guggenheim Foundation, asking for money on behalf of Mathews. At this time Mathews, who had been in Mexico for about a month, told Moe there was "no such arrangement as the one suggested to you by Mrs. Mathews [to send payments directly out of the grant]. For the last ten years I have been sending an allowance and had planned to continue it from the bank at home." "Since she is always needing money and I am not sure of my bank balance at home, you may send her fifty dollars . . . as a part of the November allowance, but do not send her anything except upon specific request from me." Ginger and Phyllis, apparently struggling, continued to call Moe against Jo's explicit wishes. At least a few times during his nine months in Mexico, Mathews asked Moe to send them one-hundred-dollar checks. In January 1943, Ginger accused Mathews of being in arrears with payments. According to the divorce agreement, for the "support, maintenance, and education" of their children, he was to pay her one hundred dollars a month until John turned twenty-one, then fifty dollars a month until Virginia reached her majority. In December of that year, Mathews received a citation to appear in district court: "The old trouble, Virginia is demanding for her own use the money which I have been spending on the children's education," he claimed. "Such vindictive dramatics come each time she loses her job or my picture appears in some national publication." In 1946, the court ordered him to pay Virginia $225.[26]

In her introduction to *Twenty Thousand Mornings*, Susan Kalter claims Mathews supported his children's education, but on the whole it appears he contributed little. In 1943 Virginia attended Goucher College for a single semester, which Mathews paid for, and John Hopper boarded at St. George's School, a preparatory school near Newport, Rhode Island. According to John's daughter Laura, however, her father was not dependent on Jo but received a generous scholarship to St. George's thanks to the persuasiveness of his mother, who according to Laura and her sister Christine "Chris" Winslow Mathews, could "talk your shirt off." Laura amplified:

> Grandmother could talk anyone into anything, and she would talk people into giving my father almost a free ride. So he went to St. George's. When he was there, all the other kids had funds they could draw from to get haircuts, buy things for their dorm or clothes. And he didn't *have* a fund because there wasn't any money. His father visited him at one point, and the school said to him, "Your son doesn't have anything in his account," and his response to that was, "Oh, then he must not need anything." [Laughs] And this man had headrights, an oil income, and

> he really didn't have to work a day of his life. So, to know that your kid is not able to get a haircut, and not have a problem with that: that was very hurtful to my dad.[27]

Gail Mathews said the only money her father-in-law spent on his own children's education was to pay for Virginia's single college semester and contribute some toward John's last year at St. George's (1943–44), where he spent five years. Given Jo's miserliness, it is ironic that his son played Scrooge in Dickens's *A Christmas Carol* at St. George's. He also starred as Richard III in the Shakespeare play of that name.[28]

Ginger and Phyllis, aided by their mother, Gertrude, raised Virginia and John H. Mathews, and at times they struggled. According to Virginia W. Mathews's biography in her poetry book, she taught foreign languages, did "personnel work and accounting, and was employed by the government during World War II." John H. Mathews's eldest daughter Sara Mathews Dydak said she also taught piano lessons. Laura commented, "My grandmother had various odd jobs. She had been brought up rich, and had a finishing school education, where she learned French and how to dance, but didn't learn how to use a typewriter."[29]

One unlikely source of income was young John Hopper Mathews. During the mid- to late 1930s, when he was nine to thirteen years old, John was a professional child actor on radio and Broadway, and as a "professional choir boy," sang soprano at the Church of the Heavenly Rest in New York. On Saturday mornings during 1936–37, he was heard on *Raising Your Parents*, a live Blue Network radio show, as a member of a panel of children that answered questions sent in by kids. In 1937–38, he was, ironically, *The Rich Kid* in a radio drama series. Both John and his mother appeared in multiple scenes for the movie newsreel series *The March of Time*. In 1939, John played a bit part on Broadway in *Set to Music*, a successful musical revue with lyrics by Noël Coward, and he was an alternate in *Dear Octopus*, a Broadway dramedy starring Lillian Gish, the First Lady of American Cinema. It is unknown whether his father knew of these performances. Laura said her dad worked on stage and in the studio because "there was no money, and he was the one who could pull some in. Although he's proud of all that, the fact is, when you have to send your kid into New York at age twelve to make money, you know you've got a problem. He was supporting them, his mother and her sister, pretty much."[30]

It was within this context that Ginger and Phyllis planned for John and Virginia to meet their long-lost father, whom they apparently had not seen in nearly a decade, in a surprise visit. Jo wrote a letter to his lover, Elizabeth Hunt, narrating this powerful event. On Tuesday, February 30, 1939, Mathews was working in his room at the

Powhatan Hotel in Washington, DC, during a trip on behalf of the Osage Tribal Council. The front desk called his room and said a young man wished to see him. Jo asked his name, but the youth was already heading up, so he "prepared to meet such a forward young man in the manner which such presumption deserved." The visitor knocked confidently and Mathews opened the door to find a five-foot-tall, slender young man topped by "a shock of brown curly hair," standing with impeccable poise.

"Is this Mr. Mathews?" the young man asked.

"Yes."

"My name is John Mathews."

"Come in."

Young John went to the window and looked out. "Washington is quite busy."

Jo agreed.

"I suppose you know who I am?"

Emotions running wild, Jo replied, "You are myself at the age of twelve, come to visit me."

"Then Daddy, don't you think you'd better kiss me?"

"You don't think it would be out of line?"

"Oh no, not in the least—I have seen Daddies kiss their sons."[31]

Instead of embracing and kissing his long-lost son, Mathews awkwardly walked to his coat, pulled out his pipe, and burned his fingers trying to light it. He remarked that across the street was a man whose hair looked exactly like a bird's nest. Then John said, "Sister is downstairs—shall we go down and see her?" Jo made an unnecessary change of clothes and, holding hands with his son, headed down to the lobby. They talked of science, and John opened up. Mathews found his son possessed more knowledge in certain areas than he did. "We talked of electrons in the Ether, and of the possibilities of final destruction of the universe in tiny electrons. I had to swing to Natural Science, where I felt more comfortable." John went on to work as a research scientist. Savoie Lottinville happened to be in the same hotel at the time, and that evening Jo told him the story of unexpectedly meeting his son after a long absence, which recalls a scene from Irving's "Rip Van Winkle." "God, it was strange!" Jo told Savoie, who was moved. Pondering this moment more than four decades later, Lottinville wrote Brandt: "This is the stuff of which white tears are made."[32]

Reaching the hotel lobby, Jo found a tall, "wholesome, beautiful girl-woman." She approached her father with sparkling eyes. "I don't know when my arms opened, and I don't know how long we stood there with her warm face against mine, and my nose in smothering curls." He sat with his son and daughter, holding hands. He became aware of Ginger and Phyllis, who approached smiling. "Ordinarily my nervous system would have been jarred at the sight of Virginia, but in the emotional jolt I had just received, there was no room for another emotion—not even hate. I stood and shook hands." He dismissed the women, telling them he would see them for dinner at 6:30. He took his offspring up to his room, and they held hands and made plans for the day. They went to the Department of the Interior building and ate lunch with four officials Jo knew, including C. L. Graves, superintendent of the Blackfeet tribe. The next day he took Virginia and John to the Smithsonian Institution, and before they left that evening, he gave two hundred dollars to his estranged wife. During Jo's trip to the east coast, he visited with his children three more times. Joe Brandt, then director of Princeton University Press, set up two meetings at his home in New Jersey, and Jo also visited them at their home in Maplewood. He felt an ephemeral passion for fatherhood. "Isn't that a wonderful word, 'Daddy,'" he asked Elizabeth. "I feel that I can write an essay on it." But apparently he did not see Virginia again until 1943 and John not until 1944; and in 1945, they fell out of his favor for a time.[33]

Jo's lack of parental attention and financial support had repercussions. One of them was a scenario of financial insecurity in which Ginger "dated" a series of men, most married, some prominent, including an owner of department stores, who were willing to provide for her family. When asked how Ginger supported the family after John was too old to be a professional choirboy or child actor, his daughter Chris Mathews revealed with a sigh, "What I know is that she had a lot of boyfriends, who were probably married, and they helped out the family. I'm a little reluctant to say that, but she was like a professional girlfriend. That helped pay the bills, if you really want to know the truth." Ginger did not enter these relationships for emotional comfort or to have a man around. "It was very calculating. She knew whom she had to date, and what she had to do, to get taken care of," Chris said. Laura used the phrase "serial mistress" to describe her grandmother's tactics. Their source was their father, John, and their aunt, Virginia, who once rattled off a list of men Ginger had dated in the 1930s–40s. John H. Mathews told Chris that his mother was "promiscuous" and saw many men romantically. Under the reality of scattershot support from Mathews, such were the reduced circumstances of this former debutante, whose grandfather was the president of Singer Company. Chris and Laura each said the unique characteristics of their father and Aunt Virginia were explained by their odd upbringing.[34]

John H. Mathews believed his mother should have remarried after it became clear Jo would never return to her, but she could not stop loving him. He said many people thought Ginger was wonderful; some asked if she would consider remarrying.

But Chris confirmed that for decades Ginger carried the torch for Jo and therefore never remarried. In this regard Laura finds Ginger's poem "Love (in two parts)" significant. Part I reads: "His love is dead? All well and fine / His life he'll live alone? Well, I'll live mine! / He 'never loved'? How could love 'die'? / He speaks in riddles. Solve them? By and by. . . . // Those talks of love—I thought them true. / No matter now, because, I never knew! / Fool's paradise; I did not know. / I could not judge him then, I loved him so! // And even now, I feel regret, / Because I love him still, and can't forget!" Then, in Part II, "(written fifty years later)," she appends: "The pain, the deep despair I felt has ended / Because, at last, my broken heart has mended." Fifty years passed between Jo's leaving Ginger and his death.[35]

When Mathews proposed to Elizabeth Palmour Hunt in the spring of 1945, he distanced himself from his son and daughter again. Seemingly he planned to concentrate his energies on his new family: the widow Elizabeth and her children, John and Ann Hunt. About a week before he remarried, Mathews claimed to be irate with his two children when they didn't reply, or reply fully enough, to his letters. In late March he visited his lawyer, Paul Humphrey, and changed his will. "I have become fed up with my children's attitude in ignoring me," Jo wrote. "I have written each month to each of them, and have not received one scratch from my son John and only fluffy little notes from Virginia, which are simply pats on the back of old dad who has been attempting to get some answer from her about her plans for the future. I shall make my will so that they will not receive my property until after Elizabeth's passing—this will not be effective of course until after my marriage to Elizabeth." John and Gail Mathews stressed Jo *never* sent regular letters. Virginia even said that a decade earlier, her father failed to reply to a letter from his son John, then nine years old. In 1956, Mathews changed his will yet again to bypass his children and leave his money to the next generation: "this afternoon with Lillian to Paul Humphrey's office to make a new will, leaving all my property to Sara Mathews [b. 1955], after Elizabeth's passing. During her lifetime she shall have full benefit of the property." Later, however, he changed his will yet again to reinstate his children.[36]

Virginia H. Mathews's 2009 oral history interview with Karen Neurohr, recorded some eighteen months before her death, contains much valuable information. Unfortunately, Virginia suffered from a propensity for prevarication, compounded by dementia late in life. The credibility of the interview is marred by misinformation and sometimes tactless fabrications about her father, her brother, and especially her stepbrother, John Hunt. Thus, nearly everything Virginia said must be treated skeptically. In 1957, Jo said Virginia grabbed "fantasies out of the air, materializing them in words as statements of fact. She is not a clever fictionist, but she seems, as canny as she is, never to be aware of her inconsistencies." Her brother, John, said when telling stories she would fabricate when she didn't know all the facts. John's daughter Laura described her as "a fibber." Among her many fabrications, Virginia claimed her father was a Rhodes scholar and she told both Russ Tall Chief, who interviewed her late in her life, and attorney Harvey Payne that her father battled the Red Baron himself in the skies over France. Perhaps her most outlandish yarn was her claim to have been in the presidential motorcade in Dallas when John F. Kennedy was shot on November 22, 1963. Virginia did meet President Lyndon B. Johnson when, as a representative of the American Library Association, she had a White House meeting with Lady Bird Johnson, who was a fan of her father's books.[37]

Although Virginia wished she had been close with her father, and perhaps convinced herself she had been, this was really not the case until the mid-1960s. Throughout her life, to interlocutors she referred to Mathews as "Daddy," even though he was almost entirely absent from her childhood and adolescence. Her claim that she started visiting her father almost every summer beginning in 1941, at age sixteen, is highly exaggerated. During her visits, Virginia said, "we spent hours reading and talking and he told me stories of when he was a little boy. He took me to visit Osage elders and to the Osage 'hand games' where he delighted in my success with concealing game objects."[38]

In 1943, Jo visited Virginia in Baltimore at Goucher College, remarking in his diary she had become a "freshman year fatty," but was "strikingly beautiful, with rosy cheeks, curly hair and sparkling eyes." He found it strange to be called "daddy" and introduced to her friends as her "father." He had rarely thought of himself as such. In 1948, when Joseph Brandt, then living in Monsey, New York, arranged for Mathews to meet Virginia in his home, Jo's diary suggests he had not seen her in years. He was hardly complimentary: she was "large and conspicuously fat," but her face remained beautiful. Though she was only twenty-three, she looked forty. "How odd that my little companion of Pasadena should be a large, sensible woman, head of a department at Brentano's [bookstore] New York." In the early 1950s, she worked in Paris as a children's book buyer.[39]

Virginia visited her father in 1954, 1956, and 1957. Mathews wrote after the last visit: "Virginia looks like her mother, has far too many of her mother's characteristics," plus those of the boastful Regnier family line. "If one had been breeding for stability, dependability, adult and mature commonsense, the mating between a descendant of the Regniers and the Hopper-Winslows would have been most carefully avoided." Virginia, then thirty-two years old, indulged in "illusions of dramatic and important accomplishment, a little of grandeur." Jo had expected her to stay with Lillian and Marie in their home on Grandview, but she instead stayed with him at The Blackjacks because she was "snubbed" by her aunts, who were hosting favored niece Sarah Jo Caudill. As they shared drinks, "her Hopper-Winslow cupidity began working," he wrote, suspicious of her motivations:

> She thinks that my will is still in favor of John and herself, and she need not ingratiate herself further with me, but she must vie with Sarah Jo for the favor of her aunties. She recognizes no snub, and is cold and calculating. Our association is not a particularly pleasant one, since I feel that she really has no feeling for me, and I am not sure whether my tepid feeling for her is induced by her lack of feeling, or by the memories of Hopperism which she inspires by many little characteristics . . . which at one time put knots in my stomach.[40]

Over the next decade, however, Jo warmed up toward his daughter. Virginia visited The Blackjacks each October in 1966, 1967, and 1968. In 1967, after speaking with Virginia by phone, Jo wrote to Brandt, "we are very close, and she is lovely, and very fond of Elizabeth."[41]

Mathews never became close with his son, however. After attending the Naval Academy Preparatory School, John H. Mathews studied engineering at the U.S. Naval Academy in Annapolis, Maryland, at government expense. John's uncle, Ohio Congressman Michael Feighan, helped secure his nephew's appointment, which Jo helped arrange. While studying at the all-male academy, he continued acting as a regular cast member of the Masqueraders, even playing "the girl" in a production of *Boy Meets Girl*, which scandalized an admiral's wife. He loved books and classical music and was respected for his rationality and individualism. Like his father, John believed in cultivating the whole person, so he rose early to run or swim before reveille, and "his idea of a restful leave was a bicycle tour of Canada," the yearbook recorded. He completed four years at the Naval Academy and graduated with the class of 1950.[42]

Circa 1949, John met his future wife, Mary Abigail "Gail" Painter, during a Tea Dance at an Annapolis hotel. Daughter of Dr. Sidney Painter, a medievalist at Johns Hopkins, Gail was genuine, bright, and pretty, and she and John hit it off. Gail was then at Bryn Mawr College, a prestigious women's liberal arts school near Philadelphia. Her sister, Julie Painter, was an alumnus of and later became a dean at Bryn Mawr, and Gail and John's daughter Laura Mathews graduated in the class of 1980.[43]

After John finished at the Naval Academy, the U.S. government paid for him to study for four years at the Eidgenössische Technische Hochschule in Zürich, Switzerland, a top-ranked STEM university where Einstein had studied. Accompanying him, Gail studied at the University of Zürich. John H. Mathews unconsciously followed in his father's footsteps by going to Switzerland to study, and marrying there. John and Gail wed in a civil ceremony at the town hall in Kussnacht, Zürich, on July 27, 1951, followed by a ceremony the next day at the English church in Zürich. They had three children: Sara (b. 1955), Laura Inslee (b. 1958), and Christine Winslow (b. 1961). Jo Mathews enjoyed sending his granddaughters letters and postcards with special pen-and-ink drawings of birds and animals.[44]

After returning to the United States in 1959, John and Gail earned master's degrees from the University of Michigan, in physics and history, respectively. They moved back east to work in Washington, D.C. Gail later earned a master of library science degree and became a school librarian. In late 1962, John and Gail moved into a house in Bowie, Maryland, where they remained until 1997. John became a U.S. government physicist in the National Research Laboratory in Washington, D.C., and conducted classified military research, including working on an atomic-powered marine tanker. As a scientist he worked for the Naval Research Laboratory, the Pentagon, the Army, and the Air Force, reaching the top ranks of civil service. John published an article in *Nature* and, especially during the 1960s, presented his research on continental drift and other subjects at many prestigious national and international scientific conferences, with abstracts published in various journals and reports. Polylingual, he presented a paper in French at a major conference in Helsinki, Finland. This became the source of a weird misunderstanding between father and son. During a visit to The Blackjacks, John told his father he planned to go to Helsinki for a conference, but Mathews somehow thought his son was telling him to "go to hell." Furious, Jo vowed he would never talk to his son again. Elizabeth made peace and told him not to be so rash.[45]

Virginia was the catalyst for any interaction between John and his father, according to Chris Mathews. John resented the fact that his father was absent during his childhood, and made few efforts to reconnect once he and John did meet, so he was not inclined to initiate a relationship with his estranged father. In 1969, John visited his father over the course of a few days but stayed elsewhere. Jo took him to the Osage Tribal Museum and the Osage County Historical Museum and presented him with a copy of *Wah'Kon-Tah*, remarking in his diary only that John was a "phenomenal eater." In March 1971, Virginia and John came out to The Blackjacks together for a few days to visit their father and Elizabeth. John brought a tape reel of his three daughters singing and playing instruments, which pleased Jo, and took home a reel of "wildlife voices" and Osage dance music. They drank and enjoyed home-cooked

John Hopper Mathews with a painting of John Joseph Mathews, 2013. *Photo by the author.*

food. Jo described Virginia and John as gourmets and overweight, but sharp and quick-witted. "I am delighted by their visit, but was not quite ready for it; I never am ready, I believe." Virginia returned to The Blackjacks for two days in November.[46]

After John left the Naval Research Laboratory, he taught at the high school and community college levels, as well as at Bowie State College, before becoming an awarded tutor for Traveling Tutors, where he helped countless students get into Ivy League schools. He also did translation work. John and Gail retired to Allensville in Amish country in remote central Pennsylvania, in part to be near two of their daughters. John Hopper Mathews, an appealing, funny, articulate, and highly intelligent man, died on February 2, 2015, and his wife, children, and grandchildren memorialized him in a service in Allensville in March.[47]

Virginia W. H. Mathews also forged a long and successful career and won many awards and recognitions. In early childhood she was educated by governesses, and in 1942, she graduated from the Beard School for Girls, a college-preparatory country day school in Orange, New Jersey. After a semester at Goucher College, she claimed to have taken courses at Columbia University and the University of Geneva, where her father had studied. She was a book buyer for Brentano's bookshops; a marketer for Longmans, Green (the publisher of *Sundown*); a mentor, activist, and children's book author and reviewer; and a librarian and author or editor of books on library science. She was an active member of the American Library Association and the National Book Committee for decades, and a consultant for the Center for the Book at the Library of Congress. She was also a consultant for Children's Television Workshop, which developed *Sesame Street*. Conscious of her Osage heritage, Virginia was a founder of the American Indian Library Association, and she strove to develop tribal libraries across the country. Imbued with a strong sense of social justice, she worked to make libraries accessible to the underprivileged. She met three first ladies: Barbara Bush, Lady Bird Johnson and, like her father, Eleanor Roosevelt. The American Indian Library Association named a scholarship in her honor in 2012. According to Chris Mathews, Virginia was always deeply devoted to her mother. She bought houses for Ginger and Aunt Phyllis, who remained inseparable throughout their lives.[48]

Virginia lived with a longtime partner and companion named Virginia "Ginny" B. Huie, who was her wife in every sense but legal recognition. Virginia's aunt, Phyllis Hopper, was also a lesbian. In fact, according to Laura and Chris, Ginny had been Aunt Phyllis's girlfriend before Virginia started seeing her. Born in 1920, Ginny was a Southerner who moved to New York to pursue a career as an opera singer. She was a paid chorister and managed an actor. Virginia and Ginny had a stormy relationship. Ginny could be volatile. Once when John Mathews and his family were visiting the couple, Ginny stormed out of the house after a fight. Virginia asked her brother to pursue Ginny and persuade her to return. He tried, but Ginny summoned a policeman and told him a stranger was following her and she was afraid. John was mortified.[49]

After living in Connecticut for many years, in 1971 Ginger and Phyllis moved to Southern Pines, North Carolina. After several of Ginger's poems appeared in the local newspaper, in 1987 she published her poetry collection *Captured Moments*. She passed away in April 2000 at age 102, preceded by Phyllis a couple of months earlier. Ginger's daughter, Virginia, returned to Pawhuska late in life, reconnecting with her father's legacy. In November 2009, she participated in the designation of both Mathews and the Osage Tribal Museum as Oklahoma Literary Landmarks, with a keynote address by Carter Revard. The mayor of Pawhuska declared November 15–21, 2009, John Joseph Mathews Week. Virginia lived in Oklahoma for a few years before returning to central Pennsylvania, where she died on May 7, 2011. She was buried beside Ginny, who died in 2008, in Machpelah Presbyterian Cemetery in Belleville, in Amish country, largely thanks to the efforts of Chris Mathews. As I paid my respects to this couple, who were regular attenders of the Presbyterian church, an Amish man driving a horse and buggy passed by.[50]

Chapter Five

OSAGE LITERARY MAN

> You are young men. You have the thoughts of white men, but you have the interest of your people in your hearts. Do what you think best. You know how to say things so that people will understand. Old men should advise young men, but those things which we meet today are not the things which I know about. The things which I know are gone. If you let your white man tongues say what is in your hearts, you will do great things for your people.
>
> —Chief Fred Lookout to Mathews and other mixed-blood councilmen

During the early 1930s, John Joseph Mathews built his sandstone home on the Osage prairie and established his literary career. He continued to publish in the *Sooner Magazine* and wrote a column called *Our Osage Hills* for the *Pawhuska Journal-Capital.* With the keen encouragement of his friend Joseph A. Brandt, he published *Wah'Kon-Tah: The Osage and the White Man's Road* (1932) with OU Press, promptly becoming a nationally recognized author. His second book, a novel, *Sundown* (1934), was issued by Longmans, Green of New York City. In the mid-1930s, Mathews turned his attention to serving his tribe. In 1934, he began a two-term (eight-year) stint on the Osage Tribal Council and worked to establish the Osage Tribal Museum, which opened in 1938. Across the decade, through literary, cultural, and political efforts, Mathews invested in his Osage heritage and people.

Shortly after Jo fled his marriage and returned to Pawhuska, Walter Campbell visited him there in December 1929, and they had a great time. Since Jo was living at the Mathews home on Grandview Avenue in Pawhuska, Campbell socialized with his mother, Jennie, and sisters, Lillian and Marie. Jo wrote Walter, "Each member of the family looks forward to your next visit, so pleasant was your recent one. I personally find it easy and delightful to entertain guests who like to ride, shoot, dance, and talk," and "if they happen to be old friends, the pleasure is double." The two men continued to see each other regularly. In March 1930, Mathews visited the Campbells in Norman. Listening to Jo's Oxford stories, Walter thought his experiences represented fantastic material for a novel. Afterward Jo wrote, "I am convinced I have a gold mine at my fingertips. I think I shall just cut loose and start writing, then come to you and we can decide if I have really done anything." He began enthusiastically, but soon ran out of steam. In June, he walked his youngest sister, Florence, down the aisle of Immaculate Conception Church, when she married Michael A. Feighan of Cleveland, who was finishing a Harvard law degree.[1]

Back home, separated from his wife and two little children and feeling uninspired, Mathews was at a loss for a time, unsure of his next move. He sought diversion. In the midst of a spiritual crisis in December 1930, he wrote Campbell a memorable letter, which Robert Dale Parker published as an appendix to *The Invention of Native American Literature*. Confessing "I need you tonight," Jo told of partying with a younger, free-spirited crowd, joyriding to Independence, Kansas, a name that to him seemed ironic. These jejune jazz agers, having taken libertine lifestyles as far as they could, were jaded and incoherent. Jo's disillusionment came to a head as a bored Kansas coed half his age fondled his chest and offered her body to him. Mathews was thirty-six when he wrote this "Lost Generation" letter to Campbell. Much older than these flaming youths, he had been raised with Victorian values. Instead of escape or sexual excitement or whatever he had hoped to find, he found weary degeneration among denizens of a prairie Wasteland. "Legs, sex, orgies, speed, alcohol, abnormalities, exaggerated frankness, and flitting around the candle of lust, have lost their thrill; they have become flat and stingless and the devotees are stupefied and listless, like children tired of their toys." Surrounded by white decadence, Mathews turned his imagination to a fantasized notion of Osage traditional religion, grasping at something familiar from boyhood that might supply a spiritual anchor. He was inspired to supplicate Wah'Kon-Tah, the Great Mystery. "Oh Wahkanda, drive into my soul the spirit of the prairie, which gave birth to mine own people, that in my creations I might glorify them, and thereby glorify you Oh Wahkanda, by speaking a language that is a true one." At the time he dismissed this reverie as "crazy thoughts," but in fact it was a serious statement of intent that would guide his future literary efforts.[2]

Given Jo's experiences during the Great War, his wanderings in Europe and northern Africa, and his drifting at home, in many ways he resembled an iconic Lost Generation literary figure. Critic Rita Keresztesi has placed *Sundown*, along with novels by D'Arcy McNickle and Mourning Dove, in a tradition of "ethnic modernism." Mathews was a contemporary of Ernest Hemingway, William Faulkner, and F. Scott Fitzgerald. For his love of hunting, nature, and manly, alcohol-soaked gatherings, Mathews garnered comparisons to Hemingway, and like "Papa," attended bullfights and hunted in Africa. "The hunting jackets that he invariably wore completed what might have been an irritatingly macho image," had not his soft-spoken humor, regard for nature, and tribal knowledge "rendered him a wilderness sage, a gentler sort of Hemingway," Terry Wilson writes. Both men projected earth-attuned, rugged, masculine images. In their work, both writers subtly dealt with sexuality and invented Native characters. Mathews admired Hemingway and in 1953 read for the third time "The Killers" and "The Snows of Kilimanjaro." Unlike his stepson—author John Hunt, discussed in chapter 6—Jo did not prize Faulkner, and he rarely mentioned Fitzgerald, surprising because as Carter Revard has pointed out, college scenes in *Sundown* share a certain satirical flavor with Fitzgerald's novel of Princeton University, *This Side of Paradise* (1920).[3]

In his mid-thirties, between 1929 and 1934, Mathews became a professional writer with the strong encouragement of Joseph Brandt and Walter Campbell. During this period, Mathews published several short pieces as an editor of the *Sooner Magazine*. Some of these pieces are specifically Osage in context; for example, the tribute "Passing of Red Eagle" (1930) and "Ee Sa Rah N'eah's Story" (1931). One of the best, most moving stories he wrote for the *Sooner Magazine* is "Hunger on the Prairie" (1930). This unusual story expresses his Osage outlook in that its characters are animals. It evokes the harsh conditions of wintertime on the Osage prairie and the struggle to survive. One feels great sympathy for birds and other little creatures who tirelessly hunt for food. The winters of 1929 and 1930 were blizzardy. Jo remembered January 1930: "I was coming out from town, with [cousins] Tony and Arthur Fortune. I had a hundred pounds of feed for the quail, and they had the groceries. The car slid gently off the ridge and broke through the crust of the drifted snow in a ravine."[4]

From spring 1930 through summer 1931, Mathews wrote a regular column called *Our Osage Hills* for the *Pawhuska Journal-Capital* newspaper; published at least once a week, sometimes even thrice, this column has been almost completely forgotten. *Our Osage Hills* pieces discuss animals, nature, ecology, hunting, conservation, and geology of the Osage reservation, as well as occasionally Osage Indian history and culture. These columns were linked with Jo's position as an officer of the Izaak Walton League in Pawhuska, a conservationist group, alongside his friend Ralph S. Tolson of the Tolson Agency. Formed in 1922, the Isaak Walton League is one of America's oldest conservation groups. Walton, a seventeenth-century English author, wrote *The Compleat Angler*, which celebrated fishing in prose and poetry. In the 1930s, the league was instrumental in establishing a wildlife refuge in Osage County. They stocked the range with animals and the streams with fish. From one point of view, Mathews's ecology and conservation efforts seem ironic, since he was a relentless hunter. But one of the objectives of conservation in that era was to protect populations of animals and keep rivers clean so that sportsmen would have a continuing population of animals to kill: "Man the hunter must protect his game if he wishes to enjoy it in the future," Mathews wrote. "He came to this realization almost too late: it came in the Osage when we saw our streams polluted with oil, and our game destroyed by transients connected with oil development who killed in all seasons with barbaric unconcern."[5]

His debut work, *Wah'Kon-Tah: The Osage and the White Man's Road*, rapidly made Mathews a nationally recognized Indian author. Released in November 1932, it was based upon the "staid, meticulous diary of a Quaker Indian agent," Major Laban J. Miles, the son of Benjamin Miles, an Iowa farmer, and Elizabeth Miles, who both taught Osage children and ran a small Osage boarding school in Pawhuska before returning to Iowa to teach Natives there. Their son Laban met his destiny in 1878 when he was appointed agent to the Osages. Miles served the tribe in this capacity for many years and during various administrations, from 1878 to 1885 and 1889 to 1893. For fifty-eight years, he was linked with the Osages, "a friend to the Indians and active on their behalf." Although Miles left Pawhuska in 1893 when military officers replaced Quaker Indian agents, he maintained his interests in the town and spent time on the reservation, eventually returning to make his home there. Throughout his lengthy career of service, Miles kept a journal recording his experiences, an important record of Osage history. After Mathews returned to Pawhuska, he met with the elderly Laban Miles and they conversed at length as Jo took notes. Shortly before Miles died in April 1931, he contacted Mathews and said, "I haven't got long and I want you to have my notes, my diary. It says plain old Quaker facts. You may have it, it's yours." Miles often felt frustrated that he was unable to express his feelings and understanding of the Osages in his writing, so he hoped his young friend might glean something from them.[6]

It was fortunate that Brandt apparently coaxed Mathews into writing *Wah'Kon-Tah*, since Mathews did not initially jump on Miles's suggestion to use his papers, notes, and interviews as material for a book. "I didn't think much of it until I started reading it," Mathews admitted to Guy Logsdon. In April 1931, Jo drove to Norman to see Joe and his remarkable wife, Sallye Little Brandt.[7] Mathews told the Brandts of his conversations with Miles, adding he would inherit the agent's notes. This elicited an excited response. During the visit, Brandt handed Mathews a clipping of Miles's obituary and said he wanted a book for OU Press: "Go home and write it." In 1940, *Time* claimed Brandt "chased" Mathews across the continent in an airplane to spur him to complete *Wah'Kon-Tah*, and the magazine later said Brandt "wheedled" the book out of Mathews. "Jo-Without-Purpose," as he called himself retrospectively, benefited from such prompting. The critical and commercial success of the book, the latter largely the result of Brandt's placing it with the Book of the Month Club, inaugurated Mathews's literary career.[8]

Miles's valuable journals had already attracted literary interest. No less than the novelist and playwright Edna Ferber had tried unsuccessfully to acquire his journal while researching Osage County for her novel *Cimarron* (1929), which dramatized Oklahoma land runs and was adapted into two well-received films. In 1928, while Jo was in California, Ferber spent time in Pawhuska, her model for the fictional town of Osage. Jo's relative Phillip Fortune claimed Ferber stayed at the Mathews family home and interviewed Lillian about local history. While in Oklahoma, she took in sights "never seen on land or sea." In Pawhuska, she found "Osage Indian houses built of brick, filled with plush and taffeta and plumbing," and in the backyard, "tepees in which the owners preferred to sleep."[9]

In the early 1930s, Mathews and Campbell reciprocated hearty respect for each other's work. In January 1933, Mathews wrote his friend: "Our two books, *Wah'Kon-Tah* and *Sitting Bull*, seem in quite a different way to say the same thing, and certainly the relationship between the Sioux and the Osage is brought out. Our individual Indians have the same reactions and philosophy." Of his forthcoming project, Mathews said in June 1931 both Brandt and OU President W. B. Bizzell were "rather keen on the prospect." Campbell was apparently surprised and envious at the attention his protégée was receiving from OU Press. In 1967 Brandt wrote Mathews, "I suppose no publisher in history ever reposed so much confidence in an unpublished author as I did with you. W. S. never got over it." After Campbell's protracted struggles to achieve literary success, Mathews seemingly waltzed into a book contract.[10]

After returning to Pawhuska, Mathews found Laban Miles's son, Oakley, and asked him if he had an old house somewhere. Oakley's neighbor had an abandoned shack, eighteen miles northeast of Pawhuska on Rock Creek, and Oakley helped Jo clean it out. The budding Osage author dived into an ascetic existence, his key possessions being a dog, a horse, and a typewriter. He used a bucket to shower and ate canned goods and whatever he hunted or fished. He brought a record player and listened to recordings of Native music for inspiration. This was a trial run for his future life at The Blackjacks. When news of Mathews's project spread across Osage communities via the "moccasin telegraph," elders sought him out to share stories about the early days of the reservation, augmenting his Osage perspective. Mathews commenced writing on July 4, 1931—a symbolic date, since he asserted his independence and in Nietzschean fashion willed himself to become a writer. During this stretch, Mathews chose to isolate himself not only to write the book, but also to avoid contact with his estranged wife. Composition flowed organically: "I wrote that book just like a wood thrush would sing. He's not conscious of it, he just sings." Mathews modestly stated, "I didn't have any idea that people would read it or that people would be interested. I just wrote it because I had to write it. If I hadn't finished it when I did, I might have gone deer hunting and forgotten about it."[11]

Wah'Kon-Tah is literary nonfiction, a history of the Osages covering 1878–1931 from the point of view of Major Miles. Not only is *Wah'Kon-Tah* of historical importance, it is also nuanced and heteroglossic, with an epic sweep that inspired Brandt to dub Mathews "the Osage Homer." Mathews wished to write a book "based on the diaries and notes but livened by his imagination," so he shone the modest light of Miles's Quaker gray prose through the prism of his lyrical imagination. Seemingly afraid of being sentimental, Miles wrote in an austere style. "He didn't praise himself or his religion, he simply told the facts as he saw it," Mathews said.[12] In contrast, Mathews called the book he wrote based on that prose "the story of a period, and atmospheric history." Essentially a "human interest document," it is a "dual sketch showing the influence of Major Miles, the Quaker Friend, on the Indians and in turn the influence of the Indians on Major Miles." Fitting into the genre of history or ethnohistory, to Brandt it was "a spiritual history of the Osage Indians." With little concern for chronology, Mathews dramatized diverse traits comprising Osage tribal culture and its interface with Euro-Americans, stressing the "spirituality, dignity, and humor of the Osages who grudgingly acculturated to the white man's road, adapting aspects of the new way for their own purposes," as Terry Wilson writes. *Wah'Kon-Tah* benefits from Jo's mixed-blood perspective: "Bilingual and bicultural, Mathews effectively meshed Miles's written documents with Osage oral remembrances to create an informal history of early reservation events," states Wilson. Actually, though Mathews spoke some Osage, he was hardly fluent. During the 1930s he used a translator when interviewing full-blood elders, and in 1958 he told a reporter that he only spoke "pidgin Osage."[13]

Beginning in the 1870s, Friends (Quakers) had a significant effect on Osages in Indian Territory, and vice versa. In *The Osages*, Mathews writes of Friends: "In the laissez faire atmosphere of the U.S. Grant administration and the greedy fever which it inspired in a nation, there was a spiritual light which became effective since it was integrated with the national government and therefore had the government's power behind it, but was not tarnished." Friends gradually earned the trust of Osages, who had interacted with Jesuits and Catholics on their previous reservation. While Mathews sometimes refers to white "chicanery" in his history, the Osages believed Quakers "didn't employ chicanery to gain their ends." While Friends could at first seem intolerant, their honesty was "not really aggressive. Rather it was like a benign wall which one must finally learn cannot be dented." In 1914, a Quaker historian stated, "year after year," many Friends "served at the Osage Agency and in other parts of the Indian country with results that have been gratifying." Mathews, his sisters, and their contemporaries were reared by a generation that had regularly interacted with Quaker agents and missionaries. As a young man, William Mathews worked for Miles's predecessor, Isaac Gibson, and lived neighboring him and Laban, a friend. Will Mathews helped reorganize the tribe, and though he sometimes disagreed with Laban's policies, they respected and admired each other. As a child, Mathews frequently played in the retired agent's home on Grandview Avenue, and as a young man, reconnected with him.[14]

After dropping out of the University of Iowa and operating a general store in West Branch, Iowa, Laban Miles was appointed agent to the Osages in 1878. Like all Indian agents at that time, he was given an honorific military title, an irony for a pacifist Quaker and a reminder that the Bureau of Indian Affairs was once a wing of the Department of War. Miles was an uncle of future president Herbert Hoover, whose childhood was partly spent in West Branch. Laban's wife, Ontario-born Agnes Minthorn Miles, was sister to Herbert Hoover's mother, Hulda. After Hulda's husband, Jesse Hoover, died, relatives helped care for their children, especially when she traveled around the state preaching as a Quaker minister. In 1882, two years after his father died, eight-year-old Bert Hoover lived among Osages for about nine months, in the care of Uncle Laban and Aunt Agnes. With his cousins, Hoover constantly mixed with Osage children at the agency, learning "aboriginal lore of the woods and streams," making bows and arrows, swimming, playing tribal games, and attending First Day School, Hoover wrote.[15]

Though imperfect, Laban Miles was a benign wall, a quiet force of nature. "A much-admired agent," Miles was recalled five years after his first retirement, at the Osages' special request, to serve another term. Gentle yet fearless, Miles was to some a superlative ally of the tribe. Osage historian Louis Burns lauds the major's "characteristic gentleness of spirit." In the mid-nineteenth century, during a dire period, "despite its faults, and there are many, the Bureau of Indian Affairs appeared on the scene to prevent the total extinction of the Osage people." Earlier actions by the War Department "had all but destroyed the Osage people," but "three outstanding BIA Agents were at least partly responsible" for saving them: A. J. Dorn, Isaac Gibson, and Laban J. Miles. Their job was not easy, they erred, but "they should be remembered by the Osage people," Burns stresses. Miles did everything in his power to help the tribe, and to bring peaceful resolution to disputes between them and whites. E. E. White, special agent to the Osages during the 1880s, said the principal chief told him he was a good agent, "just like Major Laban J. Miles."[16]

Mathews finished writing *Wah'Kon-Tah* on Thanksgiving 1931 and quickly conveyed the manuscript to Brandt. One challenge publishers face is attracting book buyers' attention to an unknown author's first book. One approach is to solicit a foreword by a famous person with a connection to the subject, in this case, the president! Thinking big, in January 1932 Brandt, Mathews, and Oklahoman author George Milburn drove a rickety Ford all the way to Washington, D.C., on a quixotic quest. The meeting was arranged through a friend of Jo's, Oklahoma Senator Thomas Pryor Gore, a populist and Gore Vidal's grandfather and mentor. Mathews wrote Gore requesting help in arranging a meeting with Hoover. Though Hoover did not write a foreword, being slightly busy dealing with the Great Depression, he offered useful material about his time in the Osage Nation as a boy, which was milked for promotion. One might wonder why the Oklahomans did not try to visit Hoover's part-Osage vice president, Charles B. Curtis, the only Indian vice president in history (he also possessed Kaw and Potawatomi ancestry). Curtis, however, was fiercely pro-assimilationist, his Curtis Act (1898) brought the General Allotment Act to the Five Civilized Tribes of Oklahoma, and he declared he was "one-eighth Kaw but 100% Republican." Mathews was a Democrat.[17]

During the summer of 1932, Mathews carefully planned his own Osage house, a one-man, two-room home built from reddish, yellow, and umber native sandstone. Through early 1936, it was known prosaically as "the Shack," but eventually Jo dubbed it The Blackjacks, after the modest variety of oak found on the prairie, whose low branches form a natural barrier. "When they become older and larger, the lower limbs die and slant downward, forming a perfect protection against anything large enough to harm them. These dead limbs are as hard and as tough as steel lances, capable of tearing hide or clothing," Mathews noted in *Talking to the Moon*. Oklahoman author Elizabeth Alden Settle wrote, "there is something about a settlement that a blackjack does not like." That Jo named his custom-built home after these trees, which ranchers dislike due to their recalcitrance, symbolizes the isolation and protection he desired. Inspired by Mathews, Osage critic Robert Allen Warrior coined the term "Blackjacks discourse" as his way of "declaring a boundary around my intellectual practice and seeking a modicum of individual determination over the way new ideas came into my intellectual and critical space." Mathews mounted a barrier between himself and society, difficult to penetrate. He wanted a place to write, reflect, observe nature and animals, hunt, and escape disapproving sisters and gossips. The Blackjacks was moreover a refuge where he could evade the pesky demands of his abandoned wife, Ginger, and where he and his favored guests might converse, eat, and drink their fill undisturbed. Only three decades later did he have a telephone installed.[18]

Working with a contractor, Jo stressed his desire for a fireplace that would draw well and be the centerpiece of the edifice. The second room was a screened-in kitchen area, and a screened-in back porch was later added. In the 1960s, an outbuilding was constructed of concrete blocks. A well served the house—later a pump system brought water into the house—and an outdoor shower nozzle was mounted on the side of the home. Mathews furnished his modest house with a small writing desk, a couch, and a red leather easy chair, in which he loved to "graze" his personal canon of "mood books," smoke his pipe, or just muse, staring into the blazing fire. He decorated his den with bearskin rugs, animal trophies, framed pictures of Indians, and eventually, his book covers. Jo moved into The Blackjacks on July 24, 1932. Walter and Isabel Campbell spent the first night with him, excited to have a getaway from the kids.[19]

A critical and commercial success, *Wah'Kon-Tah* was a Book of the Month Club alternate selection for November 1932, a first for a university press book. When this news arrived, however, Mathews could not be found, since he was in Colorado, fishing rainbow trout. Mathews retrospectively wrote to Brandt, "this made no difference; Ole Simon coiled his bullwhip and lashed out at John-Without-Purpose, and ordered him home." As an OU Press and Book of the Month Club author, he had obligations, especially now that *Wah'Kon-Tah* was garnering literary hype rarely afforded to a university press book. In October, Mathews undertook an eventful trip to New York City to promote the book, meeting publishers, editors, journalists, and radio talk show hosts. He went reluctantly, failing to remember the posters he was supposed to transport. Betty Kirk, an OU Press employee and friend of Lynn Riggs, wrote Brandt: "Jo arrived with no display material, nonchalantly, and I was so dejected I almost wept." From Norman, Brandt replied to Kirk, who was promoting the book in New York and had been pessimistic about Jo arriving: "The difficulty about Jo was that he really could not afford to make the trip, which may seem strange, but I know enough about his financial situation to know that is true." Later Kirk reported, "Jo has been a model of cooperation in working with the book and he has so many valuable contacts here."[20]

In November, Betty and Jo went to meet an advocate, Henry Seidel Canby, a Yale professor and a founding editor of *Saturday Review of Literature*. Canby, along with *Saturday Review* editors Amy Loveman and Christopher Morley, were jurors for the Book of the Month Club. Then a well-known author, Morley approached

Mathews, raved over his book, and spoke congenially of Oxford. Southwestern regionalist authors also lauded *Wah'Kon-Tah*. Mary Austin, author of *The Land of Little Rain* (1903), and Oliver La Farge, anthropologist and author of *Laughing Boy* (1929), a Pulitzer Prize–winning novel about Navajos, both wrote glowing reviews. On the radio, Lewis Titterton, an English NBC executive and fan, interviewed Mathews for the *Books and Characters* series.[21]

Jo's rich cultural and historical knowledge and writing talent, combined with his publisher's enthusiasm and promotional savvy, garnered big success for the book. Moreover, Mathews's energetic promotion of it provided momentum for his career. Even despite the Depression, the book sold fifty thousand copies through the book club and thousands more at stores. This broad readership contributed to mainstream American readers' understanding of Osages, and more broadly, Lower Plains Indians. To celebrate Jo's success, in January 1933 newspaperman Walter Ferguson and columnist Lucia Ferguson honored him with a lavish reception for more than one hundred guests at their home in Tulsa. Jo's friends and allies came out in force; Joe Brandt was present that evening with Sallye, and so was Grant Foreman—author of *Indian Removal* (1932) and *The Five Civilized Tribes* (1934)—who established the Civilization of the American Indian series for OU Press. Also in attendance was the man who encouraged Brandt to start OU Press, William Bennett Bizzell, president of OU from 1925 to 1941 and namesake of its new library. *Wah'Kon-Tah*'s illustrator, Pawhuska artist Mary Todd Aaron, attended, along with Betty Kirk and Lillian Mathews.[22]

The next month, a snowbound Mathews wrote Brandt that he expected three interesting visitors in the spring. First, Tulsa artist Roger Lane wished to paint Mathews. Then, Freddie Lookout would visit for a week to discuss the Peyote ritual. Freddie feared that the stories his father, Chief Fred Lookout, had told him would be lost if not written down. "This, I am almost whitemanishly eager to do," Jo wrote. After naming these future guests, Jo made a romanticized request for Joe Brandt's presence: "Then after Freddie leaves, comes, may I hope? One elongated, pink-haired editor of the University Press. He, I hope, will come about the time of rose planting. I shall have roses in the blackjacks. There will be no secret about the object of his visit. I shall have my cottonwoods and my locusts planted by then, but we can grub about the place and perhaps dig up the wild roses which would eventually be under the projected lake, if not transplanted."[23]

Jo's New York trip led to long-established publisher Longmans, Green soliciting a novel. Mathews acceded to his new publisher's request with what he claimed was little enthusiasm, quickly composing an evocative, semiautobiographical novel called *Sundown*. Dedicated to Campbell and published in November 1934, it became his

Formal photograph of John Joseph Mathews, 1932.
Courtesy of the Mathews family.

most studied work. *Sundown* set a paradigm followed by novelists of the Native American Renaissance, such as Leslie Marmon Silko and N. Scott Momaday: the homecoming of an alienated Native veteran who struggles with his identity. With some exceptions, the novel's events and chronology follow the trajectory of Jo's youth. The most significant difference is that Challenge Windzer's mother is full-blood Osage rather than French Catholic, instantly making Chal's point of view much more Indigenous than his creator's. Focusing on Chal's struggle to negotiate competing Euro-American and Osage formations of masculine identity, and his resulting feelings of alienation, frustration, and purposelessness, *Sundown* lacks the narrative arc of a traditional novel, instead presenting an alternative version of its author's life. Although the book features vivid scenes and a broad scope, it tends to meander. A reviewer for the *New York Times* said that although the style was impressive, "the book has a decidedly inarticulate quality, as if the problem he is trying to state had been only half comprehended and is hence not susceptible of clear statement."[24]

The vague, shrouded quality of the text bespeaks repressed material. Since Mathews wrote of the development of Chal's sexuality and masculinity, often in homosocial contexts, the book portrays male same-sex dynamics and impulses, and the repression of same. This topic has been discussed in critical work by Robert Dale Parker, Mark Rifkin, and myself. In this light, the "inarticulate quality" seems strategic. Mathews claimed he wrote *Sundown* "without any inspiration," since he would have preferred to be hunting, and repeatedly said he never read the novel after publication. But one evening in 1948, he read much of *Sundown*, which he had "always deprecated," and found it interesting, "not in the least bad." Mathews, motivated by a desire to fulfill a promise he made amidst "confusion," in a rapid stream of unconscious prose, wrote a novel inspired by his life that repeatedly suggests his protagonist's repressed same-sex interest. Mathews's disavowal of the novel's importance, to himself and the literary world, suggests he may have become aware of the novel's homoerotic aspect after its publication. Bolstering this theory, his daughter Virginia stated that in writing *Sundown*, her father showed "he had conquered himself. He created Chal out of what he had expunged from his own life."[25]

After *Sundown*, Jo's literary career trailed off for several years, but not because of a lack of reader and publisher interest. During the spring of 1936, Brandt and Mathews discussed a book project, which eventually became *The Osages*, a collaboration between OU Press and New York publisher Simon & Schuster. Jo dropped the ball, however. Brandt wrote, "Schuster would like to see your outline 'as this would help determine to how large an extent both of us could go in financing the research.' He wants a rather detailed and comprehensive outline." Mathews replied he would prepare an outline "almost immediately." But in September, Brandt inquired, "What progress on the outline of our book? I should have this sometime soon, for otherwise Mr. Schuster will feel that my influence has waned to such a degree as to be worthless." In retrospect, Mathews realized he should have done more to further his writing career. Instead, he squandered opportunities to build on the momentum of his two books. After *Sundown*, more than a decade would pass without another full-length work. Around the time *Sundown* was published, the *Pawhuska Journal-Capital* reported he enjoyed "hunting coyotes with greyhounds, quail and duck shooting, collecting material for a handbook on Birds of the Osage, collecting material for a dictionary of the Osage language, and raising pit game chickens, pheasants, and Irish setters." The dictionary and bird guide were not completed, although he studied the Osage language in his research for future books.[26]

While his literary career trailed off in the mid-1930s, his role in tribal politics took off. Following in his father's footsteps, Mathews was elected to the Fourteenth

Osage Tribal Council in June 1934, representing the Progressive Party, and he served two four-year terms. The council then was mostly a business group that managed oil and gas affairs and leased land. It was composed of ten councilmen led by Principal Chief Fred Lookout and Assistant Principal Chief Harry Kohpay. Among the councilmen were Louis DeNoya, George V. Labadie, and future chief Paul Warren Pitts. The Progressive Party dominated, being the party of the principal and assistant chief, and three out of eight remaining councilmen. In July, an Osage inauguration ceremony at the Pawhuska Indian Village featured a parade, a barbecue, and speeches by Chief Lookout, Mathews, and prominent oilmen such as E. W. Marland and Frank Phillips; the latter had been adopted into the tribe. Also present was Wild West showman "Pawnee Bill" Lillie. Kiowa and Pawnee dancers performed at the ceremony.[27]

Some full-blood Osages were displeased that Mathews and other Progressive mixed-blood councilmen would represent them. Although mixed-bloods were the majority of Osages, the council had for decades "carefully nominated and elected a fullblood chief and assistant chief as well as some councilmen," Wilson writes. After the election results were announced, the full-blood party registered a formal protest with Commissioner of Indian Affairs John Collier, but nothing was found amiss. In 1941, a full-blood protested to the tribal council that Mathews tried to run the show. The full-bloods argued the council was overly dependent on Mathews because of his education. Mathews's election to the tribal council spoke less of Osages' identification of him as Native and more of their regard for his education, ability to navigate white society, and dedication to Osage interests. Even the traditional Osages who voted for Mathews did not necessarily fully accept him as Osage. He was aware his Osageness was "always suspect in the minds of some." Along with some other mixed-blood councilmen, Mathews "scrupulously maintained an awareness" of the views of both mixed-bloods and full-bloods when "considering matters of tribal interest and welfare." Mathews was an articulate, reliable tribal spokesperson whose ideology squared with that of Collier. When Washington dignitaries visited, he was the first to speak.[28]

In the 1960s, dissatisfaction with Osage tribal government manifested in a group called ONO (Osage Nation Organization). If, as has been claimed, Yoko Ono broke up The Beatles, ONO sought to break up the headright system, replacing it with one requiring a minimum one-quarter blood quantum, which would have excluded Mathews. In this context, some Osages falsely called the Mathews family "no bloods" behind their backs, a derogatory term referring to families who got onto the tribal rolls unscrupulously, according to Romain Shackelford.[29]

The council elected in 1934 helped the Osages through the Great Depression. The enormous headright payments of the 1920s were over and the tribe had to adjust. Allotted Osages with headrights received $23,000 in 1921, but only $500 in 1932. In Washington, D.C., Mathews argued that despite headrights, the Osages suffered from the Depression as much as their white neighbors. Mathews ardently supported Collier, whose goal was to develop skills and create jobs, bringing "relief and recovery to the nation's suffering tribes," Wilson writes. When President Roosevelt appointed Collier in 1933, a turn toward acknowledging tribal sovereignty and the government's duty to tribal nations began. He championed through Congress the Indian Reorganization Act (IRA), "the Indian New Deal," which boldly altered U.S. policy, encouraging tribal self-government and consolidating individual allotments back into communal tribal land.[30]

In October 1934, Collier and Oklahoma Senator Elmer Thomas visited Pawhuska during their tour of the state, heatedly debating the IRA, or Wheeler-Howard Act, and its application to Oklahoman Indians. Digging at the Osages, Thomas vowed to reject any law that would forever exempt from taxation the "lands of rich Indians." In Pawhuska, with vocal support from Mathews, Collier excoriated past abuses and "mismanagement of Indian affairs," stressing that the allotment system caused Native Americans to lose "most of their land since 1887." The history of federal policy was an "unbroken record of betrayal by the government, of massacre and rapine." Collier accused Oklahoma of treating its Indigenous people worse than any other state had: "White men are appointed guardians of wealthy Indians, and what they suffer at the hands of their guardians is plenty."[31]

While in Pawhuska, Collier worked closely with Mathews and the Osage Tribal Council. Jo took responsibility for generating Osage support for the IRA, against the influence of Senator Thomas. Oklahoman legislators disliked the bill because it would slow the swift pace of exploitation of Natives and their resources. Mathews convinced the council to support the IRA, and stated in the media: "Those opposed are those who have lived off the Indian for years. I didn't think I would find the press so prejudiced and unfair." In May 1935, Mathews spoke during a meeting of Osages at the Pawhuska Indian Village roundhouse to discuss Collier's plan. Despite the tribe's efforts, Thomas and state lobbyists were able to exempt the Osages from the IRA against their wishes, and worse, Thomas became chairman of the Senate Indian Affairs Committee. In late November, Mathews, Chief Lookout, Assistant Chief Kohpay, and other councilmen traveled by rail to Washington, D.C., to meet with Secretary of the Interior Harold Ickes, Collier, and Oklahoma congressmen. In 1936, Congress passed the Oklahoma Indian Welfare Act, which extended many

IRA provisions to many of the state's tribes—but not to the Osages—because of devious lobbyists. The tribe again requested not to be excluded from such legislation in the future.[32]

In January 1935, Mathews wrote a lengthy obituary of John Lyman Bird, early trader to the Osages. John Bird had worked for Will Mathews at the Osage Mercantile and the Citizen's National Bank, and was the father of Jo's longtime friend Jack Bird. Bird loved the Osages and spoke their language fluently. For their part, the Osages called him Wah Shinkah (similar to *wazhinka*, "bird," in Osage). He collected artifacts, pictures, and books related to the tribe, and long before Mathews, had artists come to Pawhuska to craft portraits of full-bloods. In 1923 the Osage Tribal Council purchased his collection; fifteen years later it became the foundation of the Osage Tribal Museum's collection. When Mathews visited Bird to interview him prior to his death, Bird carefully considered what he said about the Osages. Because so many lies had been published, he wanted only verifiable facts to be printed. He told Jo to put this in his book: "The Osages of my day were gentlemen in every sense of the word—in a day when there were few white gentlemen in this country."[33]

Mathews made several public appearances during this period. Appointed to the State Board of Education by his friend, Governor E. W. Marland, in February 1935 Mathews drove to Stillwater and the campus of Oklahoma A&M (later Oklahoma State University) to address the State League of Young Democrats. A student reporter opined that Mathews did not resemble an Indian, "except for his dignity" and his hands—"the beautiful, slender, tapering hands of an Indian." Mathews also maintained strong ties to his alma mater, and served on the board of the University of Oklahoma Association. In October, Ernie Hill, editor of the *Sooner Magazine*, adapted Mathews's life story into a radio drama broadcast on WSM Nashville as part of a special OU radio program. In 1936, Mathews was awarded an honorary Phi Beta Kappa key in Norman, something he could not have earned as an undergraduate because of his uneven grades.[34]

Excitement filled Pawhuska in March 1937 when First Lady Eleanor Roosevelt visited, and Mathews was part of the hoopla. At the Osage arbor in the Indian Village, Chief Fred Lookout gave a welcome speech, and the tribe showered their distinguished guest with presents, including traditional blankets. The tribal council presented Mrs. Roosevelt with an inscribed copy of *Wah'Kon-Tah*. Mary Todd Aaron, the book's illustrator, gave her a plaque made from a woodcut depicting Osage dancers. The first lady got her wish to see Osage dances, which took place in the traditional brush arbor. After the dances, six thousand people lined the streets to witness a parade honoring the First Lady.[35]

Mathews's articulate voice was heard over the airwaves several times. In April 1937, NBC Blue Network broadcast nationwide "Romance of the Osages," a special half-hour radio program that Mathews wrote and hosted. Involving many full-blood and traditional Osages, the show was sponsored by the Bureau of Ethnology and recorded at the Tulsa Chamber of Commerce. In describing Osages and their appearance of "natural dignity" to listeners, Jo made a rare feminist statement: "Contrary to popular belief," Osage women are not "drudges shoved into the background of everyday life, but are the heads of their homes, in many instances lending valuable assistance to their husbands in business dealings." Chief Lookout recited in Osage a traditional story, translated by his son, Freddie. Jo narrated the origin of the namesake of Pawhuska. Chief Pah-Huh-Skah's name translates to "White Hair," referring to the powdered wig he was surprised to discover when he went to take an English officer's scalp. He thought it *wakon*, "spiritual mystery," and the wig became a talisman that protected a warrior in battle. Jo also narrated the origin of the Osage song "Pawnee Crying on a Hill," which an Osage choir then sang, along with a Peace Song, dedicated to Osage men who served in World War I. Finally, Mathews told the story of Coyote and Little Red Bug, which, he explained, demonstrated the themes of Osage humor, dignity made ridiculous, and the moral that all beings are important, regardless of size. Official singers and dancers made separate studio recordings of traditional Osage songs. Mathews was sent four aluminum records of the program from New York, and in 1959 he audiotaped them. The whereabouts of these recordings is unknown.[36]

In May, Mathews caused a kerfuffle among pallid Pawhuskans when *Tulsa World* reporter Harry LaFerte quoted him at length, and the controversy raged into June. "Riches of Osage Plundered by White Greed," the headline accused, and a subhead promised: "John Joseph Mathews Reveals How His People Are Victimized." The backdrop of the article was an ongoing federal investigation into Osage guardianship fraud, expected to break into a major scandal. In numerous instances, Euro-Americans had gotten themselves named court-appointed guardians of vulnerable Osages with headrights, such as orphaned children. Cash shortages had been found in seven out of eight cases investigated. Verdon Adams, biographer of FBI investigator Tom White, wrote that "some of the most despicable crimes" against Osages were committed by "respected members of the white business and professional community from under the shelter of these guardianships. This was the safe way to rob an Indian and was used by many stalwart members of the white community."[37] The Osage Agency asked for three special agents to investigate. Assistant Commissioner William Zimmerman said guardianship accounts of a thousand Natives were being scrutinized, with several million dollars at stake. Mathews asserted there was "brazen theft in many instances." According to LaFerte, insiders believed the inquiry into guardianship fraud was "merely the first step in an inevitable, sweeping probe of all Indian financial affairs," which would be sensational. During the week the scandalous story broke, Chief Lookout, Mathews, and other councilmen traveled to the nation's capital to confer with government officials about pending legislation and litigation affecting the tribe.[38]

In LaFerte's article, Mathews described means by which unethical whites had exploited Osages. Speaking with detachment, the "cool precision of the scholarly scientist," Mathews said, "*Osage* is a magic word. It means money." Every community grows around an industry of some sort, but Pawhuska's "only industry is the Osage. This community has grown and flourished on Osage money. Everyone here—the doctors, the lawyers and the merchants—are dependent on Osage money for their livelihoods." Mathews then declaimed, "Greed!" with a "sudden gesture, extending his hands at arms' length, then drawing them back against his chest with clutching fingers." LaFerte's description here generated much criticism. In a letter to the *Journal-Capital* responding to this criticism, Jo claimed he was never "emotional or sensational" in the interview. LaFerte quoted him as saying, "Greed, the white man's greed, has caused the Indians many griefs. Unscrupulous men have stooped pretty low at times to get hold of Osage money." Conniving lawyers imported alluring women from other cities to marry lonely Osage men, "with the understanding that they would soon seek a divorce and ask heavy alimony," yielding large fees for the lawyers. Echoing the situation he had dramatized in *Sundown*, Mathews told of corrupt doctors who gave Osage patients opiates to addict them, then sold them drugs at exorbitant prices. Repairmen charged Osages outrageous bills. Then, Mathews made a remark reflecting social Darwinism but also protest: "Being a biologist, I realize that certain natural laws must prevail when one race is held in subjection by a stronger one. And as I grow older, I become more tolerant. Yet I cannot ignore the wrongs my people have suffered. We have tried and are still trying to have those things remedied. But the greedy people are the most numerous. Theirs is the 'louder voice.' Politicians who wish to keep their jobs listen to the 'louder voice' rather than to us when we seek redress."[39]

The response from non-Native Pawhuskans was loud and defensive. A front-page editorial in the *Pawhuska Journal-Capital* declared the *Tulsa World* was scandal-mongering as usual; the incidents Mathews cited were few and were the exception, not the rule. Pawhuskans had "nothing to hang their heads about and they should not let anger provoke them into any action that might impair the friendly relations that have always been enjoyed between the Indians and other residents," the editorial disingenuously argued. In his June response, Mathews said LaFerte visited him at The Blackjacks and asked him to comment on the recent exploitation charges directed toward guardians, but he replied he knew little about the situation. LaFerte said he intended to write a series of articles on the exploitation of the tribe after the guardianship story broke, so Mathews volunteered to give him some general background. Usually cool as a cucumber, Mathews "felt quite hot and on the verge of perspiration" when he was handed the editorial reacting to LaFerte's piece. Mathews realized he was made to appear a sensationalist. He reasoned no one of high principle should have been offended by what he said, and most locals knew him well enough to understand his "interest in the Osages and the community is not manifested by vindictiveness." He tried to appease Pawhuska, a town with skeletons in its closet, by saying "let us as loyal citizens allow the past to remain as history and not disturb its dust, even ejecting it from consciousness so that the psychology of hope for the future will not be disturbed by ghosts." Despite LaFerte's predictions, no major scandal broke over Osage guardian exploitation, and the results of the investigation are unclear. Lawsuits involving guardians were filed in 1937, but they did not have broad impact. Why the scandal fizzled out is a mystery.[40]

During a tribal council meeting in Pawhuska that John Collier attended, Mathews first raised the concept of an Osage museum. Aligning with Collier's advocacy of tribal culture and sovereignty, Jo proposed the Osages should have a place to meet to exchange ideas, perpetuate tribal traditions, and store regalia—a museum. Immediately enthusiastic, Collier asked about projected costs. Mathews admitted no plans or estimates had been made. He then wrote a proposal to the Works Progress Administration (WPA), asking for $250,000. BIA Assistant Commissioner William Zimmerman endorsed the plan to the WPA, which granted the request and added $3,000. Mathews also garnered support from the Smithsonian Institution, which supplied artifacts. In the summer of 1936, construction began on the site of the old Osage Agency chapel and schoolhouse. Replicating the style of those former buildings, the museum was built of native sandstone, many blocks taken from the chapel building. In May 1938, the Osage Tribal Museum (recently renamed the Osage Nation Museum)—the first ever tribally owned and operated museum—held colorful opening ceremonies, including a lavish parade with celebrants attired in Native garb. Wilson wrote that "an Osage aura dominated the all-Indian dedication on one day followed by a mixed ceremony organized by Pawhuska civic organizations the next." Lillian Mathews, a respected local historian, was a fine choice as the first curator.[41]

Spearheaded by Mathews, in 1938 the tribal council applied for and received WPA Federal Art Project funding to commission more than a dozen portraits of full-blood Osage elders. Chicago artist Todros Geller, from a Ukrainian Jewish family, painted at least a dozen of the portraits, still on display at the museum. In the "Moccasin Prints" section of *Talking to the Moon* Mathews told amusing stories of the arrangements for and execution of preliminary sketches of the full-blood subjects, revealing Jo's easy rapport with these Osage elders. Also in 1938, Stanislav Rembski, a Polish-born artist who settled in Baltimore, painted a seven-foot portrait of Chief Fred Lookout, which hung in the museum for fifty-eight years. Somehow Rembski was never paid his commission, though, so in 1996, at age one hundred, he repossessed the portrait, only to have it stolen by his wife's godson in 1997, then returned to him. After Rembski died the next year, "Chief Lookout" was auctioned.[42]

Mathews's second term as councilman ended in 1942 and he was not reelected. With Mathews absent, the museum suffered. The composition of the council changed, and during the wartime 1940s, the Osage Tribal Council withheld funding from the museum and it found very few donors among Osages. The original exhibits were placed out on loan and the museum was forced to close for nearly four years, from July 1943 to May 1947. Garrick Bailey claims "most of the council and most of the Osages didn't care" about the tribal museum during the 1930s and 1940s. Perhaps many Osages were not then ready to see their material culture displayed in glass cases—especially the religious items they had put away or literally buried, never to be disturbed lest a curse be incurred. Not until the 1950s would tribal support for the museum develop, when local Osage families began donating artifacts. Desperate to keep the museum open, at one point Mathews acquired money from the Pawhuska City Council. In spring 1968 the museum was open only sporadically, because funds were lacking to pay the curator's salary.[43]

Between publishing and tribal politics, Jo's activities ensured he was not always solitary during the long period when he lived alone at The Blackjacks. He hosted numerous guests, including celebrities, at his sandstone home. Ernie Pyle, a Pulitzer Prize–winning World War II correspondent who represented the view of the common soldier, visited circa spring 1939, on one of the several visits he made to Oklahoma during a seven-year jaunt crisscrossing America, reporting eclectic experiences in a syndicated column for Scripps-Howard. The *Pawhuska Journal-Capital* reported, "A former Pawhuska doctor, Dr. Paul Hemphill, was stationed at an army hospital in Italy. Ernie Pyle was admitted as a patient. After visiting together, Pyle told him, 'Be sure to remember me to Joe Mathews when you go home.' Pyle had been a guest in the Mathews home a few years before and he, like, others, had drunk of Bird Creek waters." Ernie and Jo, both known for storytelling and drinking, surely shared many laughs together. In 1945, Pyle was killed near the island of Okinawa.[44]

In the fall of 1940, the European author Emil Ludwig relaxed at The Blackjacks. During the 1920s, Ludwig had become internationally famous for his biographies blending fact and fiction, a genre called "romance biography." Born in the German Empire to a Jewish family, Emil Ludwig was known for his biography of Napoleon, and *Jesus Christ, Son of Man*, which caused a stir in 1928. Ludwig's admiration for Mathews was revealed in Joe Brandt's 1938 review of *Out of Africa*, where he placed the author, Isak Dinesen, in a "small but precious clan of writers who are not only clairvoyantly aware of the kinship with nature, but able to share their kinship in unforgettable prose. Most nearly, in *Out of Africa*, Miss Dinesen reminds one of John Joseph Mathews, whom Emil Ludwig has called the 'Lord Byron of the Osage.'" Indeed, *Out of Africa* became one of Mathews's favorite books. He was also fond of Ludwig's writings. In 1954, he reread Ludwig's *The Nile: The Life Story of a River*, calling it "an inspiration."[45]

The French author André Maurois, who also penned "romance biographies" of French and British authors and poets, visited The Blackjacks during the mid-1940s while he was teaching at the University of Kansas City in Missouri. Maurois was interested in gay writers, including Oscar Wilde; in 1950, his biography of Marcel Proust was excerpted by *Der Kreis*, an early homophile magazine printed in Switzerland. In 1966, while Jo was working on his autobiography, he "grazed" in Maurois's *Olympia*, a biography of Victor Hugo, and other works for hints.[46]

Senator Thomas Pryor Gore paid a visit to The Blackjacks after he left the Senate in 1937. No doubt Mathews and Gore, whose boyhood blindness did not impede his political dream, talked politics, Indian affairs, and literature, swapped stories, and listened to birds and animals. As a lawyer, Gore worked on behalf of three tribes until his death in 1949. OU Professor Paul Bigelow Sears was a good friend and repeat visitor. In a letter to Sears, Mathews listed other visitors who had walked upon his Osage prairie: Ludwig, Gore, Brandt, Chief Fred Lookout, and "Shelby McGraw, the best cowwooly in the Osage." Mathews also knew Ben "Son" Johnson, stuntman, rodeo rider, and Western movie star whose family had a ranch not far from Mathews family land. In *Talking to the Moon*, Mathews describes a tree that seemed to grow on a "flat sandstone rock without visible soil support." Every time Mathews gazed at it, he felt "Paul Sears, famed botanist and friend, should be here to appreciate it with me." Sears published *Deserts on the March* in 1935 with OU Press. This landmark work was one of the earliest books to convey ecological principles to the general reading public and to address the causes and pressing dilemma of the Dust Bowl. Mathews brought several copies to Washington, D.C., on his trips on behalf of the Osage Tribal Council, and gave them to politicians such as Gore. In spring 1937,

Mathews invited Sears and Brandt out to The Blackjacks to see the prairie chickens dancing. Sears wrote Jo in thanks: "We all had a grand time and came back rested and refreshed. We needed all of this accumulated energy, however, to withstand the onslaught of our better halves when they found out that we had really gone nearly 200 miles to watch prairie chickens dance." He joked, "The next time I think we shall have to select some less innocent objective to maintain our prestige."[47]

During June 1938, Jo made a pleasurable visit to Pineville, Missouri, with longtime friend George Milburn, who was then writing radio plays, and his wife. Milburn was born in Coweta, Indian Territory, in 1906. After studying at Oklahoma A&M University and the University of Tulsa, drifting in New Orleans and elsewhere, and publishing joke books and other pulpy ephemera, in 1928 Milburn enrolled at OU where he met his wife, delicious Vivien Custard, "the prettiest coed I could find," he told *Esquire*. Millburn established himself in the 1930s as a regionalist storywriter and novelist who set most of his works in the small-town eastern Oklahoma he knew so well.[48]

At Halliburton's department store in Oklahoma City in April 1939, Mathews participated with Milburn in a remarkable authors' tea that highlighted the thriving regionalist and Indigenous literary scene. The featured literati in attendance were a rich sampling of Oklahoman writers of the time, especially Indians and authors of the Southwest. Among them was the mystery novelist and instructor at OU, Todd Downing (1902–74), a mixed-blood Choctaw from Atoka who studied in Mexico and wrote about the country in articles and novels. Downing was probably a gay man. John Milton Oskison (1874–1947), a mixed-blood Cherokee novelist (*Brothers Three*), biographer (*Tecumseh and His Times*), journalist, and editor was there, along with Stanley Vestal (W. S. Campbell) and Grant Foreman. Also from OU came poet and modern languages professor Kenneth Kaufman and Everett E. Dale, "Oklahoma's premier historian" and namesake of Dale Hall and Dale Hall Tower at OU, who wrote of the frontier and Indians. Being among this gathering of distinguished authors was an unforgettable experience. With two books under his belt, one of them with a New York publisher, Mathews could hold his own amidst such esteemed company.[49]

Chapter Six

THE HUNTER AND THE HUNTS

> The Indian is a poet. He is very religious, and he appreciates beauty. Being so very close to nature, he is filled with the rhythm and harmony of nature, yet he is cruel, as nature is cruel.
>
> —John Joseph Mathews

After Mathews returned to Pawhuska for good in late 1929, he began socializing with a younger married couple, Henry and Elizabeth Hunt. At the time of Mathews's return, Elizabeth was a graceful, attractive woman in her late twenties with a melodious voice bearing a slight Southern accent. Born Elizabeth Palmour on December 12, 1903, she had roots and family in Gainesville, northern Georgia. In grade school and college, her charm and kindness earned her the nickname "Sweetie." Elizabeth hosted parties at her girlhood home in Muskogee, "a place where even squares can have a ball," according to Merle Haggard.[1]

Elizabeth graduated from Central High in 1920. That fall 1920, Elizabeth and Henry each enrolled at the University of Oklahoma, narrowly missing Mathews, who had graduated in the spring. Jo was nine years older than Elizabeth; because of his enlistment, he was in his mid-twenties by the time he graduated. Elizabeth was a budding writer. With playwright Lynn Riggs, who was in her cohort, she wrote unsigned features for *The Whirlwind*, the new student humor magazine, and joined the Cubs Club (Student Press Club) and Entre Nous (French Club). Although it has been claimed that Riggs knew Mathews at OU, it is unclear when their paths would have crossed. After Mathews graduated the previous spring, he commenced a long hunting trip, then sailed for England, while Riggs was living in Los Angeles. Elizabeth became an active member of Delta Delta Delta sorority, and her sisterhood showed in her involvement with Tri-Delt alumni events into the 1960s.[2]

Elizabeth and Henry soon met and fell in love. Henry Clinton Hunt was born on December 29, 1901, in Tennessee, the native state of his parents, Mary Love Tharpe and John Clinton Hunt, namesake of Henry's future son. By 1910, Henry's family had moved to Shawnee, Oklahoma; they later moved to Oilton, a boomtown adjacent to the Cushing-Drumright oilfield near the border of Osage County. During 1918–20, Henry studied at OU's preparatory high school in Norman prior to matriculating at OU. Hunt was in Norman during 1919–20 when Mathews returned to his studies after the war, so it is possible the two men met. Henry studied arts and sciences and joined the Sigma Alpha Epsilon fraternity.[3]

Although Elizabeth intended to graduate with the class of 1924, she did not return to Norman for her junior year. Instead, on New Year's Day 1923, Henry and Elizabeth were married in the oil town of Haskell, Muskogee County, with only a "few intimate friends" present. The Muskogee paper said the wedding would "come as a surprise to the younger set." The couple dropped out of university and made their home in Henry's hometown, Oilton.[4]

Six months later, the society page of the *Muskogee Times-Democrat* announced that Elizabeth, "prior to her marriage, one of Muskogee's most popular young girls," was in town for a month visiting her mother, Irma Clover Palmour; perhaps there was trouble in the marriage. The couple's frequent moves as Henry pursued business opportunities may have created strain. The couple moved first from Oilton to Okemah, hometown of Woody Guthrie; then to Muskogee, where their first child, John Clinton Hunt, was born on July 24, 1925. They then relocated to Shidler, in western Osage County. Established in 1921, Shidler was a lawless oil boomtown, already declining by the close of the decade. "Osage County in the 1920s was the epitome of the Wild West," writes Osage scholar Carol Hunter. Boomtowns, which popped up "almost overnight, became infamous for narcotics and bootleg whiskey." Finally, the family settled in Pawhuska in 1928.[5]

Henry and Elizabeth expanded their family on July 9, 1930, with the arrival of Elizabeth Ann Hunt, known as Ann. In Pawhuska, Henry advanced his career, becoming local manager of a finance company, and by 1931, he was head of Pawhuska's Chevrolet agency. Some auto dealers in Pawhuska made exorbitant profits from oil-rich Osages. Having a car then was the "ultimate symbol of Progress on the Indian reservation."[6] Osages bought cars "in quantity before learning to drive, gladly hiring chauffeurs."[7] National press stories hyping the Osage oil boom reported that if a wealthy Osage crashed his car into a ditch, he just shrugged and bought a new one, at a "special" price. Within a year after taking over the Chevy dealership, Hunt suffered some sort of "nervous breakdown" and left his position. By 1932 he was a bulk distribution oil agent for Phillips Petroleum, so even during the Depression, the Hunts seemed to be financially stable. The business he operated was "one of

Pawhuska's prominent wholesale gasoline and oil enterprises," and Hunt co-owned one of the stations the bulk agency served. Granted, Osage headright payments dropped by more than one-half between 1930 and 1931. Yet despite their reduced income, Osages "continued to be exploited throughout the 1930s," Wilson writes, and some Osages spent their money extravagantly, having little understanding of savings, credit rackets, and other scams. Henry's worries seemed to be more personal than financial in nature.[8]

Amidst the suffocating summer heat of Oklahoma, to which the night offers scant respite, in the depths of the Depression, under occasional clouds of the Dust Bowl, Henry Clinton Hunt made it clear he did not want to live any longer. On the night of Thursday, August 11, 1932, shortly before 11:00 P.M., Henry sent Elizabeth downtown to obtain medicine for him. Where she could have acquired it at that time of night in a small town is unclear. After Elizabeth drove away, Hunt walked into the garage of their home on 201 E. Seventeenth Street and found oblivion with the aid of a twelve-gauge shotgun. He was thirty years old. Hearing the blast, neighbors rushed to investigate, finding a gruesome tableau. Ann Hunt, nearly two years old, was asleep inside the house. John, seven years old, was in California visiting his aunt and uncle. He returned with his grandmother for the funeral. Henry's suicide, ensuing events, even autobiographical fiction by John Clinton Hunt, all raise questions about what led up to that awful night. Never before has the story been told of what precipitated the suicide of a young businessman with a lovely wife and two small children.[9]

John Clinton Hunt, who lives in France, said his parents and Jo were "close friends," a trio who socialized together. Mathews was "very good friends of my father and my mother" in Pawhuska. "It was a threesome." He does not know exactly "what the relationship was other than their just being friends." However, he heard rumors: "some would say that there was a relationship between my mother and Jo which was more than just friendly, and it came as a very hurtful surprise to my father. . . . Many things tied them together. It has been said that what destroyed this unity was the fact that my mother and Jo fell in love. . . . It's certainly not something that would be out of the question. They were all three very special people. They found each other, and in their own ways, they loved each other." Ann Hunt told her son, attorney Peter Hunt Brown, that Jo and her mother were romantically linked prior to Henry's suicide. Whether or not Jo and Elizabeth carried on an affair while Henry was living, their mutual love may have become apparent to him.[10]

The relationship between the Hunts and Mathews is complex. It suggests Mathews unilaterally followed his desires, eschewing conventional morality and his Catholic upbringing. Mathews is consistently Darwinian and Nietzschean in his outlook, celebrating strength, health, intelligence, and beauty as their own natural ends, an ideology he reframed as traditional Osage philosophy. In *Beyond Good and Evil* Nietzsche argued such attributes were good and the absence of them bad. He critiques the concept of "evil" as a specious product of "slave morality" (such as Christianity) that self-servingly protects the weak, espousing mercy and pity, and limits strong individuals by preventing them from exerting their will to power and rising above the herd.[11]

Borrowing from novelist Thomas Wolfe, with whom he drank and socialized in Santa Fe in 1935, Mathews referred to "the herd" as "the man-swarm" and "the great sheep swarm of America," whose attitudes were conditioned by government and media.[12] Mathews was "very scornful, very impatient of weakness, especially in himself," his daughter said.[13] An elitist, he believed in his own considerable talents and strengths, and in the power of will. As he wrote his sister Marie from Oxford, "one may do anything one wants to do if he wants it badly enough and will work hard enough to achieve it."[14] Savoie Lottinville said Mathews "had a touch of contempt for the dull and unthinking" and was "highly selective" in his social life. Virginia averred her father could be cold to those he regarded as intellectual inferiors.[15] In 1961 he wondered, "Why couldn't the culture of the Patricians live on, instead of yield to the 'age of the common man?'" The common man would remain common, used as a tool by the church, by fascists, or by communists, he believed. Although the "common man" is useful in his greed, ambition, and vindictiveness, "to the powerful ones, his 'Age' is a chimera believed in only by himself."[16]

Mathews subscribed to social Darwinism and natural selection. In February and March 1951, he corresponded with evolutionary biologist Julian Huxley, who inspired the title of his unpublished novel, "Within Your Dream."[17] In his books and diaries, Mathews ideologically interweaves traditional Osage philosophy with the theories of Darwin and Nietzsche. For example, in the introduction to *The Osages*, Mathews said "there was no Right or Wrong concerning the European invasion; it was only a biological incident as far as the Neolithic man was concerned."[18] By moving to The Blackjacks, Mathews sought to live naturally, close to the earth, interacting and competing with other species.

Mathews's Osage analogue to *Beyond Good and Evil* manifested in a stunning poem, "After the Afghan," which he composed circa 1933 from the point of view of a traditional Osage. He described his tribespeople as historically strong, fierce, and ruthless in warfare. They reigned over a vast swath of the Lower Plains, repelling other tribes' incursions on their claimed hunting grounds:

> When I die I shall come before Wah'Kon-Tah—The Great Mystery.
> I shall tell him this thing:
> I shall tell him that I have been very cruel, for the sport to be found
> In Cruelty.
> I shall say that I have killed my brothers when I was not hungry—
> For sport I killed my brothers.
> I shall say that I have seen the straight white road cut the hills and
> The forests, but the road, the black ribbon,
> That wound through the hills and writhed like a great snake whose
> Head is hidden, I followed.
> I shall say that to know that which was around the sweeping bends,
> I followed this road.[19]

Mathews refers to the treatment of both human beings and their animal brothers in this poem, as he assumes the persona of a merciless, pitiless warrior. In light of Mathews's hybrid ideology, one may postulate he viewed the mutual attraction that arose between Elizabeth and him as natural, thus good, not to be resisted out of conventional morality. Henry, seemingly possessing an erratic personality and self-destructive tendencies, probably seemed to Mathews an ill-suited partner for Elizabeth and perhaps even an unsuitable father.

If Mathews did not know Elizabeth Hunt until after his permanent return to Pawhuska in October 1929, the "beautiful brunette of charming personality" quickly caught his eye, and he caught hers. A suave, tall WW I aviator and Oxford graduate, Mathews was on the cusp of literary success with his first book, released in November 1932. He intrigued Mrs. Hunt, who had aspired to write. Three decades later, Mathews reflected, "I was young in 1932, and lived a very interesting and romantic life, and I was handsome." He attracted many women, and Elizabeth was no exception. Henry probably worried he had been, or would be, cuckolded. The idea of the cuckoo and the cuckold was a topic Mathews pondered in his personal writings in both the 1920s and the 1970s.[20]

Pining away in a New York City hotel eleven weeks after Hunt's suicide, Mathews wrote a love letter to Elizabeth, addressing her by his pet name for her, "Dibbs." This letter alone would make speculation about a prior relationship unavoidable. Mathews poured out his affections to the widow: "I believe that if anyone should ask me what I desired to see more than anything else tonight (in the big middle of New York life) I should say I desire to see you—that, oddly enough, is the way I feel." Their love affair developed quickly after that. Since Elizabeth and Jo were not married until 1945, few realized their romance went all the way back to fall 1932, if not earlier, and this story has not been told before now.[21]

In the wake of her husband's tragic death, Elizabeth assumed management of the Phillips Petroleum bulk station in Pawhuska, and ran it for more than a decade. During a time when it was rare for women to manage businesses or work in the petroleum industry, this was a bold move. In 1933, Elizabeth, the "only woman dealer," hosted an all-day meeting of Phillips dealers at her home. By 1935, and through the early 1940s, Elizabeth lived at 1712 Grandview Avenue, in a white house with a Spanish-tiled roof, around the corner from the house she and Henry had lived in. Elizabeth evidently brought an aesthetic touch to her business. In 1935, Jo wrote from Washington, D.C., "I feel a great responsibility with people thinking you are crazy in your Station decorating activities—It causes something to come up in my throat." In 1943, Elizabeth faced a financial crisis, on the verge of losing her gas station unless she raised $1,000 quickly. "Her pitiful tragedy touched me," Mathews wrote. He decided to borrow $1,500 from D. J. Donahoe, a Ponca City businessman who was the father of his friend Edward. Two days later, however, Mathews wrote, "Dibbs is out of business now and I shall probably have the pickup out here after this week." By the end of the year, Elizabeth was working in a tent factory to support the war effort and to stay afloat economically. By 1944, with both of her children away at boarding schools, Elizabeth either moved again or acquired a second property at nearby 1706 Leahy Avenue.[22]

As Jo and Elizabeth continued their romance, he invited her to visit him at The Blackjacks. As a gift for Christmas 1934, Mathews wrote Elizabeth a poem. Although he occasionally wrote verse, few poems exist, so his offer to share the "peaceful marvel" of his home on the range with her is special and touching. In the poem, one of two he gave her titled "DIBBS," Mathews sought to persuade her to spend time with him at his Fortress of Solitude by evoking "wild winds that sing across this tranquil blue," and "cold days that ring like tempered steel." "Send out the ships of your fancy," he invited, and "dream dreams you have never dared."[23]

Over the decade of 1932–42, Mathews spent most of his time alone at The Blackjacks when he was not hosting guests there or visiting Pawhuska. In 1962, Mathews recalled that after the success of *Wah'Kon-Tah*, "neurotic women came out to the Blackjacks to see me, and two of them at different times came to stay with the romantic bachelor who lived in The Blackjacks with only his bird dogs. This was more sex than literature." Dibbs, alone or with the children, visited The Blackjacks many times before 1945, the year they married and she moved in. John Hunt spent days and weekends at The Blackjacks, hiking and fishing, and he and

Mathews developed a relationship that was "not unlike father and son." After Jo and Elizabeth married, they spent considerable time away from The Blackjacks. Prairie fires and ice storms sent them into town for days, weeks, or in the case of the worst fire, half a year. In *Talking to the Moon*, Mathews states, "one summer, during a severe drought, a great prairie fire swept up over the ridge," destroying all life except some blackjack trees and his home. He did not return to the ridge until the following spring. After 1945, for diversion he and Elizabeth regularly took extended summer road trips.[24]

In the 1930s especially, Mathews wrote several affectionate postcards and letters to Elizabeth when he was away. In January 1935, while serving on the Oklahoma Board of Education, Jo wrote from Shreveport, Louisiana: "Dibbs, darling, I am so anxious to get back to you that I work harder than anyone, in order to occupy my mind. You are with me constantly. I love you!" Later he wrote, "As I drove along last night I thought constantly of you," concluding, "I am no more a solitary person." In March, while in Washington, D.C., on tribal council business, he wrote emphatically: "You are so much a part of everything I experience, and there is an inevitableness about the whole thing. We must be together from now on—there is no other way."[25]

Mathews, however, remained legally married to Ginger for thirteen years after he left her and their two children. They were finally divorced in October 1941, and Mathews married Elizabeth Hunt in April 1945. Jo and Elizabeth's simple wedding took place at Kay County Courthouse in Newkirk, near the Kansas border. Neither romantic nor traditional, it involved no family members. On Thursday, April 5, 1945, Mathews wrote in his diary: "To Ponca. Picked up Edward [Donahoe], then to Newkirk. There we picked up Neil Sullivan at the Court House, and Edward and Neil acted as witnesses as Dibbs and I were married. Back to Ponca City and to Wetumps for a scotch and soda, then to Dee and Helen Donahoe's for more scotch and sodas. Thence to Edward's aunt, then to dinner and we spent the evening at Wetumps. We let Edward off at his house, then to the Jens-Marie [Hotel] for the night in a rather stuffy room." Wetumps Road House, a longstanding watering hole, sat just outside the Ponca City limits. Built in 1922, the Jens-Marie Hotel in its first decade was the site of many big oil deals involving Jo's friends E. W. Marland and Frank Phillips.[26]

Following the marriage, Elizabeth Mathews moved into Jo's cozy home. Although it had been nearly thirteen years since Henry Hunt's death, some Pawhuskans considered Elizabeth and Jo's marriage "a scandal," according to Bobbie Tolson. Others wondered how graceful Elizabeth was persuaded to live a rugged existence out at The Blackjacks, with no toilet and, until the 1960s, no telephone. In the

1970s, Elizabeth gave an answer to a friend. She and Jo hosted two couples at The Blackjacks for a wild game dinner of game Jo had hunted: quail, rabbit, even his beloved prairie chicken. They were Frederick F. Drummond, third-generation Osage County rancher, his wife Janet ("Pert"), rancher M. Lee Holcombe, and civic leader Janet Theis Holcombe, who had been in the same sorority as "Sweetie." It was a pleasant evening marked by "flowing conversation." As was typical, guests did not eat until late—midnight—and Jo did most of the cooking. Fred asked Elizabeth privately what made her decide to live with Jo in primitive fashion. She replied, "I never knew when he would be gone, or what was going to happen."[27]

Elizabeth was a tireless helper and collaborator. She routinely typed and edited Jo's longhand manuscripts, reading back what he had written for hours on end and suggesting improvements. Elizabeth provided great assistance with the research and writing process for the last two books Jo published in his lifetime, and with his autobiography. Judy Taylor, who worked at the Osage County Historical Museum as a young woman and became its curator, said, "I know that Elizabeth helped him with his books. She was his right arm, and his left arm." In 1961, a grinning Mathews told a reporter, "This is a real husband and wife team. We're inseparable. I don't know what we would do without each other." They hunted, fished, and worked together, and "Elizabeth did such a fine job typing the manuscript that the first draft was accepted." Osage artist Romain Shackelford once told Jo he wanted to write a book, but joked he could not write his own name. "Neither can I—Elizabeth does the correcting," Jo quipped. He thought her "very artistic." Dibbs told a reporter, "I just do what has to be done." The following year, in gratitude Jo bought her a ring with seventeen diamonds, one for each year of their marriage.[28]

Elizabeth was an incisive critic of her husband's prose. In a 1951 letter to his friend, Texan author and folklorist J. Frank Dobie, Mathews thanked him for sending a card and his essay, "Books and Christmas." Reporting he and Dibbs enjoyed it "to the hilt," Jo shared her response: "A few more of us need that mellow appreciation of living." Dobie makes readers "feel warm on the inside, and appreciate the fact that life holds so many beautiful things. I wish you could attain that mellowness. He seems to have confidence in words to express what he feels, and this gives the reader confidence. You seem to make your reader restless by your lack of confidence in words to express what you feel." This evaluation reveals Elizabeth's honesty, acuity, and appreciation of style. In her editorial role, she tempered some of Mathews's equivocation and pretension. Meanwhile, Elizabeth maintained her own literary ambition; in 1946 Mathews critiqued her short stories and mailed one, along with two stories by her daughter, Ann, and one of his own, to his agent in hopes of publication.[29]

Mathews is often credited with being largely responsible for the foundation of the Osage Tribal Museum; lesser known is the fact that in the late 1960s and early 1970s, Elizabeth and Jo helped develop the Osage County Historical Museum (OCHM) and played major roles there. The museum opened in its current location at the old train depot on Lynn Avenue in 1968; that year, Mathews did a signing party for the reissue of *Wah'Kon-Tah*. The Mathewses worked closely with curator Betty Smith. Assistant Judy Taylor recalled Elizabeth and Jo coming to the OCHM every day it was open: "That was his pleasure." Throughout this period, they regularly ordered and displayed volumes for the museum's "Book Corner," Dibbs's domain; Jo signed his books and managed the bookkeeping. Mathews developed an accounting system the museum used for decades. During this period, under the byline "Mrs. John Joseph Mathews," Elizabeth wrote a *Book Corner* column for the Pawhuska newspaper, in which she reviewed books on the history of the West and Indians for sale at the museum. Diaries reveal Jo ghostwrote several of these for her.[30]

Dibbs was unusually devoted to Jo. Judy Taylor said Elizabeth was "so sweet" and made sure Jo got "whatever he wanted. She was sure good to him." Aging gracefully, Elizabeth spoke softly and slowly. Comically, she once became jealous of one of her husband's girlfriends from the distant past. Judy attended a conference at OU and struck up a conversation with an older lady, who asked her, on learning she was from Pawhuska, "Do you know Johnny Mathews?" Surprised, Judy asked her if she meant John Joseph. The woman said Mathews was her "first love" back in college. When Judy next saw Jo and Elizabeth at the museum, she told them this story. Dibbs "blew a fuse," Judy said, upset by Jo's flame of fifty years ago![31]

In the mid-1930s and 1940s, Mathews got to know Elizabeth's children, John and Ann Hunt. Although Mathews became a mentor and role model to John, he never made a strong connection with Ann. Still, according to Ann's son, Peter Brown, Mathews "was her father, the only father that she ever knew"; unlike John, she did not remember Henry Hunt. Ann lived in Pawhuska through 1944 and during some summers thereafter. She socialized with a small group of friends. One of them, Melvin Tolson, described her as attractive, studious, and private; attorney William "Bill" H. Mattingly recalled her as intelligent and reserved. In August 1944, Ann was sent to Mary A. Burnham School for Girls in sylvan Greenfield, Massachusetts. Jo, who escorted Ann there, enthused over the school and Ann's roommate. During vacations, Ann stayed with her mother and Jo at The Blackjacks, sleeping on a cot. During summer 1946, Ann sometimes stayed with a friend in town. In spring 1948, Elizabeth and Jo made a month-long tour of thirteen states, attending Ann's

Elizabeth Mathews, spring 1972. *Courtesy of the Mathews family.*

graduation from Burnham and John's from Harvard. Ann then rode with her mother and Jo back to Oklahoma, and stayed with them through early September 1948. Mathews put Ann to work typing up the final draft of his Marland biography. Mathews also wrote several short stories in this period, and Ann was inspired by his productivity. "Three of us in one room is not a condition which makes work easy," Mathews noted, "but that is the best we can do apparently." Given that The Blackjacks was designed for one person, it was a bit cramped. Jo and Elizabeth were steady drinkers by then, and the home lacked privacy and indoor plumbing.[32]

In 1948, Ann won a regional scholarship to Radcliffe College, a women's college coordinate to then all-male Harvard. Mathews did not give Ann financial assistance during her college years. During a 1951 vacation in Hawaii, visiting her aunt, Ann met and fell in love with Anthony Preble Brown of Burlingame, California. Son of Emily and Hillyard Brown, a vice president of Standard Oil of California, Tony was a World War II naval veteran who went to Harvard and earned a law degree from Stanford. After Ann graduated from Radcliffe, Ann and Tony were wed in April 1953, in a quiet home ceremony with no attendants. The lack of bridesmaids suggests that Ann left her past behind. Melvin Tolson said it was as though "she had walked off of the face of the earth." Bill Mattingly reckoned Ann "outgrew most of us intellectually and otherwise." Ann very rarely returned to Pawhuska following her marriage. After a honeymoon at Lake Tahoe, where the Brown family had a vacation home, Ann and Tony settled in San Francisco, where he practiced law. The Browns had four children: Diane (b. 1954), Peter Hunt (b. 1955), Henry Palmour (b. 1959), and Samuel Clinton (b. 1960). Most of their names pay homage to Henry Hunt and his family members or to the Palmour family.[33]

Ann's relationship with Mathews was complicated by the emotions stirred up on reading her brother's first novel, published in the spring of 1956. *Generations of Men* was inspired by John Hunt's upbringing in Pawhuska and his return visits in the 1940s. It won the 1956 Spur Award for Best Novel of the West and was nominated for a National Book Award. He dedicated it to Elizabeth, "whose love and courage created an unforgettable example," and to the memory of his namesake grandfather, "J. C. Hunt, a fox-hunting man." Hunt sent Mathews a copy. "The jacket is attractive, and the blackjack thereon is quite well done," Jo commented, not mentioning that its design was remarkably similar to that of *Talking to the Moon*, as was its literary style at times. *Generations of Men* narrates the return of Jeff Beecher, like Hunt a Harvard graduate, to his Oklahoman hometown. He searches for the motivation for his father's suicide, which, like Henry Hunt's, occurred in the family garage. Jeff's mother is recently deceased, and in loco parentis, Jeff yearns for guidance, finding it in a dignified country bachelor Hardin Buck, a mixed-blood Chetopa Indian (Hunt's longtime stand-in for Osage), whom Jeff admires and adopts as a father figure. After learning he has a terminal illness, Buck too commits suicide, devastating Jeff, who loses a second "father" to suicide. Hardin wills his sandstone home to Jeff, to whom he is deeply but mysteriously linked.

Buck is modeled on Mathews in several ways: the boyhood spent roaming the range with horse and dog, the unflagging love of hunting and nature, the years of study in England, the sandstone house he built on the blackjack prairie, his development of a tribal museum, his hiring of a Chicago artist to paint portraits of full-blood elders, and more. Henry's sister, Robbie Hunt Hon wrote Elizabeth, congratulating her on John's novel and its reception in Tulsa. "The characters are wonderful—especially Hardin Buck, whom we of course recognized as Jo." Of Samuel, the character based on her father, she said although he is somewhat altered, "still he *is* Pap and I loved him and read about him with a mixture of laughter and tears."[34]

Jo and Elizabeth visited Ann and Tony in California in the summer of 1956, a few months after the publication of *Generations of Men*. The visit was more than a little awkward. Early on, Ann fled the house unexpectedly, and throughout the visit was distraught and critical of her mother. "Soon after we arrived, Ann left for Palo Alto, and we knew not why until tonight," Mathews wrote. After dinner, Jo and Ann sat down together and discussed her visits to a psychiatrist, prompted by her troubled state of mind. Ann did not know the source of her problem, and felt "dammed up like a stream." Soon it emerged that John's novel had come as a shock. As the baby sister, not yet two years old when her father killed himself, Ann was sheltered from much of the event. The novel raised questions she was exploring with her psychiatrist. "I asked her if she thought she might have been happier if she had been allowed to remain—as I put it—benighted. She said that she might have been." Ann had an appointment with her therapist while her mother and Jo were visiting, but she did not want to tell Elizabeth because it would cause needless worry. Mathews viewed this charitably, but thought Ann was becoming "a depressive" who showed resentment toward Elizabeth.

> Certainly she is a strange person. She seems to have a special attitude toward Dibbs, and at times I have wondered if she does not actually hate her. Dibbs is self-conscious and clumsy in her presence and can never say the right thing at the right time, and everything she says seems to annoy Ann. In Ann's company, Dibbs is really shown up as a rather speciously interested person as to Ann's affairs. Ann has for years . . . brought out the characteristics in her mother which are least attractive. Her mincing hypocrisy is sharply brought out by Ann's censorious silence, which we always called the "silent treatment."[35]

Peter said Ann was bitter about her father's suicide and largely blamed Elizabeth for what happened. A great deal remained unspoken between Ann and Jo. "But tonight there was no conclusion," Mathews writes. "Ann seemed to want to talk and yet never threw any light on her difficulties." He blamed a rich meal and champagne for his complacency; he seemed unwilling to ask questions that might help to illuminate her issues.[36]

In California, Ann and Jo analyzed Hardin Buck. Mathews writes, "We talked of John's book, and she seems to have an urge to draw some parallelism between her father's suicide and John making his leading character commit suicide. She seemed to think that John, in building up Hardin Buck into a very noble character, both sane and courageous, then having him commit suicide, in some way expressed John's desire to justify his father's self-destruction." Mathews never mentioned in his diary that Buck was modeled on him. Considering all the emotions latent in the dynamic between the Hunt children and Mathews, it is interesting that John Hunt chose to have the Mathews proxy kill himself. Reviewer Edith Copeland asked Mathews about the native ceremony in Buck's burial scene. He said that aside from some poetic modifications, the scene was based upon traditional Osage practice. It foreshadowed Mathews's own ceremony twenty-three years later.[37]

During the 1950s Mathews tended to be quite critical in his diary. His criticism extended to the Brown family, whom he found arrogant and materialistic; Hillyard Brown's splendid home, the tropical trees, and the swimming pool were pleasant, but Mathews regarded the family as philistines. "All but Emily [Tony's mother], who is only a Brown by marriage, the Browns have a species of smugness that seems to exclude practically everything from importance except golf, bridge, baseball, the Forty-Niner professional football team, the Republican Party, and capitalism." Ann's husband sometimes annoyed him too: "Tony needs the point of my rapier occasionally, but out of respect for Ann's difficulties, I kept it sheathed. A meat ax might be the proper weapon anyway. He is rather a bearish extrovert, at once likeable and exasperating in his extrovert smugness." Jo found it ironic that Ann, who "resented being advised in any matter," was now living with a know-it-all. "Her present need of psychiatric treatment, he obviously believes is due to negligence or persecution by Dibbs during Ann's childhood, while he blithely keeps her nerves raw by his criticism and invasions."[38]

What Mathews recorded regarding Ann's anxiety and negative feelings toward her mother is corroborated by her sons, and even paralleled in John Hunt's literary output. Ann told her son Peter Brown that Elizabeth and Jo were together as a couple immediately following Henry Hunt's death. In 2005 John Hunt published "Family Business" in *News from the Republic of Letters*. In this extract from the never-published novel "If You Leave Me . . . Take Me with You" (2011), the narrator and his sister, Katherine, sit in a motel room in Grey Horse, Hunt's longtime stand-in for Pawhuska, talking and drinking liquor. Brought together only by their mother's funeral, they stay at their usual motel in what they call the "Family Room," where their mother and stepfather, Graham Tucker, had been reduced to living due to poor health, forced to move into town from their small home on the prairie called the Crosstimbers—all paralleling real life. Katherine, exasperated by her brother's inquiries into the past, snaps, "the minute poor old Wesley was in his grave, Susanna ran straight to Tucker's arms. And then covered the whole thing up, and never told us one damned thing." She complains they were then sent to distant boarding schools as soon as possible. Ann told Peter she thought Mathews was never enthusiastic about having stepchildren, and he concluded Mathews was "really not interested in being a father." Given that Mathews had abandoned his own two children, "maybe it was not particularly ethical, kind or compassionate for him to take up with Elizabeth, knowing she had two kids," Peter remarked.[39]

In "If You Leave Me . . . Take Me with You" Katherine drops a bombshell on her brother. She claims Graham Tucker, a character resembling Mathews in many ways, was her real father! Her brother roundly rejects this. Peter Brown thought it was possible his mother believed she was Jo's biological daughter, but he had no idea if this was true. Granted, the narrative is fiction, even though it parallels reality in many ways. Hypothetically, if Mathews were Ann's biological father, Jo and Elizabeth would have had to become intimate fairly soon after his return home in October 1929. That decade, Mathews had fantasized about having his child raised by another: "If one, like the Coo coo, could lay eggs in someone else's nest and choose a new mate each year!" Jo may even have met Elizabeth before fall 1929, either during his 1928–29 extended holiday visit before he returned to California and left his wife permanently, or possibly back in spring 1920 when he chauffeured prospective sorority pledges.[40]

Regardless of whatever tensions may have been simmering, during at least three summers in the early 1960s, Jo and Elizabeth drove their AMC Rambler through Kansas, Colorado, Wyoming, Utah, and Nevada to visit the Browns at Lake Tahoe, California, where they enjoyed views of mountains, trees, and especially birds such as mountain quail. Mathews took many photographs and films. In 1962, Mathews lovingly created a book for little Henry Palmour Brown, with pen-and-ink drawings of his beloved birds and animals of The Blackjacks. In 1963 Jo and Elizabeth visited with Ann, Tony, and the children at Tahoe, and Jo read them his story "The White Sack." His treatment of Ann and Tony in his diaries became softer, and he expressed appreciation for their hospitality. From the mid-1960s on, however, Ann and her children rarely saw "Pop Jo" or Elizabeth, and the Browns are seldom mentioned in Mathews's diaries or letters. One exception was in 1975, when Ann, Henry, and Sam Brown visited their grandmother and Pop Jo in Pawhuska. By then Jo was an octogenarian and drinking heavily, but Henry and Sam were invited to attend the colorful, entrancing June I'n-lon-schka dances, and they were "blown away" by the experience. After they returned home, they persuaded their mother to send away for fry bread ingredients and make it for them.[41]

Ann and Tony Brown separated in 1964 and divorced in 1965. Both wanted custody of the children, and the divorce was contentious and painful. Though Tony was a lawyer, Ann won custody. She never remarried, and in fact, according to Peter and Henry Brown, after the divorce, their mother never had a close relationship with anyone. Needing to develop a career to support herself and her four children, she worked first as a bank teller, but that did not meet the family's needs. Because she could not find adequate employment with her BA from Radcliffe College, Ann attended nursing school at night for two years. She then pursued a nursing career, mostly at Kaiser Permanente Hospital in San Francisco, and lived in Palo Alto.[42]

Peter said neither of his parents was content. Tony Brown, who passed away in 2012, was dissatisfied despite being rich and successful, although he enjoyed having his children at his home every other weekend. Ann was never truly satisfied. She did not like Pawhuska and was not close to her family. Ann tried to be a good mother, but happiness eluded her. Peter's younger brother Sam called her "a tortured soul." She went through much therapy, which did not seem to help. Like John F. Kennedy, she suffered from Addison's disease, an adrenal gland disorder that can cause irritability and depression among its many symptoms. Peter said his mother attempted suicide in the mid-1980s, when she was in her mid-fifties. Elizabeth Ann Hunt Brown died on Christmas Day 1998. Although Peter came from a line of unhappy people—his grandfather Henry Hunt and both his parents—he said, "I've been happy, at least," and Sam echoed his sentiment. Despite the dysfunction in his family, he said, "I'm a very happy person" with a "very fortunate life."[43]

John Hunt recalls his stepfather as a highly educated man of "great distinction" and sophistication, whom he admired and in some ways emulated. Mathews became a mentor, inspiration, and father figure to Hunt and, eventually, an affectionate grandfather to Hunt's two children, Diana Palmour Hunt and Mead Kinghorn Hunt. "I needed him in so many ways that I could not define," Hunt said. "For I had lost my father, and quite obviously Jo was there to fill the gap. Though as far as I can remember, this was never discussed in my presence, no matter how important it was to all concerned." Mathews and his stepson forged a meaningful relationship, and Jo strongly influenced John's intellectual outlook and literary ambition. "As for my desire to become a writer, his influence was clearly there," Hunt said. "Though in fact we never talked about it . . . that would not be his way." Influence came through example. John followed in Jo's footsteps, becoming a literary novelist who drew from biography, engaging Osage County land and history. Years after first leaving his hometown, Hunt's feelings about his stepfather were complicated by stories he heard that made him wonder about the dynamic between Mathews, his mother, and his father prior to Henry's suicide.[44]

Hunt wrote:

> I did not think of John Joseph as my father. My memory of my father, Henry Hunt, stayed with me vividly and painfully through the years. But at the same time, Jo was a welcome substitute not only for the

> Henry who was gone, but in his own right. I loved them both, though in different ways. But Henry was my father, and Jo was my friend. Stepfather or whatever. Remember that he was a powerful, personal presence on his own. But he did not encourage the idea of his playing the role of substitute father. This was a subtle and somewhat delicate matter, important to be lived even if not defined. But, yes . . . there was definitely an element of father and son, even though we never tried to define it in specific detail.[45]

John enjoyed much of his boyhood, including fishing and hikes with Mathews. Bill Mattingly described him as highly intelligent and a nice guy to boot. Yet John grew up in Pawhuska during tumultuous times. The 1920s and 1930s were marked by rampant exploitation of Osages by many white residents. Amidst this atmosphere of corruption and economic depression, John's father took his life. Pawhuska looked normal on the surface, but concealed a dark heart. In his second novel, *The Grey Horse Legacy* (1968), Hunt wrote, "They thought it was like any other town—neat lawns and sprinklers and elm trees full of locusts in the summer, a country club and a dozen or more churches, square dancing, pie suppers . . . all that, but something more . . . you can smell it in the air, and it doesn't smell like oil. It smells like blood . . . the whole place smells like a rendering factory." In 1940, at age fifteen, John was enrolled at Lawrenceville School, a British-style boys' preparatory school in New Jersey, considered a feeder school to Princeton University. In his cohort was playwright Edward Albee.[46]

Hunt's life followed the pattern of his stepfather's in several ways. Just as Jo was a fraternity brother at the University of Oklahoma, so was John, briefly, in the 1940s. They both left studies at OU to join the military during a world war, becoming a second lieutenant; neither was shipped overseas or sent into combat. In June 1943, Hunt visited his mother and Jo on his way to Marine Corps Reserves training in Louisiana. They must have been worried for him, because on June 3, 1943, Jo lost his nephew, Henry Ben, son of his eldest sister Josephine. After graduating from Notre Dame, Henry Ben became an ensign in the U.S. Naval Corps, assigned to be a fighter pilot. During training, he died in an accident near Malabar Field, Florida. This painful loss and Jo's memory of his nephew as a boy inform his unpublished short story, "No Time." Hunt was more fortunate; after training as a marine, Hunt remained stateside until he was discharged in 1946. He entered Harvard that year, where he edited the *Student Progressive*, published by the Harvard Liberal Union. In September he hitchhiked from Cambridge to Pawhuska to visit his mother and Jo. John graduated in 1948.[47]

In October 1948 John married Barbara Helen Mead, a Radcliffe College student from Glens Falls, New York, at her parents' home. They moved to Paris and took classes at the Sorbonne. John wrote fiction, enchanted by the Hemingway ideal of the American émigré in Paris. In July 1949 their daughter Diana Palmour Hunt was born. Returning to the States in 1950, John studied at the Iowa Writers Workshop at the University of Iowa and taught in the Classics Department. There he penned a libretto for *Ethan Frome*, the first opera by his Harvard friend Douglas Allanbrook, adapted from Wharton's novel. At Iowa Hunt befriended author and editor Robie Macauley, with whom Hunt later worked in Paris. In 1951, Hunt, with his friends Keith Botsford and Seymour Lawrence, tried to meet revered Welsh poet Dylan Thomas, who was visiting Iowa City. Lawrence later became an editor at Atlantic Monthly Press, and Hunt's first novel was published during Lawrence's tenure there. After Lawrence became vice president of Knopf, that press published Hunt's second novel, *The Grey Horse Legacy*. While at Knopf, however, Lawrence rejected "Boy, Horse and Dog," the first volume of Mathews's autobiography.[48]

Hunt was offered a teaching position at Thomas Jefferson School in St. Louis, a small experimental academy for boys. He taught Greek, French, History, and English, and coached track and basketball. "He was brought up on the principle that man ought to give equal value to mind and body," Jo wrote Frank Dobie. Mathews and Hunt already had connections to the school, since the headmaster, Robin McCoy, was from Pawhuska. McCoy had mentored John and tutored him in ancient Greek while he was at Lawrenceville, though McCoy did not teach there.

In March 1952, John and Barbara's son, Mead Kinghorn Hunt, was born; in April, Jo and Elizabeth visited the Hunts at their home in Sappington, outside St. Louis. Mathews was an affectionate grandfather to Diana and Mead. As he did for Ann and Tony's children and for his granddaughters, he wrote a series of letters and cards illustrated with pen-and-ink drawings of animals to remind them of their visits. In 1954, John, Barbara, and Diana visited Elizabeth and Jo at The Blackjacks. "Little Diana came to me and presented a fifth of White Horse Scotch," Mathews wrote. She stayed with her grandparents for about a week while her parents traveled to Texas. That year, Mathews told Dobie that John and Barbara were "interesting young people" who wished to meet Dobie while visiting Austin. In August 1958, Jo and Elizabeth drove all the way to Ontario, then spent twelve days with the Hunt family at their current residence in Lake George, New York. Jo enjoyed natural beauty and inventing stories to tell the "insatiable listeners" Diana and Mead. In 1963, Mathews arranged for a bookseller to send Dobie a copy of *The Voice of the Coyote* so that he could inscribe it to eleven-year-old Mead Hunt, a big fan.[49]

Through Harvard contacts, in 1955 Hunt was recruited by Central Intelligence Agency officer Cord Meyer to become a case officer for the CIA. Around this time, his first novel was accepted for publication. Hunt was assigned to work undercover in Europe with the Congress for Cultural Freedom (CCF), which was waging a cultural cold war in Europe, organizing concerts, festivals, and readings; publishing books; and funding journals promoting ideology of the Non-Communist Left (NCL). Over seventeen years, the CIA funneled tens of millions of dollars into the CCF and similar projects. Funding for the CCF was largely controlled by Meyer, who had been named head of the CIA's International Organizations Division in 1954. Frances Stonor Saunders writes that Meyer oversaw the agency's "greatest single concentration of covert political and propaganda activities." A World War II veteran, Meyer was an elitist Ivy Leaguer, and the early CIA was surprisingly literary and modernist. Saunders reports Meyer followed the footsteps of James Jesus Angleton, "the CIA's legendary chief of counter-intelligence." Angleton, who introduced poet Ezra Pound to Yale and founded a magazine of verse, was the nexus of "the P source"—*P* for "Professor"—referring to the agency's numerous Ivy League links.[50]

After CCF Director Michael Josselson suffered his first heart attack in 1956, Meyer sent Hunt to Paris to relieve him of some responsibility. Hunt moved to Washington, D.C., for a time, probably for training, before returning to Paris. In early 1956, Jo and Elizabeth visited John, Barbara, Mead, and Diana in Washington, D.C. Mathews knew the Hunts were moving to Paris for John's government work, but how much he knew of the details is unknown. Hunt worked for the CCF in Paris as an undercover CIA officer for more than a decade. He became what he described as operations officer to Josselson's executive officer, and worked closely with Robie Macauley. In 1960 Hunt began running the Paris office and dealing with the CIA directly. The small-town boy found himself in control of great power and resources. Without the influence and guidance of Mathews, arguably Hunt would not have had the education, literary skills, or global viewpoint to assume such a position.[51]

In a way, it is revealing of Mathews that his protégée Hunt, whom he began to think of as a son, was recruited by the CIA to battle communism with cultural warfare. Mathews was vociferously anticommunist, so he would have praised his stepson's work in Paris. His unpublished story "The Liberal View" satirizes American Marxists and Soviet sympathizers. In 1962, Mathews labeled proletarian literature of the 1930s (such as *The Grapes of Wrath*) "*very* clever communist propaganda," believing it championed underdogs to vindictively attack capitalism. Mathews condemned the self-righteous liberalism he perceived at Harvard when he attended John's graduation. Students sneered at "Fascism-colored America" and "Big Business," laughing "smugly at the country which gives them a greater freedom than has ever been attained by man before, because they are self-conscious liberals who believe in a Utopia suggested by cloistered idealists of the Harvard staff, or through reading myopic fanatics. The atmosphere is restricted for a few. 'A Negro,' says John Hunt with vindictive pride, 'will lead the line to the BA section.'" Asked about his politics in 1972, Mathews replied, "Let's say I'm not a communist." Indeed Mathews took a hard line against communism during the Cold War and thought the United States ought to flex its military muscle more often. This squares with his Osage identity, since his clan was of the Hunka (Earth) people, a war people.[52]

The political winds changed as Lyndon Baines Johnson became president and ramped up the Vietnam War, opposed by the NCL. By 1967, exposés in leftist, then mainstream publications revealed the CCF was basically a front for the CIA. Hunt and Josselson were compelled to resign their positions. In a secret ceremony on a houseboat on the Seine, Hunt was awarded a "CIA medal for services rendered," a dismissal of sorts. Hunt then became executive vice president of the Salk Institute for Biological Studies in La Jolla, California. Hunt's employment there seems odd, since his degrees were in English and creative writing, so he was probably placed by the CIA. Because of the CCF scandal, "some of the younger scientists were uncomfortable" about hiring him, Suzanne Bourgeois writes.[53] Hunt left in 1970 and went on to hold senior management positions at the Aspen Institute, the University of Pennsylvania, Le Centre Royaumont pour une Science de l'Homme, and the Institute for Advanced Study in Princeton, New Jersey.[54]

The Grey Horse Legacy, Hunt's second novel, appeared in 1968 while he was at the Salk Institute. It is set in the 1920s in a town just like Pawhuska and in 1960s Paris. It portrays a father and son, Andrews and Amory Thayer, explores the ethical dilemmas of each, and deals with the Osage Reign of Terror murders. Like his first novel, *The Grey Horse Legacy* draws from Hunt's biography and Osage County history. The year before, Jo had assisted in suggesting possible chapter and book titles. At the request of the *Lincoln Star*, Mathews wrote a "very conscientious review" of the book. It was neutral, mostly summary, but Mathews did analyze and critique one metaphor. Hunt wrote, "we are all of us just wild geese in winter," driven by incomprehensible forces to unknown destinations, and he titled part III "Wild Geese in Winter." Mathews argued this line encapsulated how the last two generations, glib and intellectual, had become detached and alienated from the life-giving earth. Geese know exactly where they are going, he said, only becoming confused by human-caused light pollution. "It seems a shame that John Hunt didn't add the above to his 'Wild Geese in Winter.' His simile would not only have inspired more confidence in his bewildered, searching creation, [protagonist] Amory Thayer and his peers, but would have been rather more realistic and dramatically poignant." Amory "of course" did not find what he sought, since despair is "possibly the 'happy ending' of the 1960s," he remarked. Still, Mathews made the plot sound compelling. He respected and valued Hunt. In 1967 he wrote, "John never fails to send gifts which I appreciate deeply—from Merton College cufflinks to sweaters and books from Paris."[55]

In the summer of 1965, Hunt visited his mother and Jo at The Blackjacks with Mead and Diana. Tape-recorded by Mathews, the family had fun failing to sing "Home on the Range" in tune, and Mathews declared, "this is a very pleasant visit." During the 1960s, John Hunt separated from Barbara, and by 1968, he had divorced her and married a Frenchwoman, Chantal Pepin de Bonnerive Loiseau, who worked for the CCF in Paris. Oddly, again Hunt followed his stepfather's pattern, leaving his first wife, a son, and a daughter, and marrying a widow with two children. In 1969, Mead Hunt, seventeen, and Diana Hunt, twenty, along with their friends George Landman, who sported a "startling growth of kinky hair," and Sandie Slater, drove out from California in a Volkswagen camper van to visit Elizabeth and Jo. Mathews, allergic to hippies, radicals, and mystics, wrote, "I had a good chance to study rather speciously, the objectiveless, sophomoric wisdom of earth-detached," idealistic "world-changers, through the persons of Mead and George."[56]

In 1981, collaborating with Jimmy Carter's speechwriter Martin Kaplan, John Hunt wrote *Knights Errant*, a play about Richard Nixon and Alger Hiss. It premiered at the INTAR in New York in 1982 and was staged at the Kennedy Center. The play dramatizes the reflective, private side of Nixon. Hunt moved to Cambridge, Massachusetts by 1985, becoming founding chairman and CEO of BioTechnica International until his retirement in 1990. He and Chantal then returned to Paris. By 1997, they were living in Provence in a "rehabbed three-floor apartment nestled back among medieval valleys and streets of the town of Uzés," Carter Revard wrote. By 2005, John and Chantal had moved to Lyons, her birthplace, where they remained.[57]

Jo's devoted partner, John and Ann's mother, Elizabeth Palmour Hunt Mathews, passed away on November 7, 1982. Her intelligence, her talent, and the assistance she provided Mathews have too often been overlooked. This is reflected in the fact that although I have researched her life, read her obituary, and laid flowers on her gravestone, I do not know her middle name, though I believe it to be Ann. Dibbs

Gravestones of Elizabeth Hunt Mathews and Henry Hunt, Muskogee, 2014.
Photo by the author.

lived with Jo for a third of a century, loving, helping, and being there for him. It was not always easy living in that isolated, small home on the range. She chose not to be buried beside Mathews out at The Blackjacks, as many might have expected. Instead, she was laid to rest next to her first husband, Henry, who predeceased her by fifty years, and her parents, in placid Greenhill Cemetery in Muskogee, the town where she grew up and where her son, John, was born.[58]

Chapter Seven

MEXICO

> I wanted to . . . find perfect solitude and look into the perfect emptiness of my mind and be completely neutral from any and all ideas. . . . To be in . . . some hut in Mexico . . . and rest and be kind, and do nothing else, practice what the Chinese call "do-nothing."
>
> —Jack Kerouac, *The Dharma Bums*

A few months into Mathews's second term on the Osage Tribal Council, he decided he was fed up; his duties were wearing on him and he yearned for respite. Although the responsibilities of his role as a tribal councilman may have disturbed his comfort and led to increased visitors at The Blackjacks, nothing compelled him to run for re-election to the fifteenth council in June 1938. In September, Mathews told Walter Campbell that he would be visiting Norman to discuss with him applying to the Guggenheims for a scholarship. He had decided he "would like very much to get away from Osages for a year," and applied for a grant in order to write a book. But one can hardly escape the Osages when one is Osage.[1]

Mathews did not write the proposed book, which he said he was nearly ready to write—that is, unless one considers a book published more than two decades later. One can see how his manuscript proposal, aiming to explore the clash between the beliefs and practices of Indigenous peoples of North America and of Euro-American invaders and settlers, related to *Wah'Kon-Tah*, and especially his 1961 tribal history *The Osages: Children of the Middle Waters*, which scarcely mentions Mexico. The choice of location seemed arbitrary, mostly a means of distancing himself from personal and political entanglements. Leaving for nearly a year in the midst of his four-year term on the Osage Tribal Council may have been slightly irresponsible, but he was transparent with the Guggenheim board, noting in his application that in order to write the proposed book, "I must get away from the Osage in order to concentrate my efforts on this rather difficult project. I am a member of the Osage Tribal Council, and in addition to the ordinary affairs of the tribe, I am constantly asked to solve individual problems by members of the tribe, [so] my mind is occupied by a variety of inconsequential personal affairs." Perhaps remarkably, the Guggenheim Foundation found his rationale of wanting to escape the tribe for a year worthy of funding. One would think that living alone out on the prairie in a hunting lodge would provide enough isolation to write.[2]

Although isolation was his main goal, Mathews preferred Mexico because he hoped to find there an "advanced stage in the development of the adjustment of an indigenous race to the changes brought about by a European invader." Initially, he did "not plan to do research there," since his project was regional, but he hoped to gain impressions observationally. To some degree, Jo's experiences in Mexico enhanced his understanding of Indigenous peoples. The best piece of evidence for this might be his 1963 story "Alfredo and the Jaguar," set in a remote area of Mexico, told from the point of view of Indigenous characters.[3]

Having been awarded a $2,000 grant, Mathews was slated to depart for Mexico in early September, but as usual, he proceeded whimsically. In mid-October he was in Laredo, Texas: "I have taken my time—in fact have loitered along the way," he admitted in a letter to Dibbs. A week later, though, he was in Mexico City, where he frequently strolled, smoking his pipe or a Mexican cigarette he liked. Because of high taxes, he decided to forego hard liquor and drink wine. He enjoyed his solitude and anonymity, telling Dibbs that nothing was "apt to interfere with my pleasure."[4]

By mid-November, Mathews was enjoying life at Rancho Bassoco, an hacienda within walking distance of Cuernavaca, a small city fifty-four miles south of Mexico City, a haven for elites offering beautiful flora, pleasant weather, and a large international community. His coffee was served to him by Carlos, a "grinning Indian boy" with whom he made small talk in Spanish on the patio. "After absorbing the rays of the early sun, I go back into the house, have my cold shower, then draw the typewriter lazily toward me and start work." Jo played table tennis, walked, rode horseback, and ate lunch on the porch. At 5:00 P.M. he took a lesson in Spanish phonetics, for which he put on a suit. He never truly mastered Spanish, however. More than Spanish, he spoke English, especially with Americans living at his hacienda, or French with the Swiss émigrés in Mexico City whose businesses he patronized. On the whole Mathews pursued "pleasant living," one of his mottos. On Sundays, he enjoyed regular massages and relaxation in the sauna: "I have found a very pleasant Turkish bath, in fact an Aztec bath," he wrote Elizabeth. "Like the Indians of the Plains, the Aztecs are also worshippers of steam-bathing." In what might have been an odd line to write to a woman who was his romantic partner, Jo said he was massaged by "a magnificent Indian, who has a body like a bronze god."[5]

Jo's writing in Mexico may have been unrelated to the manuscript that eventually became *The Osages*. He was probably composing *Talking to the Moon*, finding that distance made it easier to reflect on life on the Osage prairie. It is unknown how much writing he produced in Mexico; he regularly had difficulty working. Perhaps more than anything else, Mathews was on a ten-month vacation. By mid-November 1939, he had been in Mexico for about a month but had done "very little on the project." Even when he spent hours trying to write, he wasn't productive. He confessed to Elizabeth, "I wish you wouldn't have so much confidence in my ability to do this project—'I intend to write a book'—as I am rather afraid of it. The conditions are almost perfect, but yet I really went off half-cocked as far as material was concerned." On the bright side, he discovered a new research trail at the National Library in Mexico City. As time passed, he increasingly diminished the overall importance of the finished product. "Possibly the book 'haint no big thing,' but this scholarship has been a GOOD thing for me. I feel that I am at last achieving some sort of orientation." Distance enabled him to clarify his own critical perspective as an Osage intellectual and historian.[6]

Jo lived at the hacienda with two other guests, Bud and Mike Disney, two "young New York newspaper people" on holiday for six months. It was then common for well-off North Americans and Europeans to take lengthy vacations in Cuernavaca. Loren G. "Bud" Disney, Jr., born in Muskogee, was a journalist and nephew of Jo's friend, Congressman Walter Disney, and Mignon "Mike" Disney was a magazine editor. Bud and Mike were having marital troubles and their noisy spats sometimes disturbed Jo's attempts to work. In December 1939, to escape the Disneys' "screaming divorce threats" and an annoying guest who was staying with them, Jo invited Jon, "a very sensitive boy of 24," to accompany him on a road trip to Acapulco, 180 miles away, for about a week. Jo and Jon swam in the ocean, sunned on the beach, and conversed in French for hours, which sounds like a romantic getaway. Back at the hacienda, Mike had returned to New York, but Bud remained in Mexico.[7]

At Cuernavaca, Jo received a few visitors. In November, newspaperman Walker Stone, a longtime friend, spent a weekend with Jo. As ruggedly masculine as his name implies, Walker Stone was born in Okemah prior to Oklahoma statehood and graduated from Oklahoma A&M in Stillwater. George Milburn and his wife, Vivien, who were staying fifty-three miles away at Taxco, also visited. Mathews looked forward to seeing George, but he did not care for Vivien. "I shall make no special effort with Viv. I do not have the time," he vowed. "George can sit quietly in the sun as Walker did, and not disturb the flow of life here, but Viv—she'll have to find something to do about entertainment." Sallye Brandt called Vivien a "beautiful, irresponsible child." Jo need not have worried; the visit went smoothly because, he believed, Viv "made a special effort" although he had resolved not to himself. Milburn was a repeat visitor to The Blackjacks during the late 1930s and 1940s, once arriving with novelist Edward Donahoe.[8]

In January 1940, Mathews traveled widely in his Buick Estate Wagon and recorded observations of Indigenous people. On New Year's Day, Mathews left Cuernavaca for "the wilds" of Guerrero, staying in its capital, Chilpancingo. In a remote area, as Jo drove through grassy streets, he "was stared at by Indians," whom, he hyperbolically claimed, "had never seen a white man before." Driving his big new automobile in the presence of indigenes, Jo's feeling of being an alien "white man" emerged, a feeling he experienced repeatedly. "My Station Wagon was a miracle, and as I drove along the narrow little trails which passed for roads, the Indians, especially the children and the women, fled from the roads like wild things." Though Mathews found the Indigenous peoples of Mexico to be interesting, he usually observed them from a distance and did not always identify them by tribe-specific names.[9]

He took a short vacation in Acapulco, and then, while making his way back north, in the small town of Chilapa, east of Chilpancingo, he suffered a dubious, protracted parking hassle with Mexican authorities. In his diary, he described the ordeal at length, since he believed it gave him "greater insight into Mexico and the Mexican character" than anything else he might have experienced. His narrative provided material for the unpublished, satirical short story "Only a Blonde," in which his experience is transferred to a leftist Radcliffe College student who separates from her group of young Americans. Mathews returned to Cuernavaca but soon took a short trip to Mexico City, then embarked on "another adventure," this time "into the wilds of the States of Puebla and Veracruz." Regarding his work with the Osage Tribal Council, he noted he was obliged to respond to regular letters from Superintendent Charles Ellis.[10]

In March, Mathews drove all the way back to Pawhuska for a month's vacation from his vacation. Pointing his Buick homeward, he stopped in Ciudad Valles to view its stunning ravines and waterfalls. Jo wrote his contact at the Guggenheim Foundation, Henry Moe, on March 12, saying that he was on his way home for a vacation; he would have told him of his intentions earlier, he said, but he had previously planned to spend the month in Oaxaca and Yucatan. "Certain personal matters in Oklahoma need my immediate attention, and I shall spend about three weeks there. I hope that this will not be contrary to the Foundation's wishes." The nature of these personal matters is unclear, but they may have related to his first wife's efforts to obtain a divorce and alimony from Mathews. Moreover, Elizabeth's daughter, Ann, was not well and would require surgery in June and July.[11]

Returning to Mexico, Mathews arrived late at the first Inter-American Conference on Indian Life, held in gorgeous Pátzcuaro, Michoacán. He attended as a representative from Oklahoma, in place of his and BIA Commissioner John Collier's adversary, Senator Elmer Thomas. Jo found the city's Indigenous-colonial look charmingly "picture-bookish," with adobe and wood buildings, plazas, markets, and a lake. The conference, largely organized by Collier, began on April 14, 1940, but Mathews didn't arrive in Pátzcuaro until April 18, with no explanation as to why he was late. Jo wrote, "Collier was very busy, running about, when I arrived. He seemed abrupt and a little cool. I am not sure whether it was coolness due to my delayed arrival, or whether he was so preoccupied that he was scarcely conscious of me." The reason for the chilly reception did not matter to Mathews, since he felt slighted by Collier. "If there is not some recognition of my presence by tomorrow, I shall leave for Guadalajara and Mazatlán." Considering that Collier was a friend and that this hemispheric conference was Collier's "baby" and a groundbreaking event, Jo's attitude seems petty. The next morning, Mathews listened to lectures in the Socio-Economic Section, and he was reminded of the League of Nations. His roommate was future BIA Commissioner William Brophy.[12]

Collier visualized the initial Inter-American Conference on Indian Life as a clearinghouse for hemispheric Indian issues. The conference was, the *Oklahoman* reported, mainly "a white man's meeting to work out common problems" and an "exchange of information on population and culture as a basis for research through which to improve health, law, education, art, and general administration of community affairs." There were numerous delegates from nineteen nations and seventy-one social scientists presenting more than one hundred papers, but only forty-one Indigenous people from twenty tribes in Mexico, Panama, and the United States, who met for ten days to discuss Indigenous issues. Jo was initially skeptical and wary of the nationalist suspicion shown by some delegates. But his attitude quickly changed as he realized the participants were working together. In fact, he claimed he had never seen an organization work harder than the delegates at the conference. He mostly listened but was pleased at how things resolved. The conference "ended in a spirit of cooperation and amity," and Jo believed that something might actually be done to improve "the status of the Indian" and generate "better understanding among the American countries." Mexican President Lázaro Cárdenas hosted a luncheon for the delegates, followed by native music and dancing. Songs in the Purépecha language of the Tarascan, or Purépecha, people, to which President Cárdenas belonged, filled the air.

Soon after his belated arrival, Mathews met up with D'Arcy McNickle, tribal activist and another of the few American Indian novelists writing in the 1930s, along with BIA officials Walter Woehlke and Allan Harper. McNickle, who had published *The Surrounded* four years earlier, accompanied Collier's American delegation as an advisor. Mathews later went with McNickle, Woehlke, and an old friend, German-Jewish anthropologist Paul Kirchhoff, to a fun dinner event at which they were entertained by Mexican and Indigenous dancers. Kirchhoff taught in Mexico and did groundbreaking work in the culture area of Mesoamerica, a term he coined. During the mid-1930s, when Dr. Kirchhoff was living in America seeking political asylum, he spent an afternoon with Jo and Elizabeth. Kirchhoff fondly recalled the "very pleasant afternoon" the three of them had spent and asked after Elizabeth. Fortunately, they did not talk politics: Kirchhoff was a communist activist with militant ties, while Mathews was staunchly anticommunist. Critic James H. Cox remarked that during this meeting, the authors of two crucial Native American novels of the 1930s (Mathews and McNickle) had an opportunity to discuss "what American Indians could learn from indigenous Mexicans and Mexican policy."[13]

Delegates to the Pátzcuaro conference drafted seventy-two non-binding resolutions as the foundation of a new hemispheric Indian policy. They recommended that every nation "establish an agency to help Indians build up a viable communal life by providing needed land, credit, and co-operative farming techniques." American governments should "protect Indian culture, use Native languages in educational programs, participate in an inter-American exposition of Indian art, grant Indian women social equality, develop schools of rural medicine, proclaim an 'Indian Day,' and establish anthropology departments at universities training experts in native administration." Delegates also drafted a convention authorizing a permanent Inter-American Indian Institute (IAII) after ratification by five countries.[14]

Following the conference, Jo enjoyed about a week exploring Guadalajara. A "very cultured Italian" architect and artist who had lived in Guadalajara for three decades visited Jo at his pension. With the émigré, Jo visited Chapala, a beautiful, tranquil town favored by American poets, writers, and artists. In 1945, Tennessee Williams spent a couple of months there at the house of his friend, gay poet Witter Bynner, who mentored Lynn Riggs, and wrote the first draft of *A Streetcar Named Desire.*[15]

Jo then journeyed to Mexico City, where he researched archival material and sought guidance from a Mexican anthropologist. While he was there, Robert Capa, a Hungarian photojournalist for *Life* who met Jo while taking pictures at the Pátzcuaro conference, called him and they dined at a French restaurant. Already famous for his war photography, Capa was then on assignment in Mexico for six months because his visa extensions ran out and he could not stay in America. Like Jo, Capa spoke French and loved French wine and cuisine.[16]

Meanwhile, Elizabeth Hunt was not having much fun back in Pawhuska. In December 1939, Jo received three unhappy letters. She was worried about finances and her business, and found it hard to raise a teenaged boy and a nine-year-old girl with no father figure around. If Mathews had been providing any financial support, that money was likely suspended when he decamped. Early in his trip he wrote, "I hope Phillips are not worrying you . . . about my account. I shall send the cheque to you as soon as there is sufficient money accumulated in my account." Things became much worse at home in Pawhuska in June 1940 when Ann's illness required her to have exploratory surgery. During this operation, a cyst was discovered. Jo tried to reassure Elizabeth that "Annigan," who was almost ten, would be fine. Jo felt that the surgeon, whom they referred to as "Cap," was exaggerating the danger to Ann and worrying her unnecessarily. He said that he was more worried about Elizabeth than Ann: "I can see you with jack-boot pelvic bones, hollow eyes, and that terrible lost-marbles look on your face." Another letter from Elizabeth prompted him to confirm: "you have certainly lost your marbles." Concerned, Mathews called Cap, who told Mathews that Ann's cyst was not serious enough to necessitate his return.[17]

In late May and early June 1940, Jo again returned to Acapulco, then took in Xochimilco, an attractive borough of Mexico City noted for its Indigenous history and canal system, and watched bullfighting in Mexico City. At the ruins of Teotihuacan, he was awed by the Pyramids of the Sun and the Moon and the Temple of the Feathered Spirit. In June, Jo moved from Cuernavaca, driving 500 miles north to Tamaulipas, because "screams of newsboys selling stories of an incredible war" upset him for hours. From June through August, Jo lived in a remote area at the Hacienda Santa Engracia, near a lake sharing that name "in the wilds of the state of Tamaulipas," north of Ciudad Victoria. This suited him perfectly. In 1940 Santa Engracia was a new hotel offering lush gardens, horseback riding, hunting, and fishing. During July, when Mathews was not hunting, fishing, or working, he sat for a portrait by Pedro Rodríguez. The artist flattered Mathews's vanity but captured something authentic. Mathews described it as portraying "a man placidly surveying the world and appreciating it for what it is. That is the way I see myself."[18]

Jo drove with Pepe, the hotel's cook, southwestward over the mountain and onto the high plateau of central Mexico in the state of San Luis Potosí. He returned to the hacienda due to an intermittent illness that he called malaria or fever. After he recovered, he resolved to leave for home earlier than planned, hoping to arrive in Pawhuska early enough to help John Hunt prepare for his first year of boarding school. In mid-August Mathews first reported he had been sick in bed three days, and two days later he had fever dreams. After that, the fever completely left him, but the quinine he was taking to combat malaria gave him insomnia. Suffering from intense heat, Jo wrote, "This is no place for a white man with work energy, and certainly no place for one just getting over an attack of malaria." He headed north on August 22, 1940, and returned to Pawhuska by the end of the month, curtailing his fellowship year by almost two months.[19]

Henry Moe, his contact at the Guggenheim Foundation, did not hear from Mathews for over a year after he left Mexico. In a short letter, Mathews wrote, "I imagine you have wondered about me at times. The following will give some idea of how I have spent the last year." Specifying no dates, Mathews said that he contracted fever while "nosing about in the Jungle with the Indians," and "eventually was well enough to come back." He claimed, "during the last year I have fought the fever which produced an annoying lassitude. I think I have just about recovered." He also said that he "lost only about a month of my Fellowship year in Mexico."[20] Subtracting his month back in Pawhuska, he was in Mexico only a little more than nine months out of a year-long fellowship. On the pretext of illness, Mathews explained away his failure to produce the manuscript proposed to the Guggenheims. He also claimed that he had been working on a second text about the history of peyote, and needed to focus on that because two of his sources, Osage elders, had been sick recently and might pass away. Therefore, he was going to focus exclusively on "the Peyote story" and lay aside his fellowship manuscript for the nonce. No peyote book or scholarly article was ever published under his name, but Mathews devotes much of the chapter "Moonhead" in *The Osages* to the subject, and was likely the author of an unsigned 1961 piece for the Pawhuska newspaper about the Native American Church.[21] Undermining his claim of lethargy, within weeks of his return home he traveled to Washington, D.C., and New Jersey with John Hunt and ate "like a bearcat," the teenager told his mother.[22] Moreover, in early 1941, Jo was active with community functions and Osage Tribal Council business.

Moe next heard from Mathews in February 1943, when he claimed that he had been doing nothing but trying to get into the war effort, despite the fact that he had completed a draft of *Talking to the Moon* by then. Mathews asked Moe for a recommendation for a "commission in the service under the Provost Marshal General's Office," connected to "the military administration of conquered lands." He also wanted to return to military aviation, even though he would turn fifty that year and had not flown a plane since 1919. Despite all of the ink he spilled about the war in his diaries and letters, and a lengthy trip to Washington, D.C., to investigate options, Mathews contributed nothing to the war effort. He was offered at least three different opportunities to work for the U.S. government, but he turned them down: a job with the "Economic Administration" in India, a special "cloak and dagger" intelligence mission abroad, and the writing of a biography of President Harding. Elizabeth, in contrast, lost her business and ended up toiling in a factory making tents for the army, waking up at 5 A.M. each workday. A year before his death, Mathews exaggerated in his diary, "I have never worked a day in my life."[23]

Chapter Eight

THE TRAGEDY OF LORENE SQUIRE

> That was the only time I ever heard Atticus say it was a sin to do something, and I asked Miss Maudie about it. "Your father's right," she said. "Mockingbirds don't do one thing except make music for us to enjoy. They don't eat up people's gardens, don't nest in corn cribs, they don't do one thing but sing their hearts out for us. That's why it's a sin to kill a mockingbird."
>
> —Harper Lee, *To Kill a Mockingbird*

On returning to Pawhuska from Mexico, Mathews resumed activity with the Fifteenth Osage Tribal Council. During this period he made regular trips to Washington, D.C., to meet politicians and negotiate with the government. The council was still led by Chief Fred Lookout, whom Jo greatly admired and whose life he chronicled in a long article for the *Oklahoman* in 1939 (which could not have hurt Jo's influence upon him). Lookout served as assistant principal chief in 1908–10, and principal chief in 1912–14, 1916–18, and from 1924 until his death in 1949. Over the years, Lookout's son Freddie liked to visit The Blackjacks and would sometimes talk to Jo for hours on end. In his loquaciousness he differed from his dad.[1]

Weeks after his homecoming, in September 1940 Mathews traveled to Washington, D.C., on Osage business, and delivered John Hunt to Lawrenceville School in New Jersey. Mathews wanted to talk to several people in the capital, so he was not the ideal guardian for a fifteen-year-old. One evening, Jo got into a lengthy conversation with Osage councilman and cattleman Louis DeNoya, Congressman Wesley E. Disney, and a third person, while John, getting hungry, went to a restaurant by himself to find dinner. Disney, a friend of Jo's, served in the House of Representatives as a Democrat from 1931 to 1945. He was the uncle of Bud Disney, who disturbed Jo in Cuernavaca with his marital spats.[2]

In 1941, councilman Mathews wrangled with the federal government and businessmen—including his friend, oilman Frank Phillips, who had been adopted into the tribe by Chief Lookout and the Thirteenth Tribal Council at the F.P. Ranch in 1930, and in a formal ceremony at Woolaroc in 1931. Phillips wanted to construct the Hulah Dam on the Caney River northwest of Bartlesville in the Osage Hills, ostensibly to eliminate flooding. (*Hulah* means "eagle" in Osage.) Mathews opposed the dam's construction, believing its true purpose was more recreation than flood control, and the proposed lake would cover a great deal of Osage tribal land. The Pawhuska Chamber of Commerce tried to enlist the tribe's support, but the tribal council declined. Traveling to Washington, D.C. for two weeks, Ted Byron Hall, Choctaw-Cherokee superintendent of the Osage Agency, along with Osage tribal councilmen, met with government officials. Backed by a report authored by Mathews, they lodged a formal protest against plans to construct the dam. Spearheaded by Mathews, the council's protest of the Hulah project delayed construction for several years.[3]

In August 1943, Jo and Elizabeth Hunt drove to Bartlesville because she wanted to meet with Phillips, presumably regarding the loss of her business. Phillips had been Elizabeth's employer since she had taken over her late husband's gas station and bulk distribution station. Jo did not join her as she socialized with Frank and Jane Phillips; instead, he got a haircut. As Elizabeth dined with the couple in their home, Frank accused Jo of being "the cause of the floods in Bartlesville this spring because he had opposed the construction of the Hulah dam," which Mathews found "childish and rather silly."[4]

Despite their differences, Phillips provided funds for Mathews to research and write both *Life and Death of an Oilman* and *The Osages*, though he died before they were published. Jo told author Richard Rhodes that he and Elizabeth ate picnic lunches atop Phillips's mausoleum on Woolaroc grounds. Frank had had a working telephone line installed in his tomb, and Jo always hoped he would hear it ring.[5]

In 1941, the tribal council finally enfranchised Osage women, granting them the right to vote and run for office in tribal elections. In 1935, Wesley Disney had introduced H.R. 4323, which would have extended suffrage to Osage women, but the tribal council, including Mathews, denied it with Resolution No. 6. Three years later, faced with a petition demanding women's voting rights, the council still did not yield. Publisher and former councilman George E. "Ed" Tinker advocated for extending suffrage, but could not sway the council. Mathews argued that the vote was denied not only to women but also to absentee Osages and a third class: younger "restricted males who had inherited headrights from original allottees."[6] Mathews reasoned that "if you stand on the ground of justice, in many cases, some of those young people have a greater interest in this big business than some of those who are on the roll." Tinker agreed, but believed extending voting rights beyond tribal rolls would require an act of Congress. Mathews pounced: "The minute Congress gets fooling with it, five or six thousand applicants to be enrolled will come forward; anything that would tend to open the roll is dangerous." Finally, the council was pressured to accede by a 1940 amendment to the 1906 Dawes Allotment Act stating "Osage women 21 and over, whose names appear on the quarterly annuity roll" could vote and run for tribal office, followed by two strongly worded missives from John Collier urging the council to reconsider.[7]

In March 1942, Mathews presented at the University of Oklahoma Symposium on American Literature and Education, addressing "The Indian in American Literature," paralleling the lecture on "The Negro in American Literature" by poet, critic, and Howard University professor Sterling A. Brown. Influenced by jazz, blues, and spirituals, Brown published his first book, *Southern Road*, in the same year as Jo's debut. One hopes Mathews and Brown had a chance to converse. Also presenting was New Critic Cleanth Brooks, who co-wrote with novelist Robert Penn Warren *Understanding Fiction*, which anthologized "Head by Scopas," by Jo and Warren's friend Edward Donahoe.[8]

"April is the cruelest month," T. S. Eliot wrote in "The Burial of the Dead," part 1 of *The Wasteland*. A decade after Henry Hunt's suicide, tragedy again befell Jo and Elizabeth, in the person of Lorene Squire, a gifted young artist from rural Kansas who was already "one of America's foremost photographers of wild life." Jo and Elizabeth shared her interest in photographing birds and animals.[9]

Born in October 1908 and raised in Harper, Kansas, Lorene as a child went on a bird-hunting trip with her uncle, who taught her how to shoot. Little Lorene had an epiphany, suddenly aglow with love for the birds she had been hunting. She decided right then she would devote her life to shooting birds with a camera instead of a rifle. Staying true to her childhood dream, she had her first photograph published in *Nature* at the age of fifteen. Shortly after graduating from the University of Kansas in 1932, she commenced a career as a nature photographer, while still living with her parents, Harris and Lillie Mae Squire, in her hometown in rural south-central Kansas. Over the next decade, she published copious bird photos shot in various locales in the United States and Canada in *Life* (several times), *Field and Stream*, *Saturday Evening Post*, and elsewhere. In 1938, *The Beaver*, a magazine published by Hudson's Bay Company, sent her to the Arctic to shoot wildlife and human scenes of the North. That year Squire published her atmospheric book of black-and-white photos and essays, *Wildfowling with a Camera*. In 1941 *Life* tagged Squire "the famous bird photographer" and lavished eight large pages on her waterfowl photographs. Squire was "reaching a peak in her profession where she was not only famous," but also "had no competition among women." Even though Lorene seemed "slight, even fragile," she was known for her intrepid approach to capturing avian images—for example, crawling long distances through mud on her hands and knees.[10]

Lorene traveled to Osage County on assignment for *Life*, to capture the "booming" and foot-stamping contests among male prairie chickens, the dawn dances Mathews loved to share with spring visitors. She approached Mathews for assistance. On Saturday, April 11, 1942, Jo, Elizabeth, and Lorene drove to Ponca City to find equipment. On Monday, the *Pawhuska Journal-Capital* reported that state highway patrolmen told them that the group was returning to Pawhuska late that night, with Mathews at the wheel of his 1940 Buick Estate Wagon, Elizabeth in the passenger seat, and Lorene riding in the backseat. Reportedly "blinded by the headlights of a car they were meeting," which was presumably oncoming or parked on the opposite side of Highway 60, Mathews's car struck a culvert.[11] The *Tulsa Tribune* named two highway patrolmen as sources in reporting the car "ran off the pavement onto the soft shoulder," traveling 109 feet before "crashing into a concrete bridge abutment."[12] In the days before cars had seatbelts, this was a serious accident. Elizabeth suffered rib fractures, lacerations, and "possible internal injuries," and was still in hospital two nights later. The Pawhuska paper reported that "Mathews was thrown from the car and was said to have struck his head on the pavement, causing a serious head injury." The *Oklahoman* reported he was "critically hurt," but the *Tulsa Tribune* and the *Lawrence Journal-World* said he was only "slightly injured," and having suffered "only a minor scalp laceration, did not require hospitalization," and returned home.[13]

Lorene Squire was transported to Pawhuska Municipal Hospital, suffering from a fractured pelvis and shock. She died on Sunday morning. Her body was returned to Harper, Kansas the same day, where she was buried aside a modest headstone in Harper Cemetery. She was survived by her parents and a younger brother, Harris G. Squire, who later was a captain in the army during World War II. In *Talking to the Moon* Mathews writes, "I have made so many pitiful failures that I have developed a great admiration for wild-life photographers." This was the closest he ever came to acknowledging Squire's death. Squire was a spirited, gifted young artist cut down in her prime by a senseless accident. She possessed a beautiful soul and charmed everyone she met. Colonel "Hal" Sheldon said Lorene was "one of the finest individuals I've ever known, so secure in her own integrity, so intelligent, and so gay." She conveyed her idealism and devotion to her beloved waterbirds in delightful prose: "The years will never change my ambition to picture all manner and variety of waterfowl in characteristic formations of flight, from the smallest snipe to the proud, great-winged Canada Goose. That this ambition can never be entirely realized doesn't make any difference."[14]

Those "generations of men" possessing a love of the hunt—such as Old Bill Williams, Will Mathews, Jo Mathews, and John Hunt—find great pleasure in shooting plover, ducks, geese, and other waterbirds. Though Mathews and Squire both loved the prairie and the birds that made their home there, Squire had believed since her girlhood epiphany that killing harmless birds was a sin. Mathews grew to love photographing birds, but sometimes he would still push aside the camera to reach for his rifle. While Elizabeth sometimes accompanied Mathews on his hunting jaunts, she too preferred to capture and display animals on film, not as heads mounted on the wall.

Mathews was not arrested in connection with the accident, and no evidence of speeding was found. Yet details of the evening that preceded Squire's death remain somewhat mysterious. Back in 1942, the two-lane Highway 60 was curvy and narrow—locals called it "Lizard Lane." Attorney Harvey Payne said that stretch was the site of many accidents, and he called one concrete bridge abutment that sat fairly close to the road a "death trap." Yet Mathews had traversed Highway 60 to and from Ponca City countless times. It is unknown who was in the oncoming car, but it seems odd that the headlights were so blinding as to drive him off a familiar road. The Pawhuska paper reported that the trio went "to search for equipment for Miss Squire's photographic work and were returning to Pawhuska at the time of the accident." They had "planned to set up the photographic equipment before daylight on Sunday morning in the northern part of Osage county, and had sought a fence electrification attachment to protect Miss Squire's cameras from cattle in the pasture where pictures were to be taken, it was said." Unable to find the equipment in Pawhuska, they went to Ponca City, Kay County. It seems odd that Jo, Elizabeth, and Lorene returned to Pawhuska so late at night to set up the equipment in northern Osage County, a land mass comparable to Delaware. Presumably they would prefer to set up the equipment during the day. If they drove to Ponca City during the daytime on Saturday, they were still there that night, and Jo and Dibbs may have been drinking. During the 1940s, they socialized and imbibed with friends there, including the alcoholic author Donahoe and interviewees for the Marland biography ("Marland men" had a reputation for tippling). After a book-signing party in Ponca City in 1961, Jo and Elizabeth picked up a bottle of Amontillado sherry and drove back home over the prairie. On the way they "nipped at the Sherry, following an old tradition," Mathews wrote. It stands to reason Mathews would want to show off the charming Lorene to his Ponca City friends while they were in town on a Saturday, and that he would have had a few drinks. It may otherwise seem odd that he lost such complete control of his vehicle. But we can only speculate on the circumstances.[15]

Likewise we cannot know Mathews's thoughts on what happened the night of the accident and to what degree he felt responsible for Lorene's death and Elizabeth's injuries. It must have been an awful, painful experience with a difficult emotional aftermath, one that he and Elizabeth kept to themselves. Squire was a kindred spirit, a woman who earned his respect. Jo's injuries delayed plans for a dedication program in May for a new records building at the Osage Agency, a three-story, native-stone edifice.[16]

Among certain Osages, a story is still told about Mathews and the accidental death of a visiting young artist or writer. According to the story, the accident resulted from a curse Mathews brought upon himself and her by violating taboo—opening a sacred medicine bundle to show his guest, whom, it is said, wanted to see it. Mathews acquired Wah Hopeh bundles for the Osage Tribal Museum. In *Talking to the Moon*, he explained how Osages collectively put away their traditional religion—deciding "its medicine is bad and should be forgotten"—and took up the Native American Church's peyote ceremony or Christianity, plus the I'n-Lon-Schka June dances, instead. Attorney Geoffrey Standing Bear, Principal Chief of the Osage Nation as of 2016, said that his grandmother Mary Lookout Standing Bear knew Mathews, and in his research Mathews visited with family members, asking many questions about medicine bundles, pipes, and other ceremonial materials and their usage in the late nineteenth century. They told Mathews to stop asking, since "we, the Osages, put those things away," Standing Bear said. He and other Osages mentioned stories of individuals who attempted to revive the old religion going insane or otherwise being cursed. Mongrain Lookout of the Osage Language Center—grandson of Chief Fred Lookout and Julia Pryor Mongrain Lookout, herself the descendant of a chief—recalled his father, Henry, telling Mathews that he should not write about details of the old ways. These old things must stay in the past, Henry Lookout told Jo.[17]

Sometime in the early 1940s, a son of Spotted Horse, an elder who had heard Mathews was acquiring sacred bundles for the museum, visited Mathews and raised the subject. His father had an urgent message.

Mathews cut in, "He says for me not to open one?"

"He says you must not open one of the bundles. He says you alltime ask too many questions about them bundles. . . . You oughtn't to do that; it's bad. He says you'll sure die if you fool with them things. Osage have put them bad things away, he says. He says we must follow word of Moonhead now."

Moonhead, or Moon Head, was John Wilson, a Caddo-Delaware-French spiritual leader who brought peyote to the Osages, and cultivated a group of devoted followers among them.

Mathews asked if it was acceptable to have bundles at the museum.

"I guess that's all right, but . . . don't fool with them bundles." Only the person authorized to place the bundle in the museum could handle it, he said, emphasizing his message in different iterations.

"All right," Jo acceded.[18]

Still, the son urged that Spotted Horse wanted to discuss this matter in person. Kenneth Jacob Jump wrote, "When sacred bundles were unearthed and put on display in museums, the older members of the tribe would not enter the building. The inherent religious beliefs were so inbred that fear made one cautious when such desecration was found." Given Mathews's Oxford-trained scientific outlook, he probably opened a Wah Hopeh bundle for motives of historical inquiry and curiosity, perhaps bringing bad medicine on himself, his friends, and his family. Misfortune indeed befell the Mathews family twice: two out of three of his nephews died within fourteen months of the accident. Florence's son Michael A. Feighan, Jr., age eleven, was killed by a drunk driver in July 1942; and Josephine's son, Henry Ben Caudill, died in a military training accident in June 1943.[19]

In May, while Jo and Elizabeth were convalescing, the *Saturday Review of Literature* published an article by Mathews, "Scholarship Comes to Life: The University of Oklahoma Press." In 1941, Jo's friend Everette Lee DeGolyer—geophysicist, oilman, bibliophile, OU graduate, and founder of OU's well-known History of Science collection—purchased the *Saturday Review* and became chairman of its editorial board. The article was largely a tribute to Jo's friends Brandt and Lottinville for their development of a university press spotlighting Southwestern regionalism. Mathews and his literary friends, such as Stanley Vestal (Campbell), George Milburn, J. Frank Dobie, Kenneth Kaufman, and Laura Adams Armer, contributed to this regionalist project, along with John M. Oskison, Todd Downing, Grant Foreman, E. E. Dale, Mari Sandoz, Oliver La Farge, Mary Austin, Frank Waters, and Paul Horgan. But Jo's article was no puff piece: He offered an honest critique of what he regarded as the overly academic tone and diction of OU Press books, claiming that most were marred by "scholarly smugness." (His publisher at the time was Longmans, Green.) Academic self-expression was remarkable, but manifested only on the "culture-literature plane," in the "old culture symbols of scholars" instead of in the "sap-filled living language of the earth." Mathews said the "people of the hills, the blackjacks, the shortgrass, the desert, and the mountain creeks have not yet interpreted the soil through their own idioms, metaphors, dialects, and song."[20]

Sometime in late 1942 Henry Seidel Canby of the *Saturday Review* sent Jo Mari Sandoz's biography *Crazy Horse*, requesting a review. Jo told Elizabeth in February 1943 he had quite enjoyed the book and mailed in a review. The magazine had, however, already published a review by Stanley Vestal the month before. Apparently, Jo was so far wide of his deadline that the magazine had given up on receiving anything from him.[21]

Having healed from his accident, in October 1942 Mathews visited the Menominee Indian Reservation, northwest of Green Bay in Wisconsin. Working with the Menominee tribal agency, headquartered in the small town of Neopit, he used his zoological and ecological knowledge and powers of observation to write a report on wildlife of the woodland reservation. The Menominee forest is the home of old-growth trees, bears, otters, and cormorants. During this visit, Mathews proposed a wildlife refuge in the forest, but also sought refuge for himself after several busy years on the tribal council and the tragedy of Lorene Squire.

He explored the reservation with a forester named Libby and ventured out with an official named Lyle and two Menominees, George Kenote and Jerry Grignon, to "shoot the rapids on the Wolf River in a boat and shoot ducks—there were more rapids than ducks, however." Most of his activity was out of doors—pleasant work, but chilly, he complained. He took a trip south to Chicago with Lyle to visit the "Indian office and the forestry people." He was surprised that the forestry wildlife supervisor enthusiastically accepted his proposal for a refuge and "general conservation on the Menominee." Consequently, a "Division biologist" was sent to Chicago to provide scientific assistance. Over the next decade, however, the Menominee tribe was snubbed by the federal government, a victim of federal Termination Policy, which reversed Collier's progress of the 1930s and early 1940s by severing federal recognition for Indian tribes deemed no longer to require government assistance. Kenote and Grignon, Jo's duck hunting companions, were two of the individuals who, on behalf of the tribe, sued the U.S. government in 1967, demanding recognition of their historical hunting and fishing rights. After the courts ruled in their favor, Menominees regained federal recognition and sovereignty over their lands when Congress passed the Menominee Restoration Act, signed by President Nixon in December 1973.[22]

Along with a letter to Elizabeth narrating this trip, Jo sent a special humorous message to Ann Hunt, written in an "Indian" voice on a postcard fashioned from a piece of birch bark (the traditional writing medium of Woodland tribes), conveying the idea that it was getting awfully cold on the reservation and he wished to return home soon. Perhaps Jo's loving attention to twelve-year-old Ann, who had survived a cyst two years before, was his recognition of how quickly the lives of people we care about can be extinguished.[23]

Chapter Nine

THE MOON AND MARLAND

Oh, if Ernest had not gone after strange gods!

—Alfred Marland

The year 1945 was pivotal for both global history and Mathews personally. In April he married Elizabeth, and in June, he published *Talking to the Moon*, the fruit of much labor, close observation, and meditation on his beloved Osage blackjack prairie and its wildlife, and to a lesser extent, his Osage people. He then quickly threw himself into his next project—a biography of his late friend Ernest Whitworth Marland (1874–1941), an oilman, politician, philanthropist, and aesthete known as "E.W." or "Ernie" to his friends. To Mathews, Marland's life "had the essentials for Greek drama," and the two men shared a love of art, culture, horses, hunting, and England. Mathews and Marland both possessed geological knowledge and a close understanding of the land. Mathews devoted at least five years—much longer than he had expected—to researching and writing his biography of Marland.[1]

Ironically, one of the witnesses at Mathews's wedding was a man famous for mocking Marland. Author Edward Donahoe is a crucial figure in the story of Marland and Mathews and is interesting in his own right. On April 5, 1945, Mathews married Elizabeth Hunt, his longtime devoted helper and lover. Jo and Elizabeth's efficient wedding at the Kay County Courthouse in Newkirk, Oklahoma, was witnessed by Edward Donahoe, who had scandalized his hometown by ridiculing E. W. Marland in 1937 via a fictional proxy in his roman à clef *Madness in the Heart*. Beyond Edward's role as witness, the Donahoe family was central to the celebration of Jo and Elizabeth's nuptials, and they did not skimp on the booze. The Donahoes, along with other Ponca City friends, provided Jo with an alternative social group that was lively and fun, without the intrusiveness of gossipy Pawhuska.[2]

Mathews was familiar with the social set of elite Ponca City nouveaux riches—oilmen, geologists, white and French-Osage ranchers, and their scions. Edward came from a prominent Ponca City family, attended Notre Dame, and graduated from Harvard. In the 1920s, he joined the New York City publishing scene, working for H. L. Mencken's magazine *American Mercury* and briefly for publisher Alfred A. Knopf, which printed the *Mercury*. During the early 1930s, Donahoe spent a portion of each year in Nashville with his Harvard friend (and perhaps lover) Tom Mabry, a Vanderbilt University professor. In Nashville, Donahoe became acquainted with prominent faculty such as author and poet James Weldon Johnson and his wife, Grace Nail Johnson, at Fisk University, a historically black university, and New Critic Allen Tate at Vanderbilt University. Tate was incensed when he was invited to an integrated party hosted by Donahoe and Mabry, and attended by Johnson and Langston Hughes, who was in town for a poetry reading.

During this period, Edward met and rapidly became close friends with the Harlem Renaissance novelist Nella Larsen, the author of two late-1920s novels dramatizing racial identity and social relations: *Quicksand* and *Passing*. Mutual friend Mabry seems to have introduced Edward and Nella, who was recently divorced from Dr. Elmer Imes, a professor of physics at Fisk University. Edward apparently became attached to her, and they even collaborated on an unpublished novel. At one point marriage seemed likely, but Edward parted with Nella and eventually returned to Oklahoma to marry another woman; little was heard from Larsen again. Donahoe's ties to Nella Larsen, Langston Hughes, the Johnsons, and author, patron, and photographer Carl Van Vechten make him a marginal figure of the Harlem Renaissance, even though he was a Euro-American from Ponca City, Oklahoma. As late as 1961, Hughes wrote Van Vechten, inquiring of Donahoe's whereabouts; the sad answer was a sanitarium in Albuquerque. From the 1920s through the 1950s, though, Donahoe spent his inheritance traveling in Europe, Mexico, and Connecticut, where he bought a house in the late 1930s.[3]

Donahoe drank heavily, and novelist Kay Boyle and New Critic Robert Stallman—literati who knew Donahoe—believed Edward's excess was spurred by his closeted homosexuality. Donahoe's short story "Head by Scopas," in which two male friends ski naked down a mountainside in the Swiss Alps, was anthologized in the widely taught *Understanding Fiction*, edited by Robert Penn Warren and Cleanth Brooks. In the story, the protagonist tells of how he and his friend "tumbled in the snow, laughing," made "figures and faces in the snow, and drew intricate patterns" with their skis, "occasionally falling down like collapsing kites, laughing and shouting" in their "icy graves." The protagonist's friend, Alan, has lupus and consequently a scarred, discolored face, but he has found a woman who finds his face to be beautiful, like an ancient "Greek fragment." Critics have argued over the work's homoeroticism. In an article, critic Sandra Spanier quotes correspondence between Boyle and Stallman. In response to Stallman's fecund analysis of symbolism he found in the story, Boyle wrote to Stallman, "I, too, know Donahoe and love him dearly." She argued that the only meaningful analysis would be one contemplating the author's "dark, sad shadows of homosexualism and alcoholism," which lend "power and distinction to the story." Stallman, contradicting the New Critical bent of his own published interpretation, admitted in his response to Boyle that the story was about "a couple of homosexuals, one of whom turns away from his friend on falling in love with a girl," but since Stallman knew Donahoe, he "could not publish this kind of interpretation."[4]

Although Donahoe was romantically linked with Larsen, and in 1939 married Helen Bishop, a woman from a rich Oklahoma family, these women were either "beards" or deceived, or he was bisexual. Surely Mathews, who spent much time with him, had some intimation that Donahoe was either gay or bisexual. Susan Kalter, in her introduction to *Twenty Thousand Mornings*, labels Mathews as monolithically homophobic because of occasional negative remarks about particular types of gay men he made in his diaries over the course of more than fifty-five years. But the matter is hardly so simple, as his dateless adolescence and a couple of his experiences in Mexico suggest. He had occasional romantic homosocial feelings, his novel *Sundown* deals with same-sex dynamics thematically, and he frequently associated with friends and family members who were gay or lesbian. Donahoe, one of Jo's best friends and a witness at his wedding, was bisexual if not gay; his first wife's sister, Phyllis, with whom he lived in Pasadena, was a lesbian, as was his daughter Virginia, who formed a de facto marriage with her partner; and his nephew Bill Feighan is a confirmed bachelor. Thus, it is most reductive to pigeonhole Mathews as simply homophobic.

After the wedding, Elizabeth Mathews moved into The Blackjacks—the sandstone, ridgetop house on the Osage prairie Jo had built—and became his coworker in preparing four books, two of them posthumous. With this felicitous new arrangement, Jo felt "like a form of life that has finally found refuge—from myself as well as from many other things." "I am now 'mature,' and if there is anything in me, it will now come out." His marriage to Elizabeth gave him optimism, much-needed help, and shelter from the storm of doubt and insecurity about his choice to remain at The Blackjacks, amongst other internal struggles.[5]

Talking to the Moon, Jo's favorite among his books, was the summation of a decade of observation of animals and nature, and to a lesser extent, of geopolitics. Its publication after lengthy revisions and edits was a milestone. He integrated excerpts from his unpublished political manuscript "Without the Sword" into later chapters

Mathews at The Blackjacks, circa 1945. *Courtesy of the Osage Nation Museum.*

of *Talking to the Moon*, but prior to that, he had juggled the two manuscript ideas with some frustration. Savoie Lottinville at OU Press received the philosophical and political ideas Mathews expressed in "Without the Sword" with ambivalence. An anonymous reader for the press was critical of Mathews's perceived lack of political acumen. Lottinville agreed, explaining that "Without the Sword" would be publishable only after extensive rewriting. Stung, Mathews railed against the ivory tower in 1943: "I am often annoyed with scholars. They take pride in having facts, but their coloration of the facts through their idealism would be disastrous if they were men of action and political influence. Let them sit smugly where they can do no harm, and strut before the youth of the Universities." The reader, blinded from Mathews, was actually Cortez A. M. Ewing, an influential professor of political science and author, who had a fellowship named in his honor at the instigation of Speaker of the House Carl Albert, a former student.[6]

Talking to the Moon successfully combined two different foci, ecological and political, into a poignant study primarily concerned with the natural environment of the Osage hills and prairies, while also describing Osage culture and traditional elders. A critical success and the favorite of many Mathews aficionados, *Talking to the Moon* is an expansive meditation on nature. It eloquently discusses animals' and humans' biological drives and what he called *ornamentation*—an organism's expression not necessary for survival. Critic A. LaVonne Brown Ruoff calls it the "most sophisticated and polished autobiography by an Indian author to be published up to 1945."[7] Yet for an ostensible autobiography, it includes little personal material. For example, Elizabeth and her children, John Hunt and Ann Hunt, who visited The Blackjacks; and his own children, John and Virginia, are not mentioned. At the time of its publication, the book was overlooked in the midst of turbulent global events, including Pacific warfare, the horrific U.S. atomic bombings of Hiroshima and Nagasaki, and Japanese surrender.

The end of World War II enabled Mathews to move on from a psychological state of tentative waiting to devoting himself to his next project, a biography of E. W. Marland, a book he had considered since the 1930s. Mathews was perhaps the ideal biographer of Marland. "Not only had he enjoyed an intimate relationship with Marland," Terry Wilson writes, "he also benefitted from being a trained geologist, amateur naturalist, political observer and activist, as well as a contemplative dweller within the scenes he described."[8]

Ernie Marland was a young man from Pittsburgh who went West to exploit the oil beneath Ponca and Osage lands, becoming "King of Ponca City." An amateur geologist, Marland was innovative in using new technology to locate drilling sites. He was also a charismatic philanthropist and profligate spender who made and lost two fortunes, then eventually made a comeback as governor of Oklahoma during the mid-1930s. Marland was a polarizing figure, "at once a hero—to some, almost a god—and a man who inspired the most intense hatreds," Mathews wrote. Marland is known for bringing the iconic *Pioneer Woman* statue to Ponca City. But behind the scenes, his former close friend supposedly turned archrival Lew Wentz—who traveled to Oklahoma from Pittsburgh with Ernie—stepped in to bankroll the sculpture when Marland's fortunes dissolved.[9]

As close as Mathews and Marland were, their friendship was ambivalent. Mathews regretted the harmful effects of oil derricks and roughnecks on tribal lands and in Osage society. In 1908, one of Marland's first big oil strikes was on land he leased from Willie Cries for War, known as "Willie Cry," adjacent to a sacred Ponca resting place with fully visible wrapped bodies on scaffolds. Mathews writes, "It was interesting to a Pittsburgher to see the well-wrapped bodies, swung onto braided mats supported by four poles. But the silent Poncans awaiting the call of the Great Mysteries did not hold E.W.'s interest long." Ponca Chief White Eagle had been persuaded by the Miller brothers of the famous 101 Ranch, who leased Ponca land, that it would be all right to lease this land to Marland. White Eagle had misgivings, however: he told Marland "he was bringing bad medicine" to everyone involved.[10] He was right.

Marland's surveying, exploration, and drilling of Ponca and Osage homelands (along with the activities of other oilmen) led to dramatic change to both the physical landscape and tribal culture. Because the Osages wisely retained their collective subsurface mineral rights even when they sold land, the tribe became quite wealthy for a time. But they suffered cultural stress from the flood of money and ensuing opportunists and exploiters. Protagonist Chal's response to the despoiled landscape in *Sundown* suggests Mathews regretted the befouling of tribal land. Yet upon graduating from OU in 1920, Mathews initially planned to ask Marland for a job working for his oil company abroad, then decided to attend Oxford instead. Beginning in 1920, the Burbank oilfield on the western Osage reservation brought in vast sums for Marland and Osages with headrights.[11]

Despite Marland's exploitation and desecration of Osage lands, Mathews admired him. Because of his relatively privileged upbringing, Mathews did not blame individual entrepreneurs, geologists, or fieldworkers for the negative effects of industry, instead focusing his ire on low-class "human predators" who arrived later to exploit the Osages after their wealth ballooned between 1917 and 1929. Even in his final years, Mathews found Marland appealing, telling Ponca City reporter Louise Abercrombie: "He was rather unusual because he was both a humanitarian and an ambitious man." In *The Rhetoric of History*, a masterpiece in its own right, Savoie Lottinville cited Mathews's preface to *Life and Death of an Oilman: The Career of E. W. Marland* to exemplify how a preface might evoke a zeitgeist and offer a "glimpse of some of the rascals in it."[12] In his preface, Mathews said he was attracted to Marland's unique personality and his "strange poetic mind," which distinguished him from the "other acquisitive builders of an earlier period of the Age of Freedom." Mathews and Marland possessed deep knowledge of the land and the geologic strata beneath. Both were aesthetes, avid hunters, and Anglophiles. Marland's father was English and in his heyday, Ernie brought polo fields, ponies, and fox hunting to Ponca City, and even imported English fox hunters. "He was a gentleman" and a fascinating failure, Mathews thought—vain, affected, hedonistic, extravagantly philanthropic—and symbolic of the closing of the Age of Freedom. Mathews and Marland enjoyed an "amicable relationship until the end," Bob Gregory said. Despite claims that Mathews mirrored the negative attitude of his protagonist Chal toward the oil industry, Mathews's opinions were much more nuanced. On a

1936 trip to Weatherford, Oklahoma, he found himself surrounded by oil derricks and wrote Elizabeth, "I wish you could see the activity and the result in shining silvery derricks catching the morning sun. I agree with E.W., they are beautiful."[13]

Mathews called his portrait of Marland a "personal impression rather than a biography constructed from documents." Very late in life, Mathews said he knew Marland well for a long time and was "an admirer and observer" of him. Jo "didn't do any guessing," he stressed, relying upon his "own experiences and relations with Marland." Mathews left himself out of the biography entirely, though, so we find no specific record of interactions between the two men. Early on, he became a family friend of the Marlands.[14]

At age twenty-nine, Ernie Marland married Mary Virginia Collins, who went by her middle name. A Philadelphia court stenographer, she was the daughter of Marland's friend, Judge Sam Collins, Sr. In 1908, the couple moved to Oklahoma from Pennsylvania. Virginia's sister lived in straitened circumstances in Flourtown, Pennsylvania. In 1912, it was decided that her two children, George and Lydie Miller Roberts, would live with their aunt and uncle in Oklahoma. Realizing they were unable to have children of their own, in 1916 Virginia and Ernie legally adopted teenaged George and Lydie, who took the Marland surname.

In her younger years, Virginia hosted parties at the Marlands' first mansion on Grand Street, organized charity events, and traveled with Ernie. Over time, however, Virginia's health suffered, and she eventually became an invalid. She died in June 1926, following years of illness and, allegedly, alcoholism. In January 1928, Marland annulled Lydie's adoption and, in July, took her as his bride. Predictably, the press cried scandal. "National reaction was harsh—ranging from scorn to ridicule. Ponca City was more understanding, certainly, but slightly dazed. He was 54; she was 28, and she had never been remotely serious about any other man," Bob Gregory explains.[15]

Mathews's relationship with Marland had deep roots, as he knew Ernie from childhood. Beginning in 1908, he witnessed Marland bidding at oil lease auctions under the "Million Dollar Elm" that stood near the Mathews home on Grandview. Moreover, Jo knew Lydie and George soon after they moved to Ponca City. Circa 1915 George attended OU for a year and probably socialized with Mathews. George later studied at the University of Pittsburgh and Yale University. Mathews was privy to the Marlands' opulent lifestyle, attending parties at their first mansion on Grand Avenue, built during 1914–16. Their lavish home boasted the first indoor swimming pool in the state. The Gatsbyesque soirées and balls the Marlands threw in both this and their second mansion, the palazzo on Monument Road, remain the stuff of legend. Other families of Jo's acquaintance, such as the Donahoes and the Soldanis, joined the fun. A 1922 group photo of a Shakespearean costume party proves Edward Donahoe was part of the Marlands' circle. Edward, as Othello, stands next to George, as Hamlet; Edward's brother Dee stretches out on the floor as Julius Caesar.[16]

Mathews majored in geology at the University of Oklahoma and knew several professors and students who became part of Marland's team. Lucia Ferguson stated Mathews was "a pal to scores of Marland employees," and Walter Campbell (under the nom de plume Stanley Vestal) wrote that Mathews was associated with Marland men not only as a student at OU, but also as an officer during the World War I period. The team included Dr. Irvine Perrine, who was an OU professor for a couple of years; Perrine's student W. C. "Cap" Kite, who became Marland's chief geologist while still an undergraduate; and football hero F. P. "Spot" Geyer, known for his precise "spot pass." In 1915, All-American Geyer captained the Sooners through an undefeated season and was posthumously inducted into the College Football Hall of Fame. Mathews was in the Pick and Hammer club with Cap and Spot. Marland met Perrine in 1912. The state geologist had run into unnamed problems, so Perrine drove up to Ponca to help. In the lobby of the Arcade Hotel, Marland wheedled out of Perrine an informal crash course in the geology of the Red Beds Plains geological region as they talked late into the night. Thereafter Perrine drove up from Norman to Ponca City on weekends and holidays to survey the fields with Marland, finally leaving OU to work for him full time. In spring 1915, while Mathews was a geology student, Perrine and Kite both joined the geological department of Marland's company. That term, Mathews earned an "A" for a paper on the "stratigraphy of the Red Beds on which we stood." When Marland made his first big oil strike on Ponca land, he gained recognition for finding oil on the Red Beds Plains, covering much of western Osage County, which until then had generally been believed to be bereft of oil.[17]

Mathews was abroad or in California during Marland's 1920s heyday, and so fell out of the Marland sphere, missing the construction of the second Marland home, "The Palace on the Prairie," a dazzling Florentine mansion lavish with ornate decor and art treasures. Ironically, by the time the manse was finished in 1928, E.W. and Lydie were only able to live there for less than a year because of E.W.'s lost fortunes and the exorbitant cost of maintenance. The couple later dwelled in the outlying chauffer's cottage. In 1929, Marland lost his business to what he called the "Wolves of Wall Street" after a hostile takeover by the J. P. Morgan Company, and in November he resigned as president of Marland Oil Company. Marland Oil became Continental, then Conoco Oil. Mathews and Marland both financially overextended themselves prior to the Depression, leaving them vulnerable to the crash.[18]

While Marland was governor of Oklahoma, Mathews got to know him much better. During the 1930s, Mathews visited the Marland mansion "often, and when he was governor he had his offices there" in Ponca City. State politics was Marland's revival, beginning with his service in the U.S. House of Representatives in 1933–34. In the midst of the traumatic Dust Bowl, Marland was elected governor in 1934 on a pledge to bring the New Deal to Oklahoma. Mathews actively supported Marland's campaign, publishing a long endorsement in the Pawhuska newspaper. His piece is discursive, surprisingly manipulative, and marred by logical fallacy. In October 1934, Marland gave a campaign speech in Pawhuska at the Kihekah Theater, along with his friend, Congressman Disney; onstage was Chief Lookout.[19]

Immediately after entering office, Marland appointed Mathews to the Oklahoma Board of Education, even though Mathews had no experience in this area. Mathews spent eighteen months on the board, but was highly active only during the first. In January 1935, he visited several schools in Louisiana and Oklahoma. Alongside the state superintendent, a delegation including Jo visited African American elementary schools and a rural high school near Shreveport, and enjoyed a rendition of "Swing Low, Sweet Chariot." "I am extremely glad I came," Mathews enthused in his diary. On returning to Oklahoma, they visited Durant, Sulphur, Edmond, and Oklahoma City. Mathews was working long days, rare for him.[20]

Marland, however, later asked Mathews and another board member, Chester Westfall, to resign their positions because they were not qualified. "I was 'axed' from this board, fortunately, before I neglected my blackjacks too much," Mathews remarked in *Talking to the Moon*. Mathews was facetious to a reporter: "the request for my resignation was an acknowledgement of my services to the state." The state superintendent said "the law provides there must be two practical school men with four years' experience" on the board. Yet observers discerned other motives behind the ouster. Mathews and Westfall reportedly had fought to prevent Oklahoman public schools from becoming "regimented politically," and Marland allegedly had tried to force all state employees to donate to or work for his senatorial campaign. In addition, Mathews said rumor had it he "intended to introduce Latin and Greek into the schools," but his "'axing' had, in fact a political significance. Under the influence of a natural background freshness, one can go too far."[21] The fact that Marland in essence fired Mathews did not, however, dampen their friendship long.

Marland was perhaps an idealistic governor, and some of his achievements were notable. But on the whole, he was not skilled in working the system to get things done. If nothing else, he put his own stamp on the position. As Bob Gregory elaborates, "The Oklahoma City oilfield had opened about five years earlier, but the state was getting none of the money. Marland changed that. He called out the National Guard, declared the state capitol grounds a zone of martial law, and staked the first well." His duty as "Dust Bowl Governor" was unenviable. Even though "much of his economic recovery program was not put into effect," Marland's efforts "brought relief and hope to many thousands of Oklahomans and started the state back on the road to economic recovery," Michael Everman claims. On the other hand, Marland's administration was associated with corruption, and at times he feared impeachment. In 1937, Marland displeased Mathews when he granted parole to Ernest Burkhart, a key player in the 1920s Osage Reign of Terror murders.[22]

By the early 1930s, Mathews already envisioned a biography of his colorful and eccentric friend. Between 1932 and 1951, the project "was never far from Mathews' mind," Lottinville wrote. The period after Marland's term as governor was a time of disappointment, as he ran for the Senate twice and lost, in 1936 and 1938. Mathews accompanied Marland during this period, when he and Lydie had been forced to move into the chauffer's cottage. Reminiscent of *Citizen Kane*, the former millionaire sat and talked, invited friends to swim, put on his swimming trunks, but just watched. "He wasn't bitter, just unhappy," Mathews told Gregory. "He didn't complain to us who knew him well, who were with him quite often." Mathews sat poolside and spurred Marland's memories with judicious questions.[23]

At first, Mathews intended to collaborate on the biography with Seward Sheldon, Marland's former treasurer and a newspaper editor for the *Cleveland Press*. While in Cleveland, Ohio, in April 1943, Mathews conversed with Sheldon at length. Since Seward had been Marland's treasurer and had acted as a liaison between Marland Oil Company and J. P. Morgan, he knew the gory "details of the company's finances and its bizarre history." Mathews said he "finally got Seward to agree that we should collaborate on a book" narrating a "vignette of a phase in the development of America, especially its wild exploitation of natural resources." It is unknown why the collaboration did not continue. Mathews had gone there not only to discuss co-authorship with Sheldon but also to have his *Talking to the Moon* manuscript typed up by a secretary hired by his brother-in-law, Congressman Michael Feighan, husband of his youngest sister Florence.[24]

Marland, whom Mathews dubbed an emblematic man of his times, died in 1941, at age sixty-seven, of a heart condition. In the mid-1940s, as Mathews researched more intensely, old friends connected to Marland re-emerged. In 1946, Sheldon hosted a cocktail party for Mathews at the Jens-Marie Hotel in Ponca, inviting twenty-one of Marland's friends and associates he thought could be useful to Jo's research. No doubt Jo gained contacts and potential insights. More notable, however, was a visit from Jo's old Ponca pals Lydie and George Marland, accompanied by Edward Donahoe. In August 1943, Mathews wrote that he went into Pawhuska to meet them at Elizabeth's house. "Glad to see Edward and Lyde [*sic*] again, having last seen both of them when they came to visit me at the hospital April a year ago [after the car accident]. Edward brought me a most beautiful pair of fur gloves, which his friend Lord Cecil Churchill had left after his visit in Hollywood. We sat in temperature of at least 107 at Dibbs' house and drank mint juleps. Later George Marland joined us. We had dinner in the yard." George, who was in the oil business, had moved to Tulsa after his adopted father's death.[25]

This meeting of Edward, Lydie, George, Jo, and Dibbs two years after Marland's passing is surprising. For one thing, in 1937 Donahoe, the black sheep of his prominent family, had published *Madness in the Heart*. Recalling Truman Capote's scandalous roman à clef *Answered Prayers*, the novel was the *Answered Prayers* of Ponca City for its defamation of Marland and other local figures through fictional proxies.

Donahoe's novel centers on a family curse and a father's revenge on his daughters, and includes a cast of minor characters based on real persons. One of them, clearly resembling Marland in the 1920s, is vain, aloof, and cruel. His criticism of his wife's weight gain and drinking leads her to take her own life. Virginia Marland's official cause of death was pneumonia, but she was rumored to have killed herself; her friends claimed Marland was callous and unfaithful. Kim Brumley, author of *Marland Tragedy*, believes Edward had inside knowledge of the "guarded details of Virginia's death." A sybarite, Marland loved youth and beauty, in men and women alike, and when Virginia became ill and her beauty faded, Marland grew cold and had little sympathy for her suffering. "He refused to be without youth; it must be around him in the persons of others, since his own was gone. His attitude toward Virginia's illness and death" seemed to be one of "hurt vanity," Mathews wrote. *Madness in the Heart* caused Donahoe to be ostracized by residents of his hometown, who called him crazy for maligning the Marlands and his own family. Edward's father, D. J. Donahoe, Sr., reportedly bought all available copies and burnt them.[26]

Mathews was not left out of Donahoe's roman à clef. He is styled as Raoul de Noailles, an incidental character jocosely reflecting Jo's French ancestry and suavity. The narrator describes Pawhuska and the millions paid to the tribe: "A great deal of this money was squandered in riotous living. Some of it was stolen by the kind of white rogues who have swindled the Indian since Puritan days in New England. A few of the more imaginative Osages used their money, while they had it, traveling and living in Europe." Like Mathews, this Pawhuskan "went to Oxford, where his success was extraordinary. Because he was handsome, amusing, extravagant, and a great hunter like his forebears who hunted buffalo across the plains, he was a favorite of the English aristocracy." The protagonist first meets Raoul in London in 1921, a year when Jo visited London at least twice. After Raoul returned to America, he "retired to his ranch in the Osage Nation and devoted himself to writing about his own people." Since Mathews saw Donahoe several times in 1937, the year of the novel's publication, he was no doubt aware of his characterization.[27]

At Oxford, Mathews had befriended the Earl of Cardigan ("Card"), whom he later introduced to Edward when the latter traveled to England in 1935. An author of several books, Cardigan provided the model for the Earl of Chawton in *Madness in the Heart*. In 1948, Card stayed for several days with Edward. Mathews, who had not seen Card for a quarter-century, came up to visit, and Donahoe threw him a party at the home of his brother and sister-in-law. But before the party ended, Edward was "taken home in a rather stupid condition; he had 'fallen from the wagon,' after two weeks of sanity." The previous fall, Mathews spent a weekend with Edward in Norman to attend a Sooners football game. At that time, he concluded that Donahoe was "deteriorating through constant drinking" and might be called an alcoholic.[28]

Mathews, who drank heavily throughout his adult life, found a foil in Edward, against whom he could differentiate his own regular, sometimes heavy, drinking from that of a "real" alcoholic. From the 1920s on, Mathews sometimes drank to excess and suffered hangovers. Beginning in the 1950s, his diaries detail frequent liquor store purchases, which until 1959 entailed driving to Elgin, Kansas, because Oklahoma was dry. At The Blackjacks, he dumped his empties in the ravine; in 1956 he remarked, "it seems quite impossible that so much can accumulate so fast." Mathews's visits to Ponca City to meet with former Marland associates usually involved drinking; Marland's men were "awesomely heavy drinkers—and the alcoholic causalities are legend," Gregory writes. Although Mathews habitually drank, he never appeared drunk; thus, some regarded him as a functioning alcoholic.[29]

If Mathews was depressed by Edward's dissolution, he was uplifted and inspired by the visit of his old Oxford chum, Lord Cardigan. "I hadn't realized how isolated I have been, and how limited to conversation about local affairs, cattle and business. It is inspiring to be assured that there are people in the world whose interests are much like mine, and that I am not a queer sort of person out of step with the man-environment of my community, therefore out of step with the world of man-civilization." Throughout his life, Mathews worried over being "queer" and "out of step," as did his protagonist Chal in *Sundown*. An Anglophile, Jo's enthusiasm for Cardigan reveals Oxford nostalgia and a longing to be among elegant, cultured people. In 1954, Jo worried about his lack of intellectual stimulation: "I have become as a tree, I am taking root. I have begun to live by the thought and standards of this community of mediocrity. I seem unable to help myself. Is it too late?"[30]

Mathews spent a great deal of time in the postwar 1940s conducting interviews with Marland's friends and associates. In 1946, he and Elizabeth traveled to Ponca to visit Jane Clark, who had remained a close friend to Marland until the end, and had at one time lived in his mansion. They talked about E.W. for ten hours straight, then all morning and afternoon the following day! On the first night of their visit, Mr. Cosgrove of Continental Oil and his wife came over, and they talked of Marland until midnight. Cosgrove said he would give Mathews a letter of introduction to George Whitney of J. P. Morgan in New York. These were key players in the Marland drama. Mathews found his interlocutors willing to help, believing with him that Marland was a subject worthy of a biography.[31]

Closest of all to Marland was not a wife or lover, but rather one of his "handsome young men," John Hale. In 1946 and 1948, Jo visited with John and his wife, Cecilia Hale in Ponca five times to discuss John's intimate friend, Ernie. The most important person in Marland's mature life, Hale was the tycoon's personal secretary through thick and thin, even when Ernie could not pay him. In 1929, Marland made Hale the president of his new company, E. W. Marland, Inc. John possessed an aura of sensitivity and refinement that both Marland and Mathews loved. He had a "special mixture for his pipe and could talk about wine and food and books and art," Mathews wrote. In *Life and Death of an Oilman* the reader learns much more about Hale than either of Marland's wives; moreover, the story of Ernie and John's emerging relationship is narrated as a courtship. Whereas most readers felt Mathews treated Marland fairly in the biography, Hale was critical in his review. Although he praised *Life and Death of an Oilman* as a "magnificent job done in a masterly manner," he felt Mathews too often belittled Marland and attributed his successes to luck: "his misfortunes are attributed to his bad judgment, vanity, lack of ruthfulness and the fact that he was born a gentleman. Favorable comment is usually weakened by a qualifying word or phrase." Hale closed his review by wishing Jo had "dealt with more sympathy and had placed more emphasis on the qualities of sincere kindness, innate gentleness of spirit, and boon companionship in E.W. which inspired the loyalty and affection of his friends."[32]

The long and winding road to publication of *Life and Death of an Oilman* is a drama in itself, the cast of which featured Joseph Brandt at Henry Holt, Savoie Lottinville at OU Press, and Bill Couch at the University of Chicago Press, as the manuscript shuttled between these three publishers. These shifts followed the career path of Brandt. He founded OU Press in 1928 and remained there for a decade before becoming director of Princeton University Press. In 1941, Brandt was appointed president of OU, but left in 1943 amidst controversy to become director of the University of Chicago Press. In July 1945 he moved on to New York, becoming president of the major publishing house Henry Holt. In 1944, after visiting Brandt in Chicago to work out details of publishing *Talking to the Moon*, Jo wrote Elizabeth to report success: the University of Chicago Press offered "$2,500 and a Newbury [*sic*] scholarship to do Marland." After spending ten days in early 1945 in Chicago, Mathews noted that his Marland manuscript was "due at the end of the year." This deadline was later pushed back to the end of 1946, but Mathews still did not meet it.[33]

Mathews had difficulty fulfilling his deadlines in part because the scope of the project was broader than he had anticipated. In late 1945, Mathews wrote in his diary of feeling daunted by the complexity of his subject, who represented diverse aspects of the American character. Marland took on myriad symbolic meanings: "He begins to embody man in America: the acquisitive, selfish, dreaming, generous, vain, childish man, fumbling for God and searching for beauty; expressing himself under the influence of the pleasant history of the United States," Jo wrote in his diary. By March 1946, Mathews had done much research but had written only a synopsis, which he sent to Chicago. Mathews waxed poetic to Brandt: "He 'fits my pistol' perfectly, but his story looms like a mountain, with myself at the bottom of a canyon that receives only noonday rays of light. It seems that I shall never be able to look at it from the plain." Mathews had no idea then that it would take him nearly six years to write, revise, and finally publish the book. "I didn't realize what I was getting into when I first conceived the idea of biography. It is really optimistic of me who never wrote in this form to choose a gem with so many facets," he wrote Brandt. Mathews did not actually finish the first draft until 1949.[34]

By 1948, Mathews had re-envisioned his book less as a formal biography and more as an impressionistic account appealing to a popular audience. Therefore, the University of Chicago Press, which had published *Talking to the Moon*, now seemed less than a perfect fit. With Brandt having moved on, the new director, Bill Couch, concurred. In 1948, Couch took steps to get out of the contract. Chicago had expected a complete manuscript by the end of 1946; two years later, Couch wrote Lottinville, asking him if he would take over the contract. Couch remarked that he had not heard from Mathews and had no idea when the manuscript would be finished. He stressed he had not told Mathews about this offer, and would wait to hear back from Lottinville. If OU Press wasn't interested, then Couch would probably offer the contract to Brandt at Holt, he said.[35]

One might have anticipated that Lottinville, having worked closely with Mathews for many years, would be happy to publish the Marland biography, but this was not then the case. Four years previous, Lottinville was stung upon learning Mathews would publish *Talking to the Moon* with Brandt at Chicago, and not with OU Press, as he had believed. Savoie had been working with Jo on an early draft of this work. In late 1944, Savoie sent Mathews a terse note; he had just read an article by Brandt in the *Chicago Sun* forecasting publication of *Talking to the Moon*. "Old loyalties, I suppose, are strongest, but I had no idea that you were doing anything but revising the manuscript for us. I guess I was mistaken." Lottinville's understanding of the scenario is supported by letters from 1944. Lottinville worked for two years to obtain funding, finally securing foundation funding for a "substantial advance" for the book. Had he not learned the book was going to Chicago, he would have written Mathews within days to tell him of this good fortune. A month later, Jo wrote a long response to Lottinville's note, explaining his decision and why he had not shared it, citing "animal defense" in a time of economic pressure. Despite careful explanations, Mathews seemed unapologetic, claiming his move was a necessary "business proposition."[36] Having worked so hard to secure funding, Lottinville was not sympathetic to Jo's rationale that he went to Brandt for economic reasons.

Savoie replied to Couch that after careful deliberation, he felt the best course of action would be to offer the Marland book to Brandt at Henry Holt. Brandt was the major reason Chicago had planned to publish the biography in the first place. Had Lottinville not been let down, doubtless he would have taken on the Marland contract, because, as he wrote Couch, he believed an "editor working closely with Mathews can do both himself and the author a lot of good. That's what I was doing on the book you ultimately published." He opined, "under discipline, Mathews is a superlative writer, as witnessed by *Wah'Kon-Tah*: without it, he may not jell at all."[37]

Lottinville was a generous person attuned to Jo's wavelength. He told Mathews that when he read Brandt's announcement, he felt like a "jaybird who was blithely flying along and suddenly had all of his tail feathers knocked off by an eagle." Revealing a deep understanding of Mathews's milieu, he continued: "By way of animal defense, I'm going to stay under the blackjacks and eat acorn until my tail assembly grows out again. I see no need of squabbling with the eagle (Ouashashe Hule) or his companion (Chicago Hule), because we have hunted these prairies, each in his own way, and with an understanding of the ecological role of the others, for so long that squabbling would be repugnant. After all, balance and repose make the most fundamental law of nature, and disturbances always adjust themselves to it." His tail feathers grew back; by 1948, the two had patched up their friendship, thanks to an overture from Lottinville.[38]

Once Lottinville passed on the Marland contract, Couch wrote Brandt at Holt, offering it to him. Couch asked Brandt, as he had asked Lottinville, not to tell Mathews of the offer. Regardless, Brandt wrote Mathews in February 1948, expressing his sincere hope that Holt could publish the Marland book and requesting a new précis to learn how Jo's concept of the book had changed. Mathews replied, expressing his pleasure in the proposed transfer. Optimistically, Jo assured Brandt he could have the manuscript complete in time for publication in the fall. Mathews was eager to work with Brandt again, as they had done in the early 1930s, and wanted his Marland bio to be "published by a commercial press." Two weeks later, Brandt begged Mathews to send him the first seven chapters "almost immediately," and in March, assured Jo he wanted to work quickly "to get this three-way decision resolved."[39]

Mathews was interested in Holt not only because of his changed vision of the Marland book, then tentatively titled "The Wolf of Reality," but also because he felt he needed to earn money by writing. Mathews added a stepson and stepdaughter to his family when he and Elizabeth wed in 1945. His first wife continued to pursue him for financial support, and that year a court ordered that Mathews pay up. During the postwar 1940s, writing became for Mathews a means of earning needed income, not simply the leisured pursuit of a cultured gentleman with an assured "natural income" from his Osage headright. "As matters stand with me," he told Brandt in April 1948, "I shall probably spend the rest of my life writing, and for the first time in my life, I am really serious about it. It must be either that or politics, since I can't live on my independent income. Hence the sooner I become associated with a commercial press, the better for my comfort."[40]

Under financial pressure, in 1948 and 1949 Mathews wrote a series of short stories he viewed as fundraisers for the Marland project. Unfortunately, he did not publish any. Although many of them were well crafted, his literary agent, Brandt and Brandt (no known relation to Joe), returned half of them and could not place the rest deemed to have potential. Mathews, who wrote with nuance, was a commercial failure in the late 1940s story market, perhaps because his style seemed slightly old-fashioned to modern magazine editors who admired Ernest Hemingway, F. Scott Fitzgerald, and the latest sensation, J. D. Salinger. One interesting story Mathews wrote during this period was "The Apache Woman," which tells of a party of Osage warriors raiding an Apache camp, wishing to collect a scalp to appease Wah'Kon-Tah. They find only empty lodges until they discover a figure dressed in the elaborate garb of a chief, whom, they realize, is actually a sick old woman in disguise. Before learning her identity, one warrior hits her with a coup stick and another drives an ax into her skull. This Apache ruse was not only a great insult to the Osages, but also a devastating injury: she transmitted smallpox to them. Soon the Beaver Band of Osages was "wiped out." Mathews concludes that intertribal conflict on the Plains had advanced to the level of biological "virus warfare."[41]

Along with stories, in 1949 Mathews dashed off a novel called "Within Your Dream." In 1951, Jo told J. Frank Dobie that the novel manuscript, now lost, was "on the laps of the gods in New York" and he had heard nothing definite. It tells the story of "a boy whose family scratched at a sandstone ridge here in the Osage. He, through his acquisitiveness and energy, rose from this boyhood semi-starvation to tremendous wealth (oil again). His tragedy was that, having acquired his millions, he became childish and pitiable in his middle age in his attempt to project his then unutilized energy into the fields of thought and culture." Mathews revised this manuscript through 1955 and met a deadline with Boston publisher Little, Brown, only to have the novel rejected. At the close of 1949, Mathews reflected he had "worked harder at the typewriter" that year than ever before. "I shall continue to write for the next four months of the year," and on through 1950, "not awaiting the judgment of the gods, not letting" whatever "they hand down, good or bad, disturb my industry the least bit," Mathews vowed. But all work and no play made 1949 the dullest year ever. "The magic of living was gone—because I had played the fool the few preceding years."[42]

Holt did not pick up the Marland contract. Traveling to New York in the summer of 1948, Jo found trouble afoot at the publisher. Brandt had been asked to fire employees and felt insecure about his own job. Given these financial losses, Holt was reluctant to buy the contract. "So they hesitated and criticized, and suggested some re-writing. I agreed with them about some re-writing, but 'considerable' revision I couldn't see." After his visit, Mathew declared, "I would never consent that they take the Marland; it will stay with the Chicago Press." In any event, the next month Brandt left Holt to start a journalism school at UCLA. Without Brandt, there was scant interest in publishing the book. With Holt no longer an option, the contract remained at Chicago, where Jo submitted the full draft manuscript in 1949. After review, Jo received a letter from associate editor Fred Wieck. "His readers were very kind to me," Jo said. They wanted him to make some cuts, inject "more anecdotes and conversation" to lighten the "tragic tone," and enliven the "dull spots" so they match "what he [Wieck] called 'brilliant passages,'" Jo wrote Brandt.[43]

Storm clouds appeared on the horizon, however. After Jo made the requested changes for Chicago and the manuscript was prepared for publication in fall 1950, "at the last minute Couch got some idea that there ought to be more about the first Mrs. Marland." Mathews bristled. "This very unpleasant phase I sidestepped rather gracefully, since I had known Lydie and George since boyhood, and since there is still much bitter feeling in the family and among the acquaintances of both sides," Mathews told Lottinville. Virginia's friends said Marland mistreated her; supporting this assessment are Virginia's drunken public accusations of Ernie's flagrant adultery, described in Gregory's "The Marland Mystery." Her friends' account of their later marriage seemed a "Greek tragedy in which she played the most tragic role during the last years in the big house on Grand Avenue," Mathews wrote in the biography. He refused to elaborate further in print, not wanting to hurt Lydie and George, and perhaps also following the maxim "judge not, that ye be not judged." Instead he asked for the contract to be cancelled; Couch happily complied. Jo expressed his bitterness and frustration to Brandt: "That damnable, hag-ridden Marland MS is still unpublished, partly due to my stubbornness and partly due to Couch's whims." Thus, Virginia Collins Marland is rarely mentioned in *Life and Death of an Oilman*, and when she is, Mathews equivocates rather than criticize his old friend.[44]

Mathews then began to think of his first publisher, OU Press, as a fitting home for the book, hoping that Lottinville would respect his desire to be discreet about Marland's domestic life. Jo told Lottinville he was actually pleased by the Chicago debacle, because he planned to transform the biography into fiction, reasoning it might make a "first-rate novel" rather than what he modestly deemed a "second-rate biography." Before he did so, however, he wanted to see what Savoie thought of the manuscript as it stood. "The point is I can't bring myself to destroy the MS in its present form without letting you see it." Savoie declared, "I find in it some of the best writing you have ever done." The Flying Dutchman manuscript finally found a home![45]

In May 1951, Jo had an opportunity to check facts with a crowd of Marland people who gathered in Ponca for the dedication of the E. W. Marland statue by Jo Davidson. A renowned sculptor who lived for a time in his own studio at the Marland mansion, Davidson also crafted likenesses of George and Lydie—with whom, it was rumored, he carried on an affair. In his memoir, *Between Sittings*, Davidson wrote of E.W. after his death: "What an extraordinary man he is. What a lonely soul—having all the world can give, materially, but nothing can give him spiritual and sentimental peace." After the celebration of Marland, Mathews felt he had E.W. down cold.[46]

Life and Death of an Oilman was released in October 1951. The biography has not received as much scholarly attention as Mathews's other books, in part because at first glance it seems outside the concerns of Indian literature. An Osage critical perspective occasionally emerges in the biography, however. For example, Mathews notes the government was indiscriminate in punishing tribes who supported the Confederacy in even the slightest degree: "After the Civil War, the United States government made new treaties with the Indian tribes. The fact that the Cherokee and the Osage had been divided in their loyalties between the North and South, and that parts of each tribe had fought with the Union armies, had little significance to men bent on housecleaning. They forced the Cherokee to cede parts of the Outlet, and they placed thereon, in diminished reservations, the Osage, Pawnee, Ponca, Otoe, Missouria, Nez Percé (later Tonkawa), and the Kansa." This of course led to conflict between the Cherokees and other tribes. Later, during frenzied construction of roads and derricks, an Osage elder out on the prairie looking for his horses stops to observe, "them White mens ack like tomorrow there will be no more worl'."[47]

This critical perspective also shows in a sketch Mathews made for the book. Lottinville, finding Jo's art too amateurish, commissioned drawings by J. Craig Sheppard, most of them based upon sometimes superior work by Mathews. Simple and often charming, Jo's ink sketches represent more richly the role of Ponca and Osage land and culture in the Marland saga than Sheppard's professional counterparts do. Most strikingly, Mathews limned Marland's first oil-producing well on Ponca land adjacent to a sacred Ponca resting place. In the right foreground is the oil derrick, and in the left background, appearing fairly close by, are several Ponca dead on raised scaffolds; in Sheppard's version, however, the derricks are missing, de-emphasizing the sacrilege committed.[48]

During Marland's final slippage into the great beyond, Mathews imagined scenes from his life flashing by, haunting him with visions of Poncas whose resting place he defiled. At the time he first surveyed the land, Marland had expressed "perfunctory wonderment at the burial customs of the Ponca," but immediately turned to examining the hill for drilling prospects, loving the clanking of wells that to him sang, "dollar, dollar, dollar." The Ponca dead were not to be forgotten so easily, however, emerging from the depths of memory in his final moments. This image forms an effective critique of Marland's dealings with Indians. Marland was hardly the worst example in this regard, however. To his credit, among many other philanthropic acts, he financed an Osage language dictionary to be produced by the Smithsonian. Bob Gregory says one reason Mathews liked Marland was "he didn't try to screw Indians." Yet Marland's ignorance showed when he stood to speak before a group of Osages at a tribal feast, people whose land he exploited and whose traditions and culture were undermined by oil riches. Mathews describes him turning to a friend—surely Mathews himself—and whispering, "What shall I say—I don't know what to say. Tell me what I ought to say."[49]

In Mathews's next project, *The Osages*, which occupied him for much of the next decade, he refocused on his people. In a sense, he had been researching this book all of his life. In the meantime, his financial worries were abated by the relative success of *Life and Death of an Oilman* and an increase in headright payments. In 1952, Jo was happily surprised at the amount of his first royalty check for the book. The biography was a critical success, praised in the *New York Times* by J. Frank Dobie, who had visited Jo and Elizabeth at The Blackjacks. The Texan called it wise and mature in style, perspective, scope, and interpretive power, and praised Jo's deep knowledge of Osage and Ponca land. For his part, Jo was relieved to be done with the project. He was never satisfied that the biography was truly finished, since he doubted he had successfully conveyed Marland's embodiment of "individualism's last stand." To Lottinville he confessed, "I shall always look at this child in the beautiful green jacket, at its beautiful form and typography, and think of it as a rather doubtful Caesarian birth." Readers and critics disagreed. Lottinville shared that Edwin C. McReynolds, a prize-winning history professor at OU who in that decade published *Oklahoma: A History of the Sooner State* and *The Seminoles*, proclaimed it a masterpiece "absolutely indispensable to an understanding of the development of Oklahoma." In 1956, Mathews recalled in his diary that upon requesting an inscribed book, businessman and bibliophile Everette DeGolyer quipped good-naturedly that the book's title should have been *Life and Scenery of an Oilman*.[50]

Jo's turn away from oilmen and industry to a renewed, enlivened relation to his Osage culture was emblematized by his and Elizabeth's hosting of Rita Lottinville and her daughters and friends at the I'n-Lon-Schka dances in Hominy in summer 1952. Both his renewed focus and his role as intermediary between Euro-Americans and Osages are suggested by this happy experience at Hominy. Jo and Elizabeth drove into Pawhuska to dine with their guests at the Duncan Hotel, then all eight drove to Hominy to experience the vivid Osage dances. Standing in a row, the "five very attractive young girls" watched intently: "diminutive Elinor Lottinville, then Sara Crocker from Groton, Massachusetts, daughter of Groton's headmaster. Next was Jean Valentine from Boston, then Mary Jean Caldwell, daughter of Princeton's football coach. Then Marie Lottinville, Rita and Dibbs on the end. Harry Redeagle with bells tinkling and scalplock quivering came over to shake hands with each girl. Paul Pitts (newly chosen chief) came over" too. Mathews offers an indelible image of cross-cultural interaction and respect. Mathews reconnected with Osage culture and renewed friendship with the Lottinville family after a stressful patch with Savoie, who later sent his thanks: "No bunch of women ever had a grander time than ours did in your and Elizabeth's company." It was a bright moment, one that no one involved would forget.[51]

Chapter Ten

SLOW MELT THROUGH TIME

The Osage history book at home . . . started at the Ice Age and proceeded through time in a slow melt.

—Dennis McAuliffe, Jr., *Bloodlands*

From 1952 to 1962, Mathews traveled with Elizabeth, assisted the tribe, and researched, wrote, and promoted a masterpiece, *The Osages: Children of the Middle Waters* (1961). Especially during the late 1950s, Mathews was hard at work on his massive tribal history. His research entailed trips to the University of Oklahoma, the Oklahoma Historical Society, and many other places, study of Osage vocabulary, and consultation with scholars such as anthropologist Alice Marriott. Most enriching, Jo conducted extensive interviews with full-blood elders and other Osages, which took him inside traditional homes and expanded his sense of connection to his tribal heritage. For example, in 1959, Mathews visited Freddie Lookout and his sister Mary Lookout Standing Bear to discuss ancient Osage customs. "It was extremely comfortable to sit and talk with quiet, unpretentious people. Their voices were low even in disagreement. I suddenly remembered why I have always admired the Osages." Jo interviewed Freddie several times.[1]

After the arduous path toward publication of *Life and Death of an Oilman*, Mathews needed a break. In February 1952 he said he had accomplished little since late November, "when quail season opened." Three months were "given over to hunting, reading and traveling. Wonderful!" Mathews didn't loaf for long, though; by April he was in a preliminary research stage, studying maps and documents. During this period, his financial situation improved, facilitating his investigation.[2]

Mathews remained an advocate for the Osages on crucial tribal issues. During the early 1950s, the Osages—with special help from Mathews, George Labadie, and Buddy Gray—fought to have the tribe removed from the misguided, even cruel federal termination bill. The tribe was one of ten that Congress regarded as fit to sever from federal recognition and oversight. The urgent need to reject the loss of tribal sovereignty and support temporarily united the Osages, who had splintered into factions, as they would again later in the decade. During 1952–53, Mathews helped write a report, *The Osage People and Their Trust Property*, elucidating ways in which the tribe had been exploited, to support the argument that federal trusteeship of the Osages should continue. In 1953, he visited the Osage Agency to urge the tribal council to develop "definite policy to put against that of the Federal Government." According to Roberta Ulrich, no termination bill hearings were held for tribes other than the Osages, "who lined up the entire Oklahoma congressional delegation to oppose their termination bill," showing their clout.[3]

In early 1952, Jo traveled to Washington, D.C., on behalf of the Osage Tribal Council, though he was not at that time a councilman. He paid a visit to his youngest sister, Florence, and her husband, Congressman Michael A. Feighan, who was raised in an affluent Irish-Catholic household in Lakewood, Ohio, adjacent to Cleveland. Michael's father, John Feighan, co-founded Standard Brewing Company in Cleveland, which produced Erin Brew, befriended John F. Kennedy's father, Joseph, and later became a successful banker. Michael graduated from Princeton and earned a law degree from Harvard before joining four brothers in the Feighan law firm. Beginning in 1937, Feighan sustained an epic political career, serving in the U.S. House of Representatives as a Democrat representing Ohio from 1943 all the way to 1971. During Michael's twenty-eight years in Congress, Florence "organized her own Capitol Hill home tours for disabled servicemen and their families," served as president of the 78th Congress Club, and advocated for American Indian rights, according to the *Washington Post*. After losing their firstborn son in 1942, Michael and Florence were left with two children: William "Bill" Mathews Feighan (b. 1934) and Florence Marie "Fleur" Feighan (b. 1940). Michael Feighan, who knew President Kennedy and worked closely with President Johnson, was one of Mathews's numerous political connections in Washington. In 1949 Mathews stayed with them while he met with the commissioner of Indian affairs in Washington, D.C. During his 1952 visit, Mathews ironically evoked Florence and Michael's untidy domestic life. To him, the family embodied jittery Cold War "tensions of the age," and Bill and Fleur ignored their parents.[4]

Over the decades, Mathews interacted with many powerful officials in the capital and received various offers of positions. During his 1952 visit, Cy Fryer of the State Department offered Mathews "a job in either Iran or Ethiopia." In the 1940s, Fryer had been superintendent of the Navajo reservation under Collier, who held him in high esteem. While Mathews lunched with former BIA commissioner William

Zimmerman, in walked Edward B. Swanson, assistant director of the Oil and Gas Division of the Department of the Interior, wanting to talk about *Life and Death of an Oilman*. Swanson said that even though Mathews "didn't give E.W. enough credit," the biography was a "damned good picture of E.W. and the oil industry." Later, Swanson invited Jo to his office to ask if he would be interested in writing the history of the Gulf Oil Company. "The Venezuela part of it sounds good," Mathews replied. Paralleling Collier's philosophy, he continued, "I am at present deeply interested in South America from the point of view of Hemispheric unity." He didn't take the offered position, however, or write the history of Gulf Oil. Nor did he pen the biographies of Senator Thomas Gore, Judge R. L. Williams, oilman Bill Skelly, or President Harding, all projects proposed to or considered by him. Instead, he focused on his tribe and gradually produced *The Osages*, one of the grandest books ever written by a Native author.[5]

In the 1950s, Mathews faced challenge, loss, and disillusionment. In February 1952 he experienced a humbling revelation about humanity and the meaning of adulthood, or the lack thereof, its specific prompt unclear. "The older I become, I wonder that I ever took man at his own valuation. It is only just now I realize the grown-upness in man was always an illusion. Somewhere in my mind is a criterion, inspired, nurtured through the years, that is artificial and has always been invented by man's own egotism and assumptions," he wrote. "Only just now am I able to see man as a boy grown in body, and assuming a dignity which is not his. Like his gods and his other creations, it is pure illusion." Human beings lacked the natural "dignity of a bull wapiti, a range stallion or a lion." To Mathews this was "a terrible thing to understand. It separates one from his fellowmen in some subtle manner, and weakens hope and ambition." In May, Jo remained depressed and wondered why he had even set out to write. "Today I feel that writing is stupid. If you write for money, you must write for the great mass of Christians, who love sex, murder, and God. If you write for the personal pleasure" of writing, you won't be understood. "If you must write literary merchandise, you would do much better going into oil or cattle, and keep your conscience clean." Give the masses what they want, "gasoline or meat, and let some cheap hack give them sex and murder and God."[6]

To lift his spirits and evade heat and cabin fever, in the summer of 1952 Jo and Elizabeth set out on a long trip around the United States in their station wagon. They traveled through the Southwest, including the canyon of the Rio Grande; and in Taos, New Mexico, Jo enjoyed the arts and ambience, but disparaged the poor public image he thought some Indians projected. The couple motored across vast plains, through the woodsy and rural Midwest, venturing north to Ontario, Canada.

In Minnesota, Mathews castigated the shameful state of the stolen forests, which he said had been made nearly uninhabitable by German immigrant louts with "intense acquisitiveness and cold, calculating shrewdness." The homelands of the Chippewa, Menominee (which he studied and helped preserve), Sauk and Fox, Winnebago, and Potawatomi tribes were expropriated by "every device from trading to killing, to be turned over to be exploited." For centuries, Indians had dwelt and hunted in these ancient forests, leaving them healthy, but "within a decade (or two) the immigrant had destroyed a magnificent coniferous forest and rendered the soil useless," he wrote in his diary, exemplifying his Osage critical perspective and empathy with other Indigenous peoples. Jo and Dibbs returned home on Independence Day.[7]

That year, young Carter Revard, a graduate of Bartlesville College High and the University of Tulsa, was awarded a Rhodes scholarship to study at Oxford. In a letter to Mathews penned on Christmas Eve 1951, Savoie Lottinville, a past Rhodes scholar, said he hoped Mathews was pleased with Revard's selection. "He is a remarkable youngster in many respects, and I think that he is going to do us great credit at Oxford. Like another of the Big Hill Band, he was not present when the gong rang. But if he continues to dream as well as he has done in his short twenty years, I think the world will be enriched by him." Apparently, Revard was still asleep when his interview was to have begun, leading Lottinville to compare him to Mathews, who missed his entire first term at Oxford. Mathews was initially surprised at the choice of Revard, since he did not esteem the youth's biological and adopted families. Seemingly, despite the honor of the Rhodes, it took a while for Revard to earn Jo's full respect. Still, in May 1952 Mathews attended a tribal council meeting to suggest they "resolve to express appreciation," from the council and the tribe at large, to the first Osage Rhodes scholar. Born in 1931, Revard grew up in the Buck Creek Valley in Osage County, twenty miles east of Pawhuska. He was raised by his mother, Thelma Louise Camp, of Irish and Scots-Irish ancestry, and his full-blood Osage stepfather, Addison Jump, a son of Jacob and Josephine Strikeaxe Jump, and older brother to Arita, Louis, and author Kenneth Jacob Jump. Norma C. Wilson writes that while Revard is "only a small part Osage" and does not remember his biological father, McGuire Revard, he "grew up with four half-brothers and sisters who were half Osage." In 1952, Revard received his Osage name, Nonpehwahtheh (Fear Inspiring) from Josephine Jump and other elders during a naming ceremony.[8]

In August, Mathews attempted to pay Revard a visit, to congratulate him and offer advice on Merton College. He drove to a small white house sitting on a "windy hill" near Highway 60, close to the edge of Osage County west of Bartlesville, but Carter was not home. A man stepped outside to talk to him, but three others, two women and a tall man, all unidentified, only peered through the windows. Mathews did not gain a favorable impression, and his private remarks were scathing, all too typical of his 1950s diaries.

> From these shiftless and ignorant people came the current Rhodes Scholar, Carter Revard. He is a Revard bastard, without the right of the name, and yet this is the first time the name Revard, the Osage Revards, has been lifted above the morass of mental miasma and moral lassitude. Beautiful, they have been only. Beautiful animals. Beautiful and lustful women, and dark men of Gallic handsomeness and lazy salacity. They had no vitality for criminality, and they respected the badge of the law's guardians. From these beautiful women who yielded without poetry or music or romance, and darting-eyed men, chalking their cue sticks as they apprise themselves in a convenient mirror, had now come this bastard of a Revard who will enter Oxford this autumn.[9]

In light of Revard's subsequent PhD from Yale; his teaching career at first, Amherst College, then for most of his career, at Washington University in St. Louis; and his highly regarded publication of medieval scholarship and poetry, reading this passage today is jolting. That said, Revard's memoir *Winning the Dust Bowl* reveals that the "criminality" absent from the paternal line of Osage Revards was ample on his maternal side. His uncle Carter Camp, a belligerent bootlegger, was imprisoned for attempting to rob a bank in the town of Marland, and during his capture he was shot by police. Carter survived that injury and was later paroled, only to be "shot to death trying to hijack a shipment of extra-good whisky." Uncle Aubrey Camp, also a bootlegger, was "beaten to death in the Pawhuska jail," Revard writes. Revard perhaps aims to mythologize the antics of these scofflaws in a chapter called "Family Values,"[10] but does not mention that violence-prone white bootleggers and thieves dwelling on the fringes of the reservation were a type who commonly preyed on Osages to varying degrees during this period. Such men were the villains of the later chapters of *Sundown*. Chal and his friends, including young women, are degraded and addicted by "white man's whisky"—"everyone carried a flask of corn whisky now"—and Running Elk, a full-blood who was addicted to heroin, is shot in the head by a gang of white conspirators murdering Big Hill men during the Reign of Terror on Osages, paralleling actual events of the 1920s.[11] The infamous murders were only the most outrageous form of rampant exploitation of Osages by whites. Regardless of Mathews's feelings about Carter's bloodlines, over the years, his attitude warmed as he acknowledged Revard's continued successes. In the early 1960s, Revard wrote a positive review of *The Osages* for *American Oxonian*, concluding that what Thucydides was to the Greeks, Mathews was to the Osages; Mathews penned a note of thanks in return.[12]

In the 1970s, Revard began to teach and write American Indian literature. In 1978, Professor Revard invited students from Washington University to visit his Osage County homeland. They were given a traditional dinner by his Aunt Arita and Uncle Kenneth Jump. Kenneth had told Jo his nephew was visiting the area with students. Via Kenneth, Mathews graciously offered to give them a special tour of the Osage Tribal Museum, and the group met him there. With visible pleasure, Jo related witty anecdotes of the making of the portraits of Osage elders that had been commissioned for the museum, funded by the WPA's Federal Art Project. Although this was Revard's sole meeting with Mathews, Jo was a major inspiration to him, and the dedicatee of his poem "Rock Shelters." Today, Revard is revered as a major voice in Indian literature and criticism.[13]

Just as Mathews inspired many authors, Osages and others, so was he inspired by his favorite authors and books, which he oft revisited. Cherished volumes such as *Don Quixote*, stacked on a small table next to his leather easy chair by the fireplace at The Blackjacks, comprised his "mood books," in which he would "graze" at leisure. In 1952, Jo read Thoreau's *Walden; or, Life in the Woods* (1854). Elizabeth Mathews called *Talking to the Moon* Mathews's *Walden:* "It is a book that Thoreau or Muir might write, but it is a *Walden* of the plains and prairies, of the 1930s and 1940s, by a Native American." While she and other critics called *Talking to the Moon* the Osage *Walden*, Jo might have countered that *Walden* is the transcendentalist *Talking to the Moon*. "I am entertained by parts of it," he wrote in his diary, "but I have never known why it has become a classic, a sacred thing. I much prefer White's *England Have My Bones*, and Mathews' *Talking to the Moon*, and the greatest of these is Gontran de Poncins' *Kabloona*." This is ironic, since Mathews modeled some passages on Thoreau's evergreen. For example, Mathews lyrically proclaims: "I came to the blackjacks as a man who had pulled himself out of the roaring river of civilization to rest for a while; out of the flood where formerly only his head had been over the surface." This resonates with Thoreau's raison d'être: "I went to the woods because I wished to live deliberately, to front only the essential facts of life, and see if I could not learn what it had to teach, and not, when I came to die, discover that I had not lived. I wanted to live deep and suck out all the marrow of life."[14]

Mathews repeatedly listed *Kabloona* (1941) and *England Have My Bones* (1936) among his favorite books. Not only did he celebrate the "greatness" of *Kabloona* in his diary, Mathews even listed it in the bibliography of *The Osages*. *Kabloona* is a lively, peculiar narrative by an aristocratic French adventurer who lived among the Inuit people of the Canadian arctic. It offers fascinating accounts of life inside igloos and behind dog teams as Poncins negotiates cultural differences and comes to understand his hosts' communistic norms. *Kabloona* is marred by chauvinism, however. "There is no learning to know the Eskimo through an exchange of ideas," he writes. "Properly speaking, the Eskimo does not think at all. He has no capacity for generalization."[15]

Mathews also cherished and identified with the memoir *England Have My Bones* by T. H. White, best known for *The Sword and the Stone* (1938) and the Once and Future King trilogy, the source for the musical *Camelot* and a touchstone for Michael Moorcock, J. K. Rowling, and Neil Gaiman. This memoir is a comical, whimsical book by an eccentric Englishman who, like Mathews, chose to seclude himself in the countryside. Fishing, hunting, dogs, and flying lessons—all subjects of interest for Mathews—feature in the book. White's earthy sense of place and his modus operandi resemble both Thoreau's and Mathews's: he wanted to become closer to the earth and natural rhythms. Oddly, though, he begins by denigrating aborigines: "Red Indians, I believe, are unsure of the distinction between themselves and the outside world," uncertain "whether *it* is raining or *they* are spitting." He then patronizingly states, "I understand that most races were like this, in the youth of the world, and I am sure that children are like it still." White presents his idea of the "Indian" only to serve his metaphor about the alienation of modern life: "nowadays we don't know where we live, or who we are. Intelligence seems to be merging again into the Red Indian void from which it sprung."[16]

Jo's "beloved T. H. White" was an odd duck. Queer and melancholy, allegedly a closeted gay man who fell in love with a boy, he had few friends and never developed a real relationship with a woman. To escape guilt-inducing desires, he isolated himself. Reading *England Have My Bones*, it is clear White fancied Johnny Burn, his handsome flight instructor. At the local pub with Johnny, White admits Johnny "must be a flatterer, a rogue," but "he could have my heart." Johnny could "get away with anything," even murder, because as a skilled pilot he does something flawlessly, which makes him irreproachable. When psychotherapy failed to "cure" White's homosexuality, he increasingly turned to alcohol and devoted "fantastically loving attention to his setter bitch, Brownie," according to critic John Crane. Mathews, who doted on his setter bitches and even wrote poems about them, enjoyed White's *The Once and Future King*, *The Goshawk*, and *The Book of Beasts*.[17]

Whenever Mathews took breaks from laboring on *The Osages* in the 1950s, he often grazed in books by the Anglo-Irish novelist Joyce Cary, and in the massive *Travels in Arabia Deserta* (1888) by English traveler Charles Montagu Doughty.

Doughty's tome, which influenced Mathews's style, was rediscovered by T. E. Lawrence (whose *Seven Pillars of Wisdom* Jo cherished) and experienced a resurgence in the 1920s. Jo savored Cary's comic novel about art, *The Horse's Mouth* (1944), which he dubbed the "most interesting novel in English" but felt slightly guilty about pleasure-reading amidst work on *The Osages*. "If I had any free time from reference, I should do much better by reading in Doughty, whose style I shall cross with mine in *Wah'Kon-Tah*, for the Osage book," he wrote. *The Horse's Mouth* centers on Gully Jimson, an aged, ribald trickster-artist trying to make ends meet by hook or by crook. Though the novel is sometimes marred by misogyny, it aligns with Jo's philosophy of the integrity of individual talent. Mathews read Cary's *Mister Johnson* (1939) multiple times, calling it "one of the really great novels." With a comic tone and energetic pace but a tragic ending, the novel, set in Nigeria where Cary had been a colonial officer, focuses on hapless Johnson, a childlike Nigerian colonial subject. The novel was acclaimed, but its portrayals of Africans spurred Nigerian writer Chinua Achebe, who sensed "distaste, hatred, and mockery" in them, to write his own novel, *Things Fall Apart* (1958), which is much better known today. Reading *Lolita* in 1959, Jo understated, "Nabokov is quite as clever as Joyce Cary." Another favorite was E. M. Forster's *A Passage to India*.[18]

Author and activist D'Arcy McNickle, with whom Mathews socialized in Mexico, was a major contemporary of Mathews. Jo thought of him in August 1952, while he and Elizabeth were on holiday, driving their station wagon northwest through Colorado, Wyoming, Yellowstone National Park, Idaho, Montana, and British Columbia, following the Continental Divide. In Browning, Montana, Jo and Dibbs visited the relatively new Museum of the Plains Indian, and the Blackfeet Nation. At Glacier National Park in Montana, driving in the Flathead reservation, Mathews recalled *The Surrounded*, set on that craggy landscape. Along with *Sundown* and John M. Oskison's *Brothers Three* (1935), *The Surrounded* (1936) was of the few Indian novels published in the 1930s; precious few novels by Indigenous authors featuring major Native characters were published after them until N. Scott Momaday's *House Made of Dawn* spearheaded the Native American Renaissance in 1968. McNickle, who was enrolled in the Confederated Salish and Kootenai Tribes but whose mother had First Nations Cree ancestry, grew up on the Flathead Reservation in St. Ignatius, Montana. *The Surrounded* centers on Archilde Leon, a mixed-blood fiddle player who returns to his father's ranch after living in Portland, Oregon. In 1954, in a Tulsa hotel lobby, Jo ran into D'Arcy, who was in Oklahoma representing his organization, American Indian Development (AID). McNickle told Mathews he had a new novel, *Runner in the Sun*, based upon pre-Colombian life on the Mesa Verde.[19]

Farther north, as they were leaving their motel at Kelowna, in the southern interior of British Columbia, Mathews and Dibbs were approached by a grotesque "beery wretch" wielding a crutch and cane because his foot was in a cast. He apologized for being loud the night before, and seeing their license plate, asked what part of Oklahoma they were from. When Mathews replied the northern part, the bloated man shared he had been in Tulsa in 1921, which was a flashpoint of racial tension. He had participated in a violent civil disturbance lasting two days in spring 1921, which devastated the relatively prosperous black neighborhood of Greenwood that some nicknamed the Black Wall Street. The tragedy has been called the Tulsa Race Riot, but it ultimately was a massacre perpetrated by a mob of whites against outnumbered blacks. More than a hundred people were killed, around eight hundred were injured, and thirty city blocks were burned, leaving more than a thousand families homeless. The man continued, "They give me a gun and said, 'whin yu see black, shoot.'" The Tulsa Police Department, fearing Greenwood was flaring into a "negro uprising," deputized white men carelessly, handing out guns and badges like door prizes. When Mathews, who was at Oxford at the time, replied he "had heard of that race riot," the man laughed hideously, then shoved his face even closer to Jo's and cackled some more: "hee, hee, they burnt their houses 'nen had to turn 'round and build 'em some new ones." Mathews wrote, "I felt unclean for several hours." This dark and suppressed chapter of Oklahoman history followed them all the way to Kelowna, like Victor Frankenstein chasing his monster.[20]

Along with bringing diversion and enrichment, these road trips appealed because they distanced Mathews from family entanglements. During this period Mathews was vexed by his unmarried younger sisters, Marie, and especially Lillian, who lived in the Mathews family home on Grandview. Lillian then held the purse strings of the Mathews family estate. Many younger interviewees, including Jo's granddaughters, portrayed Lillian as stern, disapproving, even scary. Lillian stringently disapproved of Jo's first wife and was not crazy about Elizabeth. She raged against modern inventions such as parking meters, in rants that younger folk found curious. Yet rancher Frederick F. Drummond, at age ninety-three, recalled Marie and Lilly as kind, polite, attractive ladies. In fall 1952, to obviate dealing with his sisters, Mathews rashly signed over all his interest in the Mathews family estate, excluding Osage Realty stock, to Marie and Lillian "without consideration." "Marie and Lillian are going through a change of life," he wrote. They thought if Mathews died suddenly, "a great confusion about the estate" would ensue. By handing over his interest, Mathews believed he would be "amputated from the family organism." He declared, "I shall thus be not involved with the family, and we shall all be happy."[21]

Mathews then turned to his tribal history project in earnest. In 1953, Mathews wrote Lottinville, congratulating OU Press on its twenty-fifth anniversary and outlining his huge project, "an idea that has buzzed about my consciousness for years. It's the story of the Osage tribe from the beginning. I'll attempt to move these people across a stage." His strategy to fill in the "rather wide spaces between documentary evidence" was an intuitive approach to use material he had gathered from speaking with the elders. His work would be a different kind of tribal history that incorporated oral tradition, a precursor to what Choctaw author LeAnne Howe calls tribalography, a method marshaling collective experiences of self, family, clan, tribe, and ancestors into a meaningful form to "inform ourselves and the non-Indian world about who we are." It took Mathews years, however, to find a groove for writing the book.[22]

During the 1950s and 1960s, for a couple who lived remotely, Elizabeth and Jo enjoyed a fairly active social life. They spent warm evenings with friends and Jo's maternal relatives of the intertwined Girard, Fortune, and Galvin families. Jo's Girard cousins were Alice Everett, Nick Fortune, "Dottie" Girard, and Marie Girard, children of his uncle Nicholas and aunt Amelia "Minnie" Girard. After rancher Tom Galvin married Marie Girard, he and Jo became good friends. Early on, Jo became friends with cousin Tony Fortune, his wife Mayme, and their son Nick, who was adopted by Jo's aunt Minnie Girard. Tony and Mayme's other son, Arthur P. Fortune, was a guitar and mandolin picker who had his own radio show. He became a mail carrier, as did his wife, Floy. Jo socialized with Arthur and Floy's son, Phillip A. Fortune, who worked at the Pawhuska Post Office for three decades. Phillip, a cultural historian, owned a massive collection of classic country and western records and is an aficionado of both western swing bandleader Bob Wills and the rodeo and Western movie star Ben "Son" Johnson—not to mention Hayley Mills. Phillip attended Jo's funeral with his father, Arthur.[23]

Among several rancher friends of Osage County, Mathews had a longstanding relationship with the prominent Drummonds. In 1946, Mathews wrote in his diary about Frederick G. Drummond, his wife, Grace Ford Drummond, and their "very attractive children." One child was Frederick Ford Drummond, who graduated from Oklahoma State University and talked to Jo in 1952 about applying for a Rhodes scholarship. He ended up earning an MBA from Stanford but struck up a friendship with Jo. Jo and Dibbs enjoyed socializing with him and his wife, Janet. Fred played a large role in the establishment of the Tall Grass Prairie Preserve in Osage County and was a founding member of the Oklahoma Nature Conservancy. In 2014 the Nature Conservancy purchased from the Mathews family the land on which The Blackjacks sits, and in 2015, restored The Blackjacks house, thanks largely to the efforts of Pawhuska attorney and Mathews aficionado Harvey Payne, director of the Tall Grass Prairie Preserve.[24]

Jo and Dibbs also socialized with Paul and Gladys Jordan Buck, and their boy, Jordan "Son" Buck, ranchers who leased the Mathews land and lived in the (since razed) ranch house on the property. Paul and Gladys were regulars at New Year's Eve parties and other gatherings hosted at The Blackjacks, and in his diaries Jo mentioned Son Buck and later his boy, P. J. (Paul Jordan). Sporting her trademark cowboy hat, Gladys—like Paul—rode horseback, cared for cattle, and patronized a barbershop, not a beauty salon. Jo once ran into Gladys Buck while they were each gathering blackberries. In 1969 he described her as "energetic and effective" in everything she did, from "'chouncing' cattle to baking a cake." The Buck family leased the Mathews family land for about seventy-five years, but was not offered an opportunity to buy it, said P. J. Buck, who ran a company called Blackjack Oil.[25]

Mathews was a visible presence in the community during this period. Through entertaining speeches as well as his books, Jo brought pleasure to strangers' lives. In 1954, he served as emcee for a popular tribute dinner for Dr. Roscoe Walker, a third-generation physician and surgeon who served Pawhuska for forty years. During the 1950s and 1960s, Mathews was in high demand as a guest speaker for organizations such as the Kiwanis, Rotary, and Lions clubs, colleges, and historical societies, appearing at commemorative events, meetings, conferences, and classes. In 1955 he visited classes at Oklahoma A&M in Stillwater for three days, and spoke at Bacone College's Diamond Jubilee. Founded in 1880 as Indian University, Bacone had close ties to Muscogee Creeks and Baptists. Jo's friend, the artist Acee Blue Eagle, fostered the Bacone style of intertribal Native art there.[26]

Despite such activity and community recognition for Jo, 1954 was marked by doubt and depression. He struggled to revise his novel manuscript, "Within Your Dream," into publishable form, and again doubted the importance of writing. Depressed by financial obligations, he faced an existential crisis. "I have begun to wonder again why I ever came back here to live 'temporarily' during the depression of 1932–37. Can I get out of the rut of pleasant living at 60? Each day I select some successful man to envy." *Pleasant living* was a motto of his, with which he signed letters and books. In 1963, Dobie replied to one of his letters: "Living pleasantly isn't enough. Producing something is what counts."[27]

If 1954 was a "most upsetting year" for Mathews, 1955 was even worse. He suffered several losses and failed to produce much writing. He was occupied with gardening and raising chickens as much as anything else. In January, his mother fell, broke her hip, and was confined to the Pawhuska hospital for several weeks. Florence flew into town to join her family and visit her ailing mother. Pauline Eugenia Girard Mathews went to heaven on March 24, 1955. Beloved by the community, generous with advice and flowers, Mrs. Mathews won the *Journal-Capital*'s Mother of the Year award in 1948, even though her youngest child was born forty-five years earlier. A devout Catholic, Jennie attended Immaculate Conception Church on Lynn Street in Pawhuska from its inception in 1915, and her funeral there was packed with mourners.[28]

At the time of their mother's death, Josephine had been ill and was an inpatient at St. Mary's Hospital in Winfield, Kansas. Mathews had visited her in November. Josephine Mathews Caudill died a month after her mother, and her funeral was also held at Immaculate Conception. Josephine had separated from Henry Benjamin Caudill by 1926, and they were divorced by 1930. It was said Henry was rarely present and did not contribute much to the family. Josie's grandson Howard J. Schellenberg III said that in the 1930s, after the divorce, Josephine traveled to New York, London, and Paris to socialize with celebrities and heiresses she had met during her earlier years of travel. During her absences, Lillian and Marie were largely responsible for raising and managing the education of her son, Henry Ben, and daughter, Sarah Jo. Sarah Jo Caudill graduated from St. Mary's College in 1944, married Army Captain Howard J. Schellenberg, Jr., in 1948, and lived in the Washington, D.C., area. Sarah Jo and Howard raised three adopted children: Howard, Maria, and Jeanne. In 1965, Lillian, along with Sarah Jo and her children, visited The Blackjacks and enjoyed a picnic.[29]

Returning to Jo's gloomy 1955, it intensified when the Ridge suffered the worst dust storm since 1936. Darkness was relentless. In May, Mathews drove to Norman to attend Rita Lottinville's funeral. He had visited with her and Savoie several times in 1954.[30]

In January 1956, Mathews had an unsettling encounter with his dentist, Dr. Noel Kaho, historian and booster of Claremore, Oklahoma. Noel researched local heroes Lynn Riggs and Will Rogers; in 1941 he published *The Will Rogers Country*, and after Riggs's death in 1954 he was a key planner of the Lynn Riggs Memorial at the Claremore Museum of History. During Jo's visit, Kaho spoke frankly of his marital difficulties. To Mathews, the doctor and his wife's marriage, even their heterosexuality, were dubious. After remaining a bachelor for years, Kaho "finally married a rather queer woman with a daughter." Jo inferred from others "she is sexually irregular, and is obviously badly adjusted. He is now spending money for psychiatric treatment." In a heteronormative culture, perhaps Noel and his wife were a lesbian and a gay man posing as heterosexual. If Kaho were closeted, this would cement his identification with the closeted gay man Riggs. Mathews thought Noel "has always been extremely self-centered and childishly greedy for publicity, and his petty jealousies and certain mannerisms have been more feminine than childish." Dr. Kaho told Jo about his new project, which Jo found "incongruous and startling." During a perusal of Riggs's papers, Kaho discovered a poem dedicated to Riggs's young lover, a Mexican man named Tico. When Mathews read the poem, he called it "a cry from the 'well of loneliness,'" alluding to the lesbian novel by Radclyffe Hall. The poem addresses "Hamlet, and a lone cowboy on the range, a solitary light in a lonesome ranch house window; an upstairs window in a lonely, shabby ranch house on the Plains." With eyes aglow, Noel announced his plans to ensure the poem "will be published by the University of Oklahoma Press as the 'jewel' of the State's 50th Anniversary celebration in 1957." Kaho planned to approach first Governor Raymond D. Gary, then OU President George Lynn Cross, with the proposition, hinting Lottinville was "to have orders from above." Mathews concluded, "Noel is a very unpleasant character when certain facets of his character are turned toward one. How ridiculous would be the poem, no matter how good, written by a pansy to his male sweetheart published as the 'jewel' of the anniversary ceremonies of a rugged, virile state."[31]

Mathews reflected, "If this 'jewel' happened to be published, this would be the second time this part Cherokee aesthete had inadvertently made a contribution to his rugged male state through misinterpretation due to Public vanity." Jo recapitulated a remark George Milburn made in his essay "Oklahoma": the state's history would make a first-rate comic opera—an assessment that opened Milburn to attacks from editors and writers who had come to Oklahoma from other states. "Then came along Hammerstein & Rogers and made Lynn's reactive play *Green Grow the Lilacs*—really a satire—into a rollicking Comic opera, calling it *Oklahoma*. Oklahomans swelled with pride like the southern mountaineer who was called a Neanderthal man by a harassed bridge builder," he wrote in his diary.[32]

Mathews showed his typical denigration of homosexuality. His professed homophobia was not only a manifestation of his culture's prejudices, it also likely helped him to build a psychological wall between his ego and his own occasional same-sex interest. Throughout much of his life, Mathews feared being seen as "queer." While occupying the subject position of heterosexual, he occasionally acknowledged being drawn to other men, and perhaps more than anything else life offered, he enjoyed homosociality, interacting with intimate groups of men in hunting parties. His serial formation of what critic Emily Lutenski calls "tribes of men," alluding to the title of John Hunt's novel *Generations of Men*, is a significant pattern in his life, and he appreciated male pulchritude.[33]

In April 1956, Jo received a visit from his daughter, Virginia. In light of his thoughts on the Kahos, it is unclear whether Mathews realized she favored women. Virginia, then a school and library consultant with Longmans, Green & Company of New York, the publisher of *Sundown*, was in Pawhuska to speak at the Oklahoma Library Association convention. She addressed children's librarians, and her father delivered the keynote speech, "Books and Libraries in Oklahoma." This was just one of many visits she paid during the 1950s and 1960s.[34]

While Jo and Elizabeth were in Washington, D.C., in summer 1957, they dined with Florence and Michael Feighan and their teenaged daughter, Fleur, at the Congressional Club—on whose advisory board Florence served—then visited at their apartment. Fleur recalls her Uncle Jo was a superlative storyteller, and he and her father were quite fond of each other. Lively, witty conversation filled the dining room. Fleur's older brother, Bill Feighan, confirmed Jo was a raconteur, a sought-after guest for dinner parties in the capital. The Feighan and Mathews families kept up ties. In 1959, Florence, Michael, and Fleur visited Pawhuska after traveling in Asia. In July 1967 Michael, Florence, Bill, Lillian, and the Bucks came out for a barbecue at The Blackjacks, a "delightful evening of conversation and the usual excellent food which Dibbs loves to produce." Around Christmas 1968, the Feighan family, with Marie and Lillian, visited Jo and Elizabeth, and Bill visited the next fall. For Christmas, Bill gave Uncle Jo a book by mystic Edgar Cayce, but upon receiving it Mathews admitted he was "hopelessly earthy" and "not the least interested in Messianic postulations." In 1969, Mathews opined that Bill, then thirty-five, had "become a sort of self-appointed missionary for the mystical postulations of at least three soothsayers." When Bill asked Uncle Jo if he had read the book, and urged him to do so, Mathews countered by asking if Bill had read *his* books, especially *Talking to the Moon*, to understand *his* philosophy of life. Embarrassed, Bill admitted he had not, and Jo was shocked. This exchange, which he later regretted, led Mathews to cut the visit short. In the early 1970s, various combinations of Feighan family members visited Jo, Dibbs, Marie, and Lillian, who retired from the Osage Agency in 1969.[35]

In Washington, D.C., Mathews assisted a group called Osages United, who were lobbying to amend a key bill being heard in the House, which would renew the Osage government for twenty-five years. Osages United sought to extend tribal voting rights to Osage tribal members living out of state. Jo and Elizabeth arrived at the Roger Smith Hotel in July 1957, and Mathews began attending hearings before the House Committee on Insular and Interior Affairs. His group was only one of four arguing for various amendments to the bill. The *Oklahoman* reported that a simple bill had "kicked up a fuss among tribal factions":

> Three tribal cliques and an association for white landowners expressed conflicting views to the House Indian Affairs subcommittee, which took no immediate action. It decided to refer the dispute to the [BIA]. One source of intra-tribal friction is the fact that only those members who hold headrights, or fraction of a headright, are allowed to participate in quadrennial elections of the [Osage Tribal Council]. Protesting this as "unfair and undemocratic" was Mrs. Lottie Pratt, Hominy president of Osage Association, Inc., a group of tribal members of half-blood or more.[36]

The Osage Association sought to make all Osages at least twenty-one years of age, regardless of headright status, eligible to vote for councilmen. Mathews thought that Pratt's protest was motivated by her being a descendant of "Wah Ti Ankah, the Stormer" and her "primitive urge to satisfy traditional *amour propre*," and the sole "path to her objective is insurgency and muddled vindictiveness." He denounced her group as capricious and nonsensical. Mathews's group, Osages United, wanted to amend the bill to reorganize the election of council members by geographical districts. Mathews, his friend Buddy Gray of Pawhuska, plus James Mosier of Denver represented the group, which included artist Romain Shackelford. Their plan called for five districts representing Oklahoma and three for the rest of the country; this change would give representation to two hundred eligible Osages living in California. All these efforts were in vain, however, since none of the amendments pitched by these factions became part of the final bill.[37]

In April 1958, this group very much wanted Mathews to stand as a candidate for the Osage Tribal Council, despite his repeated protests that he lacked the time. They made their message clear:

> Waked up in the middle of the night by a car horn. Saw a group of Osages out of the kitchen window standing in the headlights. Thought they might go away, but they remained and finally I went out in pajamas and raincoat. It was Buddy Gray, Bennie Harrison and Romain Shackelford, who were much excited about my becoming a candidate for the Osage Council this June. Suddenly they have decided they need me. After saying "NO" quite definitively, I said I should let them know tomorrow. The answer will still be no.[38]

The next day, he met with Buddy Gray and about eighteen others at "Raymond Redcorn's in the Indian Camp." They pleaded with him to let them enter his name as a candidate. "They even hinted that I was 'letting them down' by not doing so. . . . I was made quite unhappy." At the Gray ranch with Buddy, his wife Margaret, and Romain, Jo refused for a third time to be a candidate. This third denial brings to mind the Apostle Peter. In retrospect, it seems he should have done what these Osages asked of him.[39]

Around this time, Mathews drove to Marshall, Oklahoma, to participate in Angie Debo Recognition Day. Artist Acee Blue Eagle also attended. Debo's brave book *And Still the Waters Run*, completed in 1936, exposed the exploitation of the 1887 Dawes Allotment Act as it was imposed on the Five Civilized Tribes. Mathews reviewed the manuscript for OU Press and admired the published book. The historian Shirley Leckie describes the book as a "crushing analysis of the corruption, moral depravity, and criminal activity that underlay white administration and execution of the allotment policy." As such, the manuscript caused controversy, especially since some of the players were still living. OU Press withdrew as publisher; it was produced instead by Princeton University Press in 1940, under Brandt's directorship. Mathews provided a blurb for the dustjacket. In 1946 Angie Debo, with music teacher and radio broadcaster Harold Leake and his wife, Dorothy, visited Jo and Elizabeth. The quintet shared musical and literary interpretations.[40]

In fall 1958, Jo and Dibbs traveled to New Mexico, Mesa Verde National Park in Colorado, and Yellowstone National Park.[41] The following year, Jo's old friend, the newspaperman Walker Stone, invited Dobie and Mathews to join him to hunt at Rancho Seco, in Medina County, southwestern Texas. The ranch was owned by their mutual friend Ralph A. Johnston, a Houston oilman and OU geology major who grew up with Stone in Okemah. Stone brought along his boss, Roy Howard. The bond formed among Mathews, Dobie, Stone, Johnston, and to a lesser extent, Howard, was deep and heartfelt. Dobie wrote, "deer and the wild turkeys are positives of the hunt, but what we most anticipate and cherish in memory is the comradeship and talk around an evening fire that seems to emanate from our genial host." In conversation the next year, Jo waxed rhapsodic over their bond and their irreverent repartee. Dobie declared he could not remember ever being so merry. Mathews replied, "You've been perfectly free"; in society, "you've had to restrain yourself," but here, you're "able to sit around the fire and actually be free with your thoughts." This freedom entailed the absence of women.[42]

In November 1960, on his second Texas hunting trip, Mathews made a long journey to pick up Dobie near Austin before heading west to Rancho Seco. Dobie dedicated *Cow People*, published in 1964, the year of his death, to Stone and Johnston, and wrote about the men's keen relationship therein and in his newspaper column. "I knew Stone as a student in my English class at Oklahoma A&M College forty years ago." Then editor of the college newspaper, Walker was Dobie's "most memorable pupil." Years later, Stone sent Dobie *Talking to the Moon*, written by his friend since youth. Dobie wrote that over the decades, Stone "kept on actively remembering" him, and Johnston and Stone "kept remembering each other." Johnston began inviting Stone to hunt on his ranch, then asked him to choose his own hunting party. If all this mutual remembering sounds romantic, these men did enjoy each other's company immensely, reflected in the correspondence between Dobie and Mathews, and in tape-recorded conversations from their trips. To Dobie, the ideal hunt is spending "plenty of hours outdoors" and at night, being convivial with "genial companions in fine conversation, the *summum bonum* of civilized life," which involved drinking liquor liberally. Mathews agreed, telling Dobie that at Seco and Pobre, he relished "four delightful companions" and "conversations that linger in one's memory like a song." Mathews enjoyed playing his "Rancho Seco Tapes" of vivacious and sometimes ribald conversations to open-minded guests, such as his artist friends, famed portraitist Charles Banks Wilson, and sculptors Jim Hamilton and Romain Shackelford, who heard them in 1971.[43]

Jo and Frank Dobie formed a special bond. They made the long drive back to Dobie's Rancho Paisano outside of Austin, which he bought the previous year. Mathews had known Dobie only through his books and brief correspondence, but was pleased to know him well: "upon meeting you, every brush stroke of my imagined picture of you was there, with delightful and supplementary highlights of personality." Prior to their third hunting trip in 1961, Frank told Jo it was not necessary for him to make a such a long trek to retrieve him, as he had in the past, since he could take the train or a bus. Yet he added: "Of course, I'd be mighty glad to see you. You'll understand what I'm trying to say." Affection lay beneath the surface. Frank complimented *The Osages*, which he was reading, for "its majesty as an earth book." He concluded another letter: "I'm surely more eager for our hunt and comradeship than I am for Christmas."[44]

Prior to the second trip, in September 1960, Mathews spent a week in Levelland, in northwest Texas, with a friend of three decades, Dr. David Parsons, nicknamed "Chief" or "Doc Parsons." A Choctaw who had lived in Pawhuska, Parsons earned a PhD in history from the University of Oklahoma, dissertating on "The Removal of the Osages from Kansas." He ran a drugstore in Levelland for decades, was a cotton farmer, and held oil interests. As Mathews was completing *The Osages*, he needed to consult Parsons, "who knows more about a two-year period of Osage history than any man alive." For a week they discussed Osage history, pored over historical documents, manuscripts, and photos, and listened to recorded music. They read aloud together *Level Land* (1935), a southwestern poetry collection by Kenneth Carlyle Kaufman, a modern languages professor both had known. The Levelland reporter who interviewed Mathews for three hours said more than anything, Jo was genuine, evincing "warm feeling for his fellow-man and a capacity for putting anyone around him at perfect ease." Kaufman, managing editor of *Books Abroad*, the predecessor of *World Literature Today*, praised Mathews's first book, *Wah'Kon-Tah*. A room in the Bizzell library and the Modern Languages building at OU are named for Kaufman.[45]

Mathews completed *The Osages* in 1961. In January he and Elizabeth conducted final research at OU's Phillips Collection and carefully drew maps for the book's endpapers. Jack Haley, a former archivist, told Terry Wilson the couple made multiple research visits, "Mathews resplendent in an off-white hunting jacket which he wore habitually and Elizabeth preparing their meals on a folding camp stove." The book done, he and Elizabeth set out on a 4,500-mile jaunt across the West, through Kansas, Colorado, Utah, Nevada, and California. Following their return, beginning in August, Jo and Elizabeth appeared at several events to promote *The Osages*, published on August 16 by OU Press.[46]

The Osages is powerfully written in a literary style eschewing footnotes. Jo's magnum opus was crucial to many Osages who yearned to understand their tribal legacy and family history in the face of rapid change in the twentieth century. Author Charles H. Red Corn explained that his father introduced him to Mathews, some of whose writing he had read. He was "surprised such a distinguished man was so open." Later, after the publication of *The Osages*, which Red Corn found stunning, he bumped into Mathews on the sidewalk of Kihekah Avenue in Pawhuska. Charlie told Jo many young Osages were appreciatively reading *The Osages*, which they nicknamed the "Big Green Book," and he was sure it was influencing their lives for the better. Standing with distinctive bearing, Mathews removed his pipe from his mouth and quipped, "So, I am proselytizing," after which he laughed a little, conveying his pleasure in learning that Osages appreciated his books. During a hometown book-signing event, young people gazed with awe at Mathews, who was most distinctive: tall, dignified, witty, and articulate. Mathews biographer Garrick Bailey gave further evidence of the book's influence. In fall 1961, he ran into a fellow OU student, an Osage, on the street near campus. From his bloodshot eyes, rumpled clothes, and mussed hair, he appeared to be "returning and perhaps still recovering from a night of revelry." Instead his classmate had been up all night reading *The Osages*, purchased the day before, "so engrossed in reading it that he had stayed up all night and even cut his morning classes." The classmate declared excitedly, "Now I know who I am." He realized "for the first time what it truly meant to be Osage."[47]

The Osages was enriched and enlivened by oral narratives Mathews gathered from Osage elders in the community. He filled in hazy or vacant spots in the archive with intuitive accounts of Osage history informed by tribal oral memory and "instinctive knowledge," what N. Scott Momaday has called "memory in the blood" in *House Made of Dawn* and elsewhere. Mathews drew an analogy from his natural sciences background, likening himself to a paleontologist reconstructing an incomplete dinosaur skeleton, surely recalling Dr. Sollas, under whom he had studied at Oxford. Like a paleontologist, he used knowledge and intuition in his research, but Jo's empirical and familial knowledge of traditional Osage history and culture gave him an edge, because he, as he put it, had actually seen his "dinosaur walking." His methodological metaphor is apt in some ways but problematically implies his subject, the Osages, or at least some authentic version of them, had gone extinct.[48]

Nationally, *The Osages* was received with respect and acclaim. A Smithsonian ethnologist wrote in the *New York Times* that Mathews successfully conveyed from an Osage perspective the tribe's struggle to "preserve a meaningful and satisfying system of beliefs and values in the face of numerous strong and conflicting pressures." The *Christian Science Monitor* lauded Mathews's scholarship, cultural integrity, breadth, and style. Closer to home, *The Osages* was celebrated rapturously. Writing in the *Oklahoman*, Edith Copeland pleased Mathews by placing the tome on a "short list of truly great and beautiful books of our time." The *Pawhuska Journal-Capital* called it an "exquisite leviathan" and its author the "flawless spokesman" of Osage elders. Will Rogers's niece, Paula McSpadden Love, told Mathews she was enraptured by his "beautifully and poetically written" book, to her the "greatest treasure of all times."[49]

Paula was the first curator of the Will Rogers Memorial, which opened in 1938; she and her husband, Robert Love, lived on the grounds and operated the memorial for thirty-five years. Though not a close friend of Will Rogers, Mathews spoke with him a few times, and Will never met a man he didn't like. Jo probably talked to Rogers in 1930 when the entertainer flew in to Oklahoma for the unveiling, in Ponca City, of the *Pioneer Woman* statue sponsored by Marland. Some of Marland's men, friends of Jo's, knew Rogers, and in his Marland biography, Mathews describes four of them chilling with Will in the Big Apple, sitting on the curb at Forty-Second Street and Broadway, long after the New Amsterdam Theater had closed. In 1946, Mathews checked in at the Will Rogers Hotel in Claremore, Oklahoma. He called the Cherokee attorney and judge Dennis W. Bushyhead, grandson of his namesake, a devoted Cherokee chief. Dennis's father, Dr. Jesse Bushyhead, was a first cousin of Will's and close friend of the Rogers family. With his wife Christine Bushyhead, Dennis met Jo and Elizabeth for a visit to the Rogers Memorial, located at the mansion in which Rogers had planned to retire. Mathews had known Will's widow, Betty Blake Rogers, who died in 1944, and said it felt strange not to see her there. In 1964, Mathews participated in Will Rogers Day; fifty radio stations broadcast a special program from the memorial on the heritage of Oklahoman Indians, which also featured Bureau of Indian Affairs commissioner Philleo Nash and Cherokee principal chief W. W. Keeler. In 1961, Paula McSpadden Love enjoyed the attention *The Will Rogers Book*, which she edited, was receiving. Jo and Elizabeth sent flowers to the Lewis Meyer Bookshop in Tulsa for Paula's signing party. Love expressed very deep regret over missing Jo's own party at Meyer's bookstore.[50]

Anyone promoting a book in Oklahoma in the late twentieth century was wise to get it into Lewis Meyer's hands. With his wife, Natasha, this Tulsa literary and media icon owned and operated his eponymous bookstore on Peoria Avenue for nearly sixty years, and he had his own Sunday television show on KOTV in Tulsa for more than forty years. Meyer's "enthusiastic, almost giddy, reviews were unforgettable," the *Tulsa World* recalled. In August 1961, Mathews saw Meyer reviewing *The Osages* on television. Mathews called his evaluation "not deep, but sales-effective," adding a stereotype: "He is a marvel at promotion, even for a Jew." Two days later, Jo and Elizabeth twice visited Meyer's store. During the day, they witnessed a ceremony featuring Freddie Lookout, son of the late Chief Fred Lookout, giving a "chief's pipe" to Lottinville. Mathews returned that evening for his signing party and received a good turnout.[51]

Jo and Elizabeth spent most of August promoting *The Osages: Children of the Middle Waters*. During their Tulsa visit, Jo gave several interviews to local media, and the difference in his attitude toward men and women interviewers seems revealing. Encounters with men in the media were positive. His interview with Chuck Wheat of *Tulsa World* went so well it lasted all afternoon, while Mathews enjoyed talking guns with Wheat's photographer. He appeared on Tulsa television station KVOO with Carl Myerdirk and "a girl" whose name Jo forgot, and the interview went well; the next day, Mathews talked with Dick Charles on his *Kaleidoscope* radio show: "very pleasant." Contrastingly, Mathews appeared on rival Tulsa station KOTV with Betty Boyd, to him a "very shallow, very dull person who was so absorbed in her own part and appearance in the interview" that she told viewers the subtitle of his book was *Children of the Eastern Waters*. A fixture of Tulsa media for decades, Boyd interviewed Jo's daughter, Virginia in 1968. Mathews was likewise annoyed by Louise Bland of KTUL TV, whom he described as "tall, blond and dizzy." Wringing her hands, Bland confessed she had forgotten her book and asked Mathews to feed her questions. The hometown reception of the book at two unusual venues, the G&L Drug Store and Triangle Jewelry in downtown Pawhuska, was tremendous, and the local paper noted both Osages and "palefaces" turned out to have Mathews sign his book. Amiable Mathews "had time for a hearty handclasp with his old friends and a kind word for his new acquaintances."[52]

In September, Jo and Elizabeth took a break to travel to Wyoming. Jo hunted antelope with a gun while Elizabeth shot her camera. Returning to Oklahoma in mid-month, Mathews spoke at engagements in Oklahoma City and at the Indian Women's Club in Bartlesville. In October, Mathews delivered a talk at a writers' conference at the University of Tulsa; also speaking was author and critic William Peden, editor of *Story* and champion of new writers such as Philip Roth and James Purdy. Mathews discussed "The Writer and His Region," borrowing his title from J. Frank Dobie, who published an article by that title in the *Southwest Review* in 1950 and mailed a copy of it to Mathews in 1960.[53]

Once he was finished promoting *The Osages*, Mathews traveled to southeastern New Mexico for a four-day trip to hunt bear and mule deer on a ranch owned by J. Bryan Runyan, a hunting buddy since the 1930s. Next, Mathews hunted with Dobie and Stone at Ralph Johnston's Rancho Seco in November 1961, joined there by Lyle Wilson and Peter Hurd, who played guitar and told stories. Dobie told Mathews beforehand he had liked Hurd for a long time and predicted, "I'm sure we shall all have a bully, bully time." In 1962, Mathews read Dobie's *A Texan in England* (1945) with deep appreciation and sent a laudatory letter to his friend, expressing deep regret that Frank had not been able to join that year's hunting trip at Rancho Seco, when Mathews, Stone, and Johnston were joined by Hurd and Ben Wright of *This Week* magazine. A key element to the dynamic was missing without Dobie, whom Mathews found to be "a very attractive and dominating personality," as he wrote the Texan. Dobie admitted to Mathews that when he wrote *The Voice of the Coyote* (1949), he "borrowed liberally" from *Talking to the Moon*. In 1963 as Dobie, in declining health, wrote *Cow People* and newspaper columns, he again borrowed from Mathews with the latter's blessing, this time drawing an excerpt from *Talking to the Moon* about cowhand Les Claypoole. That year, Dobie was able to join the party, which included Mathews, Stone, Johnston, Wilson, Howard, Hurd, and a new member, geologist and paleontologist Glen Evans. But since his auto accident of the previous year, Dobie seemed to Mathews a decade older and "faintly petulant."[54] Mathews had enviable luck, shooting "four gobblers before noon," then a white-tail buck. J. Frank Dobie died in September 1964. Ralph Johnston subsequently bought

Dobie's Paisano Ranch and helped transform it into a writers' retreat that has offered a temporary home to Dobie-Paisano fellows such as Sandra Cisneros. The first donors were President Lyndon Johnson and Lady Bird Johnson.[55]

During this period, Mathews earned several awards and accolades. In February 1962 Mathews received a telegram from University of Oklahoma President Dr. George Cross announcing he was one of four Oklahomans chosen by the Board of Regents of the University, the Faculty, and the Alumni Association to receive the Distinguished Service Citation in May 1962. This was the highest honor the University could award: "I feel quite worthy this morning," he remarked in his diary. Mathews presumed this citation was an acknowledgment of his publishing contributions and his service to University of Oklahoma Press as a manuscript reviewer in 1933–67. Also in 1962, he received the Award of Merit from the American Association of State and Local History for *The Osages*.[56]

Even as Jo received news of the citation, he was finishing reading a manuscript by B. B. Chapman on the Otoe and Missouria Indians, which he recommended that Lottinville publish. Mathews tended to reject or strongly criticize any living authors who were working in his field of Osage culture and history. For example, he rejected three Osage-related books outright. In 1938 he sharply criticized Sister Mary Paul Fitzgerald's manuscript *The Osage Mission: A Factor in the Making of Kansas*, revised from her dissertation at St. Louis University, for its pro-missionary bias and use of offensive terms such as "half-breed" and "squaw." The manuscript was rejected by OU Press but later published by the Press of the Saint Mary College of Kansas, as *Beacon on the Plains*, and despite its obscure origin, it has been an influential and reissued book. In *Bibliography of the Osage*, Terry Wilson called it "very well researched"; esteemed Osage historian Louis Burns called it an "especially well done history" that is "rich in Osage information." Although Mathews said he enjoyed Fitzgerald's manuscript and it was worthy of publication, and eventually used it as a source for *The Osages*, his criticism likely persuaded Lottinville to pass on the book. Perhaps he was especially critical because he sought to manage the historical record on his grandfather, John Allen Mathews, and to cover up his ancestor's nefarious deeds, but he could not in good faith reject the submission outright. Burns used Sister Mary's book as his source when he said John A. Mathews exemplified "how Osage treaty benefits were perverted." Sibling rivalry may also have played a role, since Fitzgerald interviewed Lillian Mathews, a devout Catholic, but not Jo, about their slaveholding grandfather.[57]

Despite Mathews's lengthy service as a manuscript reviewer for the University of Oklahoma Press, the language of the Distinguished Service Citation did not mention this important role or that of his book *Wah'Kon-Tah*. In fact, neither his nor Brandt's citation mentioned either man's association with OU Press, even though Brandt established it! A robed Mathews, alongside Dibbs, looking attractive in a white dress and hat, was handed his citation during OU's 1962 commencement. To Mathews this honor was particularly special, because for more than four decades he was a proud alumnus; he followed OU football on the radio or TV, and occasionally attended games in Norman. U.S. House Majority Leader Carl Albert was inducted the same year, and Mathews and Albert walked over to the Kappa Alpha house together after the ceremony. The 1962 citation marked the end of an era for Mathews. Despite continued literary endeavors, Mathews never published another book during his lifetime.[58]

In acknowledgment of the citation, the *Sooner Magazine* published Mathews's observations on contemporary Indian and southwestern literatures. Mathews was discouraged by the lack of commercial success of southwestern regionalist prose during the anxious Cold War period; likewise, he pointed out that in the 1930s it had not fit into proletarian realism either, written, he said, by "intellectual vindictive sentimentalists," whom in his opinion, had been exploited by "the *extremely* clever, insinuating termite action of Communist propaganda." Mathews—writing in the early 1960s, following an arid decade that produced very little Indian literature—could not then foresee the Native American Renaissance that would be underway by the end of the decade, building on his inspiration, encircling N. Scott Momaday, Leslie Marmon Silko, Gerald Vizenor, James Welch, Paula Gunn Allen, Geary Hobson, Janet Campbell Hale, Simon Ortiz, and more.

Chapter Eleven

EVERYTHING IS A CIRCLE

> Everything is a circle, turning like a golden eagle in the sky under the eye of Grandfather Sun.
>
> —John Joseph Mathews

After finishing *The Osages*, Mathews wrote short stories inhabited by animals for young readers, labored on his memoirs, and participated in community events. In April 1962, Jo and Dibbs drove north to Nebraska's Valentine Wildlife Refuge to photograph prairie chickens dancing. The next month, they headed south to Sulphur, Oklahoma, where Jo reminisced and imbibed with old friends at a Kappa Alpha reunion. He and another artist were the only two fraternity brothers who had not devoted their lives to acquiring wealth, he concluded. Increasingly, he and Elizabeth coped with issues related to aging and declining health, exacerbated by increasingly heavy drinking. In 1962, after finishing promotional activities for *The Osages* and learning he would receive the Distinguished Service Citation from OU, Jo and Dibbs were in the mood to relax and celebrate. "Back from town, feeling expansive, we drank a whole fifth of vodka mixed with orange juice—V&O's, we call them. Had dinner of cheese sandwiches at 11 P.M. This is second time we have consumed a whole fifth of vodka within a week." The next day, Jo drove into town to run errands, buying "beer and another bottle of vodka. If we are going to be a bottle-a-day people, we'd better have it ready," he wrote. For their "Glow Hour pleasure" they also sipped rum, scotch, gin, wines including Tokay and sherry, and especially, Wild Turkey bourbon, according to Jo's diaries of the 1960s and 1970s.[1]

Despite the drinking, 1963 was a productive year. With Elizabeth's editorial aid, Jo composed several appealing stories about animals, birds, and hunting for an intended audience of boys. In the early 1960s, responding to interest from John Hunt's friend and editor, Seymour Lawrence at Atlantic Monthly Press, Jo agreed to write a collection of animal stories, which he expected to complete in November 1963. When Little, Brown acquired Atlantic Monthly, however, the new managers objected on moral grounds to a manuscript by J. P. Donleavy on which Lawrence was working, so he left, joining Knopf in 1964. With Lawrence gone, so was interest in Mathews's manuscript. Seeking a publisher, Jo hired literary agent Robert Center, but to no avail; his manuscript was also rejected by Doubleday and Viking. Although these animal stories were not published in Jo's lifetime, thankfully, Susan Kalter collected nine of them in *Old Three Toes and Other Tales of Survival and Extinction* (2015). Also in 1963, Mathews hatched an idea for a novel dramatizing the dilemma of men and nations that had lost power, recycling the title "Without the Sword," which he had used for a different manuscript ultimately folded into *Talking to the Moon*.[2]

In 1965, Mathews began work on a new book project: his autobiography, which he planned as a three-volume work. He continued to compose and revise this work until his death. Initially, he read his own and other works to settle upon a style: "Grazing in *Out of Africa*, *England Have My Bones*, *Experiment in Autobiography* by H. G. Wells, *Talking to the Moon* and *The Osages* for atmospheric background for my incipient autobiography." At the start of July 1965, Mathews noted, "This is the day I was to finish the autobiography. Not to be deterred by chickens and vegetables, I did make a start on the first volume, *Boy Horse and Dog*. Began with 1,000 words even if I may have to redo them. [The] whole thing to be called *20,000 Mornings*." Beginning in 1966, Jo read up on World War I aviation and Oxford for deep backgrounding, utilizing the Pawhuska Public Library.[3]

Only the first volume, "Boy, Horse and Dog," is available, published under the intended series title, *Twenty Thousand Mornings*, edited by Susan Kalter. Her hands-off approach to editing and her unbalanced introduction are, however, disappointing. Too often, she uncritically accepts Mathews's self-representations. Error and speculation detract from the introduction and notes. For example, John Hopper Mathews was never referred to as "John Mathews, Jr.," and never attended Princeton. She states that Jo's father, William, "was neither a lawyer nor a judge," but indeed he served as prosecuting attorney and chief justice to the Osage Nation, despite taking no degrees. Moreover, her assertion that Mathews generously supported his children's education at the expense of his own career has now been discredited. According to eldest granddaughter Sara Dydak, Jo "rarely if ever sent child support" to his first wife and "really did not do the right thing by his family and children," a sentiment echoed by other family members.[4]

By late 1966, Mathews had written a second draft of "Boy, Horse and Dog," which he continued to edit through the remainder of his life, health permitting.

In April 1968, he began composing the second volume, tentatively titled "Hunting, History, and Girls," and intended to write one thousand words a day. Jo met that month with Angus Cameron, senior editor of Knopf publishers, who was in Tulsa working at the Gilcrease Museum; in July he followed up with a long letter pitching his autobiography. Although Jo penned thousands of words, he evidently let his resolution slide, because in 1970 he again declared he needed to write the second volume of his memoirs, with a revised working title of "Hunting, History and Romance." In 1973, he labored in earnest on volume 2, still not settled on a title. His work was interrupted by Elizabeth's hospitalization. Terry Wilson, who interviewed Mathews, reported that in 1974 Mathews completed a "massive autobiographical manuscript" consisting of *two* volumes and had showed these to press editors, whose "readers expressed misgivings about its length." Eventually, "Boy, Horse and Dog" was rejected once by Seymour Lawrence of Boston in 1967 and three times by OU Press by 1970. William Morrow expressed interest but declined the manuscript, returning it with a form letter. After receiving a number of discouraging reviews of the "massive autobiography" from publishers, Mathews decided he would continue writing if only to satisfy himself. People who visited Mathews in his final years also noted he was steadfastly working on his memoirs. In 1976 Laura Mathews, her father, John, and her Aunt Virginia visited Mathews, who spoke of his efforts on the autobiography, giving Laura the impression he had completed the entire first draft, allegedly covering his life up to the 1960s. This cumulative evidence contradicts Kalter's claim that Mathews never wrote a second volume.[5]

The second volume, along with many other papers, may have been lost or sold to private parties when an auction held sometime after Lillian Mathews died in August 1992 scattered countless Mathews family papers stored in her home. Raymond Red Corn III, who as of 2016 is the assistant chief of the Osages, described the auction as chaotic. Lillian had accumulated a massive collection. Piles and boxes of artifacts, ephemera, papers, and books were sold without rhyme or reason. Red Corn recalled that local historians "felt consternation" at precious materials being dispersed "to the four winds," carted off by collectors from all over the United States. Red Corn bought all he could afford, scoring a copy of *The Osages* he had his eye on, with endpapers that Mathews had illustrated with delightful animals as a gift to Lillian. Harvey Payne—who bought an alternate 1966 diary different from the one archived at OU—painted a similar picture. It took three weekends to auction everything.[6]

In 2011 Susan Kalter published an edition of the 1966 second draft of volume 1, "Boy, Horse and Dog." She relied exclusively on this version, without consulting Mathews's copious intervening edits, omissions, and annotations, even though

Mathews continued to work on his autobiography until his death. For example, in 1972 Jo wrote he had "spent several hours editing my MS, *Boy Horse and Dog.* I shall have to cut it quite a bit, in order to make it publishable, as well as do something about chronology; there is also too much detail." In April 1978, he wrote, "today began again on the MS by beginning again at the first sentence. I made new deletions, and shall incorporate new thoughts and ideas. The original is incredibly overwritten." In June he vowed, "When I finish editing, the MS will be about $^1/_3$ the pre-surgery size." During this period, Mathews felt "deep interest in re-writing it for possible publication."[7]

Through the 1960s, along with writing, gardening, and raising chickens, Mathews worked to acquire federal grant money from the Bureau of Indian Affairs (BIA) to modernize the Osage Tribal Museum. In May 1965, he expressed his dream of refurbishing the museum in his audiotaped diary, noting a recent day of successful lobbying in Washington, D.C., when he received encouragement from his friend, House Majority Leader Carl Albert, and from BIA Commissioner Philleo Nash. Albert, "the Little Giant from Little Dixie" who went on to become Speaker of the House from 1971 to 1977, had much in common with Mathews: both were Kappa Alpha fraternity brothers at OU who after graduation studied at Oxford. According to Elizabeth Thompson, Albert once visited The Blackjacks.[8]

The National Arts and Crafts Board awarded a grant of $86,000 to renovate the Osage Tribal Museum. Jo predicted to Joe Brandt that "get-away-from-it-all John-Without-Purpose will be compelled to transmute himself into a ringmaster all summer." To him, refurbishing the museum was only part of a grander plan. In Pawhuska, he met with the Osage Committee on Buildings and Property, and spoke with Chief Paul Pitts and councilmen George Baconrind and Ed Red Eagle, Sr., who recommended that the full council endorse Jo's plan to nominate the museum and the Osage Agency as a national monument. In June, Jo wrote Brandt, reporting the first step toward turning the Osage campus, with the museum as its nucleus, into a national monument, had been achieved. The next month Jo wrote a prospectus, and that summer he and Elizabeth drove to Washington, D.C., to present it to his allies, Congressman Ed Edmondson and Majority Leader Albert, along with BIA Commissioner Nash and Secretary of the Interior Stewart Udall. A confident Jo wrote, "They decided to approve my proposal to turn the Osage museum and campus into a National Monument."[9]

During September 1967, he worked with councilman Ed Red Eagle and other Osage officials to prepare for the grand reopening, as a stepping stone to greater recognition. With the formal grand reopening of the museum on September 30, Jo aimed to "impress those in Washington, DC who have authority in such matters as National Monuments." Though Jo was never successful in having the Osage Agency and the Tribal Museum designated a national monument, in 1974 the museum was added to the National Register of Historic Places.[10]

In 1966, Mathews painted enchanting scenes on the wall of his outbuilding, which he referred to as the "block house" in his diary. He also jokingly called it "the Time-Life Building" since he archived his collection of magazine back issues there. His whimsical paintings trace the progress of history. On August 9, he offered a key: "Nijinsky in *L'Après Midi d'une faune*, a Neanderthal man, a Medieval hunter spearing a unicorn lured by a staked-out virgin, a pre-Columbian Osage warrior, modern Osage drummer and dancer, and the Marquess of Ailesbury [Lord Cardigan] clearing a stone wall during a hunt in Oxfordshire." In 1967 he thought about adding the model Twiggy, since he thought "she might be the symbol of the national psychoneuroses," and did a preliminary color sketch. Over the years, Mathews also painted landscapes on canvas. John and Gail Mathews displayed some of Jo's atmospheric paintings in their home. His prairie landscapes ably evoke the open-sky environment.[11]

In 1967, Jo and Elizabeth were honored guests in Oswego, Kansas, where Jo was keynote speaker for the town's centennial celebration. Mathews's grandfather, John Allen Mathews, is recognized as a key historical personage because Oswego grew up near the site where he had established his trading post, blacksmith shop, and stables. Meanwhile, one of Elizabeth's ancestors, D. W. Clover, who established the first ferry across the Neosho River, had selected the name Oswego. Jo said townspeople showed "unparalleled community spirit" and enthusiasm that inspired him. Visitors had to be turned away from the packed community hall. Mathews was awarded a sterling medallion presented by local historian Wayne A. O'Connell, with whom they breakfasted the next day.[12]

Mathews made several public appearances during this period. In 1970, amidst protestors, Mathews and Osage Chief Sylvester J. Tinker spoke at the dedication of a plaque sponsored by the Oklahoma Petroleum Council and the Oklahoma Historical Society to memorialize the history of oil and gas lease auctions held under the branches of the "Million Dollar Elm," close to the Osage Tribal Museum in Pawhuska. Local media covered the event, and an interview with Jo aired on KVOO TV Tulsa. The celebrated elm stood right down the avenue from Mathews's family home, and in his youth he witnessed several auctions involving famous oilmen

Paintings by John Joseph Mathews on the outbuilding at The Blackjacks, 2014.
Photo by the author.

there. The ceremony occurred in the context of the rising Red Power movement, and an oil industry commemoration was not universally welcomed. The Shonkamoie family, "Mama, daughter and son," organized a protest, which Mathews derided as "a most ridiculous demonstration" and a performance of "tragi-comedy." While Mathews spoke at the event, Mrs. Shonkamoie stood to one side holding a sign reading, "WE DON'T NEED PLAQUES. WE NEED JOBS, HOMES, HOME REPAIRS, FOOD & CLOTHING."[13]

Jo was again interviewed for television in 1971, this time at The Blackjacks by KTUL Tulsa, and his diary records he found the director and cameraman personable and the experience pleasant. That year the *Oklahoman* reported Mathews was "working with the national arts and crafts program through the Department of Interior on a big Osage celebration." This event, held on September 30, 1972, commemorated the centennial of the relocation of the Osages from what is now Kansas to their present reservation. Jo served as co-chairman of the steering committee with Camille Pangburn and his sister Lillian, who did publicity and produced a radio show for Pawhuska's KOKN radio, which played recorded narratives about Osages for a week. Six years later, Pangburn became the first woman elected to the Osage

Left to right: John Joseph Mathews, Laura Mathews, Chris Mathews, Elizabeth Mathews, spring 1972. *Courtesy of the Mathews family.*

Tribal Council. That week, Mathews contributed "Osage Vignettes" and guided the preparation of commemorative issues of the *Pawhuska Journal-Capital* highlighting Pawhuska and Osage history, culture, and society.[14]

Jo's birthday, November 16, 1972, found him in a reflective mood: "I have now attained the 78th year of my pleasant life. I received long distance calls from Arizona and Washington, DC, and a letter from my daughter, which touched me deeply, expressing her sincere pride in being my daughter." He received gifts and a cake from Marie and Lillian. Dibbs gave Jo $25 to pick out his present at the liquor store. Stocked up with four bottles of bourbon and sherry, Mathews checked in at the Osage Tribal Museum and at the Osage County Historical Museum, where he signed the reissue of *Wah'Kon-Tah*. Elsie Blackhawk, wife of rancher Edward A. Blackhawk, hereditary chief of the Winnebago, phoned Jo from the Blackhawk Ranch on Sand Creek, to wish him a happy birthday. Mathews promised Elsie he "would do his usual pen & ink sketch" for her birthday the next day.[15]

Jo found the Osage Tribal Museum vacant the next day. A rumor was flying around Pawhuska that members of the American Indian Movement (AIM) were targeting the museum grounds; one Osage family wanted to remove their exhibits from the museum. According to the rumor, a "delegation of these cowardly fools planned to come to the Agency Campus and blow up" a time capsule meant to be opened in 2072, which had very recently been sealed into a hole drilled into the sandstone outside the tribal museum. Nothing happened. Later, Mathews encountered a skunk that raised its tail in a bluff, and he pondered "two bluffs in one afternoon: vicious bluffing of intertribal cowards and T-V lens hungry ignoramouses [*sic*], and the much more dignified and respected bluff of the skunk, who was actually bluffing *au naturel*."[16]

The rumor was not so far-fetched given that two days before, fifty AIM activists had occupied the Nebraska Historical Society Museum at Fort Robinson State Park. Mathews derided AIM protestors as "frenzied, imitative asses who had despoiled the Department of Interior Offices" during their very recent occupation of the BIA building in Washington, D.C., from November 3 to 9, as part of the nationwide Trail of Broken Treaties action. AIM occupiers overturned tables, started fires, destroyed records such as deeds and treaties, and damaged or stole hundreds of paintings and artifacts.[17]

The 1970s were difficult for Jo and Elizabeth as they faced the challenges and constraints of advancing age. From 1968 through 1970, Jo noted a series of serious nosebleeds. He felt increasingly lethargic and grew depressed at times. In 1973, both suffered from malnutrition, among other ailments, and both required surgery during the mid-1970s. Living at The Blackjacks full-time became infeasible. Without informing many of their friends and acquaintances, Jo and Elizabeth rented a room at the Kihekah Motel on West Main Street in Pawhuska, conveniently located near a Sonic drive-in and across the street from a liquor store. Their first stay was during the month of January 1973; they returned that summer and stayed there for a lengthy term extending into 1976, punctuated by visits to The Blackjacks as their health allowed. Their motel room was crammed with books, papers, guns, and personal effects. Henry Brown recalled that during a visit to his grandmother Elizabeth and Pop Jo with his brother Sam and mother Ann Hunt Brown, they found the walls of the motel room lined with empty half-gallon bottles of Wild Turkey, which, as Jo noted with precision in his diary, cost twenty dollars.[18]

In 1974, Kansan author Richard Rhodes tracked down Mathews to interview him for his book of travel writing, *Looking for America: A Writer's Odyssey* (1979).

> I found John Joseph Mathews, at the cocktail hour of my arrival, in the room he shared with his wife at the better motel. They had lived there

> most of a year, ever since a serious operation brought her into town from the stone house Mathews had built . . . too far from town for safe convalescence. Mathews was drinking Wild Turkey, and I joined him, his wife preferring rum and orange juice, the juice on doctor's orders for the potassium it contained. The man reclined on his bed on one elbow, beneath the elbow a folded blanket, in exactly the posture of the old Osage chiefs in the faded photographs taken long ago by the Bureau of Ethnology. He is a tall man, a big man, was dressed in a blue jumpsuit, his forehead Shakespearean and capped with fine white hair, his voice firm and commanding, with a touch of Oxford at the edges.

Rhodes wrote that finding the Osage author and historian in a "small Oklahoma motel room was like finding Gibbon or Herodotus there, and Mrs. Mathews was no less remarkable, her voice lilting and her face still beautiful, surrounded by abundant gray hair." Rhodes was moved: "The elderly in America seldom carry such a freight of dignity and courtliness and pride. Halfway through my life, I stored the Mathewses away somewhere, knowing how much I might need their memory at a later time." In 1974, Mathews was also interviewed by Alice Ann Callahan, serving as a major source for her book *The Osage Ceremonial Dance: I'n-Lon-Schka*.[19]

In 1976 John Hunt bought a house for his mother and Jo at 1619 Leahy Avenue in Pawhuska, at the instigation of his friend Strat Tolson of the Tolson Agency. For decades, members of the Tolson family—Ralph S. Tolson and his sons Strat, Melvin, and Ralph—had known and worked with the Mathews and Hunt families. Strat and Melvin each recalled fondly that even before seeing Mathews, one would catch a whiff of wood smoke. Strat had alerted John Hunt that Elizabeth and Jo's living situation in a small motel room was precarious. "In all honesty, it was killing him," Tolson said. When John told Strat he had decided to buy them a house, Tolson replied, "I think that would save his life." The Mathewses moved into the new house on the corner of Seventeenth Street and Leahy, known as "the old Dr. Stock house." It featured a large den that looked out over the backyard.[20]

When Laura Mathews, along with her father John and her aunt Virginia, visited her grandfather and Elizabeth in 1976, they spent time both at the new home on Leahy and out at The Blackjacks. During this visit, Jo and Elizabeth seemingly ate very little. Jo appeared to sustain himself on a mixture of milk and Wild Turkey bourbon, an odd cocktail recalled by several family members. Laura recalled there was little food in the house. Her grandfather showed them photos and home movies of wildlife and hunting trips. Chris and Laura both recalled that, during another visit, Laura argued with her grandfather about hunting, since she did not understand how he could love animals so much yet want to kill them so often. Both Chris and Laura vividly recalled being driven through a prairie fire blazing on both sides of the road, a surreal vision. Chris also mentioned that when her family visited The Blackjacks, they had to wait until late at night to eat dinner, because cocktail hour would stretch out all evening. This was typical for Mathews, who made guests wait until they were ravenous, so that they would eat with gusto. "The great trick is delay," he explained in *Talking to the Moon*. Chris recalled one night at The Blackjacks when, after eating late, she felt ill. A tipsy Dibbs insisted that Chris join her in the kitchen area, and sat the teenager on her lap to rock her, even though she was clearly too old for that. Even stranger to Chris, the rocking went on for half an hour. Sara, Chris, and Laura all found some aspects of their grandparents' lifestyle a bit unusual.[21]

In 1978 Charles H. Red Corn and his sister, Kathryn Red Corn, a future curator of the Osage Tribal Museum, paid Jo and Elizabeth a visit at their home. They found the older couple busy organizing stacks of biographical materials. Though advanced in years, Jo remained a lively conversationalist and was attentive, helpful, and humorous, Red Corn said. During this period, Jo and Dibbs organized his papers, magazines, photos, clippings, and slides, and he spent many days transcribing his taped diary entries. One April afternoon in 1978, a young teacher from Tahlequah named Susanna Mosley drove to Pawhuska to interview Mathews. She was an "intelligent interviewer" and he quite enjoyed her visit. Mosley borrowed and copied five undated poems Mathews lent her: "I Thought" (". . . a violin expressed life's yearning, / Then I heard a bull-elk's challenge burning"), "The Last Shot" ("The red bitch makes one more sally"), "Autumn Night" ("I should like to write immortal words / While the red bitch dreams of birds"), "Old Don," and "To the Bluejay." She phoned the next day to tell him she had played her recording of him reading his poems to her class. "My visit will always be one my fondest memories," Mosely told Jo and Elizabeth.[22]

On the evening of Monday, June 11, 1979, John Joseph Mathews walked on. His health had been failing for several months, and according to Henry Brown, the cause of death was cirrhosis of the liver. A decade earlier, on Jo's seventy-fifth birthday, he reflected he had "lived almost a perfect life" doing exactly what he had chosen to do. To pay tribute, the Osage Tribal Museum closed and flags in the city were flown at half-mast. Frederick Drummond recalled, however, that the Osage Agency did not close, which he felt showed a lack of proper respect by the tribe toward their spokesman and historian. Upon Jo's passing, columnist Gary Jack Willis of the *Tulsa*

Tribune, a Pawhuska native, wrote: "Some will wonder why they didn't take more time to know him better and less time for him to know them."[23]

Humor and sadness intermingled in recollections of Jo's unique life. Willis told an oft-repeated story about a woman reporter who, unable to get in touch with Mathews, decided to drive out to The Blackjacks to attempt an interview. She knocked on the door in vain until Jo came around from the back of the house, buck naked. Locals have it that Jo and Elizabeth liked to go au naturel at The Blackjacks, making Mathews a naturalist in more than one way. Willis praised Jo's nonconformity: "An Oxford man who had seen the world, Jo wouldn't let Pawhuska keep him from being himself. The town usually frowns on originality in any form." Jo's bush jacket and safari hat "just wouldn't hang right in many other closets, but he wore them and stood out from the crowd and never looked back." Gary Jack's aunt, Violet Willis, recalled Mathews as an independent, unconventional man. Michael Vaught later wrote: "Some who remember him still view him as something of an eccentric, but *unconcerned* would be a more accurate description."[24]

John Joseph Mathews influenced, inspired, or was a kindred spirit to countless Osage writers, critics, artists, historians, and intellectuals. One of the most important is professor and critic Robert Allen Warrior, whose seminal study *Tribal Secrets: Recovering American Indian Intellectual Traditions* (1995) focused on Mathews and Vine Deloria, Jr. According to Creek and Cherokee novelist and critic Craig S. Womack, Warrior's historicist and tribally specific reading of *Sundown* argues that Chal's identity struggles are connected to larger threats to Osage sovereignty; namely, "the abrogation of Osage national government, the dislocating effect of having grown up in a sovereign nation that is dismantled under the Dawes and Curtis acts." Warrior's analysis of *Sundown* entirely changed the way Womack approached Native literature from then on. Others who have looked to Mathews for inspiration include novelist and essayist Charles H. Red Corn, whose novel *A Pipe for February* (2002)—like the last section of *Sundown* (1934), John Hunt's *Grey Horse Legacy* (1968), and Chickasaw author Linda Hogan's *Mean Spirit* (1990)—was set in and near Pawhuska during the 1920s Reign of Terror. Among artists can be counted sculptor John D. Free, whom Jo introduced at an event in 1969, and Romain Shackelford, who painted Jo's portrait that year and another one after his death. Also inspired were poets Carter Revard, Kenneth Jacob Jump, and Elise Paschen, daughter of Osage prima ballerina Maria Tallchief and Chicago executive and building contractor Henry D. Paschen, Jr. Elise Paschen has "looked to his work for inspiration" and says *The Osages* "helped me with some of my work." In one of Mathews's unpublished stories titled "Moccasin Prints" (not to be confused with the section of *Talking to the Moon* bearing that heading), the daughter of an Osage chief prepares her father to meet Lord Dorset, an English ambassador to the United States. Her name is Maria, and she is a famous ballerina. The chief tells his daughter a story of George Washington's heroism at Braddock's Defeat during the Battle of Monongahela in the French and Indian War. Then a volunteer aide-de-camp for the British, Washington, due to his bravery and seeming invincibility, was referred to by Indian warriors as "the tall chief" and associated with Wah'Kon-Tah (spiritual mystery), he says. Maria's sister Marjorie Tallchief was also a celebrated ballerina. Their great-nephew, dancer, writer, and educator Russ Tall Chief, also expressed his debt to Mathews.[25]

On the evening of Wednesday, June 13, the Rosary was received at Jo and Elizabeth's house on Leahy Avenue, where he died. On Thursday morning, June 14, Immaculate Conception Catholic Church was filled with mourners for a funeral Mass. Pallbearers included Strat Tolson and Frederick Drummond. Mathews was buried in the garden of his beloved Blackjacks home, his resting place marked with a small headstone. Jo's friend, Assistant Principal Chief Ed Red Eagle, Sr., led an Osage ceremony at the burial, and a recording of Osage songs was played. Jo's relatively short ritual was not a full Osage mourning ceremony, which could continue for days. Still several full-bloods were present, as were several friends and Mathews and Hunt family members, and the ceremony became emotional. Lillian Mathews said that as Jo's casket was being lowered into the ground, a black bird no one could identify flew extremely low over them and made a mournful sound. To Lillian, this was a wondrous sign that her brother's spirit was free. Ed Red Eagle lamented: "The man who knew more about our heart and what we thought is gone."[26]

Everything is a circle
turning like a golden eagle
in the sky
under the eye
of Grandfather Sun.

NOTES

ABBREVIATIONS USED IN THE NOTES

JAB Joseph A. Brandt Collection, Western History Collections, University of Oklahoma

JFD J. Frank Dobie Collection, Correspondence, Harry Ransom Center, University of Texas

JJM John Joseph Mathews Collection, Western History Collections, University of Oklahoma

LDO *Life and Death of an Oilman: The Career of E. W. Marland* by Mathews

OCHS Osage County Historical Society

OHS Oklahoma Historical Society

OTM Osage Tribal Museum

OU University of Oklahoma

OUP University of Oklahoma Press Collection, Western History Collections

PJ-C *Pawhuska Journal-Capital*, archived on microfilm at the Oklahoma Historical Society Research Center

SR Sound Recordings, John Joseph Mathews Collection

TTM *Twenty Thousand Mornings*, by Mathews

WHC Western History Collections, University of Oklahoma

WSC Walter Stanley Campbell Collection, Western History Collections, University of Oklahoma

Chapter One **SILVER SPUR**

1. Kenneth Jacob Jump, *Osage Indian Poems and Short Stories*, 2nd ed. (Pawhuska, Okla.: n.p., 1996 [1979]), 76; Harry LaFerte, "Cabin in the Osage—Refuge for a Scholar," *Tulsa World*, June 26, 1937; Bob Foresman, "Mathews' New Book Will Be Whopper," *Tulsa Tribune*, November 3, 1958.

2. Louis Owens, *Other Destinies: Understanding the American Indian Novel* (Norman: University of Oklahoma Press, 1992), 25, 60; Terry P. Wilson, "John Joseph Mathews," in *Native American Writers of the United States*, ed. Kenneth M. Roemer, Dictionary of Literary Biography 175 (Detroit: Gale Research, 1997), 154; Gerald Vizenor, *Fugitive Poses: Native American Indian Scenes of Absence and Presence* (Lincoln: University of Nebraska Press, 1998), 105.
3. For the date of John Joseph's birth, see Guggenheim application, John Joseph Mathews Collection, Western History Collections, University of Oklahoma (hereafter JJM), 3.14; information on siblings is from "Descendants of William Shirley Mathews," in the private collection of Mary Abigail Mathews; John Joseph Mathews, *Twenty Thousand Mornings: An Autobiography*, ed. and intro. Susan Kalter (Norman: University of Oklahoma Press, 2012), 92, 141.
4. Mathews, *TTM*, 10–12, 92, 33, 36.
5. Mathews, *TTM*, 11, 65, 92; Osage County Historical Society (hereafter OCHS), "The Mathews Children," *Osage County Profiles* (Pawhuska: OCHS, 1978), 27–28; Frederic F. Drummond, telephone interview, March 25, 2015; "Marie Mathews," *Pawhuska Journal-Capital* (hereafter *PJ-C*), December 2, 1988.
6. Mathews, *TTM*, 11, 45, 65; Fleur Feighan Jones, telephone interview, January 13, 2015.
7. Mathews, *TTM*, 3–4; John Joseph Mathews, *The Osages: Children of the Middle Waters* (Norman: University of Oklahoma Press, 1961).
8. *Encyclopedia Britannica*, s.v. "Osage," Britannica.com, updated July 20, 2014; Foresman, "Mathews' New Book."
9. *Encyclopedia Britannica*, s.v. "Osage," Britannica.com, updated July 20, 2014; Rennard Strickland, *The Indians in Oklahoma* (Norman: University of Oklahoma Press, 1980), 15; Terry P. Wilson, "Osage Oxonian: The Heritage of John Joseph Mathews," *Chronicles of Oklahoma* 59 (Fall 1981): 265–66.
10. Mathews, *TTM*, 20–21, 38; Betty Smith, "OCHS Museum Notes," *PJ-C*, July 9, 1972; OCHS, "The Mathews Children," *Osage County Profiles*, 26–27; T. Wilson, "Osage Oxonian," 270.
11. "Josephine Caudill Dies at Winfield, Rites Here Friday," *PJ-C*, April 27, 1955; Mathews, *TTM*, 32–33, 50–52; "St. Louis School Was for Indians," *PJ-C*, September 29, 1972.
12. Charles H. Red Corn, "Remembering John Joseph," *Osage News*, March 22, 2011; Garrick Bailey, ed., *Traditions of the Osage: Stories Collected and Translated by Francis LaFlesche* (Albuquerque: University of New Mexico Press, 2010), 18.
13. Alpheus H. Favour, *Old Bill Williams: Mountain Man* (Norman: University of Oklahoma Press), 1962 [1936], 45–46, 53–56; Enid Johnson, *Bill Williams: Mountain Man* (New York: Julian Messner, 1952), 21–22.
14. Favour, *Old Bill Williams*, 43–45, 53, 55, 57, 69; Louise Baker and Wayne A. O'Connell, "The Story of Oswego," in *Oswego, Kansas, Original Souvenir Book: Oswego Centennial,*

1867–1967 (Oswego: Independent, 1967), 5; Johnson, *Bill Williams*, 38–41; Mathews, *Osages*, ix.

15. John A. Mathews's surname is alternately spelled in the records as Mathas, Mathis, Mathes, and Matthews. Bill Nix (Red Corn) was also known by variations of his father's and stepfather's surnames.
16. Mathews diary, June 5, 1952 (JJM 2.3); Mathews to Campbell, March 5, 1929 (WSC 32.27); Johnson, *Bill Williams*, 69–70; Stanley Vestal, *Mountain Men* (Boston: Houghton Mifflin, 1937), 251.
17. Mathews, *TTM*, 110; Favour, *Old Bill Williams*, vii, 95, 108–10.
18. Johnson, *Bill Williams*, 38–41; "Proud Moment for Oswego," *Oswego Independent*, February 2, 1951; Harry Sloan, "Mathews at Oswego, Speaks of Earlier Days," *Independent*, April [n.d.] 1967; Louis F. Burns, *A History of the Osage People* (Tuscaloosa: University of Alabama Press, 2004), 165.
19. OCHS, *Osage County Profiles*, 26.
20. Philip Dickerson, *History of the Osage Nation, Its People, Resources, and Prospects* (Pawhuska, Okla.: n.p., 1906), 71; Favour, *Old Bill Williams*, 97, 130; Mathews, *Osages*, 627–28; Mathews, *TTM*, 53–58; Burns, *Osage Mission Baptisms, Marriages, and Interments, 1820–1886* (Fallbrook, Calif.: Ciga Press, 1986), 365.
21. Mathews, *Osages*, 628–29; Wayne O'Connell, *The Story of 'Little Town' (Oswego, Kansas) and Its Founder John Mathews* (Humboldt, Kans.: Oswego Independent, 1998 [1961]), 4–5, 7; W. W. Graves, *History of Neosho County* (St. Paul, Kans.: Osage Mission Historical Society, 1986 [1949]), 180, 182–86.
22. Graves, *History of Neosho County*, 179–80; O'Connell, *Story of 'Little Town,'* 8. Schoenmakers is immortalized in the "Osage Window" at Immaculate Conception Church in Pawhuska, which shows the priest bringing the Word to the tribe. See Jodi Smith, "Catholic Church Draws Visitors from around the World," *PJ-C*, March 31, 1993.
23. Mathews, *Osages*, 632–34; Burns, *History of the Osage People*, 250–51.
24. O'Connell, *Story of 'Little Town,'* 11, 18; Philip Blair, personal interview, Oswego, Kans., July 15, 2013; Willard H. Rollings, *Unaffected by the Gospel: Osage Resistance to the Christian Invasion (1673–1906): A Cultural Victory* (Albuquerque: University of New Mexico Press), 164; Jo Mathews to Gerald Barnard, May 1, 1967, Oswego Historical Society; Graves, *History of Neosho County*, 180. I thank Philip Blair of Oswego for providing several useful sources.
25. Mathews, *TTM*, 24–25, 137; OCHS, *Osage County Profiles*, 26.
26. Mathews, *TTM*, 24–25; OCHS, *Osage County Profiles*, 26; Harvey Payne, personal interview, July 16, 2013.
27. Mathews, *TTM*, 24; Violet Willis, "W. S. Mathews, Early Day Tribe Leader," *PJ-C*, September 29, 1972; Carol Hunter, "The Historical Context in John Joseph Mathews' *Sundown*," *MELUS* 9, no. 1 (Spring 1982): 61–72; "William Shirley Mathews Deceased," *Pawhuska Capital*, March 18, 1915.

28. "Eben Soderstrom, 93, Watched Much of Pawhuska's History," *PJ-C*, February 29, 1972; OCHS, *Osage County Profiles*, 27; "Safeway Store Takes Quarters in Old Osage Mercantile Building," *PJ-C*, January 2, 1935; Raymond Red Corn III, personal interview, January 7, 2013, Pawhuska.
29. Dickerson, *History of the Osage Nation*, 8; "William Shirley Mathews Deceased"; Willis, "W. S. Mathews, Early Day Tribe Leader"; Osage Tribal Museum (OTM), *The Osage Timeline* (Pawhuska: OTM, 2013), 42.
30. "William Shirley Mathews"; Willis, "W. S. Mathews, Early Day Tribe Leader"; Dickerson, *History of the Osage Nation*, 46; OTM, "Osage Tribal Council History," Osage Nation, http://osagetribe.com/museum/uploads/otc_1906-2006.pdf (no longer online); Mathews, *Talking to the Moon* (Chicago: University of Chicago Press, 1945), 1.
31. E. E. White, *Experiences of a Special Indian Agent* (Norman: University of Oklahoma Press, 1965 [1893]), 222; Guy Logsdon, "John Joseph Mathews—A Conversation," *Nimrod* 16 (April 1972): 70.
32. OCHS, *Osage County Profiles*, 27; Mathews, *TTM*, 100–102, 98, 174.
33. Mathews, *TTM*, 12, 14–15, 18, 23; Mathews diary, October 18, 1952 (JJM 2.2).
34. Audiotaped conversation, November 16, 1960 (JJM SR 2280). On "natural reason," see Gerald Vizenor, *Native Liberty: Natural Reason and Cultural Survivance* (Lincoln: University of Nebraska Press, 2010).
35. OCHS, *Osage County Profiles*, 26–27; Mathews diary, October 18, 1952, March 26, 1955 (JJM 2.2, 2.7); Mathews, *TTM*, 23.
36. Mathews diary, October 18, 1952 (JJM 2.2).
37. John Joseph Mathews, "Ee Sa Rah N'eah's Story," *Sooner Magazine*, June 1931, 328–29.
38. Mathews, *TTM*, 13–14; OCHS, *Osage County Profiles*, 27; Willis, "W. S. Mathews Deceased"; Patti Gambill, "Mathews Home Comes Alive for Holiday Home Tour," *PJ-C*, December 2, 1992; John Hopper Mathews, personal interview, August 2, 2013; Fleur Feighan Jones, telephone interview, January 13, 2015; "Penney's Here since Back in '25," *PJ-C*, September 29, 1972; "Biographical Sketch," *J. C. Penney Papers: A Guide to the Collection*, DeGolyer Library, Southern Methodist University, www.lib.utexas.edu/taro/smu/00012/smu-00012.html.
39. Mathews, *TTM*, 45–49, 63–64; Mathews diary, August 29, 1961 (JJM 2.14); OTM, *Osage Timeline*, 38.
40. Mathews, *TTM*, 88–89; Orpha B. Russell, "Chief James Bigheart of the Osages," *Chronicles of Oklahoma* 32, no. 4 (Winter 1954–55): 384.
41. "John Palmer, Well Known Indian Dies," *PJ-C*, October 25, 1934; *The Trumpeter* (Pawhuska High School yearbook) 1, no. 4 (1912); Mathews, *TTM*, 39, 43–44, 61, 65–66, 74, 76–78, 80–82, 86–87, 137, 103–8; Violet Willis, "The Mathews Children," *Osage County Profiles*, 28; "Eben Soderstrom," *PJ-C*, February 29, 1972.
42. Mathews, *TTM*, 91–93, 95–96; Mathews diary, May 30, 1948.
43. Mathews, *TTM*, 98–100.

Chapter Two **FLIGHT/SCHOOL**

1. John Joseph Mathews, "Scholarship Comes to Life: The University of Oklahoma Press," *Saturday Review of Literature*, May 16, 1942, 30; Mathews, *TTM*, 138.
2. John Joseph Mathews, "When Brooks Field Was a Farmyard," *University of Oklahoma Magazine*, May–June 1917, 18.
3. Mathews, *TTM*, 140–41.
4. Mathews, *TTM*, 141–42; Mathews, "Boy, Horse, and Dog," 120 (JJM 4.33); Howard McCasland, "Oklahoma Goes after New Home," *Kappa Alpha Journal*, April 1916, 90; Joe [John Joseph] Mathews, "Jolly Fraternitee," *University of Oklahoma Magazine*, April 1917, 17.
5. *Sooner* yearbook, University of Oklahoma, Norman, 1915, 165, and 1916, 188; Mathews, "Boy, Horse, and Dog," 133.
6. "Indian Heiresses Invade Capital," *Washington Herald*, September 7, 1914.
7. Mathews, *TTM*, 142–43; "William Shirley Mathews Deceased."
8. Mathews, *TTM*, 144–45.
9. Mathews, *TTM*, 143–48; Pawhuska Journal-Capital, *Reflections of Pawhuska, Oklahoma*, vol. 1 (Pawhuska: D-Books, 1995), 16.
10. Daniel Francis, *The Imaginary Indian: The Image of the Indian in Canadian Culture* (Vancouver: Arsenal Pulp, 1992), 151–53; Mathews, *TTM*, 148–50; Mathews to Elizabeth Hunt, August 20, 24, and 31, 1935 (JJM 1.3); Ray Tassin, *Stanley Vestal: Champion of the Old West* (Glendale, Calif.: A. H. Clark, 1973), 35; Mathews diary, June 29, 1959 (JJM 3.12).
11. Mathews, "Boy, Horse, and Dog," 130.
12. Mathews, "Boy, Horse, and Dog," 128–32.
13. Ibid., 132; PJ-C, *Reflections of Pawhuska*, 74.
14. Mathews, "Boy, Horse, and Dog," 141.
15. Phyllis Cole Braunlich, *Haunted by Home: The Life and Letters of Lynn Riggs* (Norman: University of Oklahoma Press, 1988), 40; Elmer L. Fraker, "With Thoburn at Honey Creek," *Chronicles of Oklahoma* 34 (Spring 1956): 44–52; Fraker, "Cave Men in Wilds of Soonerdom," *University of Oklahoma Magazine*, October 1921; Bob L. Blackburn, "Thoburn, Joseph Bradfield (1866–1941)," *Encyclopedia of Oklahoma History & Culture*, Oklahoma Historical Society, www.okhistory.org/publications/enc/entry.php?entry=TH005.
16. "Local News Happenings in and about Town," *PJ-C*, August 17 and September 14, 1916.
17. Mathews, "Boy, Horse, and Dog," 139–40; Mathews, *Sundown*, 121–26, 129; Mathews, *TTM*, 166, 232.
18. *Sooner* yearbook 1917, 110; Mathews, "Boy, Horse, and Dog," 141; "Oklahoma Academy of Science," *Science* 45, no. 8: 271–72; "Local News Happenings," *PJ-C*, December 9 and December 26, 1916.

19. Mathews, *TTM*, 158–61; "Local News Happenings," *PJ-C*, January 18, January 25, and April 5, 1917.
20. Mathews, *TTM*, 161–62; *University Oklahoman*, May 2, 1917 (JJM 4.37); "Local News Happenings," *PJ-C*, May 10, 1917.
21. Mathews, *TTM*, 162–65.
22. Mathews, "Boy, Horse, and Dog," 148–50; Mathews, *Talking to the Moon*, 13.
23. Mathews, *TTM*, 166–68.
24. Mathews, *TTM*, 169–70, 173; "Local News Happenings," *PJ-C*, August 16, 1917; "Josephine Caudill."
25. Mathews, *TTM*, 169, 171–73; Gore Vidal, *Point to Point Navigation* (New York: Knopf, 2007), 170.
26. Mathews, *TTM*, 174–75, 183–86, 191.
27. Mathews, *TTM*, 177, 187–90, 192–96.
28. Mathews, *TTM*, 197–99.
29. Mathews, *TTM*, 199–200, 208, 202, 205–6, 232.
30. Mathews, *TTM*, 199, 212, 205; Mathews, "Boy, Horse, and Dog," 186.
31. Mathews, *TTM*, 187, 205, 208, 211; Mathews, "Boy, Horse, and Dog," 186–87; Mathews, *Sundown*, 211–12, 216.
32. Mathews, *TTM*, 214–15, 217–18, 221–27; Mathews diary, June 26, 1921 (JJM 1.44).
33. "Henry Ben Caudill, Jr.," Oklahoma Casualties Database, World War II, Oklahoma History Center, www.okhistory.org/historycenter/okcasualties/world-war-2-detail.php?casualty=313; Mathews, *TTM*, 230.
34. Mathews, *TTM*, 231.
35. *Sooner* yearbook, 1919, 127, and 1920, n.p.; Mathews, *TTM*, 231–32.
36. *Sooner* yearbook, 1920, n.p.; Mathews, *TTM*, 232, 138; Frank L. Dennis, "Scenes from a Scrapbook," *Sooner Magazine*, Spring 1988, 23; Peter Carlson, "When Signs Said 'Get Out,'" *Washington Post*, February 21, 2006, www.washingtonpost.com/wp-dyn/content/article/2006/02/20/AR2006022001590.html.
37. Mathews, *TTM*, 232–33; Martin Shockley, ed., *Southwest Writers Anthology* (Austin: Steck-Vaughn, 1967), 127; Tassin, *Stanley Vestal*, 13–14, 85–86.
38. Mathews, *TTM*, 233, 253; interview with Guy Logsdon, March 14, 1972, audiocassette (JJM SR 2281).
39. Mathews, "Boy, Horse, and Dog," 206–12.
40. Mathews, *TTM*, 234, 236–37, 239–40; Mathews, "Hunting in the Rockies," *Sooner Magazine*, May 1929, 279.
41. Mathews, *TTM*, 242.
42. Mathews, *TTM*, 249–52; Mathews to Walter Stanley Campbell, December 7, 1920, Walter Stanley Campbell Collection, Western History Collections, University of Oklahoma (WSC 32.27).
43. Mathews, *TTM*, 252–53; Tassin, *Stanley Vestal*, 65–66.

CHAPTER THREE **OXFORD AND EUROPE**

1. Carter Revard, e-mail to the author, August 11, 2013; Karen Neurohr, oral history interview with Carter Revard, Spotlighting Oklahoma Oral History Project, Oklahoma State University, Edmon Low Library, 2009, 8–10; Tassin, *Stanley Vestal*, 60–76.
2. Savoie Lottinville, "In Memoriam: John Joseph Mathews, 1895–1979," *American Oxonian* 57, no. 4 (1980): 238; Mathews diary, February 18, 1924 (JJM 1.44); Wilson, "Osage Oxonian"; "Six Oklahomans Are in Oxford Colleges," *Oklahoma Teacher*, January 1922, 28; Guy Logsdon, interview with Mathews, March 14, 1972, audiocassette (JJM SR 2281).
3. Lottinville, "In Memoriam: John Joseph Mathews," 238; Mathews diary, June 6, 10, 15, and 18, 1921 (JJM 1.44).
4. Mathews diary, May 2, 4, and 5, 1922 (JJM 1.44).
5. Mathews diary, June 26, 1923 (JJM 1.44). William Johnson Sollas was a British geologist, zoologist, paleontologist, anthropologist, and author acclaimed as a "geological polymath." He taught at Oxford from 1897 until his death in 1936, and in later years became increasingly eccentric. Mathews, who "loved the old gentleman," thanked his friend, ecologist and OU botany professor Paul B. Sears, for sending him an obituary of "dear old Sollas. Those old Victorians were smug and often ridiculously formal and hard on rivals, but somehow in their old, badly lighted, often musty labs, they accomplished great things." Mathews to Sears, March 29, 1937, Paul Bigelow Sears Papers, Yale University Library, MS 663, I, 40.617.
6. Mathews diary, June 3, 1921 (JJM 1.44).
7. Mathews diary, June 3, 8, 9, and 10, 1921 (JJM 1.44).
8. Mathews diary, June 12, 1921 (JJM 1.44).
9. In her introduction to *Twenty Thousand Mornings*, Susan Kalter guessed that "W.J.H." was probably a member of the Hobbs family. In her afterword to *Old Three Toes*, Kalter upgraded the hypothetical "W. J. Hobbs" to an unequivocally real person (p. 169). Kalter is clearly in error because Mathews did not socialize with the Hobbs family until three years after this time, and even then, Mathews's diary entry of March 13, 1924 indicates no family member has the first initial W. "Six Oklahomans Are in Oxford Colleges," *Oklahoma Teacher*, January 1922, 28; "Personal Notes by Classes, Class of 1920," *American Oxonian* 9, 171; "Personal Notes by Classes, Class of 1920," *American Oxonian* 10, 206.
10. Mathews diary, June 14, 17, 19, and 23, 1921; July 13–14, 1921; n.d.; September 24, 1921 (JJM 1.44); Mathews, "What Thing Is Fairest" (JJM 4.26).
11. Mathews misspells the name "Dunlop."
12. Mathews diary, June 5, 1921 (JJM 1.44); April 28, 30 1922 (JJM 1.45); "Cornmarket, Oxford, 21 Cornmarket (site of former White Hart Inn)," *Oxford History*, www.oxford history.org.uk/cornmarket/east/21_white_hart.html.
13. Mathews diary, June 24, 25, 1921 (JJM 1.44); "Activities in the Export and Bunker Trades," *Black Diamond* 69 (July 1, 1922); "Anniversary: Black Friday 15 April 1921,"

The Socialist, April 20, 2011, www.socialistparty.org.uk/issue/667/11893/20-04-2011/anniversary-black-friday-15-april-1921.

14. Mathews diary, June 26, 28, 1921 (JJM 1.44).
15. Ibid., June 27–29, 1921; July 2–7, 1921 (JJM 1.44).
16. Ibid., July 8, 10–11, 1921 (JJM 1.44).
17. Ibid., July 15–22, 1921 (JJM 1.44).
18. Ibid., July 23–26, 1921 (JJM 1.44); Rudyard Kipling, "The Ladies," in *Collected Verse of Rudyard Kipling* (New York: Doubleday, 1907), 371–73.
19. Mathews diary, July 27, 1921 (JJM 1.44).
20. Ibid., July 29–30, 1921 (JJM 1.44); August n.d., 15–16, and 18–20, 1921 (JJM 1.44).
21. Ibid., July 6, 1921 (JJM 1.44).
22. Ibid., September 23–26, 1921 (JJM 1.44); "Six Oklahomans Are in Oxford Colleges."
23. "Hobbies, etc.," University of Oklahoma Press Collection, Western History Collections 37.5 (hereafter OUP); Mathews, "Hunting the Red Deer of Scotland: The Thrill of Conquering the Monarch of the Highlands," *Sooner Magazine* 1 (May 1929): 213–14; Mathews, "Hunting in the Rockies," 263, 278–80; Mathews, "Lady of the Inn," n.d. (JJM 4.9); Mathews, "The Royal of Glen Orchy" (JJM 4.21); description of Auch Lodge in JJM to J. Frank Dobie, n.d. [late 1959 or early 1960], correspondence, J. Frank Dobie Collection, Harry Ransom Center, University of Texas (hereafter JFD). Many thanks to James H. Cox for alerting me to this correspondence, which at the time of this writing has not yet been digitally catalogued.
24. Maria Eugenia Schellenberg, telephone interview, December 13, 2015. The leopard skin was passed down to Maria.
25. Mathews diary, December 31, 1924 (JJM 1.45); January 6, 1922 (JJM 1.44); Mathews, "Gallery," *Space* 1, no. 1 (May 1934).
26. Mathews diary, January n.d., 1922 (JJM 1.44); Mathews, "Allah's Guest" (JJM 4.2).
27. Mathews diary, January n.d., 10, 13, 14, and 16, 1922 (JJM 1.45).
28. John Hunt, "John Joseph Mathews," *Encyclopedia of North American Indians* (Boston: Houghton Mifflin, 1996), 364; Logsdon, "John Joseph Mathews," 70; T. Wilson, "Osage Oxonian," 271–72.
29. *Occest (occ est)* is a northern African Latin corruption of *hoc est*, but "occast" seems to be Mathews's error.
30. Mathews, *Talking to the Moon*, 194; Gaston Boissier, *Roman Africa: Archeological Walks in Algeria and Tunis*, translated by Arabella Ward (New York: Putnam, 1899), 207; Richard Higgs, "Searching for John Joseph Mathews," *This Land*, August 15, 2013.
31. Mathews diary, June 24, 27–30, 1922; July 1–2, 1922 (JJM 1.45); Mathews to Marie Mathews, April 16, 1923 (JJM 1.22).
32. Mathews diary, July 5–20, 1922 (JJM 1.45); John O. Moseley went on to join the faculty at OU for fifteen years, teaching Latin and classical archaeology, before becoming president

of Central State Teachers College, which later became the University of Central Oklahoma. "John O. Moseley," *Wikipedia*, https://en.wikipedia.org/wiki/John_O._Moseley.

33. Mathews diary, July 31, 1922 (JJM 1.45).
34. *Calumet Chieftain* (Calumet, Okla.), June 8, 1922; Kim Brumley, *Marland Tragedy: The Turbulent Story of a Forgotten Oklahoma Icon* (Mustang, Okla.: Tate, 2009), 33.
35. Mathews diary, July 25–26, 28–31, 1922, August 5, 7–9, 1922 (JJM 1.45); "Georgette LaMotte Views Passion Play," *Musical Courier*, August 24, 1922, 39; Joseph Thoburn, *A Standard History of Oklahoma* (Chicago: American Historical Society, 1916), 5:2136–37; "The Founding Meeting of NCAI," National Congress of American Indians, www.ncai.org/about-ncai/mission-history/the-founding-meeting-of-ncai.
36. Mathews diary, August 11–15, 17–24, 26–27, 29, 31, 1922; September 17–18, 1922 (JJM 1.45); New York, Passenger Lists, 1820–1957, Ancestry.com; Mathews diary, December 31, 1924 (JJM 1.45).
37. Mathews to Marie Mathews. April 16, 1923 (JJM 1.22).
38. Mathews diary, June 26, 1923 (JJM 1.44).
39. Mathews, interview with Guy Logsdon, March 14, 1972 (JJM SR 2281); "Teapot Dome Scandal," *Encyclopedia Britannica*, updated July 5, 2015, www.britannica.com/event/Teapot-Dome-Scandal.
40. Mathews, interview with Logsdon; Emily Lutenski, "Tribes of Men: John Joseph Mathews' Indian Internationalism," *SAIL: Studies in American Indian Literatures* 24, no. 2 (2012): 39–64. Many thanks to Kathryn Redcorn, curator of the Osage Tribal Museum, for helping me with my research questions and showing me Mathews's certificate.
41. *Bankers Magazine*, January–June 1918, 301–2; Heather Carmen Martin, "Cast of Characters: Singer Presidents," *Singer Memories*, 2011, www.singermemories.com/cast-characters-singer-presidents; Karen Neurohr, "Oral History Interview with Virginia H. Mathews," September 9, 2009, Spotlighting Oklahoma Oral History Project, Oklahoma State University.
42. John Hopper Mathews and Gail Painter Mathews, personal interview, August 2, 2013; Virginia Winslow Mathews, *Captured Moments* (Madison, Conn.: Horse Pond, 1987), 40, author biography.
43. Mathews diary, June 9, 1921; January 1, 1924; February 9, 1924 (JJM 1.44, 1.45); Chris Mathews, personal interview, July 31, 2013; Laura Mathews Edwards, personal interview, August 2, 2013.
44. Mathews diary, January 1–3, 1924 (JJM 1.45).
45. Mathews diary, January 19 and 23, 1924 (1.45).
46. Mathews diary, January 25, 1924; February 10, 13, 17–19, 1924; March 13, 1924 (JJM 1.45); "Cedric Brudenell-Bruce, 7th Marquess of Ailesbury," https://en.wikipedia.org/wiki/Cedric_Brudenell-Bruce,_7th_Marquess_of_Ailesbury.

47. Mathews diary, March 6, 1924 (JJM 1.45).
48. Mathews diary, March 7 and 27, 1924 (JJM 1.45).
49. Mathews diary, March 1 and 3, 1924 (JJM 1.44); Savoie Lottinville, "Portrait of a Sooner," *Sooner Magazine*, September 1938, 13.
50. Mathews diary, April 5 and 20–22, 1924 (JJM 1.45).
51. Mathews diary, April 24, 1924 (JJM 1.45); John Joseph Mathews, "Beauty's Votary," *Sooner Magazine* 3 (February 1931), 171, 181–82.
52. Mathews diary, May 3, 7–11, 14–16, 1924; June 1–7, 30, 1924; July 1, 1924 (JJM 1.45); Neurohr, "Oral History Interview with Virginia H. Mathews," 10–12; Mathews to "friends and others of influence in the nation," n.d. [1964] (JJM 4.40).
53. Mathews diary, July 2–4, 8–9, 1924; September 3, 1924; November 2, 5, 9–18, 1924 (JJM 1.45); New York, Passenger Lists, 1820–1957, Ancestry.com.

Chapter four **FIRST FAMILY/CALIFORNIA DREAMING**

1. I refer to Mathews's first wife as Ginger, her nickname. Although Mathews and some family members would refer to her as Virginia after the couple's separation, I wish to differentiate her from three other Virginias who play roles in Jo's story: his daughter, his daughter's companion, and E. W. Marland's first wife.
2. Mathews diary, November 18–19, 1924; December 1, 26, 28, 1924 (JJM 1.45).
3. Mathews diary, December 27 and 29, 1924 (JJM 1.45); Nathan Miller, *New World Coming: The 1920s and the Making of Modern America* (New York: Scribner, 2003), 63.
4. Mathews diary, December 31, 1924 (JJM 1.45).
5. Neurohr, "Oral History Interview with Virginia H. Mathews," 12.
6. Virginia Mathews, "My Father, John Joseph Mathews," in *John Joseph Mathews: Osage Writer and Tribal Councilman, Artist, Naturalist, Historian and Scholar*, ed. Karen Neurohr and Lindsey Smith (Norman: Friends of Libraries in Oklahoma, 2009), 16–17; V. Mathews, *Captured Moments*, 40, author biography; John Hopper Mathews, personal interview, August 2, 2013; Gail Painter Mathews, e-mail to the author, February 4, 2015.
7. Neurohr, "Oral History Interview with Virginia H. Mathews," 13–14; Mathews to Walter Campbell, February 15, 1929 (WSC 22.32); *Virginia W. Mathews v. John Joseph Mathews*, D-7267, District Court of Osage County, Oklahoma, in the personal collection of Gail Painter Mathews.
8. Campbell to Mathews, November 22, 1926, and Mathews to Campbell, February 25, 1925 (WSC 32.27); Tassin, *Stanley Vestal*, 122.
9. Mathews to Campbell, March 7 and May 10, 1927; Campbell to Mathews, July 23, 1927 (WSC 32.27); Neurohr, "Oral History Interview with Virginia H. Mathews," 12–13; "Local Writer, Onetime Pawhuskan Both Work on Osage Tribal History," *PJ-C*, September 18, 1960, 7, 10.
10. Logsdon, interview with Mathews, March 14, 1972; Fleur Feighan Jones, telephone interview, January 13, 2015; William Feighan, telephone interview, January 19, 2015.

11. Travis Bogard, *Contour in Time* (New York: Oxford University Press, 1988), Appendix II: "The Casts of O'Neill's Plays"; Neurohr, "Oral History Interview with Virginia H. Mathews," 15; Patt Morrison, "Sheldon Epps: Play It Again," *Los Angeles Times*, February 26, 2010.
12. V. Mathews, *Captured Moments*, 40, author biography; *Encyclopædia Britannica Online*, s. v. "Charles Wakefield Cadman," December 6, 2009, www.britannica.com/biography/Charles-Wakefield-Cadman; "Charles Wakefield Cadman," Naxos Records, www.naxos.com/person/Charles_Wakefield_Cadman/25915.htm.
13. Mathews to Campbell, April 27 and May 10, 1927 (WSC 22.32).
14. Tassin, *Stanley Vestal*, 114–15, 127–28; Braunlich, *Haunted by Home*, 41–42, 49–54; Campbell to Mathews, July 23, 1927 (WSC 32.27).
15. From the 1820s through the 1880s, the famous trail connecting Santa Fe, New Mexico, to Franklin, Missouri, was "the major route between the Spanish Southwest and the Anglo Midwest." The Cheyenne and Arapahoe tribes were generally found north of the trail, while the Kiowas and Comanches lived south of it. Martin Shockley, ed. *Southwest Writers Anthology* (Austin, Tex.: Steck-Vaughn, 1967), 127–28.
16. Mathews to Campbell, November 12, 1928 (WSC 27.32); Campbell to Mathews, January 4 and 20, 1929 (WSC 27.32); *Virginia W. Mathews v. John Joseph Mathews*.
17. Campbell to Mathews, January 4, 1929 (WSC 27.32); Brandt to Mathews, n.d. (JAB 5.14).
18. Mathews to Campbell, February 15 and 25, 1929 (WSC 22.32); California, Passenger and Crew Lists, 1882–1959, Ancestry.com.
19. Mathews to Campbell, February 15 and 25, 1929 (WSC 22.32); Tassin, *Stanley Vestal*, 143–47.
20. Mathews, "Admirable Outlaw," *Sooner Magazine* 2 (April 1930): 241, 264; Mathews, "Singers to the Moon," *Oklahoma Today* 46, no. 5 (1996): OKT Reader section, ii–vii.
21. Brandt to Mathews, n.d. (JAB 5.14); *Joseph A. Brandt, Seventh President of the University of Oklahoma* (Norman: University of Oklahoma, 1941) (booklet reprinted from *Sooner Magazine*, December 1940 and January 1941); Mathews to Campbell, March 5, 1929 (WSC 22.32).
22. Mathews to Campbell, October 29, 1929 (WSC 32.27).
23. Gail Mathews, e-mail to the author, February 4, 2015; U.S. Census Report, 1935, Ancestry.com; T. Wilson, "Osage Oxonian," 272.
24. Mathews diary, February 18, 1943 (JJM 1.20); Romain Shackelford, personal interview, July 16, 2013; John Hopper Mathews and Mary Abigail Mathews, personal interview, August 2, 2013; Laura Mathews Edwards, personal interview, August 2, 2013.
25. Laura Mathews Edwards, personal interview, August 2, 2013; Fleur Feighan Jones, telephone interview, January 13, 2015.
26. Mathews to Henry Allen Moe, November 15 and December 30, 1939; March 12, April 24, and June 22, 1940 (JJM 3.14); Mathews diary, December 3, 6, 1943; January 25 and September 2, 1946 (JJM 1.46, 1.48); *Virginia W. Mathews v. John Joseph Mathews*.

27. Laura Mathews Edwards, personal interview, August 2, 2013.
28. John H. Mathews and Mary Abigail Mathews, personal interview, August 2, 2013. I am grateful to the late Mr. Mathews, who supplied me with a résumé, notes, and documents, a great help.
29. Sara Mathews Dydak, telephone interview, March 13, 2015; Laura Edwards Mathews, personal interview, August 2, 2013.
30. John H. Mathews, personal interview, August 2, 2013; John Dunning, *On the Air: Encyclopedia of Old Time Radio* (New York: Oxford University Press, 1998), 566; Laura Mathews Edwards, personal interview, August 2, 2013.
31. Mathews to Elizabeth Hunt, March 30, 1939 (JJM 1.6).
32. Mathews to Elizabeth Hunt, March 30, 1939 (JJM 1.6); Lottinville to Brandt, February 27, 1981 (JAB 5.12).
33. Mathews to Elizabeth Hunt, March 1 and 30, 1939 (JJM 1.6).
34. Chris Mathews, personal interview, July 31, 2013; Laura Mathews Edwards, personal interview, August 2, 2013.
35. Chris Mathews, telephone interview, September 8, 2013; V. W. Mathews, *Captured Moments*, 45–46.
36. Mathews diary, March 27, 1945 (JJM 1.47); April 12, 1956 (JJM 2.8); Neurohr, "Oral History Interview with Virginia H. Mathews."
37. Neurohr, "Oral History Interview with Virginia H. Mathews"; John Hopper Mathews, personal interview, August 2, 2013; Mathews diary, June 15, 1957 (JJM 2.10); Laura Mathews Edwards, personal interview, August 2, 2013; "American Indian Library Association Names Scholarship in Honor of Virginia Mathews," American Library Association, February 7, 2012, www.ala.org/news/press-releases/2012/02/american-indian-library-association-names-scholarship-honor-virginia-mathews; Todd Wayne Vaughan, "Presidential Motorcade Schematic Listing," 1993, Rpt. Harold Weisberg Archive, jfk.hood.edu/Collection/Weisberg%20Subject%20Index%20Files/M%20Disk/Motorcade%20Route/Item%2015.pdf.
38. Virginia Mathews, "My Father," 17; Rhonda Kohnle, personal interview, June 2, 2014.
39. Mathews to Elizabeth Hunt, February 18, 1943 (JJM 1.20); Mathews diary, June 18, 1948 (JJM 1.50).
40. Mathews diary, June 15, 1957 (JJM 2.10).
41. Mathews diary, June 27, 29 and July 1–2, 1954, April 10, 23, 1956, June 15, 1957 (JJM 2.6, 2.8, 2.10); Neurohr, "Oral History Interview with Virginia H. Mathews"; Romain Shackelford, personal interview, July 16, 2013; Harvey Payne, personal interview, July 15, 2013; Mathews to Joseph Brandt, August 13, 1951, June 27, 1967 (JAB 5.14); Mathews diary, 1966 (Harvey Payne personal collection), October 21–22, 1967; Mathews diary, October 11–15, 1968 (JJM 3.5, 3.6).
42. John H. Mathews, personal interview, August 2, 2013; Mathews to Elizabeth Mathews, August 5 and September 24, 1944 (JJM 1.21); *The Lucky Bag* (yearbook), U.S. Naval Academy, class of 1950, 310.

43. John Hopper Mathews and Gail Mathews, personal interview, August 2, 2013; Gail Mathews, e-mail to the author, December 18, 2015; Laura Mathews Edwards, personal interview, August 2, 2013.
44. Gail Mathews, e-mail to the author, February 4, 2015; John Hopper Mathews and Gail Mathews, personal interview, August 2, 2013; Laura Mathews Edwards, personal interview, August 2, 2013.
45. Gail Mathews, e-mail to the author, February 4, 2015; John Hopper Mathews and Gail Mathews, personal interview, August 2, 2013.
46. Chris Mathews, personal interview, July 31, 2013; Mathews diary, June 7–10, 1969; March 27–30, 1971; Nov 7–8, 1971 (JJM 3.7, 3.10).
47. Laura Mathews Edwards, personal interview, August 2, 2013; John H. Mathews and Gail Mathews, personal interview, August 2, 2013; "John Hopper Mathews," *Lewistown Sentinel*, February 4, 2015, lewistownsentinel.com/page/content.detail/id/561483/John-Hopper-Mathews.html%3Fnav%3D5007; Gail Mathews, e-mail to the author, December 18, 2015.
48. "American Indian Library Association Names Scholarship in Honor of Virginia Mathews," American Library Association, February 7, 2012, www.ala.org/news/press-releases/2012/02/american-indian-library-association-names-scholarship-honor-virginia-mathews; Neurohr, "Oral History Interview with Virginia H. Mathews"; Chris Mathews, personal interview, July 31, 2013.
49. Chris Mathews, personal interview, July 31, 2013; Laura Mathews Edwards, personal interview, August 2, 2013.
50. "Memorial Resolution Honoring Virginia Mathews," 2010–2011 ALA Memorial #15, 2011 ALA Annual Conference, www.ala.org/aboutala/sites/ala.org.aboutala/files/content/governance/council/council_documents/2011_annual_docus/memorial_15_virginia.pdf; Neurohr, "Oral History Interview with Virginia H. Mathews"; "Virginia Winslow Hopper Mathews," obituary, *Lewistown Sentinel*, May 9, 2011, lewistownsentinel.com/page/content.detail/id/529123/mifflin.eztouse.com/.

Chapter Five **OSAGE LITERARY MAN**

1. Mathews to Campbell, March 4, 1930 (WSC 32.27); "Feighan-Mathews Wedding Solemnized Here Saturday," *PJ-C*, June 22, 1930.
2. Mathews to Campbell, December 3, 1930 (WSC 32.27).
3. Rita Keresztesi, *Strangers at Home: American Ethnic Modernism between the World Wars* (Lincoln: University of Nebraska Press, 2005), 117; Mathews diary, March 3, 1953, October 2, 1952 (JJM 2.5, 2.3); Karen Neurohr and Lindsey Smith, eds., *John Joseph Mathews: Osage Writer and Tribal Councilman, Artist, Naturalist, Historian, and Scholar* (Norman, Friends of Libraries in Oklahoma, 2009), 3; T. Wilson, "Osage Oxonian," 284.
4. Mathews, "Hunger on the Prairie," *Sooner Magazine* 2 (June 1930): 328–29; Mathews diary, January 22, 1962 (JJM 3.1).

5. "History & Mission," Isaak Walton League of America, www.iwla.org/about-us/history-mission; Mathews, *Our Osage Hills* columns, *PJ-C*, May 29, 1931; March 23, 1930; March 26, 1930; April 2, 1930; May 5, 1930.
6. Logsdon, audiotaped interview with Mathews; Louis Thomas Jones, *The Quakers of Iowa* (Des Moines: State Historical Society of Iowa, 1914), 212; "Maj. Laban Miles, Uncle of President Hoover and Early Day Indian Agent, Taken by Death," *PJ-C*, April 13, 1931, 1–2.
7. The *Sooner Magazine* reported: "in Tulsa, Sallye Little worked for Joe Brandt, city editor of the *Tribune*, until she was lured away" by the rival Tulsa newspaper. As *Tulsa World*'s "star gal reporter, she scored scoops that made Joe's face turn red as his hair," especially since Sallye was then his fiancée. Alternatively, a 1991 account by a *Tribune* colleague says she threw an inkwell at Brandt following an argument, and then quit. They married in 1927; Joe became head of University of Oklahoma Press the next year. While managing the family's domestic life, Sallye continued her literary interests and pitched in at OU Press with proofreading and stenography. "First Lady Elect," *Sooner Magazine* 13 (June 1941): 14; "OU Presidency Sour Experience for Joseph Brandt," *Tulsa World*, July 11, 1991.
8. T. Wilson, "Osage Oxonian," 274; Logsdon, audiotaped interview with Mathews, March 14, 1972; "Sooner Back to Sooners," *Time*, December 2, 1940; "Come Down, Professor," *Time*, September 24, 1945; Mathews to Brandt, June 27, 1967 (JAB 5.14).
9. Edna Ferber, *A Peculiar Treasure* (Garden City, N.Y.: Doubleday, Doran, 1939); Phillip Fortune, personal interview, February 20, 2015; Julie Goldsmith Gilbert, *Ferber: Edna Ferber and Her Circle* (Milwaukee, Wis.: Hal Leonard, 1999).
10. "Local Writer's Book on Major Miles and Osage History to Be Published Nov. 1," *PJ-C*, October 7, 1932; "Maj. Laban Miles"; Mathews to Campbell, June 18, 1931; January n.d., 1933 (WSC 32.27); Brandt to Mathews, June 8, 1967 (JAB 5.14).
11. T. Wilson, "Osage Oxonian," 274; Logsdon, audiotaped interview with Mathews; Michael Vaught, "Osage Scribe," *Oklahoma Today* 46, no. 5 (1996): 34–37.
12. Joseph A. Brandt, "Book of the Month," *Sooner Magazine*, December 1932, 77; T. Wilson, "Osage Oxonian," 274.
13. Review of *Wah'Kon-Tah*, *New York Times*, December 18, 1932; Terry P. Wilson, Review of *Wah'Kon-Tah*, *SAIL: Studies in American Indian Literatures*,1st ser., 9, no. 3 (1985): 126; Joseph A. Brandt, "Book-of-the-Month," *Sooner Magazine* 5, no. 3 (1932): 77; T. Wilson, "John Joseph Mathews"; Foresman, "Mathews' New Book Will Be Whopper"; Stanley Vestal, Review of *Wah'Kon-Tah*, *Mississippi Valley Historical Review* 20, no. 1 (1933): 153; Louis Owens, "Disturbed by Something Deeper: The Native Art of John Joseph Mathews," *Western American Literature* 35, no. 2 (2000): 166; Joseph Brandt, "Three Osage Leaders," *Sooner Magazine* 7, no. 2 (1934): 30.

14. Mathews, *The Osages*, 681–83, 413, 440, 690; Louis Thomas Jones, *The Quakers of Iowa* (Des Moines: State Historical Society of Iowa, 1914), 21; R. Michael Barnett, "Jesus among the Middle Waters: American Christian Missionaries and the Osage Nation, 1820–1920," master's thesis, University of Missouri, St. Louis, 2004, 58.
15. Henry Seidel Canby, "A Talk with President Hoover about Major Miles," *Book of the Month Club News*, October 1932, 4; Herbert Hoover, *The Memoirs of Herbert Hoover 1874–1920: Years of Adventure* (New York: Macmillan, 1951), 4–5; "Laban Miles House," Herbert Hoover National Historic Site, National Park Service, www.nps.gov/heho/learn/historyculture/laban-miles-house.htm; Ruthanna M. Simms, "Friends and the Osages: History of Hominy Friends Church," Friends University, Edmund Stanley Library Special Collections, Wichita, Kansas, 1970, 12; "Maj. Laban Miles."
16. Barnett, "Jesus among the Middle Waters," 60; Mathews, *The Osages*, 720; Simms, "Friends and the Osages," 4–5; "*Wah'Kon-Tah* and John Joseph Mathews," four-page press release, 1932, Western History Collections, University of Oklahoma (OUP 6.1), n.p.; Elizabeth Williams Cosgrove, review of *Wah'Kon-Tah*, *Chronicles of Oklahoma* 11, no. 1 (1933): 733; Burns, *History of the Osage People*, 359, 358, 199; "Maj. Laban Miles"; Mathews, *Wah'Kon-Tah*, 335, 331; E. E. White, *Experiences of a Special Indian Agent*, 229; T. Wilson, "Osage Oxonian," 274; "A Note on the Author and Artist" (OUP 103.3); Logsdon, "Conversation with John Joseph Mathews," 73.
17. Mathews to Brandt, June 27, 1967; Brandt to Mathews, June 8, 1967 (JAB 5.14); Brandt to Mrs. O'Dell, January 6, 1932 (OUP 4.13); Gore Vidal, *I Told You So: Gore Vidal Talks Politics* (Berkeley: Counterpoint, 2013), 90–91; "Charles Brent Curtis," *Encyclopedia of World Biography*, 2004, www.encyclopedia.com/topic/Charles_Curtis.aspx; Bill Kelter, *Veeps: Profiles in Insignificance* (Atlanta: Top Shelf, 2008), 159.
18. Mathews to Brandt, February 12, 1936 (OUP 4.14); Mathews, *Talking to the Moon*, 19; Elizabeth Alden Settle, "From the Blackjacks," *Folk-Say: A Regional Miscellany 1931*, ed. B. A. Botkin (Norman: University of Oklahoma Press, 1931), 236; Warrior, *The People and the Word: Reading Native Nonfiction* (Minneapolis: University of Minnesota Press, 2005), 184–85.
19. Mathews, *Talking to the Moon*, 19; Mathews, audiotaped diary, July 24, 1965 (JJM SR 2275).
20. T. Wilson, "Osage Oxonian," 275, 277; Mathews to Brandt, June 27, 1967 (JAB 5.14); Brandt to Betty Kirk, October 19, 1932 (OUP 4.13); Kirk to Brandt, October 27, 31, 1932 (OUP 4.13); Oliver La Farge to Kirk, November 2, 1932 (OUP 6.1); Virginia H. Mathews, introduction to *Sundown* (Norman: University of Oklahoma Press, 1988 [1934]), vii.
21. Kirk to Brandt, November 6, 1932 (OUP 4.13); Mary Austin, "The Osage Indians," review of *Wah'Kon-Tah*, *Saturday Review*, November 19, 1951, 251; Oliver La Farge to Kirk, November 2, 1932 (OUP 6.1); "Interview with Lewis Titterton," *Books and Characters*, November 6, 1932, 1–9.

22. Mathews to Campbell, n.d. [January 1933] (WSC 32.27); Bob L. Blackburn, "Foreman, Grant (1869–1953)," *Encyclopedia of Oklahoma History and Culture*, OHS, www.okhistory.org/publications/enc/entry.php?entry=FO020web; Kitty Pittman, "Bizzell, William Bennett (1876–1944)," *Encyclopedia of Oklahoma History and Culture*, www.okhistory.org/publications/enc/entry.php?entry=BI015; "Author Honored at Reception," *Tulsa World*, January 15, 1933.
23. Mathews to Brandt, n.d. [February 12, 1933] (OUP 9.1).
24. "An Educated Indian," Review of *Sundown, New York Times*, November 25, 1934.
25. Robert Dale Parker, *The Invention of Native American Literature* (Ithaca, N.Y.: Cornell University Press, 2003); Mark Rifkin, "The Duration of the Land: The Queerness of Spacetime in Sundown," *Studies in American Indian Literatures* 27, no. 1 (Spring 2015): 32–69; Michael Snyder, "'He certainly didn't want anyone to know that he was queer': Chal Windzer's Sexuality in John Joseph Mathews's *Sundown*," *Studies in American Indian Literatures* 20, no. 1 (Spring 2008): 27–54; Mathews diary, September 11, 1948 (JJM 1.50); Virginia H. Mathews, introduction to *Sundown*, xiv.
26. Brandt to Mathews, March 18, 1936 (OUP 4.14); Logsdon, interview with Mathews, March 14, 1972; Mathews diary, September 11, 1948 (JJM 1.50); "Readin' and Ritin'," *P-JC*, November n.d., 1934 (JJM 4.37).
27. "Osage Tribal Council History," *Osage Tribal Museum, Library & Archives*, 2013, www.osagetribe.com/museum/uploads/otc_1906-2006.pdf; "Osage Ceremony Planned Monday," *PJ-C*, July 1, 1934.
28. T. Wilson, "Osage Oxonian," 269, 278–80.
29. Romain Shackelford, personal interview, July 16, 2013; Jean Dennison, *Colonial Entanglement: Constituting a Twenty-First-Century Osage Nation* (Chapel Hill: University of North Carolina Press, 2012), 24–25.
30. Terry P. Wilson, "The Depression Years," in *Indians of North America* (New York: Chelsea House, 2008); OTM, "Osage Headright History," www.osagetribe.com/mineral/info_sub_page.aspx?subpage_id=6; "American Indian Religious Freedom Act," American Indian Heritage Month: Commemoration vs. Exploitation, ABC-Clio, *History and the Headlines*, historyandtheheadlines.abc-clio.com.
31. "Collier Assails Indian Treatment," *PJ-C*, October 2, 1934; "Collier and Thomas Start Indian Tour," *PJ-C*, October 14, 1934.
32. T. Wilson, "Osage Oxonian," 280; "Sen. Thomas Is Named to Indian Post," *PJ-C*, January 6, 1935; "1934 Pawhuska News Headline Calendar," *PJ-C*, December 31, 1934; "Tribal Council Selects Attorney," *PJ-C*, July 17, 1934; Brian F. Rader, "Oklahoma Indian Welfare Act," *Encyclopedia of Oklahoma History and Culture*, www.okhistory.org/publications/enc/entry.php?entry=OK059; "Osage Indians to Meet," *Tulsa World*, May 26, 1935.
33. Mathews, "John L. Bird, Early Osage Trader, Dies," *PJ-C*, January 28, 1935; "Osage Tribal Museum, Library & Archives," pamphlet (Pawhuska: Osage Tribal Museum, 2015).

34. "Oklahoma Novel Writer to Talk Here This Week," *Daily O'Collegian* [Stillwater, Okla.], February 5, 1935; "Tune in October 7," *Sooner Magazine* 8, no. 1 (October 1935): 8; JJM to Brandt, April 11, 1936 (OUP 4.14).
35. "Tribal Dance Here for Mrs. Roosevelt," *PJ-C*, March 16, 1937; Mathews to Brandt, March 29, 1937 (JAB 5.14).
36. "Romance of the Osages" (transcript of radio show) Lilly Library, Indiana University; "Music and Language of Osages Preserved in Sound Recording," *PJ-C*, April 30, 1937; "Osage Program to Be Broadcast," *PJ-C*, April 28, 1937; Mathews diary, May 15, 1959 (JJM 3.12).
37. This was the "safe way" of swindling Osages short of outright murder. During the Reign of Terror on the Osages, which occurred while Mathews was abroad in the 1920s, a gang of white men conspired against and murdered at least two dozen Osages, possibly many more, plus a few non-Osages, in a nefarious plot to inherit headright payments. They covered up the killings by clumsily disguising them as accidents or suicides. Many potential witnesses who might testify were murdered. The Osage Tribal Council requested federal assistance, and J. Edgar Hoover's new FBI stepped in. Kingpin William K. Hale and his nephews Ernest and Byron Burkhart were indicted, but more were involved in or aware of the plot. Bill Hale was paroled in 1947; Byron never served time; and Ernest was released in 1959 and pardoned in 1966.
38. "Inquiry of Osage Fund Cases Loom," *PJ-C*, May 13, 1937; "Osage Group Goes to Washington, D.C.," *PJ-C*, May 24, 1937; Harry LaFerte, "Riches of Osage Tribe Plundered by White Greed: John Joseph Mathews Reveals How His People Are Victimized," *Tulsa World*, May 25, 1937; Verdon R. Adams, *Tom White: The Life of a Lawman* (El Paso: Texas Western, 1972), 47.
39. LaFerte, "Riches of Osage Tribe Plundered by White Greed"; "Joe Mathews Writes Relative to Controversial Article," *PJ-C*, June 3, 1937.
40. "Telling the World," *PJ-C*, May 28, 1937; "Joe Mathews Writes Relative to Controversial Article," *PJ-C*, June 3, 1937; A-88368, Sept. 9, 1937, 17 Comp. Gen. 226, Legal Decisions & Bid Protests, GAO, U.S. Government Accountability Office.
41. T. Wilson, "Osage Oxonian," 280–81; "New Indian Museum on Campus Nears Completion," *PJ-C*, March 14, 1937.
42. OTM, *The Osage Timeline*, researched and developed by Lou Brock (Pawhuska: OTM, 2013), 74–75; Susan Weininger, "Todros Geller," *Modernism in the New City: Chicago Artists, 1920–1950*, www.chicagomodern.org/artists/todros_geller/; Jamie Stiehm, "Man Sentenced to Four Months for Stealing Art," *Baltimore Sun*, March 9, 1999, http://articles.baltimoresun.com/1999-03-09/news/9903090047_1_stanislav-rembski-chief-lookout-godson-of-dorothy-rembski.
43. T. Wilson, "Osage Oxonian," 280; Garrick Bailey, "John Joseph Mathews, Osage, 1894–1979," in *American Indian Intellectuals of the Nineteenth and Early Twentieth Centuries*,

ed. Margot Liberty (Norman: University of Oklahoma Press, 2002 [1978]), 240; Mathews diary, April 7 and May 28, 1968 (JJM 3.6).

44. Ernie Pyle, *Brave Men* (Lincoln: University of Nebraska Press, 2001), 48–57; Ruth Randolph, "Pawhuska, Cosmopolitan City in the '20s: Art, Music, Parties, Fashion Were a Way of Life" *PJ-C*, September 29, 1972; William W. Savage, Jr., "Pulitzer Prize Winner Ernie Pyle Toured Oklahoma during Depression," *Oklahoma Gazette*, July 17, 2008.

45. Mathews diary, April 21, 1954; January 7, 1961 (JJM 2.6, 2.14); Randolph, "Pawhuska"; Joseph A. Brandt, Review of *Out of Africa* by Isak [Karen] Dinesen, *Oklahoman*, April 10, 1938.

46. Jack Kolbert, *The Worlds of André Maurois* (Selinsgrove, PA: Susquehanna University Press, 1985), 59–60; Hubert Kennedy, *The Ideal Gay Man: The Story of Der Kreis* (New York: Routledge, 2013), n.p.

47. Gore Vidal, *Palimpsest* (New York: Random House, 1995), 259; Randolph, "Pawhuska"; Sears to Mathews, June 1, 1936; April 21, 1937, Paul Sears Collection, Sterling Memorial Library, Yale University, 40.617; Mathews diary, April 29, 1952; January 4, 1958, January 18, 1962 (JJM 2.4, 2.12, 3.1); Mathews, *Talking to the Moon*, 27, 182.

48. "Oklahoma Historical Notes," *Chronicles of Oklahoma* 16, no. 4 (1934): 398; Savoie Lottinville to Mathews, September 7, 1938 (OUP 48.7); Lillian Mathews to Lottinville, November 3, 1938 (OUP 48.7); Mathews diary, November 3, 1978 (JJM 3.12); "Milburn, George," *Encyclopedia of Oklahoma History and Culture*, www.okhistory.org/publications/enc/entry.php?entry=MI018; "Backstage with *Esquire*," *Esquire*, March 1936: 26.

49. "Authors to Be Guests at City Tea," *Oklahoman*, April 18, 1939; Richard Lowitt, "Regionalism at the University of Oklahoma," *Chronicles of Oklahoma* 73, no 2 (1995): 155; Mathews diary, January 7, 1956 (JJM 2.8); "Downing, George Todd (1902–1974)," *Encyclopedia of Oklahoma History and Culture*, www.okhistory.org/publications/enc/entry.php?entry=DO013; Michael Dirda, "Reading for a Winter's Night: The Detective Fiction of Todd Downing," *Washington Post*, March 5, 2015, www.washingtonpost.com/entertainment/books/reading-for-a-winters-night-the-detective-fiction-of-todd-downing/2015/03/04/01cf5adc-c1dc-11e4-9271-610273846239_story.html; Frances Kennedy, "Twenty-Fifth Meeting," *Reports of the Oklahoma Library Commission* (Oklahoma City: Warden, 1922), 59–61; "John Milton Oskison," *Encyclopedia of Oklahoma History and Culture*, www.okhistory.org/publications/enc/entry.php?entry=OS008; "Foreman, Grant (1869–1953)," and "Edward Everett Dale (1879–1972)," *Encyclopedia of Oklahoma History and Culture*, www.okhistory.org/publications/enc/entry.php?entry=FO020 and www.okhistory.org/publications/enc/entry.php?entry=DA005.

Chapter Six **THE HUNTER AND THE HUNTS**

1. Lewis Titterton, "Interview with John Joseph Mathews, *Books and Characters*, November 6, 1932; "Miss Palmour to Wed," *Muskogee Times-Democrat*, January 2, 1923; *Muskogee Times-Democrat*, February 12, 1915, 5; 1910 U.S. census; *The Chieftain* (yearbook), 1919,

Central High School, Muskogee, 34; Merle Haggard, "Okie from Muskogee," *Okie from Muskogee*, Capitol Records, 1969.

2. Mathews diary, March 10 and August 5, 1946; April 16, 1955; January 7, 1956 (JJM 1.48, 2.7, 2.8), July 13, 1965 (JJM SR 2274); "University High School Notes," *Norman Transcript*, February 14, 1922; *Sooner* (yearbook), 1921, University of Oklahoma; Jace Weaver, *That the People Might Live* (New York: Oxford University Press, 1997), 96; James Howard Cox, *The Red Land to the South: American Indian Writers and Indigenous Mexico* (Minneapolis: University of Minnesota Press, 2012), 201; Braunlich, *Haunted by Home*, 33, 41–42.
3. "Former Norman Men Strike Big Bonanza," *Cleveland County Enterprise*, January 8, 1920; 1910 and 1920 U.S. censuses ; *Sooner* (yearbook) 1922, 324; Linda D. Wilson, "Oilton," *Encyclopedia of Oklahoma History and Culture*, www.okhistory.org/publications/enc/entry.php?entry=OI005.
4. *Sooner* (yearbook), 1922, 116, 263, 358; *Muskogee Times-Democrat*, October 6, 1922, 5; "Miss Palmour to Wed"; Ellen Collins Johnson, "Haskell," *Encyclopedia of Oklahoma History and Culture*, www.okhistory.org/publications/enc/entry.php?entry=HA046.
5. *Muskogee Times-Democrat*, June 30, 1923; Muskogee County Schools, Central High School Class of 1920, 1925 update, www.usgennet.org/usa/ok/county/muskogee/county schoolcensus/1920alumni.htm; "Mrs. Henry Hunt Takes Over Gasoline Business," *PJ-C*, August 23, 1932; Hunter, "Historical Context in John Joseph Mathews' *Sundown*," 68; Jon D. May, "Shidler," *Encyclopedia of Oklahoma History and Culture*, www.okhistory.org/publications/enc/entry.php?entry=SH033.
6. Carol Hunter, "The Protagonist as a Mixed-Blood in John Joseph Mathews' Novel *Sundown*," *American Indian Quarterly* 6, nos. 3–4 (1982): 323.
7. Terry P. Wilson, *The Underground Reservation: Osage Oil* (Lincoln: University of Nebraska Press, 1985), 128–29, 156.
8. T. Wilson, "The Depression Years"; OTM, "Osage Headright History," www.osagetribe.com/mineral/info_sub_page.aspx?subpage_id=6; LaFerte, "Riches of Osage Tribe"; "Mrs. Henry Hunt "; "Local Man Found Dead in Garage," *PJ-C*, Friday, August 12, 1932.
9. "Local Man Found Dead"; Mathews diary, July 24, 1943 (JJM 1.46).
10. John Clinton Hunt, telephone interview, December 12, 2014; Peter Hunt Brown, telephone interview, September 18, 2014.
11. Mathews defined himself as not Christian and reportedly very rarely went to Catholic Mass from his time at Oxford until late in his life. Mathews diary, May 26, 1952 (JJM).
12. Mathews diary, June 3, 1952; June 5, 1957 (JJM 2.4, 2.10); Thomas Wolfe, *Of Time and the River: A Legend of Man's Hunger in His Youth*, 1935, Project Gutenberg Australia, http://gutenberg.net.au/ebooks03/0301021h.html. Wolfe refers to the "man-swarm" nineteen times in the novel, which was highly successful at the time Mathews met him in the summer of 1935.

13. Sara Jane Richter, "The Life and Literature of John Joseph Mathews: Contributions of Two Cultures" (PhD diss., Oklahoma State University, 1985), 33.
14. Mathews to Marie Mathews, April 16, 1923 (JJM 1. 27).
15. Richter, "Life and Literature of John Joseph Mathews," 33.
16. Mathews diary, July 11, 1961 (JJM 2.14).
17. Mathews, correspondence with Julian Huxley, February and March 1951 (JJM 1.29).
18. Mathews, *Osages*, xiii.
19. Mathews, "After the Afghan," n.d. (WSC 56.5).
20. "Miss Palmour to Wed"; Mathews diary, April 5, 1962 (JJM 3.1); June 12, 1921, (JJM 1.44); Mathews, "Thoughts for MS" (JJM 3.13).
21. Mathews to Elizabeth Hunt, October 26, 1932 (JJM 1.1).
22. "Mrs. Henry Hunt"; Mathews diary, January 8, 1935 (JJM 1.8); "Former Perkins Boy Making Good," *Perkins Journal*, July 6, 1933; Mathews to Elizabeth Hunt, March 15, 1935 (JJM 2.1); Mathews diary, July 16, 18, and December 22, 1943 (JJM 1.46).
23. Mathews, "DIBBS" (JJM 1.27).
24. Mathews diary, April 4, 1962 (JJM 3.1); Mathews, *Talking to the Moon*, 29–30; John Hunt, telephone interview, December 12, 2014.
25. Mathews to Elizabeth Hunt, January 8 and 18, March 22, 1935 (JJM 1.2).
26. Mathews diary, April 5, 1945 (JJM 1.47); John H. Mathews, personal interview, August 2, 2013; Ponca City History Tid-Bits, "The Jens-Marie Hotel," Ponca City Publishing, www.poncacity.com/about/history/jens_marie_hotel.htm; Michael Koch, *The Kimes Gang* (Bloomington: AuthorHouse, 2005), 212.
27. Stratford B. Tolson and Bobbie Tolson, personal interview, January 7, 2013; Frederick Ford Drummond, telephone interview, March 25, 2015; "Janet (Theis) Holcombe, (1935–2013)" *Bartlesville Examiner-Enterprise*, January 20, 2013, www.legacy.com/obituaries/examiner-enterprise/obituary.aspx?pid=162444563.
28. Mathews diary, November 21, 1949; May 21 and July 14, 1962 (JJM 2.1, 3.1); Judy Taylor, personal interview, June 28, 2014; "Mathews Rushed as New Book Hits Stores Next Week," *PJ-C*, August 11, 1961; Romain Shackelford, personal interview, July 16, 2013.
29. J. Frank Dobie, "Books and Christmas," *Southwest Review*, Winter 1951, 1–6; Mathews to Dobie, January 3, 1951 (JFD); Louise Abercrombie, "Marland Book's Author Remembers Oilman," *Ponca City News*, April 11, 1979; Mathews diary, March 10 and August 5, 1946 (JJM 1.46).
30. Judy Taylor, personal interview, June 28, 2014; Mathews diary, December 15, 1968; March 28 and April 26, 1969; January 27 and February 14, 1973 (JJM 3.6, 3.8, 3.12).
31. Judy Taylor, personal interview, June 28, 2014.
32. Melvin L. Tolson, personal interview, July 16, 2013; Peter Hunt Brown, telephone interview, September 18, 2014; Mathews to Elizabeth Mathews, August 5, 1944 (JJM 1. 21); Mathews diary, June 28, 1946 (JJM 1.48); William H. Mattingly, telephone interview, March 21, 2015; Mathews diary, June 30 and September 5, 1948 (JJM 1.50).

33. Mathews diary, June 30, 1948 (JJM 1.50); Logsdon, interview with Mathews, March 14, 1972 (JJM SR 2281); *San Mateo Times*, April 14, 1953; "Tony Brown to Wed San Francisco Girl," *San Mateo Times*, March 12, 1953; Melvin L. Tolson, personal interview, July 16, 2013; "Descendants of Solomon Palmer," Genealogy.com; William Mattingly, telephone interview, March 21, 2015; "Anthony Preble Brown," *Monterey Herald*, August 2, 2012, www.legacy.com/obituaries/montereyherald/obituary.aspx?pid=158900845.
34. John Clinton Hunt, *Generations of Men* (Boston: Atlantic Monthly–Little, Brown, 1956); Mathews diary, March 22, 1956 (JJM 2.8); Mrs. Arthur Hon to Elizabeth Mathews, April 18, 1956 (JJM 1.31).
35. Mathews diary, June 15, 1956 (JJM 2.8).
36. Mathews diary, June 15, 1956 (JJM 2.8).
37. Edith Jameson Copeland, Review of *Generations of Men* by John Hunt, *Oklahoman*, April 15, 1956; Mathews diary, June 17, 1956 (JJM 2.8).
38. Mathews diary, June 17–18, and 21, 1956 (JJM 2.8).
39. John Clinton Hunt, "Family Business," *News from the Republic of Letters* 16 (Winter 2005): 167–68, 175; Peter Brown, telephone interview, September 18, 2014.
40. John Clinton Hunt, "If You Leave Me...Take Me with You," unpublished manuscript, 2011, 377–80; copy supplied to the author by Hunt; Mathews diary, June 12, 1921 (JJM 1.44).
41. Mathews diary, September 5, 1961; February 3, 5–7, 1962; July 9–18, 1962; August 3, 1963 (JJM 2.14, 3.1, 3.2); Sam Brown, telephone interview, March 27, 2015.
42. Peter Brown, telephone interview, September 18, 2014; Henry Brown, telephone interview, March 23, 2015; "Alison King Is Engaged to Peter Brown," *New York Times*, August 1, 1982; "Anthony Preble Brown," *Monterrey Herald*, August 2, 2012.
43. Peter Brown, telephone interview, September 18, 2014; Henry Brown, telephone interview, March 23, 2015; Sam Brown, telephone interview, March 27, 2015; U.S. Social Security Applications and Claims Index, 1936–2007.
44. Mathews to Diana Hunt and Mead Hunt [many dates] (JJM 1.34); John Clinton Hunt, telephone interview, December 12, 2014, and e-mail to the author, October 16, 2014.
45. John Clinton Hunt, e-mail to the author, October 16, 2014.
46. William Mattingly, telephone interviews, January 7, 2013, and March 21, 2015; John Clinton Hunt, *The Grey Horse Legacy* (New York, Knopf, 1968), 84; Mel Gussow, *Edward Albee: A Singular Journey* (New York: Simon and Schuster, 1999), 47–50.
47. "Marines," *Sooner Magazine* 16, no 1 (September 1943): 23; Mathews diary, December 15, 1944 (JJM 1.47); V. Willis, "Mathews Children," 27–28; "Caudill Jr., Henry Ben," Oklahoma Casualties Database, World War II, Oklahoma History Center, www.okhistory.org/historycenter/okcasualties/world-war-2-detail.php?casualty=313; "Josephine Caudill"; Mathews, "No Time" (JJM 4.16); Mathews diary, September 6, 1946 (JJM 1.48).
48. Miss Barbara Mead Becomes Bride of John Clinton Hunt," *Oklahoman*, October 3, 1948; John Clinton Hunt, e-mail to the author, October 16, 2014; "Father and Son Make Ethan Frome Sing," *Harvard University Gazette*, November 5, 1998; Ray B. West,

"Dylan Thomas at Iowa," in *A Community of Writers: Paul Engels and the Iowa Writers' Workshop*, ed. Robert Dana (Iowa City: University of Iowa Press, 1999), 255; "Seymour Lawrence Named Vice-President at Knopf," *New York Times*, April 15, 1964; Susan Kalter, introduction to *TTM*, xxv.

49. Mathews diary, March 27, 1954; August 16–25, 1958; July 8, 1961; January 21, 1973 (JJM 2.6, 2.12, 2.14, 3.12); Mathews to Dobie, March 30, 1954, n.d. [1963], JFD; Binder of letters from John Joseph Mathews to his grandchildren, Diana and Mead Hunt, 1950–1960 (JJM 1.34).
50. Saunders, *Cultural Cold War*, 234, 241–42; Robin W. Winks, *Cloak & Gown: Scholars in the Secret War, 1939–1961* (New Haven, Conn.: Yale University Press, 1996 [1987]), 442–44.
51. Mathews diary, January 21, 1956 (JJM 2.8); Saunders, *Cultural Cold War*, 237, 242, 343, 139, 363, 367.
52. Mathews diary, June 8, 1948, January 2, 1961 (JJM 1.50, 2.14); Mathews, "The Liberal View" (JJM 4.12); Mathews, "Author John Joseph Mathews Discusses the Limited Impact, Influence and Dollar-importance in Books of the Indian and the Southwest," *Sooner Magazine*, July–August 1962, 10–11, , emphasis in original; Logsdon, interview with Mathews, March 14, 1972.
53. Suzanne Bourgeois, *Genesis of the Salk Institute* (Berkeley: University of California Press, 2013), 148, 154–58.
54. Saunders, *Cultural Cold War*, 356, 397–99, 419; "John Clinton Hunt," *Marquis Who's Who*, Marquis Biographies Online, www.marquiswhoswho.com.
55. John Hunt, *Grey Horse Legacy*; "Oil-Rich Red Hawks Were Victims of Domino Theory," review of *The Grey Horse Legacy* by John Hunt, *Lincoln Star*, June 16, 1968; Mathews diary, October 11, 1967 (JJM 3.5).
56. Mathews, audio-taped diary, ca. June 1965 (JJM SR 2275); Mathews diary, May 1, 1968; September 1 and 19, 1969 (JJM 3.6, 3.8); "Chantal Loiseau Hunt" (author biography), *News from the Republic of Letters* 16 (Winter 2005).
57. "John Clinton Hunt," "Chantal Loiseau Hunt" (author biographies), *News from The Republic of Letters* 16 (Winter 2005); John Hunt, "Knights Errant," New York Public Library archives, 1982; Frank Rich, "Theater: 'Knights Errant,' on Nixon," *New York Times*, December 2, 1982; U.S. Public Records Index, vol. 1 (database); Margaret Dwyer, "Carter Revard in Cyberspace: An E-mail Sampler," in *In Honor of Carter Revard*, special issue, *Studies in American Indian Literatures*, ser. 2, 15, no. 1 (2003), 111.
58. JJM 3.13; Mathews diary, February 13, 1973 (JJM 2.12); "Elizabeth Mathews Services Wednesday," *PJ-C*, November 9, 1982.

Chapter Seven **MEXICO**

1. Mathews to Campbell, September 16, 1938 (WSC 32.27); OTM, "Osage Tribal Council History."

2. Mathews, application for Guggenheim grant, 3 (JJM 3.14).

3. Mathews, "Alfredo and the Jaguar" (JJM 4.1); Mathews to Campbell, February 25, 1925 (WSC 32.27).

4. "Mathews Will Write in Quiet of Mexico," *Stillwater Press*, August 31, 1939 (JJM 3.14); Mathews to Elizabeth Hunt, October 13 and 23, 1939; Mathews to Henry Allen Moe of the Guggenheim Foundation, October 19, 1939 (JJM 3.14).

5. "Cuernavaca," *Encyclopedia Britannica*, https://www.britannica.com/place/Cuernavaca; Mathews to Elizabeth Hunt, November 13, 1939 (JJM 1.8); December 8, 13 1939 (JJM 1.9).

6. Mathews to Henry Moe, November 15, 1939; June 5, 1940 (JJM 3.14); Mathews to Elizabeth Hunt, November 22 and December 8, 13, 1939; January 8 and 24, February 12, and May 23, 1940 (JJM 1.8, 1.9, 1.10, 1.11, 1.14).

7. Mathews to Elizabeth Hunt, December 8, 1939 (JJM 1.9); Dorothy Cameron Disney Darby, "Aunts and Unks," *The Other Disneys*, www.theotherdisneys.com/AuntsnUnks.htm.

8. Mathews to Elizabeth Hunt, November 22, 1939 (JJM 1.8); and November 23, 28, 1939 (JJM 1.8); Emery Winn, "World of Words," *Oklahoman*, July 18, 1971; Randolph, "Pawhuska"; Mathews diary, March 29, 1937 (JJM 5.14); Sallye Little Brandt, "The Milburns," *Sooner Magazine*, March 1931, 207.

9. JJM to Elizabeth Hunt, January 8, 10, 1940 (JJM 1.10).

10. Mathews to Elizabeth Hunt, January 18, 1940 (JJM 1.10); Mathews diary, January 7–8, 1940 (JJM 1.37); Mathews, "Only a Blonde" (JJM 4.29). Mathews's experiences in Mexico informed another unpublished story focusing on a blonde and her friends in Mexico, "Yellow Hair" (JJM 4.19).

11. Mathews to Henry Moe, March 12, 1940 (JJM 3.14); Mathews to Elizabeth Hunt, December 13, 1939 (JJM 1.9).

12. Kenneth R. Philp, "John Collier and the Indians of the Americas: The Dream and the Reality," *Prologue*, Spring 1979, 10; Mathews to Elizabeth Hunt, April 19, 1940 (JJM 1.13).

13. "Thomas Unable to Attend Indian Problem Parlay," *Oklahoman*, April 14, 1940; Philp, "John Collier and the Indians of the Americas," 10; Andre Gingrich, "Alliances and Avoidance: British Interactions with German-Speaking Anthropologists, 1933–1953," in *Culture Wars: Context, Models and Anthropologists' Accounts*, ed. Deborah James, Evelyn Plaice, and Christina Toren (New York: Berghahn Books, 2013), 27; Berthold Reise, "Short Portrait: Paul Kirchhoff," *Interviews with German Anthropologists, The History of Federal German Anthropology from 1945 to 1990*, www.germananthropology.com/short-portrait/paul-kirchhoff/185; Mathews to Elizabeth Hunt, April 24, 29, 1940 (JJM 1.13); Mathews diary, April 20, 1940 (JJM 1.39); Cox, *Red Land to the South*, 154–55; Dorothy R. Parker, *Singing an Indian Song: A Biography of D'Arcy McNickle* (Lincoln: University of Nebraska Press, 1994), 83.

14. Philp, "John Collier and the Indians of the Americas," 10.
15. Mathews to Elizabeth Hunt, April 19, 22, 24, 29, 1940 (JJM 1.13); Tennessee Williams, "On a Streetcar Named Success," *New York Times*, November 30, 1947.
16. Mathews to Elizabeth Hunt, May 7, 1940 (JJM 1.14); Richard Whelan, *Robert Capa: A Biography* (Lincoln: University of Nebraska Press, 1994), 165, 168–69.
17. Mathews to Elizabeth Hunt, November 13 and December 8, 1939; February 12, July 6, July 12,1940 (JJM 1.7).
18. Postcards from Mathews to John Hunt, May 31 and June 8, 12, 18, 1940 (JJM 1.18); postcards from Mathews to Elizabeth Hunt, May 30 and June 8, 12, 1940 (JJM 1.18); Mathews to Elizabeth Mathews, July 29, 1940 (JJM 1.16).
19. Mathews to Moe, June 5, 1940 (JJM 3.14); Jorge E. Degetau, "Hacienda Santa Engracia, Tamaulipas," *México Desconocido*, www.mexicodesconocido.com.mx/hacienda-santa-engracia-tamaulipas.html; Mathews to Elizabeth Hunt, Aug 1, 5, 10, 14, 16, 1940 (JJM 1.17).
20. Mathews to Moe, September 11, 1941 (JJM 3.14).
21. Mathews to Moe, September 11, 1941 (JJM 3.14); Mathews, *Osages*, 740–58; "Peyote Religion Practiced in the Osage," *PJ-C*, June 15, 1961.
22. John Hunt to Elizabeth Hunt, September 12, 1940 (JJM 1.24).
23. Mathews to Moe, February 27, 1943; May 1, 1944 (JJM 3.14); Mathews to Elizabeth Hunt, February 18, 1943; March 16, 1943 (JJM 1.20), August 5, 1944 (JJM 1.21); Mathews diary, December 4, 1943 (JJM 1.28); Mathews diary, November 1, 1978 (JJM 1.32).

Chapter Eight **THE TRAGEDY OF LORENE SQUIRE**

1. OTM, "Osage Tribal Council History"; "Fred Lookout," *Encyclopedia of North American Indians*, ed. Frederick E. Hoxie (Boston: Houghton Mifflin, 1996), 346–47; Mathews, "Chief Fred Lookout"; Mathews diary, November 7, 18, 1949; February 18, 1953 (JJM 2.1, 2.5).
2. John Hunt to Elizabeth Hunt, September 12, 16, 1940, January 4, 1941 (JJM 1.24); OTM, "Osage Tribal Council History."
3. "Chamber Committee to Talk with Osages," *PJ-C*, March 5, 1941; Mathews diary, October 22, 1963 (JJM 3.2); Michael Wallis, *Oil Man: The Story of Frank Phillips and the Birth of Phillips Petroleum* (New York: Doubleday, 1988), 314–15, 326, 29; Mathews diary, June 3, 1957 (JJM 2.10); T. Wilson, "Osage Oxonian," 279; "History of Hulah Lake," U.S. Army Corps of Engineers, www.swt.usace.army.mil/Locations/Tulsa-District-Lakes/Oklahoma/Hulah-Lake/History/.
4. Mathews diary, August 7, 1943 (JJM 1.46).
5. Mathews, *Osages*, xv; Richard Rhodes, *Looking for America: A Writer's Odyssey* (New York: Doubleday, 1979), 91.
6. T. Wilson, *Underground Reservation*, 178–79.
7. OTM, *Osage Timeline*, 61–62; Thoburn, *Standard History of Oklahoma*, 1948.

8. "Symposium on Literature Set for March 27 at Norman," *Oklahoman*, March 22, 1942; "Sterling A. Brown," Academy of American Poets, www.poets.org/poetsorg/poet/sterling-brown; Edward Donahoe, "Head by Scopas," in *Understanding Fiction*, ed. Cleanth Brooks, Jr. and Robert Penn Warren (New York: Appleton-Century-Crofts, 1943), 325–29.
9. "Photos Won Fame: Lorene Squire, Noted for Pictures of Wildlife, Dies in Accident," *Lawrence Journal-World*, April 13, 1942.
10. "Wildlife Photography of Lorene Squire Required Rugged Life," *Lawrence Journal-World*, January 15, 1948; "4 out of 5 Ducks Come from Canada: A Kansas Girl Goes 8,000 Miles to Photograph Them," *Life*, March 21, 1938; "Birds in Arctic: A Girl Photographer Follows Them to Their Far-North Breeding Ground," *Life*, April 3, 1939; "Waterfowl: They Are Now Winging South after a Wet and Happy Summer," *Life*, November 17, 1941; Lorene Squire, "Camera Shots: Photographing Fast-Flying Game Birds of the Saskatchewan Prairies," *Field and Stream*, June 1938; "Lorene Squire Photographs Taken for 'The Beaver' Magazine," Archives of Manitoba, Winnipeg, http://pam.minisisinc.com/scripts/mwimain.dll/144/PAM_DESCRIPTION/DESCRIPTION_DET_REP/REFD+13962?SESSIONSEARCH; Lorene Squire, *Wildfowling with a Camera* (New York: J. B. Lippincott, 1938); "Mourn Lorene Squire," *Milwaukee Journal*, June 12, 1942; Peter Geller, *Northern Exposures: Photographing and Filming the Canadian North, 1920–45* (Vancouver: University of British Columbia Press, 2011), 126; 1940 U.S. census.
11. "Kansan Dies after Crash West of City, Joe Mathews, Mrs. Elizabeth Hunt Also Injured," *PJ-C*, April 13, 1942.
12. "Companion of Writer Killed, John Joseph Mathews of Pawhuska Injured," *Tulsa Tribune*, April 13, 1942.
13. "Kansan Dies after Crash West of City"; "Writer Is Critically Hurt in Fatal Highway Mishap," *Oklahoman*, April 14, 1942; "Companion of Writer Killed"; "Photos Won Fame," *Lawrence Journal-World*, April 13, 1942.
14. "Photos Won Fame"; "Mourn Lorene Squire"; Mathews, *Talking to the Moon*, 235; Squire, *Wildfowling*, 15.
15. "Kansan Dies after Crash West of City"; Bob Gregory, "Marland Mystery," *Oklahoma Monthly*, January 1981, 54; Mathews diary, August 22, 1961 (JJM 2.14); Harvey Payne, personal interview, July 16, 2013; "The Mabelle Kennedy Highway–Pawhuska, Oklahoma," *Waymarking*, July 8. 2009, www.waymarking.com/waymarks/WM6YVG_The_Mabelle_Kennedy_Highway_Pawhuska_OK; Mathews, *Life and Death of an Oilman* (Norman, University of Oklahoma Press, 1951), 158.
16. Mathews diary, August 14, 1943 (JJM 1.46); "Injury to Mathews Holds Up Ceremonies," *Oklahoman*, April 26, 1942.
17. Pauline Allred, personal interview, May 3, 2013; Mathews, *Talking to the Moon*, 85; Mongrain Lookout, personal interview, May 2, 2013; "Henry Edward 'Ed' Lookout," Find a Grave, www.findagrave.com/cgi-bin/fg.cgi?page=gr&GRid=92338508; Geoffrey Standing Bear, telephone interview, July 16, 2013.

18. Mathews, *Talking to the Moon*, 85–86; Mathews, *Osages*, 742–58; Weston La Barre, "Appendix 7: John Wilson, the Revealer of Peyote," in *The Peyote Cult* (New Haven: Yale University Press, 1938).
19. Kenneth Jacob Jump, *Osage Indian Poems and Short Stories*, 40; Fleur Feighan Jones, telephone interview, January 13, 2015.
20. Mathews, "Scholarship Comes to Life," 20–21.
21. Mathews diary, December 14, 1956 (JJM 2.8); Mathews to Elizabeth Hunt, February 18, 1943 (JJM 1.20); Stanley Vestal, "Chief of the Oglalas," Review of *Crazy Horse* by Mari Sandoz, *Saturday Review of Literature*, January 12, 1943, 20.
22. Mathews to Elizabeth Hunt, November 2, 1942 (JJM 1.19); Mathews diary, April 3, 1943 (JJM 1.46); *Menominee Tribe of Indians v. United States*, Leagle, www.leagle.com/decision/19671386388F2d998_11168/MENOMINEE%20TRIBE%20OF%20INDIANS%20v.%20UNITED%20STATES ; "Menominee Termination and Restoration," Indian Country Wisconsin, Milwaukee Public Museum, www.mpm.edu/wirp/ICW-97.html.
23. Mathews to Elizabeth and Ann Hunt, November 2, 1942.

Chapter Nine THE MOON AND MARLAND

1. Mathews, *Life and Death of an Oilman: The Career of E. W. Marland* (Norman: University of Oklahoma Press, 1951) (hereafter *LDO*), vii, 120.
2. Mathews diary, April 5, 1945 (JJM 1.47).
3. Mathews to Elizabeth Hunt, October 26, 1932 (JJM 1.1); Edward Donahoe, *Madness in the Heart* (New York: Little, Brown, 1937); "Edward Donahoe," *Ponca City News*, March 22, 1967; George Hutchinson, *In Search of Nella Larsen* (Cambridge, Mass.: Harvard University Press, 2006), 416, 439; Thadious M. Davis, *Nella Larsen, Novelist of the Harlem Renaissance* (Baton Rouge: Louisiana State University Press, 1994), 403–5, 428–31; Emily Bernard, ed., *Remember Me to Harlem: The Letters of Langston Hughes and Carl Van Vechten, 1925–1964* (New York: Knopf, 2001), 316.
4. Edward Donahoe, "Head by Scopas," in *Understanding Fiction*, ed. Cleanth Brooks, Jr., and Robert Penn Warren, 325–29 (New York: Appleton-Century-Crofts, 1943); Sandra Spanier, "'Paris Wasn't Like That': Kay Boyle and the Last of the Lost Generation," in *Lives Out of Letters: Essays on American Literary Biography, and Documentation in Honor of Robert N. Hudspeth*, ed. Robert Habich (Cranbury, N.J.: Associated University Presses, 2004), 174; Robert Wooster Stallman, "The Critical Reader," *College English* 9, no. 7 (1948): 362–69; Frederick L. Gwynn, "A Bead for Donahoe," *College English* 10, no. 7 (1949): 409–10; Stallman wrote another piece defending his analysis of Donahoe's story. He did not address the issue of sexuality but rather the complaints he received, similar to Boyle's, which argued he had surely read far more symbolism into the story than the author had intended. Stallman responded with the dicta of the New Critics, arguing the intentional fallacy. Robert Stallman, "A Note on Intentions," *College English* 10, no. 1 (1948): 40–41.

5. Mathews to Brandt, April 17, 1945 (JAB 5.14).
6. Mathews diary, November 22, 1943 (JJM 1.46); folder of correspondence regarding Mathews's proposed book "Without the Sword," 1943–44 (OUP 94.5); "Cortez A. M. Ewing Public Service Fellowship," Department of Political Science, University of Oklahoma, http://psc.ou.edu/ewing.
7. A. LaVonne Brown Ruoff, "John Joseph Mathews's *Talking to the Moon:* Literary and Osage Contexts," in *Multicultural Autobiography: American Lives*, ed. James Robert Payne (Knoxville: University of Tennessee Press, 1992), 6.
8. T. Wilson, "Osage Oxonian," 286.
9. Mathews, *LDO*, vii; Bob Gregory, "The Marland Mystery," *Oklahoma Monthly*, January 1981, 54, 56.
10. Mathews, *LDO*, 81.
11. Mathews, *Sundown*, 250–51; Mathews, *TTM*, 233; T. Wilson, *Underground Reservation*, 126, 132, 134.
12. Savoie Lottinville, *The Rhetoric of History* (Norman: University of Oklahoma Press, 1976), 41–42.
13. Mathews, "Red Man's Gold," *Service*, October 1946, 12–13; Mathews, *LDO*, 89, viii–ix; Abercrombie, "Marland Book's Author Remembers Oilman"; Bob Gregory, telephone interview, July 7, 2012; Mathews to Elizabeth Hunt, April 17, 1936 (JJM 1.5).
14. Abercrombie, "Marland Book's Author Remembers Oilman"; Mathews, *LDO*, vii.
15. Mathews, *LDO*, 46–47; *Marland Estate Mansion Guest Guide* (n.p.: Ponca City, Okla., n.d.); Gregory, "Marland Mystery," 54–55; Bob Gregory, *Oil in Oklahoma* (Muskogee, Okla.: Leake Industries, 1976), 40; Brumley, *Marland Tragedy*, 27–28.
16. OU Press document related to *Life and Death of an Oilman*, April 2, 1951 (OUP 175.6); Mathews to Lottinville, November 8, 1950 (OUP 175.6); "Funeral Rites Held for George Marland," *Ponca City News*, January 21, 1957; Gregory, "Marland Mystery," 52, 61; C. D. Northcutt, William C. Ziegenhain, and Bob Burke, *Palace on the Prairie: The Marland Family Story*, Oklahoma City: Oklahoma Heritage Association, 2005 (Photo courtesy of Robert Clark, Jr.).
17. Mathews, *TTM*, 148–49; Mathews, *LDO*, 84, 79, 89–90; "The Fascinating Story of E. W. Marland," *Ponca City News*, October 14, 1979; Mathews, *LDO*, 88, 89, 131; Lucia Ferguson, "A Sad, Exciting Story," Review of *Life and Death of an Oilman*, *Memphis Press-Scimitar*, November 3, 1951; Stanley Vestal, "Oilman Marland: A Victim of His British Tradition," *Chicago Daily Tribune*, November 4, 1951.
18. Abercrombie, "Marland Book's Author"; Mathews, *LDO*, 252.
19. Abercrombie, "Marland Book's Author"; Mathews, "E. W. Marland," *PJ-C*, July 1, 1934; "Many Attend Rally Here for Marland," *PJ-C*, October 5, 1934.
20. Mathews to Elizabeth Hunt, March 7, 1935; January 8, 1935 (JJM 1.2); Mathews to Joseph Brandt, February 12, 1936 (OUP 4.14).

21. "Two Put Off State Board by Governor," *Oklahoman*, August 2, 1936; "Three Named to Education Board," *Ada Weekly News*, August 6, 1936; Mathews, *Talking to the Moon*, 25–26.
22. Michael W. Everman, "Ernest Whitworth Marland: Governor of Oklahoma, 1935–1939," in *Oklahoma's Governors, 1929–1955: Depression to Prosperity*, ed. LeRoy H. Fisher (Oklahoma City: OHS, 1983), 79, 98–99; Mathews, *LDO*, viii, 251; Gregory, *Oil in Oklahoma*, 41; Gregory, "Marland Mystery," 41; John Kobler, "Where Is Lydie Marland?" *Saturday Evening Post*, November 22, 1958, 19; OTM, *Osage Timeline*, 60.
23. Lottinville, "In Memoriam: John Joseph Mathews," 240; Gregory, *Oil in Oklahoma*, 41, 43; Mathews, *LDO*, viii.
24. Mathews, *LDO*, 131; Mathews diary, April 3, 10, 1943 (JJM 1.46); Benton Ferguson, "Seward Sheldon," *Sooner Magazine* 5, no. 4 (May 1933): 234.
25. Mathews diary, August 12, 14, 1943 (JJM 1.46); March 1, 1946 (JJM 1.48).
26. Mathews, *LDO*, 181; Brumley, *Marland Tragedy*, 56–57; Donahoe, *Madness in the Heart* (New York: Little, Brown & Co., 1937; Davidson, Tenn.: Aegis Press, 2004), 183–88, 264–65; Mathews diary, March 9, 1945 (JJM 1.47); November 8, 1948 (JJM 1.48).
27. Donahoe, *Madness in the Heart*, 158–59; Mathews to Brandt, March 29, 1937 (JAB 5.14).
28. "Cedric Brudenell-Bruce, 7th Marquess of Ailesbury," Wikipedia; Mathews diary, May 9, 19, 1948; November 9, 1947.
29. "Lord Almost Puts Up His Dukes," *Oklahoman*, May 18, 1948; Neurohr, "Virginia Mathews Oral History Interview," 19; Mathews diary, December 9, 1946, April 11, 1943; June 6, 1921; December 15, 1956; May 1, 19, 1948; March 15, 1952 (JJM 1.50, 1.49, 1.48, 1.46, 1.44, 2.8, 1.50, 2.3); Gregory, "Marland Mystery," 54; Jimmie L. Franklin, "Prohibition," *Oklahoma Encyclopedia of History and Culture*, OHS, www.okhistory.org/publications/enc/entry.php?entry=PR018.
30. Mathews diary, May 30, 1948; October 31, 1954 (JJM 1.50, 2.6).
31. Mathews diary, January 21, 22, 1946 (JJM 1.48); Mathews, *LDO*, 258.
32. Mathews diary, January 30, March 22, and September 22, 1946 (JJM 1.48); April 24 and May 8, 1948 (JJM 1.50); Mathews, *LDO*, 126–27, 199; John E. Hale, "Life and Death of an Oilman—Marland's Career," *Ponca City News*, October 23, 1951.
33. Mathews, "Scholarship Comes to Life," 20; *Oklahoman*, July 22, 1945; Mathews to Elizabeth Hunt, September 24, 1944 (JJM 1.21). It is not clear that Mathews was actually awarded a Newberry grant. Mathews diary, January 31, 1945 (1.47).
34. Mathews to Brandt, December 8, 1945 (JAB 5.14); Mathews diary, March 21, 1946 (JJM 1.48); March 31, 1949 (JJM 2.1).
35. Bill Couch to Savoie Lottinville, January 14, 1948 (OUP 103.3).
36. Lottinville to Mathews, December 12, June 1, September 15, December 19, 1944; January 15, 1945 (OUP 103.3); Mathews to Lottinville, January 11, 1945 (OUP 103.3). The earlier manuscript Savoie had seen, Mathews explained, was not the same one reviewed by Brandt in Chicago, which incorporated material from his unpublished manuscript

"Without the Sword," which was rejected in its original form by OU Press after being reviewed by Lottinville and a professor of political science.

37. Lottinville to Mathews, December 12, 1944 (OUP 103.3); Mathews to Lottinville, January 11, 1945 (OUP 103.3); Lottinville to Couch, January 22, 1948 (OUP 103.3).
38. Lottinville to Mathews, January 15, 1945 (OUP 103.3); Mathews to Lottinville, September 29, 1948 (OUP 103.3).
39. Brandt to Mathews, February 2, 17, 1948, March 10, 1948; Mathews to Brandt, March 4 and February 12, 1948 (JAB 5.14).
40. Mathews to Brandt, April 15, 1948 (JAB 5.14).
41. Mathews, "The Apache Woman," 1946 (JJM 4.3).
42. Mathews to Brandt, September 2, 1949 (JAB 5.14); Mathews diary, November 13, 15, December 1, 1949; and January 3, 13, 1955 (JJM 2.1, 2.7); Mathews to Dobie, April 17, 1951 (JFD).
43. Mathews diary, June 15, 1948 (JJM 1.50); Mathews to Brandt, July 13 and September 2, 1949 (JAB 5.14).
44. Mathews to Lottinville, November 8, 1950 (OUP 175.6); Gregory, "Marland Mystery," 54–55; Mathews, *LDO*, 47, 181; Matthew 7:1, King James Bible; Mathews to Brandt, January 3, 1950 (JAB 5.14).
45. Mathews to Lottinville, November 8, 1950; Lottinville to Mathews, January 3, 1951 (OUP 175.6).
46. Mathews to Lottinville, May 11, 1951 (OUP); Brumley, *Marland Tragedy*, 66–67; Jo Davidson, *Between Sittings: An Informal Autobiography* (New York: Dial, 1951), 220.
47. Mathews, *LDO*, 71, 118.
48. "Tentative Illustrations for Marland Book" (sketchbook; JJM 3.17); Mathews, *LDO*, 80–82.
49. Mathews, *LDO*, 81, 150, 234; Bob Gregory, telephone interview, July 7. 2012.
50. J. Frank Dobie, "Black Gold and Roses," review of *LDO*, *New York Times*, October 21, 1951; Lottinville to Mathews, January 19, 22, 1953 (OUP 175.6); Mathews diary, December 14, 1956 (JJM 2.8).
51. Mathews diary, July 26, 1952 (JJM 2.3); Lottinville to Mathews, August 12, 1952 (OUP 175.6).

Chapter Ten **SLOW MELT THROUGH TIME**

1. Mathews diary, September 9, 1958; February 15, 17, March 31, April 10, and August 13, 1959 (JJM 2.12).
2. Mathews diary, February 29 and April 21, 1952 (JJM 2.3); Mathews to Lottinville, August 1, 1952 (OUP 175.6); OTM, "Osage Headright History," www.osagetribe.com/minerals/uploads/2012_06_Osage_Hdrght_Pmt.pdf.
3. "Margaret Gray Obituary," *Barnsdall Times*, April 6, 2008, http://barnsdalltimes.typepad.com/news/2008/04/margaret-gray-o.html; Roberta Ulrich, *American Indian Nations from*

Termination to Restoration, 1953–2006 (Lincoln: University of Nebraska Press, 2010), 130; Mathews diary, February 16, 1953; January 8, 1958 (JJM 2.5, 2.11); T. Wilson, *Underground Reservation*, 184–85.

4. Wolfgang Saxon, "Ex-rep. Michael A. Feighan, 87," *New York Times*, March 29, 1992; "Standard Brewing Company," *Encyclopedia of Cleveland History*, http://ech.case.edu/cgi/article.pl?id=SBC3; Mathews diary, January 31, 1952 (JJM 2.3); "Florence Feighan, Indian Rights Advocate, Organized Hill Tours," *Washington Post*, January 25, 1980.
5. Mathews diary, February 1, 1952 (JJM 2.3).
6. Mathews diary, February 1, 7, 14, 25, 29, and May 26, 1952 (JJM 2.3).
7. Mathews diary, June 2, July 1, 21, 1952 (JJM 2.3); T. Wilson, *Underground Reservation*, 184.
8. Lottinville to Mathews, December 24, 1951 (OUP 175.6); Norma C. Wilson, "Star Legacies," in *The Salt Companion to Carter Revard*, ed. Ellen L. Arnold (Cambridge: Salt, 2007), 12–14; Carter Revard, *Winning the Dust Bowl* (Tucson: University of Arizona Press, 2001), "Osage and Ponca Family Members" photograph captions following pp. 38, 112.
9. Mathews diary, August 13, 1952 (JJM 2.3).
10. Revard, *Winning the Dust Bowl*, 144–49.
11. Mathews, *Sundown*, 248, 250–51, 258, 270, 274, 305.
12. Neurohr, "Oral History Interview with Carter Revard," 11.
13. Revard, e-mail to the author, August 10, 2013; Neurohr, "Oral History Interview with Carter Revard," 11; Carter Revard, "Rock Shelters," in *An Eagle Nation* (Tucson: University of Arizona Press, 1993), 9–11.
14. Mathews diary, August 4, 1952 (JJM 2.3); Elizabeth Mathews, foreword to *Talking to the Moon*, n.p.; Mathews, *Talking to the Moon*, 3–4; Henry David Thoreau, *Walden*, annotated ed. chap. 2, para. 16, University of Iowa e-server, http://thoreau.eserver.org/walden02.html.
15. Mathews diary, March 27, 1959 (JJM 2.12); Gontran de Poncins, *Kabloona* (Alexandria, Va.: Time-Life Books, 1965 [1941]), 113, 109.
16. T. H. White, *England Have My Bones* (New York: Putnam, 1936), 3–4, 59–60, 64.
17. Mathews, *Talking to the Moon*; John K. Crane, *T. H. White* (Boston: Twayne, 1974), 18; Mathews diary, July 11, 1961, January 18, 1962 (JJM 2.14, 3.1); Mathews, audiotaped diary, July 11, 12, 1965 (JJM SR 2275); Mathews, "The Last Shot" and "Autumn Night" (JJM 4.30).
18. Mathews diary, June 2, 1957; July 11, 1958; March 18 and May 6, 1959 (JJM 2.10, 2.11, 2.12); Joyce Cary, *The Horse's Mouth* (Alexandria, Va.: Time-Life, 1965 [1944]), 391; Cary, *Mister Johnson* (New York: Time, 1962 [1939]); "An African Voice" (interview with Chinua Achebe), *Atlantic Unbound*, August 2, 2000, www.theatlantic.com/past/docs/unbound/interviews/ba2000-08-02.htm.

19. Mathews diary, August 31, 1952 (JJM 2.3); Parker, *Singing an Indian Song*, 55–56, 59–109, 164.
20. Mathews diary, September 4, 1952 (JJM 2.3); see Alfred R. Brophy, *Reconstructing the Dreamland: The Tulsa Riot of 1921, Race, Reparations, and Reconciliation* (New York: Oxford University Press, 2003).
21. Mathews diary, October 29, 1952; November 6, 1952; February 17, 1953; January 9, 1956 (JJM 2.4, 2.5, 2.8); Chris Mathews, personal interview, July 31, 2013; Frederick Ford Drummond, telephone interview, March 25, 2015.
22. Mathews to Lottinville, January 22, 1953 (OUP 175.6); LeAnne Howe, *Choctalking on Other Realities* (San Francisco: Aunt Lute, 2013), 3
23. Phillip Fortune, personal interview, February 20, 2015; "Amelia Girard Hilbert," "Arthur Phillip Fortune," "Marie Girard Galvin," and "Nicholas Albin 'Nick' Fortune," Find a Grave, www.findagrave.com.
24. Frederick Ford Drummond, telephone interview, March 25, 2015; Les Warehime, "Drummond Ranch," *Oklahoma Encyclopedia of History and Culture*, OHS, www.okhistory .org/publications/enc/entry.php?entry=DR007; Mathews diary, January 2, 1954; January 6, 1963; June 26, 1969 (JJM 1.47, 2.6, 3.3, 3.8).
25. "Gladys Buck," obituary, June 3, 2002, USGenWeb Archives, http://files.usgwarchives.net/ok/osage/obits/gldysbck.txt; Paul Jordan "P. J." Buck, telephone interview, May 6, 2015; Mathews diary, June 26, 1969 (JJM 3.8).
26. "Osage Folk Honor Their Dr. Walker," *Oklahoman*, March 26, 1954; Mathews diary, January 3, 6, 8–11, February 13, 3, 8, 9, and June 1, 1955; April 4, 1957 (JJM 2.7, 2.10); Mathews audiotaped diary (JJM Tape 2275, Side A).
27. Mathews diary, September 23, 1954 (JJM 2.6); Dobie to Mathews, June 26, 1963 (JFD).
28. "Pioneer Pawhuska Resident, Mrs. William S. Mathews Dies," *PJ-C*, March 25, 1955; Mathews diary, October 14, 1954; February 23, 1955 (JJM 2.6, 2.7).
29. Mathews diary, November 4–5, 1954 (JJM 2.6); U.S. Indian census rolls, 1926; U.S. federal census, 1930; Howard J. Schellenberg, III, e-mails to the author, November 23 and December 31, 2015; Maria Schellenberg Johnson, telephone interview, December 13, 2015; "Josephine Caudill"; "Feighan-Mathews Wedding Solemnized Here Saturday," *PJ-C*, June 22, 1930; Mathews audiotaped diary (JJM SR 2275); "Sarah Schellenberg," *Bigheart Times*, May 17, 2010.
30. Mathews diary, April 23, 1955 (JJM 2.7).
31. Braunlich, *Haunted by Home*, 185–88; "Lynn Riggs Memorial," Rogers County Historical Society, www.rchs1.org/lynn-riggs-museum; Mathews diary, January 7, 1956 (JJM 2 .8).
32. Mathews to Elizabeth Hunt, December 13, 1939; January 24, 1940 (JJM 1.10).
33. Lutenski, "Tribes of Men." Mathews never dated in high school and was not much interested in pursuing girls or women until he was a military aviator. Throughout his life, Mathews was occasionally struck by a young man whom chance would present. Recall that while

in Mexico in 1939, uninhibited by the presence of his future wife or small-town gossips, Mathews, then pushing forty, road-tripped and holidayed in Acapulco with a "very sensitive" twenty-four-year old man with whom he conversed in French on the beach. In 1940, while in Cuernavaca, he enjoyed regular massages from "a magnificent Indian" with "a body like a bronze god." On August 15, 1958, driving through a Mohawk reservation in Ontario, he gazed on "a perfect Apollo—a young Mohawk walking down the highway" (JJM 2.12). On January 10, 1961, Jo recorded in his diary a visit from a striking, simpatico repairman: he "was young and alert and I felt confidence in him. . . . I was drawn to him" (JJM 1.14). On January 9, 1973, he was struck by a "young man with long hair and deep blue eyes" who came to The Blackjacks to repair the telephone (JJM 3.12).

34. "Oklahoma Library Association Convention Opens," *PJ-C*, April 18, 1956; "Speakers at Convention Here," *PJ-C*, April 19, 1956; Mathews diary, April 19, 1956 (JJM 2.8).
35. "Florence Feighan, Indian Rights Advocate, Organized Hill Tours"; Mathews diary, July 12–19, 1957; December 17, 1959; February 5, 1962; June 9 and September 19, 1969; June 4, 1970; August 31, 1971 (JJM 2.10, 2.12, 3.8, 3.9, 3.10); Fleur Feighan Jones, telephone interview, January 13, 2015; Bill Feighan, telephone interview, January 19, 2015; "Relatives Leave after Visit in Mathews Home," *PJ-C*, August 30, 1972.
36. "Tribal Council Bill Starts Fuss among Osages," *Okahoman*, July 16, 1957.
37. Romain Shackelford, personal interview, July 16, 2013; T. Wilson, *Underground Reservation*, 185; Mathews diary, July 16–17, 1957 (JJM 2.9).
38. Mathews diary, Friday, April 4, 1958 (JJM 2.12).
39. Mathews diary, April 5, 7, 1958 (JJM 2.12).
40. Mathews diary, July 20, 1946 (JJM 1.48); Shirley A. Leckie, "Angie Debo: From the Old to the New Western History," in *Their Own Frontier: Women Intellectuals Re-Visioning the American West*, ed. Shirley A. Leckie and Nancy J. Parezo (Lincoln: University of Nebraska Press, 2008), 67; Randolph, "Pawhuska"; Ellen Fitzpatrick, *History's Memory: Writing America's Past, 1880–1980* (Cambridge, Mass.: Harvard University Press, 2004), 133.
41. Mathews diary, September 23–October 4, 1958 (JJM 2.12).
42. Audiotaped conversation, Arroyo Seco, Medina County, Texas, November 16, 1960 (JJM SR 2280); Mathews diary, December 12–14, 1959 (JJM 2.12).
43. Mathews diary, February 13, 1971 (JJM 3.10); J. Frank Dobie, *Cow People* (Boston: Little, Brown, 1964); Dobie, "Associating with Brush Deer," *San Antonio Light*, December 17, 1961.
44. Mathews to Dobie, n.d. [circa late 1959 or early 1960]; Dobie to Mathews, November 6, November 8, 1961 (JFD).
45. "Local Writer, Onetime Pawhuskan," 7, 10; "Boswell School Speaker Honored," *Paris [Texas] News*, May 28, 1957; Mathews to Elizabeth Hunt, February 26, 1934 (JJM 1.1).
46. T. Wilson, "Osage Oxonian," 287; "Mathews Rushed as New Book Hits Stores Next Week," *PJ-C*, August 11, 1961.

47. Charles H. Red Corn, "Remembering John Joseph"; "John Joseph Mathews Greets Friends at Home Presentation of his Book," *PJ-C*, August 20, 1961; "Osage County Author Facing Busy Days with Latest Book Coming Out," *Ponca City News*, August 11, 1961; James J. Fisher, "Author's Spirit Burns with Pride in Osage History," *Kansas City Times*, November 28, 1974; Bailey, "John Joseph Mathews," 232.
48. Mathews, *Osages*, xiii–xiv.
49. John C. Ewers, "Tribal Tribute," review of *The Osages*, *New York Times*, September 24, 1961; Kimmis Hendrick, "Saga of a Tribe," *Christian Science Monitor*, October 12, 1961; Edith Copeland, "Short List of Great, Beautiful Books Added by One," review of *The Osages*, *Daily Oklahoman*, August 20, 1961; Review of *The Osages*, *PJ-C*, August 13, 1961; Paula McSpadden Love to Mathews, September 10, 1961 (JJM 1.32).
50. Will Rogers, *The Papers of Will Rogers: The Early Years, November 1879–April 1904* (Norman: University of Oklahoma Press, 1995), 371, 505–6, 292, 485; "Robert W. and Paula McSpadden Love Papers," University of Tulsa, McFarlin Library, Special Collections and University Archives, www.lib.utulsa.edu/speccoll/collections/lovemcspadden/index.htm; Phillip Fortune, personal interview, February 20, 2015; Mathews, *LDO*, 157, 202–4; Mathews diary, January 12, 1946 (JJM 1.48); "Dennis Wolfe Bushyhead," *Chronicles of Oklahoma* 14, no. 3 (1936): 350–59; "Dennis Wolf [*sic*] Bushyhead," Find a Grave, www.findagrave.com/cgi-bin/fg.cgi?page=gr&GRid=61640530; "Will Rogers Observance Set," *Oklahoman*, November 2, 1964; Paula McSpadden Love, *The Will Rogers Book* (Indianapolis, Ind.: Bobbs-Merrill, 1961).
51. Lori Roll, "The Good Humor Man Is Still Playing Strong on Peoria," *Tulsa World*, October 17, 1982; "Lewis Meyer," *Tulsa World*, January 7, 1995; Mathews diary, August 13, 17, 20, 22, 1961 (JJM 2.14).
52. "Betty Boyd," "Louise Bland," Tulsa TV Memories, http://tulsatvmemories.com/womans.html; "Former KOTV Personality Betty Boyd Dies," News on 6, KOTV Tulsa, www.newson6.com/story/13795140/former-kotv-personality-and-state-lawmaker-dies; "John Joseph Mathews Greets Friends"; "Mathews Rushed"; "Osage County Author"; Mathews diary, August 3, 15–17, 20, 22, 28, 31, 1961; January 21, 1962, October 16, 1968 (JJM 2.14, 3.1, 3.6).
53. "Mathews to Lecture at TU's Writers Conference Soon," *PJ-C*, October 7, 1961; "William Peden Short Story Collection," University of Missouri Libraries, Special Collections & Rare Books, http://library.missouri.edu/specialcollections/bookcol/peden/; Mathews to J. Frank Dobie, May 14, 1960 (JFD).
54. Yet in 1964, his final year, when the Beatles invaded the United States, causing controversy with their long hair and Cuban heels, the septuagenarian Dobie thought they "add a lot to life" and saw nothing bad about them. He held faith in younger generations, presaging a Beatles tune when he said that as a species, we are evolving, "getting better" all the time. Dobie was much more optimistic than Mathews. Stephen L. Davis, *J. Frank Dobie: A Liberated Mind* (Austin: University of Texas Press, 2009), 130.

55. Mathews to J. Frank Dobie, November 1, 1961; January 7, June 15, 1963; Dobie to Mathews, November 6, 8, 1961; March 15 and June 5, 1963 (JFD); Robert Metzger, "Hurd, Peter," *Handbook of Texas Online*, June 15, 2010, https://tshaonline.org/handbook/online/articles/fhu55web; Mathews diary, January 9, 12, 1962, October 15, 1963 (JJM 3.1, 3.2); "Ben Wright, 89, Former Magazine Publisher," *New York Times*, April 27, 2001, www.nytimes.com/2001/04/27/us/ben-wright-89-former-magazine-publisher.html; Davis, *J. Frank Dobie*, 225–28, 236.
56. Mathews diary, February 2, 1962 (JJM 3.1); Neurohr and Smith, *John Joseph Mathews*, 7.
57. Kalter, introduction to *TTM*, xxxiii–xxxvii; Lottinville to Mathews, August 9, 1938 (OUP 48.7); Terry P. Wilson, *Bibliography of the Osage* (Metuchen, N.J.: Scarecrow, 1985); Louis F. Burns, *Osage Indian Bands and Clans* (Fallbrook, Calif.: Clearfield, 1984), 172; Burns, *History of the Osage People*, 165; Sister Mary Paul Fitzgerald, *Beacon on the Plains* (Leavenworth, Kans.: Saint Mary College, 1939), 109, 111–13; Mathews, *Osages*, 627–36, 795.
58. "Distinguished Service Citations: The Reason for Recognition," *Sooner Magazine*, July–August 1962, 5; Mathews, "Author John Joseph Mathews," 10–11; Mathews to Brandt, June 27, 1967 (JAB 5.14); Mathews diary, May 27, 1962 (JJM 3.1).

Chapter Eleven **EVERYTHING IS A CIRCLE**

1. Mathews diary, April 27–28, 1962; February 2–3, 8–9, 12, 1962; May 18–19, 1962 (JJM 3.1). "Glow Hour" was a common phrase in the diaries; "Glow hour pleasure" appeared on January 10, 1973 (JJM 3.12).
2. Mathews diary, January 2, 27, October 23, 1963 (JJM 3.2); July 5, 1963 (JJM 3.3); Susan Kalter, afterword to *Old Three Toes and Other Tales of Survival and Extinction* by Mathews (Norman: University of Oklahoma Press, 2015), 138–39, 158–61; Kalter, introduction to *TTM*, xv.
3. Mathews, audiotaped diary, July 5, 1965 (JJM Tape 2275, Side A).
4. Susan Kalter, introduction and notes to *Twenty Thousand Mornings: An Autobiography*, edited by Kalter (Norman: University of Oklahoma Press, 2011), xxxix, li–lii, 263, 266, 271; Sara Mathews Dydak, telephone interview, March 13, 2015; Laura Mathews Edwards, personal interview, August 2, 2013.
5. Mathews diary, April 1, 21, July 21, 1968; January 1, 1970; February 28, 1973 (JJM 3.6, 3.9, 3.12); Rhodes, *Looking for America*, 79; T. Wilson, "Osage Oxonian," 290; T. Wilson, "John Joseph Mathews," in *Dictionary of Native American Literature*, ed. Andrew Wiget (New York: Routledge, 1994), 236; Susan Kalter, foreword and introduction to *Twenty Thousand Mornings*, xi, xviii.
6. Raymond Red Corn III, personal interview, January 7, 2013; Harvey Payne, personal interview, July 15, 2013.

7. Mathews diary, November 2, 3, 7, 9, 1966 (Harvey Payne, personal collection). Thanks go to Harvey Payne for allowing me to read the diary in his Pawhuska office and make photocopies. Mathews diary, October 7, 11, 1967; January 20, 1968; January 1, 1970; November 12, 1972; April 10 and June 3, 1978 (JJM 3.5, 3.8, 3.9, 3.11, 3.12).
8. Mathews audiotaped diary, May 27 and 29, 1965 (JJM SR 2274); Elizabeth Thompson, telephone interview with Virginia Mathews, July 2, 1997, notes in private collection of Dr. Thompson. Thanks go to Elizabeth for sharing these notes with me.
9. Mathews to Brandt, June 27, 1967 (JAB 5.14); Mathews, audiotaped diary, July 9, 21, and 23, 1965 (JJM SR 2275).
10. "Osage National Monument Proposed," *PJ-C*, September 29, 1972; Mathews diary, September 4–5, 1967 (JJM 3.5).
11. Frederick F. Drummond, telephone interview, March 25, 2015; Mathews diary, July 2, 3, 7, 9, August 9, 17, and September 6–7, 12, 18, 23, 1966 (Harvey Payne personal collection); Mathews diary, July 20, 1967 (JJM 3.5).
12. Mathews diary, April 15, 1967 (JJM 3.5); "Mathews at Oswego, Speaks of Earlier Days," *Oswego Independent*, April 16, 1967; Mathews to Gerald Barnard, May 1, 1967, Oswego Historical Society; Philip Blair, personal interview, July 15, 2013, Oswego, Kans.
13. AP wire photograph, 2012.201.B0403.0526, November 7, 1970, OHS; Mathews diary, November 7, 1970 (JJM 3.9).
14. Mathews diary, October 2, 11, 1963; October 21, 1971 (JJM 3.3, 3.10); Emery Winn, "World of Words," *Oklahoman*, July 18, 1971; Violet Willis, "Medicine Men," *PJ-C*, September 28, 1972.
15. Mathews diary, November 16, 1972 (JJM 3.11); William Mathews Feighan, telephone interview, January 19, 2015; "Hereditary Chief of Winnebagos, Blackhawk, Dies Dewey, Okla.," *Lincoln Star*, September 18, 1975.
16. Mathews diary, November 17, 1972 (JJM 3.11). Surely "ignoramouses" is an intentional pun.
17. "Indians Seize Nebraska Museum," *Washington Post*, November 16, 1972; Paul Chaat Smith and Robert Warrior, *Like a Hurricane: The Indian Movement from Alcatraz to Wounded Knee* (New York: New Press, 1996), 144, 270.
18. Mathews diary, January 10, 1973 (JJM 3.12); Henry Palmour Brown, telephone interview, March 23, 2015; Samuel Clinton Brown, telephone interview, March 27, 2015.
19. Rhodes, *Looking for America*, 76, 79–81.
20. Stratford B. Tolson, telephone interview, March 28, 2015, and personal interview, January 7, 2013; Melvin L. Tolson, personal interview, July 16, 2013.
21. Laura Mathews Edwards, personal interview, August 2, 2013; Chris Mathews, telephone interview, September 8, 2013; Mathews, *Talking to the Moon*, 98; Sara Mathews Dydak, telephone interview, March 13, 2015.
22. Charles H. Red Corn, "Remembering John Joseph," *Osage News*, March 22, 2011; Mathews diary, April 1–3, 5, 6, 9, 15, 16, 1978 (JJM 3.12); Susanna Mosley to Mathews,

August 17, 1978 (five poems enclosed, which are also found in JJM 4.30), and March 17, 1979 (JJM 1.32).

23. Mathews diary, November 16, 1969 (JJM 3.8); Frederick Drummond, telephone interview, March 25, 2015; Gary Jack Willis, "Joe Mathews, John Wayne Lived as They Decided to Live, *Tulsa Tribune*, June 12, 1979.

24. Willis, "Joe Mathews, John Wayne Lived"; "Gary Jack Willis (1944–2011)," *Bartlesville Examiner-Enterprise*, February 4, 2011; Vaught, "Osage Scribe."

25. Craig S. Womack, "A Single Decade: Book-Length Native Literary Criticism between 1986 and 1997," in *Reasoning Together*, ed. the Native Critics Collective, 60–61 (Norman: University of Oklahoma Press, 2008); Elise Paschen, e-mail to the author, April 14, 2015; Mathews, "Moccasin Prints," n.d. (JJM 4.14).

26. "Noted Writer, Historian Dies Here," *PJ-C*, June 12, 1979; "Tributes Set for Mathews; Museum Closes," *PJ-C*, June 13, 1979; Henry Brown, telephone interview, March 23, 2015; Mathews diary, November 16, 1969 (JJM 3.8). Lillian Mathews was interviewed telephonically by Sarah Richter on May 28, 1984. Sara Jane Richter, "The Life and Literature of John Joseph Mathews: Contributions of Two Cultures" (PhD diss., Oklahoma State University, 1985); Frederick Drummond, telephone interview, March 25, 2015. The quotation that forms the epigraph at the beginning of this chapter, and which I have set as a poem at its close, was spoken by John Joseph Mathews to a Kansas City journalist. James J. Fisher, "Author's Spirit Burns with Pride in Osage History." *Kansas City Times*, November 28, 1974.

WORKS BY JOHN JOSEPH MATHEWS

BOOKS

Wah'Kon-Tah: The Osage and the White Man's Road. Norman: University of Oklahoma Press, 1932.

Sundown. New York: Longmans, Green, 1934.

Talking to the Moon. Chicago: University of Chicago Press, 1945.

"Within Your Dream." Unpublished novel manuscript written in 1949 and revised through 1955. Now lost.

Life and Death of an Oilman: The Career of E. W. Marland. Norman: University of Oklahoma Press, 1951.

The Osages: Children of the Middle Waters. Norman: University of Oklahoma Press, 1961.

Talking to the Moon. 2nd ed. Foreword by Elizabeth Mathews. Norman: University of Oklahoma Press, 1981.

Sundown. Introduction by Virginia H. Mathews. Norman: University of Oklahoma Press, 1988.

Twenty Thousand Mornings: An Autobiography. Edited and introduced by Susan Kalter. Norman: University of Oklahoma Press, 2012.

Old Three Toes and Other Tales of Survival and Extinction. Edited and with afterword by Susan Kalter. Norman, University of Oklahoma Press, 2015.

Articles, Short Stories, Poems, and Select Unpublished Manuscripts

"Admirable Outlaw." *Sooner Magazine* 2, no. 7 (April 1930): 241, 264.

"After the Afghan." (Poem). N.d. Walter Stanley Campbell Collection, Western History Collections, University of Oklahoma, 56.5.

"Alfredo and the Jaguar." 1963. John Joseph Mathews Collection, Western History Collections, University of Oklahoma, 4.1.

"Allah's Guest." N.d. John Joseph Mathews Collection, Western History Collections, University of Oklahoma, 4.2.

"The Apache Woman." 1946. John Joseph Mathews Collection, Western History Collections, University of Oklahoma, 4.3.

"Author John Joseph Mathews Discusses the Limited Impact, Influence, and Dollar-Importance in Books of the Indian and the Southwest." *Sooner Magazine* 34, no. 10 (1962): 10–11.

"Beauty's Votary." *Sooner Magazine* 3, no. 5 (1931): 171, 181–82.

"Boy, Horse and Dog." (Full-length vol. 1 of three planned autobiographical volumes). John Joseph Mathews Collection, Western History Collections, University of Oklahoma, 4.33.

"Chief Fred Lookout Saw Great Changes Come to His Tribesmen of the Osage." *Oklahoman*, April 23, 1939.

"Dance at Dawn." *Oklahoma Today* 19, no. 2 (1969): 28–36.

"DIBBS." (Poem). Christmas 1934. John Joseph Mathews Collection, Western History Collections, University of Oklahoma, 1.27.

"Ee Sa Rah N'eah's Story." *Sooner Magazine* 3, no. 9 (1931): 328–29.

"E. W. Marland." *Pawhuska Daily Journal-Capital*, July 1, 1934.

"From the Osage Hills." *Sooner Magazine* 3, no. 8 (1931): 280, 308–10.

"Gallery." *Space* 1, no. 1 (1934).

"Grus, the Sandhill Crane." 1963. John Joseph Mathews Collection, Western History Collections, University of Oklahoma, 4.8

"Hunger on the Prairie." *Sooner Magazine* 2, no. 9 (1930): 328–29.

"Hunting in the Rockies: The Wary Bull Wapiti Worthy Foe of Hunter's Skill." *Sooner Magazine* 1, no. 8 (1929): 263, 278–80.

"Hunting the Red Deer of Scotland: The Thrill of Conquering the Monarch of the Highlands." *Sooner Magazine* 1, no. 7 (1929): 213–14, 246.

"Joe Mathews Writes Relative to Controversial Article." *Pawhuska Journal-Capital*, June 3, 1937.

"John L. Bird, Early Osage Trader, Dies." *Pawhuska Journal-Capital*, January 28, 1935.

"Jolly Fraternitee." *University of Oklahoma Magazine*, April 1917, 17.

"Lady of the Inn." N.d. John Joseph Mathews Collection, Western History Collections, University of Oklahoma, 4.9.

"The Liberal View." N.d. John Joseph Mathews Collection, Western History Collections, University of Oklahoma, 4.12.

"Man Not Afraid." *The Sooner* 4, no. 5 (1932): 140.

"Moccasin Prints." N.d., John Joseph Mathews Collection, Western History Collections, University of Oklahoma, 4.19.

"No Time." N.d., John Joseph Mathews Collection, Western History Collections, University of Oklahoma, 4.16.

"Ole Bob." *Sooner Magazine* 5, no. 7 (April 1933): 206–7.

"Only a Blonde." N.d., John Joseph Mathews Collection, Western History Collections, University of Oklahoma, 4.19.

"Osage National Monument Proposed." *Pawhuska Journal-Capital*, September 29, 1972.

Our Osage Hills. (Newspaper column). *Pawhuska Journal-Capital*, March 16, 1930–July 10, 1931.

"Passing of Red Eagle: An Osage Goes to His Happy Hunting Ground." *Sooner Magazine* 2, no. 5 (1930): 160, 176.

"Red Man's Gold." *Service* (Cities Service Magazine), October 1946, 12–13.

"Romance of the Osages." Transcript of radio show recorded in Tulsa, broadcast April 30, 1937, NBC Blue network. Lilly Library, Indiana University, Bloomington.

"The Royal of Glen Orchy." 1963. John Joseph Mathews Collection, Western History Collections, University of Oklahoma, 4.21.

"Scholarship Comes to Life: The University of Oklahoma Press." *Saturday Review of Literature*, May 16, 1942: 20–21.

"Singers to the Moon." *Oklahoma Today* 46, no. 5 (1996): ii–viii.

"The Thinkin' Man." N.d. John Joseph Mathews Collection, Western History Collections, University of Oklahoma, 4.24.

"The Trapper's Dog." *Sooner Magazine* 3, no. 4 (January 1931): 133, 141.

"What Thing Is Fairest." John Joseph Mathews Collection, Western History Collections, University of Oklahoma, 4.26.

"When Brooks Field Was a Farmyard." *University of Oklahoma Magazine*, May–June 1917, 18.

"The White Sack." 1963. John Joseph Mathews Collection, Western History Collections, University of Oklahoma, 4.28.

"Yellow Hair." 1946. John Joseph Mathews Collection, Western History Collections, University of Oklahoma, 4.29.

Book Reviews

Review of *Warpath* by Stanley Vestal. *Sooner Magazine* 6, no. 7 (1934): 172.

"Oil-Rich Red Hawks Were Victims of Domino Theory." Review of *The Grey Horse Legacy* by John Hunt. *Lincoln Star*, June 16, 1968.

"Ten Million Kinds of Bugs." Review of *Insect Dietary* by Charles Bruce. *Saturday Review*, June 8, 1946, 66.

Interviews

Logsdon, Guy. Interview with John Joseph Mathews. March 14, 1972. Sound Recordings 2281, John Joseph Mathews Collection, Western History Collections, University of Oklahoma. Audiocassette.

Titterton, Lewis. Interview with John Joseph Mathews, *Books and Characters*, November 6, 1932, 1–9. University of Oklahoma Press Collection, Western History Collections, University of Oklahoma, 6.1.

Lectures

"Books and Libraries in Oklahoma." Oklahoma Library Association, Pawhuska, April 1956.

"Hawks of Oklahoma." Oklahoma City Academy of Science, Sixth Annual Meeting, December 1916.

"The Indian in American Literature." Symposium on American Literature and Education, University of Oklahoma, March 1942.

"The Writer and His Region." University of Tulsa Writers Conference, October 1961.

SELECTED BIBLIOGRAPHY

ARCHIVES AND SPECIAL COLLECTIONS

Donahoe Family Collection. Vertical file. Ponca City Public Library, Okla.

J. Frank Dobie Collection, Correspondence. Harry Ransom Center, University of Texas at Austin.

John Joseph Mathews Collection. Osage Tribal Museum, Library & Archives, Osage Nation.

John Joseph Mathews Collection. Western History Collections, University of Oklahoma.

Joseph August Brandt Collection. Western History Collections, University of Oklahoma.

Joshua Lee Collection. Carl Albert Center, University of Oklahoma.

Lily Library Special Collections. Indiana University, Bloomington.

Lyde Marland Collection. Western History Collections, University of Oklahoma.

Newspaper Archives. (Microfilm). Oklahoma Historical Society Research Center, Oklahoma City.

Oswego Historical Society. Oswego, Kans.

Paul Bigelow Sears Collection. Sterling Memorial Library. Yale University.

Pawhuska Public Library Special Collections. Pawhuska, Okla.

University of Oklahoma Press Collection. Western History Collections, University of Oklahoma.

University of Oklahoma Student Publications Collection. Western History Collections, University of Oklahoma.

Walter Stanley Campbell Collection. Western History Collections, University of Oklahoma.

W. W. Graves Memorial Public Library Special Collections. St. Paul, Kans.

Interviews and Correspondence with the Author

Allred, Pauline. Personal interview, May 3, 2013, Osage Tribal Museum, Osage Nation.

Blair, Philip. Personal interview, July 15, 2013, Oswego, Kans.

Botsford, Keith. E-mail to the author, July 27, 2012.

Brown, Henry Palmour. Telephone interview, March 23, 2015.

Brown, Peter Hunt. Telephone interview, September 18, 2014.

Brown, Samuel Clinton. Telephone interview and e-mail to the author, March 27, 2015.

Buck, Paul Jordan "P. J." Telephone interview, May 6, 2015.

Drummond, Frederick Ford. Telephone interview, March 25, 2015.

Dydak, Sara Mathews. Telephone interview, March 13, 2015.

Edwards, Laura Mathews, and Sam Edwards. Personal interview, August 2–3, 2013, in their home near Saxonburg, Pa.

Feighan, William Mathews. Telephone interview, January 19, 2015.

Fortune, Phillip. Personal interview, February 20, 2015, Pawhuska Public Library, Pawhuska, Okla.

Gregory, Bob. Telephone interview, July 7, 2012.

Hunt, John Clinton. E-mail to the author, October 16, 2014.

———. Telephone interview, December 12, 2014.

Johnson, Maria Schellenberg. Telephone interview, December 13, 2015.

Jones, Fleur Feighan. Telephone interview, January 13, 2015.

Kohnle, Rhonda. Personal interview, June 2, 2014, Osage County Historical Museum, Pawhuska, Okla.

Labadie, Milton V. Personal interview, January 7, 2013, in his home in Pawhuska, Okla.

Lookout, Mongrain. Personal interview, May 2, 2013, Osage Language Center, Pawhuska, Okla.

Mathews, Chris. Personal interview, July 31, 2013, in her home in Belleville, Pa.

———. Telephone interview, September 8, 2013.

Mathews, John Hopper, and Mary Abigail "Gail" Painter Mathews. Personal interview, August 2, 2013, in their home in Allensville, Pa.

Mathews, Mary Abigail. E-mails to the author, February 4, 2015, December 18, 2015.

Mattingly, William H. Telephone interviews, January 7, 2013, March 21, 2015.

Northcutt, C. D. Telephone interview, June 4, 2012.

Paschen, Elise. E-mail to the author, April 14, 2015.

Payne, Harvey. Personal interview, July 15, 16, 2013, in Pawhuska, and at The Blackjacks, Okla.

Red Corn, III, Raymond. Personal interview, January 7, 2013, Pawhuska, Okla.

Revard, Carter. E-mails to the author, August 10, 11, 2013.

Schellenberg, III, Howard J. E-mails to the author, November 23, 24, December 31, 2015.

Shackelford, Romain. Personal interview, July 16, 2013, at his home in Pawhuska, Okla.

Standing Bear, Geoffrey. Telephone interview, July 16, 2013.

Standing Bear, Sean. Telephone interview, August 17, 2016.

Taylor, Judy. Personal interview, June 28, 2014, Osage County Historical Museum, Pawhuska, Okla.

Tolson, Melvin L. Personal interview, July 16, 2013, Tolson Agency, Pawhuska, Okla.

Tolson, Stratford B. Telephone interview, March 28, 2015.

Tolson, Stratford B., and Bobbie Tolson. Personal interview, January 7, 2013, in their home in Pawhuska, Okla.

WORKS BY MATHEWS FAMILY MEMBERS

John Clinton Hunt

Ethan Frome (libretto, written 1951–52). Music by Douglas Allanbrook. *Ethan Frome World Premiere: A Lyrical Opera in Three Acts*. 2 compact discs. Cambridge Chamber Orchestra. Recorded 1999. Mapleshade, 2001.

Generations of Men. Boston: Atlantic Monthly–Little, Brown, 1956. 2nd ed. New York: Curtis, ca. 1973.

The Grey Horse Legacy. New York: Knopf, 1968. 2nd ed. New York: Bantam, 1970.

With Martin Kaplan. *Knights Errant: A Play in Two Acts*. New York Public Library Archives, 1982.

"John Joseph Mathews." In *Encyclopedia of North American Indians*, edited by Frederick E. Hoxie, 363–65. Boston: Houghton Mifflin, 1996.

"Family Business." (Novel excerpt). *News from the Republic of Letters* 16 (Winter 2005): 107–89.

"If You Leave Me . . . Take Me with You." (Unpublished novel manuscript). 2011.

Elizabeth Palmour Hunt Mathews

Book reviews for the *Pawhuska Journal-Capital* were bylined "Mrs. John Joseph Mathews."

"From a Seven-Year-Old." *Edmond Enterprise*, August 8, 1912.

Unsigned short features. *The Whirlwind* (University of Oklahoma humor magazine), October–December 1921, February–April 1922.

Review of *Bill Tilghman: Marshall of the Last Frontier* by Floyd Miller. *Pawhuska Journal-Capital*, July 2, 1972.

Review of *The Cayuse Indians: Imperial Tribesmen of Old Oregon* by Robert H. Ruby. *Pawhuska Journal-Capital*, July 4, 1972.

Review of *The Nez Perces: Tribesmen of the Columbia Plateau* by Francis Haines. *Pawhuska Journal-Capital*, July 5, 1972.

Review of *The Cowboy in Art* by Ed Ainsworth. *Pawhuska Journal-Capital*, July 14, 1972.

Review of *New Echota Letters: Contributions of Samuel A. Worcester to the Cherokee Phoenix*, edited by Jack Frederick Kilpatrick and Anna Gritts Kilpatrick. *Pawhuska Journal-Capital*, August 6, 1972.

Review of *The Reynolds Campaign on Powder River* by J. W. Vaughn. *Pawhuska Journal-Capital*, August 13, 1972.

Review of *Together with the Ainu: A Vanishing People* by M. Inez Hilger. *Pawhuska Journal-Capital*, August 15, 1972.

Review of *The Bonanza West: The Story of the Western Mining Rushes* by William S. Greever. *Pawhuska Journal-Capital*, September 8, 1972.

Foreword to *Talking to the Moon* by John Joseph Mathews. Norman: University of Oklahoma, 1981.

John H. Mathews

"Impossible Magnetic-Field Self-Patterning." *Nature*, November 19, 1960: 651.

Mathews, John H., and W. K. Gardiner. "Field Reversals of 'Paleomagnetic' Type in Coupled Disk Dynamos." In Naval Research Laboratory Report #5886, March 27, 1963, 1–11.

Virginia H. Mathews

Stop Look Listen, illustrated by C. R. Schaare. New York: Hampton, 1947.

Going Places. New York: Hampton, 1950.

Animals and Little Ones, illustrated by Howard Hastings. New York: Hampton, 1955.

Libraries for Today and Tomorrow. New York: Doubleday, 1976.

Introduction to *Sundown*, v–xiv. Norman: University of Oklahoma Press, 1988 [1934].

"My Father John Joseph Mathews." In *John Joseph Mathews: Osage Writer and Tribal Councilman, Artist, Naturalist, Historian and Scholar*, edited by Karen Neurohr and Lindsey Smith, 16–17. Norman: Friends of Libraries in Oklahoma, 2009.

Neurohr, Karen. "Oral History Interview with Virginia H. Mathews." September 9, 2009. Spotlighting Oklahoma Oral History Project. Oklahoma Oral History Research Program. Oklahoma State University, Edmon Low Library. www.library.okstate.edu/oralhistory/digital/spotlighting-oklahoma.

Virginia Winslow Mathews

Captured Moments: A Lifetime of Poems. Madison, Conn.: Horse Pond, 1987.

SELECTED BOOKS AND ARTICLES

Abercrombie, Louise. "Marland Book's Author Remembers Oilman." *Ponca City News*, April 11, 1979.

Adams, Verdon R. *Tom White: The Life of a Lawman*. El Paso: Texas Western Press, 1972.

Arnold, Ellen L., ed. *The Salt Companion to Carter Revard*. Cambridge: Salt, 2007.

Austin, Mary. "The Osage Indians." Review of *Wah'Kon-Tah*. *Saturday Review*, November 19, 1932, 251.

Bailey, Garrick. "John Joseph Mathews, Osage, 1894–1979." In *American Indian Intellectuals of the Nineteenth and Early Twentieth Centuries*, edited by Margot Liberty, 232–44. Norman: University of Oklahoma Press, 2002 [1978].

———, ed. *Traditions of the Osage: Stories Collected and Translated by Francis LaFlesche*. Albuquerque: University of New Mexico Press, 2010.

Bernard, Emily, ed. *Remember Me to Harlem: The Letters of Langston Hughes and Carl Van Vechten, 1925–1964*. New York: Knopf, 2001.

Blackburn, Bob L. "Oklahoma Historians Hall of Fame: John Joseph Mathews." *Chronicles of Oklahoma* 74 (Fall 1996): 332–34.

Bogard, Travis. *Contour in Time: The Plays of Eugene O'Neil*. New York: Oxford University Press, 1988.

Boissier, Gaston. *Roman Africa: Archeological Walks in Algeria and Tunis*. Translated by Arabella Ward. New York: Putnam, 1899.

Bourgeois, Suzanne. *Genesis of the Salk Institute*. Berkeley: University of California Press, 2013.

Brandt, Joseph A. "Book of the Month." *Sooner Magazine* 5, no. 3 (1932), 77.

———. "John O. Moseley." *Sooner Magazine* 7, no. 5 (1935), 102–3.

———. Review of *Out of Africa* by Isak [Karen] Dinesen. *Oklahoman*, April 10, 1938.

———. "Three Osage Leaders." *Sooner Magazine* 7, no. 2 (1934): 30–31.

———. *Toward the New Spain*. Chicago: University of Chicago Press, 1933.

Brandt, Sallye Little. "The Milburns." *Sooner Magazine* 3, no. 6 (1931): 207–8, 215.

Braunlich, Phyllis Cole. *Haunted by Home: The Life and Letters of Lynn Riggs*. Norman: University of Oklahoma Press, 1988.

Brophy, Alfred R. *Reconstructing the Dreamland: The Tulsa Riot of 1921, Race, Reparations, and Reconciliation*. New York: Oxford University Press, 2003.

Brumley, Kim. *Marland Tragedy: The Turbulent Story of a Forgotten Oklahoma Icon*. Mustang, Okla.: Tate, 2009.

Burns, Louis F. *A History of the Osage People*. Tuscaloosa: University of Alabama Press, 2004.

———. *Osage Indian Bands and Clans*. Fallbrook, Calif.: Ciga Press, 1984.

———. *Osage Mission Baptisms, Marriages, and Interments, 1820–1886*. Fallbrook, Calif.: Ciga Press, 1986.

Callahan, Alice Ann. *The Osage Ceremonial Dance: I'n-Lon-Schka*. Norman: University of Oklahoma Press, 1993.

Campbell, Isabel. *Jack Sprat*. New York: Coward-McCann, 1928.

Canby, Henry Seidel. "A Talk with President Hoover about Major Miles." *Book of the Month Club News*, October 1932, 4–5.

———. "*Wah'Kon-Tah* by John Joseph Mathews." *Book of the Month Club News*, October 1932, 2–3.

Cary, Joyce. *The Horse's Mouth*. Alexandria, Va.: Time-Life Books, 1965 [1944].

———. *Mister Johnson*. New York: Time, 1962 [1939].

"Companion of Writer Killed, John Joseph Mathews of Pawhuska Injured." *Tulsa Tribune*, April 13, 1942.

Copeland, Edith Jameson. Review of *Generations of Men* by John Hunt. *Oklahoman*, April 15, 1956.

———. Review of *Life and Death of an Oilman*. *Sooner Magazine* 24, no. 5 (1952): 30–31.

———. "Short List of Great, Beautiful Books Added by One." Review of *The Osages*. *Oklahoman*, August 20, 1961.

Cosgrove, Elizabeth Williams. Review of *Wah'Kon-Tah*. *Chronicles of Oklahoma* 11, no. 1 (1933): 733–34.

Cox, James Howard. *The Red Land to the South: American Indian Writers and Indigenous Mexico*. Minneapolis: University of Minnesota Press, 2012.

Crane, John K. *T. H. White*. Boston: Twayne, 1974.

Davidson, Jo. *Between Sittings: An Informal Autobiography*. New York: Dial Press, 1951.

Davis, Steven L. *J. Frank Dobie: A Liberated Mind*. Austin: University of Texas Press, 2009.

Davis, Thadious M. *Nella Larsen, Novelist of the Harlem Renaissance*. Baton Rouge: Louisiana State University Press, 1994.

Dennison, Jean. *Colonial Entanglement: Constituting a Twenty-First-Century Osage Nation*. Chapel Hill: University of North Carolina Press, 2012.

Dickerson, Philip. *History of the Osage Nation, Its People, Resources, and Prospects*. N.p., 1906.

"Distinguished Service Citations: The Reason for Recognition." *Sooner Magazine* 34, no. 10 (1962): 5.

Dobie, J. Frank. "Associating with Brush Deer." *San Antonio Light*, December 17, 1961.

———. "Black Gold and Roses." Review of *Life and Death of an Oilman*. *New York Times*, October 21, 1951.

———. "Books and Christmas." *Southwest Review*, Winter 1951, 1–6.

———. "Can a Coyote Raise His Tail?" *Oklahoman*, March 11, 1951. (John Joseph Mathews is quoted extensively though he is not bylined.)

———. *Cow People*. Boston: Little, Brown, 1964.

———. *A Texan in England*. Boston: Little, Brown, 1945.

———. *The Voice of the Coyote*. Lincoln: University of Nebraska Press, 1949.

Donahoe, Edward. "Head by Scopas." In *Understanding Fiction*, edited by Cleanth Brooks, Jr., and Robert Penn Warren, 325–29. New York: Appleton-Century-Crofts, 1943.

———. *Madness in the Heart*. Boston: Little, Brown, 1937.

Doughty, Charles Montagu. *Travels in Arabia Deserta*. New York: Random House, 1946.

Dunning, John. *On the Air: Encyclopedia of Old Time Radio*. New York: Oxford University Press, 1998.

Dwyer, Margaret. "Carter Revard in Cyberspace: An E-mail Sampler." In "In Honor of Carter Revard." Special issue, *Studies in American Indian Literatures*, ser. 2, 15, no. 1 (Spring 2003): 109–38.

"Eben Soderstrom, 93, Watched Much of Pawhuska's History." *Pawhuska Journal-Capital*, February 29, 1972.

"An Educated Indian." Review of *Sundown*. *New York Times*, November 25, 1934.

Ewers, John C. "Tribal Tribute." Review of *The Osages*. *New York Times*, September 24, 1961.

Favour, Alpheus H. *Old Bill Williams, Mountain Man*. Norman: University of Oklahoma Press, 1962 [1936].

"Feighan-Mathews Wedding Solemnized Here Saturday." *Pawhuska Journal-Capital*, June 22, 1930.

Ferber, Edna. *Cimarron*. Garden City, N.Y.: Doubleday, Doran, 1929.

———. *A Peculiar Treasure*. Garden City, N.Y.: Doubleday, Doran, 1939.

Ferguson, Benton. "Seward Sheldon." *Sooner Magazine* 5, no. 4 (1933): 234.

Ferguson, Lucia. "A Sad, Exciting Story." Review of *Life and Death of an Oilman*. *Memphis Press-Scimitar*, November 3, 1951.

Fischer, LeRoy H., ed. *Oklahoma's Governors, 1929–1955: Depression to Prosperity*. Oklahoma City: Oklahoma Historical Society, 1983.

Fisher, James J. "Author's Spirit Burns with Pride in Osage History." *Kansas City Times*, November 28, 1974.

Fitzgerald, Sister Mary Paul. *Beacon on the Plains*. Leavenworth, Kans.: Saint Mary College, 1939.

Fitzpatrick, Ellen. *History's Memory: Writing America's Past, 1880–1980*. Cambridge, Mass.: Harvard University Press, 2004.

"Florence Feighan, Indian Rights Advocate, Organized Hill Tours." *Washington Post*, January 25, 1980.

Foresman, Bob. "Mathews' New Book Will Be Whopper." *Tulsa Tribune*, November 3, 1958.

Fraker, Elmer L. "Cave Men in Wilds of Soonerdom." *University of Oklahoma Magazine*, October 1921.

———. "With Thoburn at Honey Creek." *Chronicles of Oklahoma* 34 (Spring 1956): 44–52.

Francis, Daniel. *The Imaginary Indian: The Image of the Indian in Canadian Culture*. Vancouver: Arsenal Pulp, 1992.

"Fred Lookout." In *Encyclopedia of North American Indians*, edited by Frederick E. Hoxie, 346–47. Boston: Houghton Mifflin, 1996.

Gambill, Patti. "Mathews Home Comes Alive for Holiday Home Tour." *Pawhuska Journal-Capital*, December 2, 1992.

Geller, Peter. *Northern Exposures: Photographing and Filming the Canadian North, 1920–45*. Vancouver: University of British Columbia Press, 2011.

Gilbert, Julie Goldsmith. *Ferber: Edna Ferber and Her Circle*. Milwaukee, Wis.: Hal Leonard, 1999.

Gingrich, Andre. "Alliances and Avoidance: British Interactions with German-Speaking Anthropologists, 1933–1953." In *Culture Wars: Context, Models and Anthropologists' Accounts*, edited by Deborah James, Evelyn Plaice, and Christina Toren, 19–31. New York: Berghahn, 2013.

Graves, W. W. *Annals of Osage Mission*. St. Paul, Kans.: Graves Memorial Library, 1987 [1934].

———. *History of Neosho County*. St. Paul, Kans.: Osage Mission Historical Society, 1986 [1949].

Gregory, Bob. "The Marland Mystery." *Oklahoma Monthly*, January 1981, 50–61.

———. *Oil in Oklahoma*. Muskogee, Okla.: Leake Industries, 1976.

Gussow, Mel. *Edward Albee: A Singular Journey*. New York: Simon and Schuster, 1999.

Gwynn, Frederick L. "A Bead for Donahoe." *College English* 10, no. 7 (1949): 409–10.

Hale, John E. "Life and Death of an Oilman—Marland's Career." *Ponca City News*, October 23, 1951.

Hendrick, Kimmis. "Saga of a Tribe." Review of *The Osages*. *Christian Science Monitor*, October 12, 1961.

Higgs, Richard. "Searching for John Joseph Mathews." *This Land*, September 4, 2013.

Hogan, Linda. *Mean Spirit*. New York: Athenaeum, 1990.

Hoover, Herbert. *The Memoirs of Herbert Hoover, 1874–1920: Years of Adventure*. New York: Macmillan, 1951.

Howe, LeAnne. *Choctalking on Other Realities*. San Francisco: Aunt Lute, 2013.

Hunter, Carol. "The Historical Context in John Joseph Mathews' *Sundown*." *MELUS* 9, no. 1 (1982): 61–72.

———. "The Protagonist as a Mixed-Blood in John Joseph Mathews' Novel *Sundown*." *American Indian Quarterly* 6, nos. 3–4 (1982): 319–37.

Hutchinson, George. *In Search of Nella Larsen*. Cambridge, Mass.: Harvard University Press, 2006.

"Indian Heiresses Invade Capital." *Washington Herald*, September 7, 1914.

"Injury to Mathews Holds Up Ceremonies." *Oklahoman*, April 26, 1942.

"Inquiry of Osage Fund Cases Looms." *Pawhuska Journal-Capital*, May 13, 1937.

Isherwood, Christopher. "Los Angeles." *Horizon*, October 1947, 142–47.

"John Hopper Mathews," *Lewistown (Pa.) Sentinel*, February 4, 2015.

"John Joseph Mathews Greets Friends at Home Presentation of His Book." *Pawhuska Journal-Capital*, August 20, 1961.

Johnson, Enid. *Bill Williams: Mountain Man*. New York: Julian Messner, 1952.

Jones, Louis Thomas. *The Quakers of Iowa*. Des Moines: State Historical Society of Iowa, 1914.

"Josephine Caudill Dies at Winfield, Rites Here Friday." *Pawhuska Journal-Capital*, April 27, 1955.

Jump, Kenneth Jacob. *Osage Indian Poems and Short Stories*. 2nd ed. Pawhuska, Okla.: n.p., 1996 [1979].

"Kansan Dies after Crash West of City, Joe Mathews, Mrs. Elizabeth Hunt Also Injured." *Pawhuska Journal-Capital*, April 13, 1942.

Kaufman, Kenneth Carlyle. "The Indian's Burden." Review of *Sundown*. *Christian Science Monitor*, November 8, 1934.

———. *Level Land: A Book of Western Verse*. Dallas, Tex.: Kaleidograph Press, 1939.

Kelter, Bill. *Veeps: Profiles in Insignificance*. Atlanta: Top Shelf, 2008.

Kennedy, Frances. "Twenty-Fifth Meeting." In *Reports of the Oklahoma Library Commission*. Oklahoma City: Warden, 1922.

Keresztesi, Rita. *Strangers at Home: American Ethnic Modernism between the World Wars*. Lincoln: University of Nebraska Press, 2005.

Kipling, Rudyard. *Collected Verse of Rudyard Kipling*. New York: Doubleday, 1907.

Kobler, John. "Where Is Lydie Marland?" *Saturday Evening Post*, November 22, 1958, 19–20.

Koch, Michael. *The Kimes Gang*. Bloomington, Ind.: AuthorHouse, 2005.

Kolbert, Jack. *The Worlds of André Maurois*. Selinsgrove, Pa.: Susquehanna University Press, 1985.

La Barre, Weston. *The Peyote Cult*. New Haven: Yale University Press, 1938.

La Farge, Oliver. "The Realistic Story of an Indian Youth." Review of *Sundown*. *Saturday Review of Literature*, November 24, 1934, 309.

LaFerte, Harry. "Cabin in the Osage—Refuge for a Scholar." *Tulsa World*, June 26, 1937.

———. "Riches of Osage Tribe Plundered by White Greed: John Joseph Mathews Reveals How His People Are Victimized." *Tulsa World*, May 25, 1937.

La Flesche, Francis. *War Ceremony and Peace Ceremony of the Osage Indians*. Bureau of American Ethnology Bulletin 101. Washington, D.C.: U.S. Government Printing Office, 1939.

Leckie, Shirley A. "Angie Debo: From the Old to the New Western History." In *Their Own Frontier: Women Intellectuals Re-Visioning the American West*, edited by Shirley A. Leckie and Nancy J. Parezo, 65–96. Lincoln: University of Nebraska Press, 2008.

Levy, David. *The University of Oklahoma: A History*. Vol. 1, *1890–1917*. Norman: University of Oklahoma Press, 2005.

"Lillian B. Mathews." *Pawhuska Journal-Capital*, August 29, 1992.

"Local Writer, Onetime Pawhuskan Both Work on Osage Tribal History." *Pawhuska Journal-Capital*, September 18, 1960.

Logsdon, Guy. "John Joseph Mathews—A Conversation." *Nimrod* 16 (April 1972): 70–75.

"Lord Almost Puts Up His Dukes." *Oklahoman*, May 18, 1948.

Lottinville, Savoie. "In Memoriam: John Joseph Mathews, 1895–1979." *American Oxonian* 57, no. 4 (1980): 237–41.

———. "Portrait of a Sooner—Joe Brandt." *Sooner Magazine* 11, no. 1 (1938): 13.

———. *The Rhetoric of History*. Norman: University of Oklahoma Press, 1976.

Love, Paula McSpadden. *The Will Rogers Book*. Indianapolis, Ind.: Bobbs-Merrill, 1961.

Lowitt, Richard. "Regionalism at the University of Oklahoma." *Chronicles of Oklahoma* 73, no. 2 (1995): 150–71.

Lutenski, Emily. "Tribes of Men: John Joseph Mathews' Indian Internationalism." *SAIL: Studies in American Indian Literatures* 24, no. 2 (2012): 39–64.

"Maj. Laban Miles, Uncle of President Hoover and Early Day Indian Agent, Taken by Death." *Pawhuska Journal-Capital*, April 13, 1931.

Marable, Mary Hays, and Elaine Boylan. *A Handbook of Oklahoma Writers*. Norman: University of Oklahoma Press, 1939.

"Marie Mathews." *Pawhuska Journal-Capital*, December 2, 1988.

"Mathews Addresses Alumni." *Sooner Magazine* 6, no. 8 (1934): 8.

"Mathews to Lecture at TU's Writers Conference Soon." *Pawhuska Journal-Capital*, October 7, 1961.

"Mathews Rushed as New Book Hits Stores Next Week." *Pawhuska Journal-Capital*, August 11, 1961.

"Mathews Will Write in Quiet of Mexico." *Stillwater Press*, August 31, 1939.

McCauliffe, Dennis. *Bloodland: A Family Story of Oil, Greed, and Murder on the Osage Reservation*. San Francisco: Council Oak, 1994.

McNickle, D'Arcy. *The Surrounded*. Albuquerque: University of New Mexico Press, 1988 [1936].

Milburn, George. *Catalog*. New York: Harcourt, 1936.

———. *No More Trumpets and Other Stories*. New York: Harcourt, 1933.

———. "Oklahoma." *Yale Review*, March 1946, 515–26.

———. *Oklahoma Town*. New York: Harcourt, 1931.

———. "The Osage Nation." Review of *Wah'Kon-Tah*. *The New Republic*, November 16, 1932, 24–25.

Miller, Nathan. *New World Coming: The 1920s and the Making of Modern America*. New York: Scribner, 2003.

"Miss Barbara Mead Becomes Bride of John Clinton Hunt." *Oklahoman*, October 3, 1948.

Momaday, N. Scott. *House Made of Dawn*. New York: Harper and Row, 1968.

"Mourn Lorene Squire." *Milwaukee Journal*, June 12, 1942.

"Mrs. Henry Hunt Takes Over Gasoline Business." *Pawhuska Journal-Capital*, August 23, 1932.

Neurohr, Karen, and Lindsey Smith, eds. *John Joseph Mathews: Osage Writer and Tribal Councilman, Artist, Naturalist, Historian and Scholar*. Booklet. Norman: Friends of Libraries in Oklahoma, 2009.

Nietzsche, Friedrich. *Beyond Good and Evil*. Translated by Helen Zimmern. New York: Dover, 1997 [1906].

Northcutt, C. D., William C. Ziegenhain, and Bob Burke. *Palace on the Prairie: The Marland Family Story*. Oklahoma City: Oklahoma Heritage Association, 2005.

"Noted Writer, Historian Dies Here." *Pawhuska Journal-Capital*, June 12, 1979.

O'Connell, Wayne A. *The Story of 'Little Town' (Oswego, Kansas) and Its Founder John Mathews*. Humboldt, Kans.: Oswego Independent, 1998 [1961].

"Oklahoma Academy of Science." *Science* 45, no. 8 (1917): 271–72.

"Oklahoma Novel Writer to Talk Here This Week." *(Stillwater, Okla.) Daily O'Collegian*, February 5, 1935.

"Osage County Author Facing Busy Days with Latest Book Coming Out." *Ponca City News*, August 11, 1961.

Osage County Historical Society (OCHS). *Osage County Profiles*. Pawhuska: OCHS, 1978.

Osage Tribal Council. *Osage Indians Semi-centennial Celebration, 1907–1957*. Pawhuska, Okla.: Osage Agency Campus, 1957.

Osage Tribal Museum. *The Osage Timeline*. Researched and developed by Lou Brock. Pawhuska, Okla.: OTM, 2013.

Oswego, Kansas, Original Souvenir Book: Oswego Centennial, 1867–1967. Humboldt, Kans.: Oswego Independent, 1967.

Owens, Louis. "Disturbed by Something Deeper: The Native Art of John Joseph Mathews." *Western American Literature* 35, no. 2 (2000): 162–73.

———. *Other Destinies: Understanding the American Indian Novel.* Norman: University of Oklahoma Press, 1992.

Parker, Dorothy R. *Singing an Indian Song: A Biography of D'Arcy McNickle.* Lincoln: University of Nebraska Press, 1994.

Parker, Robert Dale. *The Invention of Native American Literature.* Ithaca, N.Y.: Cornell University Press, 2003.

Pawhuska Journal-Capital. *Reflections of Pawhuska, Oklahoma,* vol. 1. Pawhuska: D-Books, 1995.

Peyer, Bernd C., ed. *The Singing Spirit: Early Short Stories by North American Indians.* Tucson: University of Arizona Press, 1989.

Philp, Kenneth R. "John Collier and the Indians of the Americas: The Dream and the Reality." *Prologue,* Spring 1979, 4–21.

"Photos Won Fame: Lorene Squire, Noted for Pictures of Wildlife, Dies in Accident." *Lawrence Journal-World,* April 13, 1942.

"Pioneer Pawhuska Resident, Mrs. William S. Mathews Dies." *Pawhuska Journal-Capital,* March 25, 1955.

Poncins, Gontran de. *Kabloona.* Alexandria, Va.: Time-Life Books, 1965 [1941].

Pyle, Ernie. *Brave Men.* Lincoln: University of Nebraska Press, 2001.

Randolph, Ruth. "Pawhuska, Cosmopolitan City in the '20s: Art, Music, Parties, Fashion Were a Way of Life." *Pawhuska Journal-Capital,* September 29, 1972.

Red Corn, Charles H. "Osage Portraits." *Osage News,* December 12, 2012.

———. *A Pipe for February.* Norman: University of Oklahoma Press, 2002.

———. "Remembering John Joseph." *Osage News,* March 22, 2011.

Revard, Carter. *An Eagle Nation.* Tucson: University of Arizona Press, 1993.

———. *Family Matters, Tribal Affairs.* Tucson: University of Arizona Press, 1998.

———. *From the Extinct Volcano, A Bird of Paradise,* edited by Brian Hudson. Norman, Okla.: Mongrel Empire, 2014.

———. *How the Songs Come Down: New and Selected Poems.* Cambridge: Salt, 2005.

———. *Ponca War Dancers.* Norman, Okla.: Point Riders Press, 1980.

———. *Winning the Dust Bowl.* Tucson: University of Arizona Press, 2001.

Rhodes, Richard. *Looking for America: A Writer's Odyssey.* New York: Doubleday, 1979.

Richter, Sara Jane. "The Life and Literature of John Joseph Mathews: Contributions of Two Cultures." PhD diss., Oklahoma State University, 1985.

Rifkin, Mark. "The Duration of the Land: The Queerness of Spacetime in *Sundown.*" *Studies in American Indian Literatures* 27, no. 1 (2015): 32–69.

Rogers, Will. *The Papers of Will Rogers: The Early Years, November 1879–April 1904*. Norman: University of Oklahoma Press, 1995.

Rollings, Willard Hughes. *Unaffected by the Gospel: Osage Resistance to the Christian Invasion (1673–1906): A Cultural Victory*. Albuquerque: University of New Mexico Press, 2004.

Ruoff, A. LaVonne Brown. "John Joseph Mathews's *Talking to the Moon*: Literary and Osage Contexts." In *Multicultural Autobiography: American Lives*, edited by James Robert Payne, 1–31. Knoxville: University of Tennessee Press, 1992.

Russell, Orpha B. "Chief James Bigheart of the Osages." *Chronicles of Oklahoma* 32, no. 4 (1954–55): 384–94.

Saunders, Frances Stonor. *The Cultural Cold War: The CIA and the World of Arts and Letters*. New York: New Press, 1999.

Saxon, Wolfgang. "Ex-rep. Michael A. Feighan, 87." *New York Times*, March 29, 1992.

Sears, Paul B. *Deserts on the March*. Norman: University of Oklahoma Press, 1935.

Seton, Ernest Thompson. *Wild Animals I Have Known*. New York: Scribner, 1912 [1898].

Settle, Elizabeth Alden. "From the Blackjacks." In *Folk-Say: A Regional Miscellany 1931*, edited by B. A. Botkin, 236–61. Norman: University of Oklahoma Press, 1931.

Shockley, Martin, ed. *Southwest Writers Anthology*. Austin, Tex.: Steck-Vaughn, 1967.

Simms, Ruthanna M. *As Long as the Sun Gives Light: An Account of Friends' Work with American Indians in Oklahoma from 1917 to 1967*. Richmond, Ind.: AECFIA, 1970.

"Six Oklahomans Are in Oxford Colleges." *Oklahoma Teacher*, January 1922, 28.

Smith, Jodi. "Catholic Church Draws Visitors from around the World." *Pawhuska Journal-Capital*, March 31, 1993.

Smith, Paul Chaat, and Robert Allen Warrior. *Like a Hurricane: The Indian Movement from Alcatraz to Wounded Knee*. New York: New Press, 1996.

Snyder, Michael. "Friends of the Osages: John Joseph Mathews's *Wah'Kon-Tah* and Osage-Quaker Cross-Cultural Collaboration." *Chronicles of Oklahoma* 88, no. 4 (2010–11): 438–61.

———. "'He certainly didn't want anyone to know that he was queer': Chal Windzer's Sexuality in John Joseph Mathews's *Sundown*." *Studies in American Indian Literatures* 20, no. 1 (2008): 27–54.

Spanier, Sandra. "'Paris Wasn't Like That': Kay Boyle and the Last of the Lost Generation." In *Lives Out of Letters: Essays on American Literary Biography and Documentation in Honor of Robert N. Hudspeth*, edited by Robert Habich, 169–88. Cranbury, N.J.: Associated University Presses, 2004.

Squire, Lorene. *Wildfowling with a Camera*. New York: J. B. Lippincott, 1938.

Stallman, Robert Wooster. "The Critical Reader," *College English* 9, no. 7 (1948): 362–69.

———. "A Note on Intentions." *College English* 10, no. 1 (1948): 40–41.

Strickland, Rennard. *The Indians in Oklahoma*. Norman: University of Oklahoma Press, 1980.

Tassin, Ray. *Stanley Vestal: Champion of the Old West*. Glendale, Calif.: Arthur H. Clark, 1973.

"Telling the World." *Pawhuska Journal-Capital*, May 28, 1937.

Thoburn, Joseph Bradfield. *A Standard History of Oklahoma*, vol. 5. Chicago: American Historical Society, 1916.

"Tribal Council Selects Attorney." *Pawhuska Journal-Capital*, July 17, 1934.

"Two Put off State Board by Governor." *Oklahoman*, August 2, 1936.

Ulrich, Roberta. *American Indian Nations from Termination to Restoration, 1953–2006*. Lincoln: University of Nebraska Press, 2010.

Vaught, Michael. "Osage Scribe." *Oklahoma Today* 46, no. 5 (1996): 34–37.

Vestal, Stanley [Walter Stanley Campbell]. "Chief of the Oglalas." Review of *Crazy Horse* by Mari Sandoz. *Saturday Review*, January 12, 1943, 20.

———. *Mountain Men*. Boston: Houghton Mifflin, 1937.

———. "Oilman Marland: A Victim of His British Tradition." Review of *Life and Death of an Oilman*. *Chicago Daily Tribune*, November 4, 1951.

———. Review of *Wah'Kon-Tah*. *Oklahoman*, November 6, 1932.

———. Review of *Wah'Kon-Tah*. *Mississippi Valley Historical Review* 20, no. 1 (1933): 153.

———. *Sitting Bull, Champion of the Sioux*. Norman: University of Oklahoma Press, 1957 [1932].

Vestal, Stanley [Walter Stanley Campbell], and Isabel Campbell. "One Genius in a Family Is Not Enough, Say the Campbells." *Sooner Magazine* 2, no. 1 (1929): 18–19.

Vidal, Gore. *I Told You So: Gore Vidal Talks Politics*. Berkeley, Calif.: Counterpoint, 2013.

———. *Palimpsest*. New York: Random House, 1995.

———. *Point to Point Navigation*. New York: Knopf, 2007.

"Virginia Winslow Hopper Mathews." *Lewistown (Pa.) Sentinel*, May 9, 2011.

Vizenor, Gerald. *Native Liberty: Natural Reason and Cultural Survivance*. Lincoln: University of Nebraska Press, 2010.

———*Fugitive Poses: Native American Indian Scenes of Absence and Presence*. Lincoln: University of Nebraska Press, 1998.

Wallis, Michael. *Oil Man: The Story of Frank Phillips and the Birth of Phillips Petroleum*. New York: Doubleday, 1988.

Warrior, Robert Allen. *The People and the Word: Reading Native Nonfiction*. Minneapolis: University of Minnesota Press, 2005.

———. *Tribal Secrets: Recovering American Indian Intellectual Traditions*. Minneapolis: University of Minnesota Press, 1995.

Weaver, Jace. *That the People Might Live*. New York: Oxford University Press, 1997.

Whelan, Richard. *Robert Capa: A Biography*. Lincoln: University of Nebraska Press, 1994.

White, E. E. *Experiences of a Special Indian Agent*. Norman: University of Oklahoma Press, 1965 [1893].

White, T. H. *England Have My Bones*. New York: G. P. Putnam's Sons, 1982 [1936].

"William Shirley Mathews Deceased." *Pawhuska Capital*, March 18, 1915.

Williams, Tennessee. "On a Streetcar Named Success." *New York Times*, November 30, 1947.

Willis, Gary Jack. "Joe Mathews, John Wayne Lived as They Decided to Live." *Tulsa Tribune*, June 12, 1979.

Willis, Violet. "The Mathews Children." In *Osage County Profiles*. Pawhuska: Osage County Historical Society, 1978.

———. "W. S. Mathews, Early Day Tribe Leader." *Pawhuska Journal-Capital*, September 29, 1972.

Wilson, Norma C. "Star Legacies." In *The Salt Companion to Carter Revard*, edited by Ellen L. Arnold, 12–33. Cambridge: Salt, 2007.

Wilson, Terry P. *Bibliography of the Osage*. Metuchen, N.J.: Scarecrow, 1985.

———. "The Depression Years." In *Indians of North America*. New York: Chelsea House, 2008 [1998].

———. "John Joseph Mathews." In *Dictionary of Native American Literature*, edited by Andrew Wiget, 233–36. New York: Routledge, 1994.

———. "John Joseph Mathews." In *Native American Writers of the United States*, edited by Kenneth M. Roemer, 154–62. Dictionary of Literary Biography 175. Detroit: Gale Research, 1997.

———. "Osage Oxonian: The Heritage of John Joseph Mathews." *Chronicles of Oklahoma* 59 (Fall 1981): 264–93.

———. Review of *Wah'Kon-Tah*. *SAIL: Studies in American Indian Literatures*, 1st ser., 9, no. 3 (1985): 124–27.

———. *The Underground Reservation: Osage Oil*. Lincoln: University of Nebraska Press, 1985.

Winks, Robin W. *Cloak & Gown: Scholars in the Secret War, 1939–1961*. New Haven, Conn.: Yale University Press, 1996 [1987].

Winn, Emery. "World of Words." *Oklahoman*, July 18, 1971.

Womack, Craig S. *Art as Performance, Story as Criticism: Reflections on Native Literary Aesthetics*. Norman: University of Oklahoma Press, 2009.

———. *Red on Red: Native American Literary Separatism*. Minnesota: University of Minneapolis Press, 1999.

———. "A Single Decade: Book-Length Native Literary Criticism between 1986 and 1997." In *Reasoning Together: The Native Critics Collective*, edited by Craig S. Womack, Daniel Heath Justice, and Christopher B. Teuton, 3–104. Norman: University of Oklahoma Press, 2008.

INDEX

Works with no author identified are by John Joseph Mathews.

CPSIA information can be obtained
at www.ICGtesting.com
Printed in the USA
FSOW01n0355120118
42948FS

9 780806 160528